Sports Sponsorship

Sports Sponsorship

Principles and Practices

John A. Fortunato
Foreword by Tony Ponturo

McFarland & Company, Inc., Publishers
Jefferson, North Carolina, and London

LIBRARY OF CONGRESS CATALOGUING-IN-PUBLICATION DATA

Fortunato, John A.
Sports sponsorship : principles and practices / John A. Fortunato ;
foreword by Tony Ponturo.
p.   cm.
Includes bibliographical references and index.

ISBN 978-0-7864-7431-8
softcover : alk. paper ∞

1. Sports sponsorship.   2. Sports—Public relations.   I. Title.
GV716.F69 2013   796.07973—dc23   2013027512

BRITISH LIBRARY CATALOGUING DATA ARE AVAILABLE

On the cover: Baseball statistics board and global business icons
(iStockphoto/Thinkstock)

Manufactured in the United States of America

*McFarland & Company, Inc., Publishers
Box 611, Jefferson, North Carolina 28640
www.mcfarlandpub.com*

In loving memory of
John Carmen Fortunato,
December 15, 1934–April 2, 2012

Contents

Acknowledgments

This book would not have been possible without the time and efforts of many talented people. I would first like to thank all of the professionals who willingly gave up their time to participate in interviews. Their insights contributed much to my understanding of the sponsorship field. Without their knowledge, this book would have been incomplete.

My thanks to David Abrutyn, IMG Consulting senior vice president and global managing director; Paul Asencio, senior vice president of corporate sales and partnerships for the New York Mets; Jim Biegalski, senior vice president of consulting for the Marketing Arm; J. W. Cannon, UPS senior project leader, sponsorship and events; Darin David, account director for the Marketing Arm; Dan Donnelly, executive vice president and managing director with Starcom MediaVests; Todd Fischer, State Farm manager of national sponsorships; Lou Imbriano, president and CEO of TrinityOne, a marketing strategies and business consulting firm; Gordon Kane, founder of Victory Sports Marketing; John Knebel, Washington Nationals vice president and managing director of corporate partnerships and business developments; Steve Margosian, NBC Sports senior vice president enterprise sales and marketing; Christine Plonsky, University of Texas women's athletic director and senior associate athletic director external services; Tony Ponturo, former head of media and sports marketing for Anheuser-Busch; George Pyne, president of IMG Sports and Entertainment; Mike Singer, consulting director for the Marketing Arm; Keith Turner, NFL senior vice president of sponsorship and media sales; Keith Wachtel, NHL senior vice president of integrated sales; and Scott Willingham, vice president/general manager, Longhorn IMG Sports Marketing.

I would also like to acknowledge the people who helped me coordinate some of these interviews: Joe Browne, Tina Mannix, Jared Melzer, and Paul Reilly. A special thanks to Steve Margosian for introducing me to Tony Ponturo. I am honored that Mr. Ponturo contriubuted the Foreword.

In addition to the interviews, a great amount of research went into obtaining information from printed records and Web sites to provide the practitioner perspective as well. One publication in particular that I deem essential in my research in helping me keep up with the field is the *Street & Smith's Sports Business Journal*. It is certainly a goal of this book to align the theoretical foundations of promotional communication put forth in the literature with what is happening in the practical industry.

Two of my former students at Fordham University worked tirelessly in helping me track down both academic and practical sources for the book: Rebecca Cuiba and Ben Gartska. I am very appreciative of their efforts and their interest in this research. They should feel proud of their contributions.

I am grateful to the administration of Fordham University's Gabelli School of Business and the faculty members of the Business School's Area of Communication & Media Management for their tremendous support of my work. Being able to discuss ideas with them was very beneficial.

I would also like to mention my friends and former faculty colleagues at the University of Texas at Austin in the Department of Advertising and Public Relations. In my five years as a faculty member in that department, our constant discussions about so many of the topics of promotional communications informed me at every step and in many ways served as an inspiration for this project. I was honored to reference the illuminating research that many of you have conducted in this book.

Finally, I would like to thank the students who have taken my classes that serve as an inspiration for informative content. There is a great connection between quality research and quality teaching. It is often during lectures and students' feedback and questions that I think about my own research projects. I am excited to discuss what I learned in this book with future classes. I certainly hope the information in these pages helps them in their careers.

Foreword by Tony Ponturo

Sports sponsorship has become a sophisticated business with huge amounts of marketing dollars at stake. Marketing investments need to be maximized for effective branding and growing market share, while sports teams, leagues, and associations need sponsors as major sources of revenue. When successful, the sponsorship partnership should benefit both the marketing brand and the property. For the sponsor in particular, when successful, sponsorship can be a valuable strategy to satisfy a specific brand goal and the long-term strategy of brand building.

For 26 years I worked for Anheuser-Busch, eventually becoming its head of media and sports marketing. I was responsible for directing the media planning and buying functions domestically and internationally for the Anheuser-Busch beer brands. I witnessed firsthand the growth of the sponsorship business. I have learned that to excel in the sponsorship industry you need to be aware of many concepts and possess a set of skills. The industry has been desperate for a book that can provide an understanding of these concepts and an explanation of these skills needed to compete in this demanding arena. *Sports Sponsorship: Principles and Practices* answers this demand and offers the insight to succeed in this industry.

The sponsorship industry has become more complex, but I contend that certain fundamentals remain. The sponsorship process still begins with understanding the customer the brand is trying to reach, understanding the brand's goals, finding the best properties to accomplish those goals, knowing the value of the property, and exciting customers about the brand. Critical decisions need to be made: Which property should a brand sponsor? What level of investment needs to be made to achieve the brand's goals? How can the sponsorship best highlight a brand theme and better connect the brand with the consumer? And how can sponsorship best be evaluated? You must also understand the competition within the product category and the neverending quest for market share. At Anheuser-Busch our marketing team was always considering how our sponsorships could help grow market share.

Sponsorship offers unlimited possibilities with the details of the agreement having to be negotiated between the brand and the property. Each sponsorship agreement is uniquely customized. Because of this sponsorship is an industry where relationships need to be developed and fostered. The representatives of the brand and the property need to be in constant communication to develop trust and ideas to improve the sponsorship.

To help the reader better understand the sponsorship industry this book contains numerous practical examples which reflect the unlimited possibilities available through sponsorship. This book also features interviews with professionals from all areas of the field. In any field, or walk of life, it is important to learn from those who have experienced the business. The perspectives of these sponsorship professionals highlight the challenges they confront on a daily basis. These professionals provide a foundation to stimulate creativity and forward thinking about an industry that will continue to evolve.

   Sports Sponsorship: Principles and Practices discusses in great detail all the important concepts that people in the industry must know. In reading this book one will obtain the necessary understanding of the industry that will make for more effective sports sponsorships in the future.

Tony Ponturo is the CEO of the Ponturo Management Group and a partner and producer of the Kirmser/Ponturo Group.

Introduction

The setting for Game One of the 2012 World Series between the San Francisco Giants and the Detroit Tigers is AT&T Park, the stadium in San Francisco named for the telecommunications company. The game is being televised on Fox, and its pre-game show sponsored by Chevrolet has just concluded. Among the commercials during the pre-game show is Procter & Gamble's Head & Shoulders shampoo featuring Minnesota Twins All-Star catcher Joe Mauer. The end of the commercial has a visual of the Major League Baseball logo and a graphic declaring that Head & Shoulders is the official shampoo of Major League Baseball. Another commercial is for MasterCard, the official credit card of Major League Baseball, in which the company along with Major League Baseball is thanking customers who used their MasterCard in helping raise money for the Stand Up to Cancer charity. The commercial ends with the MasterCard, Major League Baseball, and Stand Up to Cancer logos.

When the broadcast returns from a commercial break just prior to the start of the game Geico and DirectTV are recognized as sponsors of the World Series through bumpers, still shots showing a company's logo set against video of the stadium or the city in which the game is being played, with an announcer mentioning the brand names. Following the bumpers the starting lineup for the Detroit Tigers appears on the screen with the Taco Bell logo and Fox announcer Joe Buck telling the audience that the "starting lineup for the Tigers is brought to you by Taco Bell; Sometimes you got to Live Mas." After announcing the names of the Tigers starters, Buck informs viewers that Taco Bell is conducting a "Steal a Base, Steal a Taco" promotion during the World Series where if a player steals a base, consumers will be allowed to get a free taco — in Game Two, San Francisco Giants outfielder Angel Pagan did steal a base giving everyone in the United States the chance to get a free Doritos Locos Taco.

The next image is Giants starting pitcher Barry Zito making his warm-up throws, with Buck telling viewers that the "opening pitch is brought to you by Budweiser. Great times are waiting, grab some Buds." While Buck is saying this, the Budweiser logo appears on the screen with a video of beer being poured into a glass.

As the first inning of the World Series is played, the signage display board behind home plate that is clearly visible on television has a Dick's Sporting Goods billboard with its brand slogan of "Every Season Starts at Dick's." The Dick's Sporting Goods logo also appears on the screen when the teams' defensive lineups are announced in the top and bottom of the first inning with Joe Buck again stating the company slogan to viewers.

When the game comes back from commercial for the bottom of the first inning, a bumper is provided for Taco Bell, whose voice-over includes the "Live Mas" slogan. The Giants starting lineup, sponsored by Taco Bell, is then introduced with Buck again providing the Taco Bell slogan. Joe Buck tells the television audience, estimated at more than 12 million viewers for Game One, that Taco Bell invites you to "Live Mas" three times before a Giant hitter comes to bat in the 2012 World Series. The bottom of the first inning features a Budweiser advertisement on the signage display board behind home plate with both the Budweiser and Major League Baseball logos and the phrase "proud sponsor" on the advertisement to clearly communicate the association between the sponsor and the property.

This description of brand exposure, communication of brand themes, and these brands trying to associate themselves with an event such as the World Series is just one example of one aspect of what a sponsorship might entail. Critical questions about this sponsorship strategy emerge: Did viewers notice the brands' advertisements? Do viewers identify and positively associate the brand with the property? Can viewers recall the specific brand when it is time to make a purchase within that product category? Will this sponsorship entice them to purchase the brand?

Any promotional communication effort has to begin with the premise that it has the potential to be influential regardless of what stage the consumer is at in terms of his or her perception of the brand or his or her need to purchase an item from that product category. Although there are many variables that determine a sale, the belief for practitioners has to be that these promotional communication efforts can move consumers along the path toward purchasing the brand. In that light, Keller (2001) defines promotional communication goals as trying to "inform, persuade, incite, and remind customers, directly or indirectly, about the brands they sell" (p. 819). Pope, Voges, and Brown (2009) state promotional communication can influence perceptions of a brand "either through interacting with existing perceptions, or by presenting information to persuade a consumer of a brand's merits" (p. 5). Mills (2011) adds, "Clearly, the goal of companies advertising their products is to obtain a positive change in attitude toward their product or service, ideally with the least amount of effort and financial cost" (p. 510).

Specific promotional communication strategies must be implemented to achieve these persuasive goals. Determining the specific promotional communication strategy is a challenge for all practitioners. It is clear several corporations are now utilizing sponsorship as a viable investment strategy and a major part of their overall promotional communication plan. IEG reported that sponsorship spending in North America in 2012 totaled $18.9 billion, and global sponsorship spending totaled $51.1 billion (IEG press release, January 7, 2013).

The rationale for sponsorship as part of a company's overall promotional communication strategy is somewhat simple; as communication technologies emerge causing media use behavior patterns to change, the audience has become splintered. Companies need to be in various places in order to reach all of their various demographic audience groups. Thus, sponsorship has become a necessary strategy for many companies to obtain brand exposure, achieve better brand recall, communicate their brand themes, and achieve a better association between the brand and the consumer with the hopes of obtaining sales (Fortunato & Dunnam, 2004; Kinney, 2006; Meenaghan, 1991, 2001; Mullin, Hardy,

& Sutton, 2007; Pedersen, Miloch, & Laucella, 2007; Shank, 2008; Walliser, 2003). Cornwell (2008) simply declares that sponsorship is a mainstream marketing activity no longer in need of justification.

Beyond providing another promotional communication method, there are distinct and unique advantageous characteristics of sponsorship that will be detailed in this book. These characteristics include:

- The ability to negotiate the parameters of the sponsorship agreement
- Multiple entry points to a property that can fit all budgetary constraints
- Multiple methods of communicating the brand name to receive exposure
- Multiple methods of having consumers interact and engage with the brand
- Opportunities to increase brand recall
- Opportunities to form and communicate a brand association with a popular property
- Opportunities to activate the sponsorship with a flexible and customizable program that addresses the brand's goals
- Opportunities to communicate a brand theme in a creative way, including fan participatory experiences
- Opportunities to immediately sell the product or increase future sales
- Opportunities for product category exclusivity and eliminating competition at a given location
- Opportunities for hospitality to reward clients and employees
- Opportunities to engage in and communicate corporate social responsibility initiatives
- Opportunities to evaluate the sponsorship on a series of metrics that can clearly demonstrate the financial value of the sponsorship strategy as well as inform and advise future promotional communication planning

Understanding the advantageous characteristics of sponsorship is critical to making it an effective promotional communication method. The characteristic of negotiation makes anything possible, it is only a matter of what the representatives from the sponsor and the property agree to, is the most distinct advantage of sponsorship. No two sponsorship agreements are alike, as the negotiated details define the difference. Each sponsorship agreement should be flexible and customized to address any specific brand goals. The ability to negotiate the parameters of the agreement ultimately provides a great opportunity for both the sponsor and the property to craft an agreement that is beneficial for each entity. The sponsor and the property are also very much partners in an interdependent relationship. The property very much needs sponsors for revenue, while sponsors very much need the property as the vehicle to reach their target audience and help achieve their overall promotional communication business goals.

There are two main steps to the sponsorship process: acquiring sponsorship rights and activating the sponsorship. A considerable investment is required by the sponsor to first obtain the sponsorship. An additional investment needs to be made to activate the sponsorship. Activation ideas need to be developed to creatively communicate a brand theme and associate the brand with the property as well as associate the brand with the consumers. Ideas for how the sponsorship will be executed and structured can emanate from people affiliated with either the sponsor or the property. Sponsorship can simply be thought of as an "ideas business."

Much of the sponsorship spending is with sports properties; therefore, sports sponsorship is the focus of this book. A sports property is simply being defined in a general manner and includes a sports league, a team, an event, or an individual player. The reasons why sponsors invest large amounts of money with sports properties will be articulated throughout the book. These reasons include brand exposure to a large, but often difficult to reach demographic audience that is passionate in its feelings toward sports teams; there is ample opportunity for the sponsor to associate itself with the sports property and its image; there are opportunities for brand exposure within games when the audience is apt to be watching to assist with recall; and sports programming is largely DVR-proof. Raynaud and Bolos (2008) summarize that brands are interested in sports "because it is big, growing and has measurable impacts of rational and emotional benefits" (p. 33). It will become clear why sponsorship with sports properties will continue to be an often used promotional communication strategy.

In trying to capture this complex industry no singular book about sponsorship can be completely exhaustive in covering the field. The sponsorship industry is constantly changing as new technologies emerge and practitioners within the industry continue to develop new ideas for brand exposure and better associating the brand to the audience. The creative talents of the people in the industry using the technologies that continue to be developed ensure that the field will look different in the coming years than it does today. The principles of sponsorship, the goals of sponsorship, the need to understand the audience, to understand the brand, and the need to develop the relationships that have to be built for the sponsorship strategy to remain effective do not change. The key is for people within the industry to have the knowledge of the sponsorship principles so that they can better apply them to the opportunities that will be available. Therefore, it is important to provide an overview of the practice of sponsorship at this critical time.

Sponsorship is not a new strategy. In the 1950s radio and television had sponsored programs, and the outfield wall of major league ballparks featured sponsorship signage. The book is not necessarily designed to focus on the history of sponsorship (for a detailed, historic review of the literature about the evolutions of sponsorship theories and practices, see Cornwell & Maignan, 1998; O'Reilly & Madill, 2009; Walliser, 2003).

This book provides a theoretical foundation of promotional communication and its role in persuasion, details the need for sponsorship as a form of promotional communication, explains the core fundamentals of the sponsorship practice, explains the key decisions the companies continuously deal with when developing their sponsorship programs, and provides a sampling of how companies are implementing and executing their sponsorships through numerous examples. These real-life examples document the complexity of the industry and provide the reader with a series of best practices that signify the opportunities available and what is possible through a sponsorship strategy. This book intends to make the reader aware of the many variables that concern practitioners in their designing and executing successful sponsorship programs. Finally, it will make the reader more observant in witnessing and analyzing the practice of sponsorship.

Chapter One provides a theoretical foundation to better understand the concept of persuasion and how it relates to promotional communication practices. One theory emphasized is the Elaboration Likelihood Model attributed to Cacioppo and Petty, which contends that individual involvement, or interest, in an issue or a product category will lead the person to evaluate the quality of the argument of those messages more critically. Theories of promotional communication help provide a guideline for best practices in the industry and an overall approach to understanding and executing sponsorship agreements. Some of the practical strategies detailed in the book will be applied to these theoretical concepts. Chapter One also focuses on the branding process and the goals of promotional communication campaigns, such as brand exposure and brand recall that contribute to consumer behavior. The advantageous characteristics of the advertiser controlling the message placement and the message content due to its financial investment are highlighted.

Chapter Two documents the need for sponsorship as part of a company's overall promotional communication strategy. It begins with a discussion of the splintered media use environment. Chapter Two also shows how sponsorship has become a plausible option in reaching a target audience. Definitions of sponsorship are offered with an emphasis on the characteristic of negotiation making anything possible and all sponsorships being unique depending on the sponsor's promotional communication business goals. The relationship between a sponsor and a property begins to be explained with the sponsor using the property as a means to accomplish any number of promotional communication business goals and the property needing the sponsor as a major source of revenue. Strategies for how the property and the sponsor approach the negotiation process are offered.

Chapter Three addresses the primary critical decision that the sponsor has to make: selection of the property. It specifically focuses on two of the variables that are always part of the selection process: the target audience and the cost of the sponsorship. All promotional communication decisions start with identification of the target audience. Selection of the property is based on these audience demographic variables. Different property selections are tailored to reach different demographic audience groups. These sponsorship property selection decisions obviously have to be made within a company's budgetary constraints. Chapter Three also highlights the concept of exclusivity, a prominent condition that is negotiated in a sponsorship agreement. Exclusivity eliminates competing brands from having a presence and depicting an association at that location or with that property. The chapter ends by indicating that companies have to be clear to define the product category rights that are part of the exclusivity agreement with any potential ambiguity in the product category creating an opening for another company to weave its way into that location or with that property.

Chapter Four demonstrates that there are multiple entry points for a sponsor to engage with a property: the event, league, team, individual athlete, or broadcast network. A major advantage of sponsorship emerges in that much like product placement, sponsorship allows for brand exposure within the context of the game when the audience is most likely to be watching and not clicking channels or walking away from the television screen. Chapter Four also has a discussion of two very noticeable sponsorships that are certainly enhanced through television coverage: stadium or arena naming rights and college football bowl games. The chapter ends by examining fans' reactions to the practice of sponsorship.

Chapter Five examines sponsorship selection based on the ability of the sponsor to form a brand association with the property. This association is enhanced if there is a strong brand fit between the sponsor and the property. Brand fit, or congruence, can be based on either an image component, when the sponsor and the property share a similar image, or functional component, when the sponsor's brand is actually used in the participation or support of the event. The concept of "purchase congruence" is also introduced where in some industries, such as the soft drink industry, sponsors have the opportunity for immediate point-of-purchase sales at the stadium or arena. Evidence of sponsorship leading to consumer behavior is provided in this chapter. Chapter Five ends with a discussion of uniform, apparel, and equipment sponsorships to illustrate how all of the beneficial congruence variables can complement one another.

Chapter Six focuses on sponsorship activation, the many strategies that are implemented to further communicate the brand's sponsorship and better associate the sponsor with the property and the consumer. Sponsorship activation can occur in a way that creatively communicates a brand theme. To help create a successful sponsorship there must be not only an investment in acquiring the rights to the property, but an investment to activate the sponsorship as well. Numerous practical examples of activation programs are provided for fans that attend sporting events and activation programs that engage consumers in other settings. A section of how credit card companies activate their sponsorships is provided. Chapter Six also reexamines the negotiation process focusing on renewal and retention of sponsors and the role that activation execution achieving a brand's promotional communication goals plays.

Chapter Seven documents the many hindrances to a successful sponsorship. These hindrances largely involve improper brand recognition of an official sponsor by the audience. These hindrances include advertising clutter, ambush marketing, and conflicts of multiple sponsorships being sold to different companies within the same product category by the league and its teams. Examples of ambush marketing attempts and remedies to ambush marketing practices are provided. The NFL beer market is profiled to better understand the conflict between the league and its teams both being able to sell official, exclusive sponsorships within the same product category. Chapter Seven ends with a discussion of other possible hindrances: company scandal and the sports fans purposely not purchasing products from sponsors who support the teams and athletes that they root against.

Chapter Eight deals with the use of individuals as a product sponsor. It reveals that many of the same variables (cost, target audience, brand fit) that influence league and team property selection, influence the selection of an individual endorser. This chapter touches on the personal characteristics of the individual that enhance the effectiveness of the endorsement strategy, most notably endorser expertise and image. The conflict between an individual being sponsored by one brand and the team being sponsored by a different brand within the same product category is highlighted. Chapter Eight also provides insight into how sponsors react when the individual endorsing their brand is involved in a public scandal.

Chapter Nine raises the prospect of sponsorship being thought of as a form of public relations as much as it is a form of advertising. The need to engage in corporate social responsibility efforts continues to emerge in the public's evaluation of these companies. It seems that one sponsorship can simultaneously achieve both advertising business communication and public relations image goals. Activating the sponsorship with a corporate social responsibility component can highlight important brand themes. In fact, to not include a corporate social responsibility initiative as part of a sponsorship might be a missed opportunity for a company to further enhance its brand exposure and image. Several practical examples of a corporate social responsibility initiative through the company's sponsorship of a property are provided.

Chapter Ten focuses on sponsorship evaluation. The possible methods of evaluation are discussed. Similar to other forms of promotional communication, evaluation of sponsorship is a difficult, but necessary task. To not conduct extensive evaluation of the sponsorship overall, and any of its activation programs specifically, appears to be a missed opportunity. Nelson and Katz (2011) explain that "marketers are challenged to gain more precise and accurate information, not only on who is the audience, but where are they and how receptive might they be to the ad message" (pp. 314–15). Chapter Ten also examines evaluation in terms of both return on investment (ROI) and return on objectives (ROO). It shows how brand goals, development of activation programs, and evaluation measures should all be coordinated and established during the initial sponsorship negotiation.

Finally, a Conclusion provides additional commentary on the sponsorship principles and practices documented throughout the book. It offers tips for how to best maintain an understanding of what is happening in the sponsorship industry.

To capture what is occurring in the field of sponsorship three main methods are used. The first is mere observation. Because promotional communication campaigns eventually need exposure to an audience, it is easy to witness some of a company's sponsorship strategies by watching games and events on television, visiting Web sites, and attending events in person. The second method is to interview practitioners from every aspect of the industry. Interviews were conducted with practitioners representing properties, both leagues and teams, sponsors, and agency personnel. The final method is to gather commentary from practitioners through quotes within media stories and press releases that provide their perspective. Researchers have identified that news releases are valuable in obtaining media coverage (Cameron, Sallot, & Curtin, 1997; Ohl, Pincus, Rimmer, & Harrison, 1995; Walters & Walters, 1992). The use of press releases in studying an organization's communication strategy has also been done in previous research (Cho & Benoit, 2005, 2006; Choi & Park, 2011).

Providing the practitioner perspective is the best approach to illuminate what is actually occurring in the field of sponsorship. Bringing together the work of academics, the work of the press covering the sponsorship industry, and the perspective of the practitioners is important because these methods help align theoretical claims with practical techniques. The practitioner perspective can be analyzed in conjunction with theoretical concepts of promotional communication in general and sponsorship specifically that have been put forth in the academic literature.

Chapter One

Promotional Communication and Persuasion

From the earliest forms of advertising using print and basic drawings to the most sophisticated techniques of today using all forms of digital media, the ultimate goal of promotional communication has not changed: to persuade (Leckenby & Stout, 1985; O'Guinn, Allen, & Semenik, 2006; Tellis, 2004). According to Perloff (2008) persuasion is intentional communication. He defines it as "a symbolic process in which communicators try to convince other people to change their attitudes or behaviors regarding an issue through the transmission of a message in an atmosphere of free choice" (p. 17). Changing people's attitudes and behaviors is a very difficult task. There are many variables influencing the persuasion process, whether it is an issue-oriented argument or a purchase decision. These variables include the quality of the argument presented and the credibility of the message source as well as receiver variables, such as if the person has an interest in the issue of the communicated message or, in the case of promotional communication messages, if it is a brand that he or she is loyal toward. Persuasion is the desired outcome for all promotional communication efforts.

Promotional communication is a general term encompassing all forms of advertising, marketing, public relations campaigns, and certainly sponsorship. In a business context, promotional communication messages are trying to influence people's opinions in order to eventually get them to buy their brand. Promotional communication is an industry reliant on understanding the brand, the consumers' needs and desires, and the communication methods available in terms of both message formulation and delivery systems. The better that people understand the theoretical framework of the persuasion process, the more effective they can be in developing their communication strategies and the better that people receiving these persuasive messages can be in evaluating and understanding these persuasion attempts.

Elaboration Likelihood Model

One of the most recognized theories of persuasion that has been applied to promotional communication is the Elaboration Likelihood Model, attributed to Petty and Cacioppo (Cacioppo & Petty, 1979; Petty & Cacioppo, 1979, 1981; Petty, Cacioppo, &

Morris, 1983; Petty, Cacioppo, & Schumann, 1983). The Elaboration Likelihood Model focuses on a cognitive process beginning with the premise that people are constantly receiving messages whose intent is to persuade, but they do not have the capacity to think exhaustively about every single message nor have the ability to completely ignore these messages. The Elaboration Likelihood Model posits that the individual involvement, or interest, in the issue will motivate him or her to evaluate certain messages more critically. Involvement with an issue is categorized along a continuum as being either high or low. As an issue or message increases in personal relevance it becomes more important for the individual to form a reasoned opinion. The likelihood of elaboration is, therefore, increased for issues that people find relevant — those categorized as high involvement.

For issues or messages that are considered high involvement by the individual, there will be the detailed evaluation of the quality of the argument being presented, and it is this extended elaboration that will be the determinant factor of persuasion occurring. Petty, Cacioppo, and Schumann (1983) explain, "People are more motivated to devote the cognitive effort required to evaluate the true merits of an issue or product when involvement is high rather than low" (p. 137). They add, "Under high involvement conditions people appear to exert the cognitive effort required to evaluate the issue-relevant arguments presented, and their attitudes are a function of this information-processing activity" (p. 137). The diligent consideration of the quality of the argument producing an attitude change is referred to by Petty and Cacioppo as persuasion occurring through a central route. Attitude changes through the central route are thought to be enduring and more predictive of behavior.

If the message does indeed provide a quality argument as intended, persuasion could be achieved in the manner desired by the message sender. However, if a quality argument is not presented, the receiver of the message could be persuaded toward the opposing point of view. Petty and Cacioppo (1979) explain that "increasing involvement with an issue increases one's motivation to process information relevant to the issue and can lead to either increased or decreased persuasion" (p. 1915). Petty et al. (1983) add, "If information is perceived to be cogent and persuasive, favorable attitudes will result, but if this information is weak and specious, unfavorable attitudes will result (central route)" (p. 138).

According to the Elaboration Likelihood Model for messages about issues that are not of major relevance to the individual, those of low involvement, there is not a comprehensive evaluation of the quality of the argument. Petty et al. (1983) explain, "Under low involvement conditions, attitudes appear to be affected by simple acceptance and rejection cues in the persuasion context and less affected by argument quality" (p. 137). There is still a chance for an attitude change, but it will occur based on attributes other than the quality of the argument, referred to as persuasion occurring through a peripheral route (see Figure One).

Elaboration Likelihood Model and Promotional Communication

In applying the Elaboration Likelihood Model to promotional communication, high involvement is categorized as the individual having a need for a particular product category

Figure One: Elaboration Likelihood Model

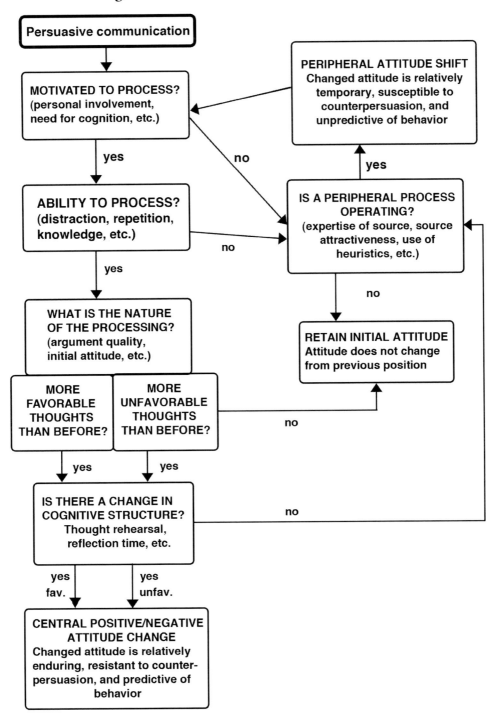

Source: Petty & Cacioppo, 1986; diagram by Petty & Wegener, 1989.

or that he or she will at least be involved in the purchase decision (i.e., a parent buying an item for his or her child). A consumer who is looking to purchase a car may pay more attention to automobile advertisements and notice car companies' sponsorships. Cauberghe and De Pelsmacker (2010) confirm that "product category involvement has an influence on the motivation to process information" (p. 8). The likelihood of elaboration is increased for product categories that people need or desire. For these high involvement product categories there will be a more deliberate evaluation of the quality of the product-relevant information and the compelling brand features presented in the promotional communication. The consumer who is looking to purchase a car will pay attention to the message content of the promotional communication and the specific brand's features, such as cost, gas mileage, safety characteristics, size of the car, or any other attributes that he or she deems relevant.

Involvement is not only based on need, but the mere motivation on the part of the consumer to learn about the various brands within a given product category because of his or her interests. For example, a person who has an interest in golf will pay more attention to promotional communication about golf equipment even if he or she does not have a need for those products at that particular time. This desire to learn about the options available is a factor in the individual's processing of the information. Kinney, McDaniel, and DeGaris (2008) state, "Involvement with the sport may translate into deeper, more elaborate processing of brand information presented via sport" (p. 176).

Low involvement is categorized as the individual not having a need, desire, or interest for a particular product category. For the product categories that are thought to have low involvement, because of a lack of motivation to learn, the assessment of the promotional communication messages will not be as detailed on the quality of the information presented. Petty et al. (1983) point out that when the individual is not interested in that product, at that moment, he or she "will not expend the effort required to think about the product-relevant arguments in the ad, but may instead focus on the attractiveness, credibility, or prestige of the product's endorser (peripheral route)" (p. 138). Through these nonargument based factors there is still an opportunity for an individual to be persuaded into a purchase. As Perloff (2008) contends, "People buy products for reasons other than tangible benefits. They buy to fulfill ambitions, dreams, and fantasies" (p. 427).

The Elaboration Likelihood Model views persuasion as occurring only through either the central or peripheral route based on the individual's involvement. Unlike the Elaboration Likelihood Model, which sees these two paths of persuasion as distinct and mutually exclusive, the Heuristic-Systematic Model, attributed to Eagly and Chaiken (1993, 1998), contends that people can be persuaded through both systematic, argument-based reasoning similar to the central route, and heuristic, simple cues similar to the peripheral route. Eagly and Chaiken (1993) explain that the two routes can be influential if they do not have highly contradictory information. They claim, "Recipients' processing of heuristic cues establishes expectancies about message validity, which, in turn, influence their perception and evaluation of persuasive arguments" (p. 329).

Note that involvement in an issue or with a product category is not a static condition. Consumers' needs for different product categories can shift at any given moment (i.e., an appliance breaks; a person suddenly has to rent a car or book a hotel). What was a low involvement product category one day can become a high involvement product category the next day. Also, when one promotional message is being sent, the sender (the advertiser) cannot definitively know the issue involvement of all of the specific message receivers (the audience)—how many of the total number of message receivers have high involvement or low involvement with the issue or product category.

These ambiguous conditions lend support to the notion of using both a quality, logic-based argument, but also a heuristic, social-attribute argument. If using the example of the promotional communication for an automotive brand as mentioned previously, the brand's features that form a quality argument could be tailored for the high-involvement individual. The promotional communication campaign could simultaneously use a memorable logo or slogan, or a celebrity spokesperson to attract the low-involvement consumer. If that low-involvement consumer then transforms to one of high involvement due to his or her newly found need for that product category there may already be a level of familiarity with the brand. That consumer now of an emerging high-involvement mindset might then pay greater attention to the quality of the argument being presented in that brand's promotional communication.

It probably behooves the advertiser to always present a quality argument in some of its promotional communication messages as well because this compelling evidence could potentially move a low-involvement consumer toward becoming a high-involvement consumer. A person might not think that he or she has a need for a certain product category; however, a compelling argument might get that person to realize that the product does not cost much, or is easy to use, or not difficult to obtain. Therefore, not using both logic-based arguments and heuristic attributes might result in a missed opportunity to engage a consumer. Ultimately, there is the opportunity to communicate effectively through both the central and peripheral route to both the high-involvement and low-involvement individual.

Branding Process

In extending the work of Petty and Cacioppo, as the concept of individual involvement with the issue or product category implies, a key mediating variable in evaluating the persuasive message is to not only examine the quality of the argument, but to examine the individuals' motivations, ability to process, and attitudes toward the messages they receive. For example, Chaiken, Liberman, and Eagly (1989) suggest concepts that influence message processing, such as a defense-motivation, a desire to form and defend a particular attitude position, or an impression-motivation, a desire to hold a socially acceptable attitude position. Wood (2000) provides a comprehensive overview of social reasons that influence persuasive change, including favorable evaluation of self and ensuring satisfactory relations. She cites the concept of "Consensus implies correctness," with people wanting to be part of the majority opinion as an influence on their attitude or behavior (p. 551).

How attitudes shape the evaluation of messages and dictate consumer behavior becomes an important area of analysis (Auty & Lewis, 2004; Eagly & Chaiken, 1993, 1998; Fishbein & Ajzen, 1975, 1981). Researchers make a necessary recognition that these attitudes have to manifest themselves at the time of behavior for them to truly be meaningful. Eagly and Chaiken (1998) state, "Individuals do not have an attitude until they first encounter the attitude object (or information about it) and respond evaluatively to it" (p. 270). Perloff (2008) explains that for the attitude to influence behavior it must come to mind spontaneously at the time a decision needs to be made and that the attitude must be the influencing agent. He states, "You can harbor an attitude toward a person or issue, but unless the attitude comes to mind when you encounter the other person or issue, you cannot act on the attitude in a particular situation" (p. 137).

One major attitude held by consumers is toward the source of the message; in promotional communication this would be the advertising brand. The consumers' attitude toward the company engaging in promotional communication attempts is critical in the branding process. These attitudes toward specific brands are learned, and they can influence an individual's thoughts and actions (Perloff, 2008). In fact, that is largely the role of the promotional communication industry and the branding process, to help shape these attitudes and guide consumer behavior.

Scholars have indicated that brands have images and personalities and the perception of the brand is largely in the mind of the consumer (Blackston, 2000; Davis, 2002; Keller, 1993, 1998). Aaker (1991) describes a brand as an implicit contract between a product and a consumer. Blackston (2000) claims that there are two characteristics of a successful relationship between the brand and the consumer: (1) trust in the brand and (2) customer satisfaction with the brand. Kapferer (2001) focuses on the customer satisfaction with the brand, explaining that a brand is a set of promises that a company makes to its customers and that the promise is built on the coherence and continuity of the brand's products. Davis (2002) similarly defines a brand as "a set of promises. It implies trust, consistency, and a defined set of expectations" (p. 3). He adds, customers "cannot have a relationship with a product or service, but they may with a brand" (p. 31). It is the consistent, quality performance of the brand that meets consumers' expectations and inspires the consistent, loyal behavior of the audience toward the brand. Pope (2010) points out that any gap between what the brand claims and what the brand's actions are creates a potential issue of brand trust.

Researchers have examined the phenomenon of brand loyalty or commitment by an individual as a major factor in his or her evaluation of promotional communication messages (Ahluwalia, 2000; Raju, Unnava, & Montgomery, 2009). Raju, Unnava, and Montgomery (2009) explain that "a committed individual feels 'tied' to the brand or position and is less willing to change that position compared to a less committed individual" (p. 21). Commitment toward a brand can too be thought of as a continuum ranging from high to low. Burns (2011) points out that the connection and commitment of the consumer to the brand has to be factored into evaluating the effectiveness of the promotional communication. He explains that a portion of consumers can be identified as non-users or rejectors, people who have used the brand previously, but have since stopped, for whom the promotional communication message will have little, if any, value. He also points out that there is a group of persuadables, which "represents an opportunity to build share" (p. 306).

The level of commitment that an individual has toward a brand even becomes a factor in assessing product information from a competing brand. High-committed individuals toward one brand have less favorable attitudes toward competing brands and form multiple counterarguments to the information that is being presented as their first line of defense in support of their own brand choice commitments (Ahluwalia, 2000; Chaiken et al., 1989; Jain & Maheswaran, 2000; Raju et al., 2009). Raju et al. (2009) claim, "A consumer who is committed to a brand will not only defend his or her committed brand against attacks, but may also view positive information about a competitive brand unfavorably" (p. 22). They add, "Committed consumers will not only resist changes to their attitudes, but they may systematically underrate competitive offerings compared to less committed consumers" (p. 22).

To alter brand commitment, Raju et al. (2009) found that competitor brands need to provide overwhelmingly strong, irrefutable evidence in order to have high-committed consumers view the competing brand favorably. Demonstrating a brand is merely comparable to the favorable brand is not sufficient to influence high-committed consumers. If strong evidence is not presented, high-committed brand consumers will continue to view competitors unfavorably.

For a competing brand, in addition to presenting an argument with strong evidence, the number of occasions that the argument is received by the consumer can help produce an effect (Jain & Maheswaran, 2000; Petty & Cacioppo, 1984). Raju et al. (2009) articulate the best scenario for a competing brand trying to receive a consumer's approval is to present an argument with overwhelmingly strong evidence and have it communicated on multiple occasions. They state, "Many strong arguments that convince high-commitment consumers of the quality of the competitor brand are needed to reduce counterarguments, and hence, enhance evaluations" (p. 32). For low brand-committed consumers, the standard for influencing favorability of competing brands is not as difficult in terms of argument strength or the number of times the message needs to be received.

Achievement of Goals Leading to Persuasion

Within this ultimate goal of persuasion there are steps in the process that need to be achieved for persuasion to occur. The Hierarchy of Effects Model of persuasion describes a sequence of awareness, knowledge, liking, preference, conviction, and purchase (Lavidge & Steiner, 1961. For an additional discussion of the Hierarchy of Effects Model see Barry, 2002; Barry & Howard, 1990; Clow & Baack, 2012; Murphy, Cunningham, & Stavchansky de Lewis, 2011). Crompton (1996) explains that a consumer decision making process has to go through four stages: awareness, interest, desire, and purchase actions. Perloff (2008) claims a change in attitude or behavior may take time with people moving step-by-step toward a solution to a problem or a decision about which brand of a product category to purchase. He believes that persuasion involves the mental state of the receiver with people ultimately persuading themselves.

In terms of practical behavior, Burns (2011) suggests some of the several levels of interaction that can be achieved leading up to the ultimate goal of consumer behavior, such as visiting the brand's Web site, downloading information, or signing up to receive e-mails. Russell (2011) summarizes that promotional communication campaign objectives include brand awareness, familiarity, affinity, recall, preference, social media effects and recommendations, purchase, and repeat purchase.

To achieve persuasion, Fortunato and Dunnam (2004) describe any promotional communication strategy, including sponsorship, as having three specific goals: (1) obtaining exposure to the desired target audience, (2) increasing product brand recall, and (3) increasing consumer behavior (i.e., purchasing the brand). The progression is that exposure and increased recall help achieve the desired behavior. While there are many variables that influence a purchase decision, it is important that behavior is thought of as the ultimate goal of a promotional communication campaign, as without revenue being earned the company will cease to exist. Baker (1999) contends if a promotional campaign does not drive sales it can be rendered unsuccessful. Russell, Mahar, and Drewniak (2005) parsimoniously state, "Marketing is concerned with increasing future sales and by extension future cash flows" (p. 67). Green (2008) claims that "at the end of the day, most brands are in business to make a profit—everything else is merely an intermediate step on the road to this goal" (p. 359). Murphy, Cunningham, and Stavchansky de Lewis (2011) add, "A marketing program is intended to plan how products or services are taken from the point of production to the point of consumption in such a way as to develop a positive relationship between consumers and the producer that will foster additional or repeat usage" (p. 23).

In trying to achieve these behavior goals, understanding what determines the effectiveness of persuasive promotional communication continues to be an issue raised by many scholars (Tellis, 2004; Till & Baack, 2005) and an obvious concern of all practitioners. For promotional communication to have its best opportunity at being persuasive it needs to be effective on two components: its message placement and message content.

The initial component of a promotional communication strategy is the placement of the message. In advertising and sponsorship the company controls the message placement component by paying a certain dollar amount for a certain location, giving it access to the audience that participates in that content or location. Companies pay large amounts of money because their investment does guarantee them message placement at the time and location desired. This guaranteed placement is designed to provide the brand exposure to the target audience needed to be achieved in promotional communication (Fortunato & Dunnam, 2004; Wakefield, Becker-Olsen, & Cornwell, 2007). McAllister (1996) emphasizes the critical aspect of the proper brand exposure, stating, "Advertisers know that that first necessary (but not sufficient) condition for persuading a potential consumer to buy a product is to force the consumer to notice the message. If the consumer does not see the ad or ignores the ad, then the advertiser's message is wasted" (p. 18).

Bellamy and Traudt (2000) explain the necessity of brand exposure, "The fundamental concept is that a recognizable brand will more easily attract and retain customers than an unrecognizable one" (p. 127). This simple exposure begins the process of making the brand salient in the minds of consumers. Ehrenberg, Barnard, Kennedy, and Bloom (2002) explain that salience is having a share of the audience member's mind, stating, "Such broad salience is vital for a brand to become and remain in one's 'consideration set' as a brand that one might or does buy" (p. 8). Sutherland and Galloway (1981) argue, "Advertising does not create needs; it merely reflects those needs that are already existent in society at the time" (p. 25). They state, "Products that are advertised heavily have a status conferred upon them—i.e., they are felt by customers to be 'the more popular' products" (p. 27). They conclude, "Advertising (media prominence) functions as a significant cue to the customer in judging what is and is not acceptable and popular with others" (p. 28).

This salience or top-of-mind awareness is particularly important when an individual needs to purchase from a particular product category for the first time. It will be the familiar brands that will leap to the minds of consumers, giving these brands a distinct advantage in the purchase decision. The brand familiarity makes consumers feel more comfortable and confident in their purchase decision. Ehrenberg et al. (2002) explain that with "'share of mind' come feelings of being familiar and feelings of assurance" (p. 11). Brand familiarity can indeed be the determining variable of behavior if consumers view the brand choices as equivalent or if the purchase will not require much evaluation of brand choices (Baker, 1999; Greenwald & Leavitt, 1984). Ehrenberg et al. (2002) even contend that persuasion does not have to be overt in promotional communication. They point out that promotional communication can simply publicize the brand and that the exposure does not have to provide an explicit comparison between competing brands to influence the consumer.

The second component for a promotional communication message to have its best opportunity of being persuasive is to develop message content that will resonate with the audience. Just as the financial investment gives the company control over the message placement, the company has control of the message content within that time or space. In the content of the advertisement, the company gets to emphasize the brand features that it chooses. Murphy et al. (2011) claim, "The message content component presents a concise statement of the key benefit the brand promises the consumer if he or she will buy the brand" (p. 96).

Through paid promotional communication and the company controlling the content, the brand is portrayed, or framed, in the manner that the company chooses. Entman (1993) explains, "To frame is to select some aspects of a perceived reality and make them more salient in a communicating text, in such a way as to promote a particular problem definition, causal interpretation, moral evaluation, and/or treatment recommendation for the item described" (p. 52). He also claims that frames "call attention to some aspects of reality while obscuring other elements, which might lead audiences to have different reactions" (p. 55). Nelson, Clawson, and Oxley (1997) add that "frames influence opinions by stressing specific values, facts, and other considerations, endowing them with greater apparent relevance to the issue than they might appear to have under an alternative frame" (p. 569).

Jewler and Drewniany (2001) point out that promotional communication must make relevant associations with the consumer and that this can be achieved through the content of the message. They add, products are not different; "It's how you present them in the ad that makes the real difference" (p. 9). There are many product categories that people purchase where the individual believes that there is little difference between the competing brands. Companies use promotional communication strategies and the branding process to try to create a brand difference in the consumers' perceptions.

The concept of a unique selling proposition was developed by long-time advertising executive Rosser Reeves (1961) and explained in his book *The Reality of Advertising.* O'Guinn et al. (2006) define the unique selling proposition as "a promise contained in an advertisement in which the advertised brand offers a specific, unique, and relevant benefit to the consumer" (p. 744). Clow and Baack (2012) explain that a unique selling proposition is "an explicit, testable claim of uniqueness or superiority that can be supported or substantiated in some manner" (p. 191). The unique selling proposition provides an attribute that can quickly be associated with the brand, facilitating the brand being learned and memorized by consumers. The unique selling proposition could be a product attribute or perhaps a brand association.

Brand Recall

Proper brand message placement and message content, such as the communication of a unique selling proposition, can help achieve the important goal of brand recall (Cornwell, Relyea, Irwin, & Maignan, 2000; Kelley & Turley, 2004; Newell, Henderson, & Wu, 2001; Till & Baack, 2005). Brand recall focuses on remembering the specific brand name at the time when the purchase decision is being made. It is not enough that consumers are aware of the product category (insurance), they need to be aware of and have the ability to recall the specific brand name (State Farm). This recall is especially important in making a purchase for the first time in a product category as discussed earlier through the concept of brand salience and is important in product categories where there are several competing brands.

Brand recall is mitigated by a number of audience demographic variables. Studies have shown that brand recall has been influenced by education level, with higher education levels recalling more brands (Kinney et al., 2008; McDaniel & Kinney, 1999), age, with younger fans recalling more brands (Kinney et al., 2008; McDaniel & Kinney, 1999), and gender, with males recalling more brands (Kinney et al., 2008). In a study of NASCAR fans Kinney et al. (2008) concluded that "brands seeking to reach younger, more educated, male targets should continue to seek NASCAR sponsorships" (p. 169).

Practitioners employ several placement methods to enhance brand recall. One simple exposure method to enhance recall is repeated exposure of the brand name (Newell & Henderson, 1998). Companies can buy large amounts of advertising time and space in multiple locations to obtain the necessary and repeated brand exposure that can help achieve recall. McDaniel and Kinney (1998) found that recency of promotional communication exposure can be a factor in brand recall. Certainly there is a temporal element to advertising placement with the message reaching the audience at the right time. The concept of recency indicates an opportune moment to enhance recall might be just prior to the purchase decision being made. Many product categories have a distinct selling season. For example, a movie that is trying to have a big opening weekend might have multiple placements on Thursday, or a company that manufactures snow-removal equipment has a peak selling season of the winter. For other product categories there is not certainty when the purchase decision will be made, as indicated earlier in the discussion of consumers' needs for products shifting.

Beyond repeated exposure or recent exposure there are a multitude of strategies involving the content of the promotional communication message that could assist in brand recall, including compelling information, humor, featuring a celebrity, displaying a logo, providing a slogan, or showing what the product packaging looks like so that customers can easily recognize it on a store shelf. A variety of these message content strategies are simultaneously employed.

A recognizable corporate logo is a prominent strategy to enhance recall and an invaluable part of the branding process. Aaker (1996) claims that a strong brand symbol can be a key ingredient to brand development and identity, making the process of recognition and recall much easier. He suggests that corporations void of a strong brand symbol are at a competitive disadvantage. He notes that brand symbols are often promoted through society by their consumers who actively pursue, celebrate, and protect these symbols as a reflection of their beliefs and values. Atkin (2004) summarizes that "brands are symbols. We live in a world dominated by commercial icons, total design initiatives, and completely integrated marketing efforts, where products are consumed less for what they are (materially) and more for what they represent (spiritually, or at least socially)" (p. 111). Brand symbols such as the Nike swoosh, McDonald's golden arches, the Mercedes-Benz logo, or the Apple icon are exemplars of corporate logos with strong recognizable visual imagery. People might prefer to wear a T-shirt with a Nike swoosh rather than a plain T-shirt. For brands that aren't the company manufacturing the shirt, it is not uncommon to see people wearing apparel of a branded product, such as a Pepsi hat or T-shirt, or co-branded merchandise, such as a T-shirt that has a Pepsi logo and the logo of a sports team.

The words used in the promotional communication are as capable of impacting brand recall as are any pictures or logos created. Howard (1997) found that familiar brand slogans can lead to attitude changes. Slogans such as "Just Do It," "The King of Beers," or "You're in Good Hands" can be attributed to their proper corporate brand by most consumers. The branding aspects of logo and slogan development become an important communication instrument based on that heuristic appeal.

These logos and slogans help establish brand prominence. Accuracy of recall and top-of-mind awareness are enhanced if a brand is already prominent (Carrillat, Lafferty, & Harris, 2005; Hoeffler & Keller, 2003; Johar & Pham, 1999; Roy & Cornwell, 2004). The question that emerges is how does a brand become prominent? Obviously the quality of the product in the establishment of the brand cannot ever be overlooked. In addition to previous use of the product by the individual, brand prominence could be established through promotional communication by the company (Campbell & Keller, 2003). Even if consumers have never tried the brand, at the outset the prominent brands have a predisposed advantage to the recall process as the public is already very familiar with them through their promotional communication (including their logos and slogans). Practitioners in the promotional communication industry certainly have to feel that their efforts can play a substantial role in the branding process and establishing brand prominence.

Individual involvement plays a role in brand recall. In their research applying the Elaboration Likelihood Model to promotional communication, specifically traditional commercial advertising, Petty et al. (1983) found that increased involvement resulted in higher recall of the product category and the specific brand being advertised. For product categories of low involvement they found that there was still product category recall, but not recall of the specific brand. Petty et al. (1983) caution that recall is not always predictive of attitude change, nor should recall be thought of as the sole indicator of promotional communication effectiveness.

Beyond interest in the product category as noted in the Elaboration Likelihood

Model, researchers have identified that if the brand is related to the property in which it is advertising recall can be enhanced (Crimmins & Horn, 1996; Gwinner & Swanson, 2003; Johar & Pham, 1999; Pham & Johar, 2001; Rifon, Choi, Trimble, & Li, 2004; Speed & Thompson, 2000; Wakefield et al., 2007). Individuals participate in media for their content, not purposely because of the promotional communication messages that will be within that content, although it should be pointed out that people do go to specific Web sites to learn about product categories and specific brands. In relating the brand to the property, in message placement an implicit brand association is conveyed between the company and the property in which the advertisement is being placed (i.e., either a media organization such as NBC or *The New York Times* or the actual content in that media location such as the Olympics or *American Idol*).

If the brand and the property are linked in some fashion it can further establish this association and enhance recall. If the association is not explicit, the message content of the promotional communication can try to amplify the connection. Advertisers might make the content of the promotional communication similar to the content in which it is placed. For example, a commercial during a football game could feature elements of football or a commercial during a prime-time program might feature one of the stars from that show.

The attitude-toward-the-ad (AAD) theory claims that consumers' responses to promotional communication can have a significant positive impact on their attitude-toward-the-brand (Kinney & McDaniel, 1996; Lutz, 1985). Researchers have found that merely liking the advertisement can lead to a positive attitude-toward-the-brand (Brown & Stayman, 1992; Gardner, 1985; MacKenzie, Lutz, & Belch, 1986). More specifically, researchers have found that the message content of an advertisement can lead to a positive feeling toward the brand (Kelley & Turley, 2004; Turley & Kelley, 1997). Finally, and more importantly, researchers have concluded that the message content of an advertisement can lead to brand sales (Ang & Low, 2000; Chandy, Tellis, MacInnis, & Thaivanich, 2001; Tellis 2004). The attitude-toward-the-ad theory contends that consumers' responses to the promotional communication can have a significant positive impact on their purchase intention, but that attitude-toward-the-ad is more significant predictor of attitude-toward-the-brand than it is a predictor of purchase intention (Brown & Stayman, 1992; Kinney & McDaniel, 1996).

The optimum condition for the advertiser is for its promotional communication to effectively combine both the message placement and message content components. To be successful on only one component is to miss out on a critical opportunity toward achieving persuasion. Success on both components in terms of ideal placement and a compelling message does not, however, guarantee fulfillment of the ultimate goal of persuading behavior. There are, after all, many variables that are a part of consumer decision making about which brand to ultimately buy. The environment in which all of this persuasive promotional communication occurs must certainly be taken into account.

Chapter Two

The Principles of Sponsorship

Achievement of persuasion or the promotional communication goals of brand exposure and brand recall are much more complicated in the current technological communication environment (Atkin & Jeffres, 1998; Cauberghe & De Pelsmacker, 2011; Edelman, 2007; Ferguson & Perse, 2004; O'Guinn et al., 2006). It can be said that every time the technological communication environment changes and causes the mass media use of the audience to change, so too does the promotional communication industry (Fortunato & Windels, 2005). Russell (2011) indicates that any promotional communication strategy "rests on an understanding of consumers' media habits and the role that media play in the context of the decision cycle on engagement and persuasion — whether those are newly encountered media, passively used media or actively sought media" (p. 134). Eastin, Daugherty, and Burns (2011) add, "The combination of advertising practice, available technology and media use has produced shifts in commercial and social communication that have become culturally defining" (p. xxv).

Advertising, and the entire promotional communication industry, used to be easier in a media environment that featured only three main television networks, national magazines, and more localized newspapers and radio stations. Advertisers could simply purchase commercial time in a few locations and reach a large portion of their target audience. In 1995, three well-placed television commercials could reach 80 percent of women television viewers. By 2003, 97 television commercials were needed to reach the same size audience (O'Guinn et al., 2006).

The media environment that now features multiple cable television channels, television on-demand capabilities, the Internet, satellite radio, and hand-held devices provides content that has splintered the audience. As audiences are provided with a multitude of communication vehicles to experience media content, competition for attention is fierce, and companies simply need to have their brand exposed at a time and in a location when their target audience is available. During that exposure period companies must then present their brand with relevant information that can help produce brand recall and help lead toward consumer behavior. Russell (2011) explains that "the objective of the old broadcast model was to reach an aggregated audience. Objectives for new media emphasize identifying and engaging niches of fragmented markets with each fragment expecting relevancy" (p. 127).

The new media environment is dominated by digital technologies. Digital media allow for participation with content at a time and place that is convenient for the audience

(Bright, 2011; Carey & Elton, 2010; Daugherty, Eastin, & Bright, 2008; DeFleur & Dennis, 2002; Tauder, 2006). Bright (2011) explains, "While traditional media are nowhere near extinction, it is clear that trends are changing such that consumers are more in control of their media consumption in both the interactive and traditional realms. Not only have media evolved to distribute a diverse collection of news and information, they have also enabled consumers with a great capability to contribute their thoughts, opinions, and personal media" (p. 35). Jim Biegalski, senior vice president of consulting for the Marketing Arm, comments that all involved in the promotional communication industry, especially the sponsorship process, have to understand that "consumers have control over the way they experience content. Properties have the content that is the fans passion point, but the consumers control the interaction" (personal communication, February 8, 2012).

This audience control over their media choices regarding content and when they experience that content only exacerbates the difficulty for the advertisers that are trying to reach those potential consumers at a desired time. For example, a movie company might have purchased a 30-second commercial on a Thursday night airing of *The Big Bang Theory* on CBS in anticipation of a film's opening weekend. However, if a person DVR'd *The Big Bang Theory* and does not view it until the following week, the commercial will not be as effective, and there is no contribution at all from that promotional communication investment to the movie company's goal of having a successful opening weekend at the box office. Those in the promotional communication industry can counter the challenge of the environment by being cognizant of the opportunities that are presented through these new communication technologies (Fortunato & Windels, 2005).

Product Placement

One response to the brand exposure and brand recall challenge of the current mass media environment has been the use of product placement. The advantageous characteristic of product placement is communicating the brand to the audience during the actual program content. Karrh (1998) defines product placement as "paid inclusion of branded products or brand identifiers through audio and/or visual means, within mass media programming" (p. 33). More recently, Van Reijmersdal, Neijens, and Smit (2009) describe product placement as "the purposeful incorporation of brands into editorial content" (p. 429). The idea of product placement is simply that if people are viewing the content (or listening to a song) they will not be able to escape the brand exposure. It should be noted that not every brand that appears within a television program, movie, or a sports telecast is a paid sponsor.

Several researchers have discussed the effectiveness of product placement as a form of promotional communication, although research is mixed as to its effectiveness (Ansons, Wan, & Leboe, 2011; Auty & Lewis, 2004; Balasubramanian, Karrh, & Patwardhan, 2006; Bressoud, Lehu, & Russell, 2010; Cowley & Barron, 2008; Gupta & Lord, 1998; Homer, 2009; Karrh, 1998; Law & Braun, 2000; Olson & Thjomoe, 2003; Russell, 2002; Russell & Belch, 2005; Van Reijmersdal et al., 2009; Yang & Roskos-Ewoldsen, 2007). Similar to any other promotional communication strategy, product placement does not automatically guarantee the brand being noticed, greater brand recall, a more positive brand attitude, or choosing the exposed brand over its competitors.

The initial challenge of the product placement strategy is does the brand get noticed? People might be so invested in watching the content that they do not notice the brand exposure. Ansons, Wan, and Leboe (2011) claim that "measures of product placement effectiveness commonly rest upon the presumption that a product placement is effective if the experience of encountering a brand within entertainment is memorable" (p. 110). Again, even if memory is achieved, there is no guarantee of positive brand attitude or brand choice (Law & Braun, 2000).

The concern of the brand being noticed can be addressed and the product placement be more effective by having brand placements within the content be of longer durations (Singh, Balasubramanian, & Chakraborty, 2000), have repetition of the brand name (Roehm, Roehm, & Boone, 2004), have an audiovisual placement rather than either an audio component or a visual placement only (Gupta & Lord, 1998; Law & Braun, 2000), and that the product is related to the content in which it appears (Bressoud et al., 2010; Russell, 2002). These techniques are not mutually exclusive and all can be incorporated into a singular product placement initiative. Bressoud, Lehu, and Russell (2010) found that placement on the screen, duration of the placement, and a verbal element along with a visual element are positively related to recall.

Digital media offer numerous opportunities for product placement. Through digital media the audience's interactivity and ability to immerse itself in the product's exposure provide opportunities for better brand recall (Ansons et al., 2011; Lee & Faber, 2007). These digital media possibilities include product placement in video games (Nelson, 2002; Nelson, Yaros, & Keum, 2006; Schneider & Cornwell, 2005). In studying video games, researchers found that brands that appeared more prominently and were better integrated into the game were more likely to be remembered than brands that only appeared on the periphery (Lee & Faber, 2007; Nelson, 2002; Winkler & Buckner, 2006).

Some companies have even developed their own branded videogames on the Internet, referred to as "advergames" (Cauberghe & De Pelsmacker, 2010; Skalski, Campanella-Bracken, & Buncher, 2011). For example, McDonald's has its own branded video game at the Web site, www.mcvideogame.com, that is a digital parody of running the McDonald's company. Participants take part in every aspect of the McDonald's industry from an agricultural section that involves growing soy and raising cattle, to restaurant management that includes making hamburgers and hiring a crew, to a corporate headquarters section where strategic decisions can be made about the brand's image.

Another negative characteristic of mere product placement is that the company often does not have the opportunity to discuss any of its brand features. This creates a need for traditional 30-second commercials or other forms of promotional communication. Singh, Balasubramanian, and Chakraborty (2000) emphasize that brand recall of product placement is enhanced if it is combined with other promotional communication activities. Therefore, researchers claim the best practice is to integrate multiple forms of promotional communication (Clow & Baack, 2012; Cornwell & Maignan, 1998; Kitchen, Kim, & Schultz, 2008; Murphy et al., 2011; O'Guinn et al., 2006; Quester & Thompson, 2001; Sheehan & Young, 2011; Shimp, 2003; Smolianov & Shilbury, 2005; Walliser, 2003). O'Guinn et al. (2006) explain, "When marketers combine contests, a Web site, event sponsorship, and point-of-purchase displays with advertising, this creates an integrated brand promotion" (p. 12).

Sponsorship Defined

Sponsorship has simply emerged as another promotional communication strategy that is part of an integrated campaign confronting the challenges of the communication environment. Sponsorship is often only one component of a larger promotional communication strategy of a company. Sponsorship does not completely replace traditional forms of advertising such as the 30-second television commercial, print magazine or newspaper advertisements, product placement, direct-mail campaigns, or in-store displays, but rather complements those activities. In a seminal article about the practice of sponsorship Meenaghan (1991) claims that "sponsorship must be implemented as part of a marketing campaign and thus integrated with other elements of marketing communications" (p. 43). Cornwell and Maignan (1998) add that sponsorship activities will be more effective if they are coordinated with other marketing communications and promotional activities. The use of multiple promotional communication strategies indicates there is value in all of these methods as each has a chance for brand exposure and brand recall potentially leading to consumer behavior.

In its most general description, sponsorship is another form of promotional communication with the basic goal to persuade. Sponsorship is an amorphous concept that can take on unlimited forms, thus making it difficult to define. There are, however, some fundamental characteristics similar in all sponsorship initiatives. Meenaghan (1991) offers one of the more recognized definitions of sponsorship, describing it as "an investment, in cash or in kind, in an activity, in return for access to the exploitable commercial potential associated with that activity" (p. 36). The definition by Meenaghan could be applied to traditional forms of commercial advertising. Corporations make the investment in sponsorship as a form of promotional communication because of the perceived and expected return on the investment. In this light, sponsorship is not different in its business objectives from any other promotional communication strategy. McAllister (1998), however, makes a distinction between sponsorship and buying a single commercial within a program. He defines sponsorship as "the funding of an entire event, group, broadcast or place by one commercial interest in exchange for large amounts and special types of promotion connected with the sponsored activity" (p. 358).

In a practical application, the International Olympic Committee (IOC) defines an Olympic sponsorship as "an agreement between an Olympic organization and a corporation, whereby the corporation is granted the rights to specific Olympic intellectual property and Olympic marketing opportunities in exchange for financial support and goods and services contributions" (Olympic Marketing Fact File, 2012, p. 10. http://www.olympic.org/Documents/IOC_Marketing/OLYMPIC-MARKETING-FACT-FILE-2012.pdf).

Sandler and Shani (1989) offer a broader definition of sponsorship, emphasizing the association that can be created between the sponsor and the property. They describe sponsorship as "the provision of resources (e.g., money, people, equipment) by an organization directly to an event or activity in exchange for a direct association to the event or activity. The providing organization can then use this direct association to achieve either their corporate, market, or media objectives" (p. 10). Because of this characteristic of explicit association Cameron (2009) claims that sponsorship works very differently than advertising. He states, "Advertising involves a two-way communication process of 'interruption' in which the consumer views a brand message. In contrast, sponsorship involves a three-way communication process in which the consumer views the brand message together with the property in a 'passion' mode" (p. 134). Cameron (2009) summarizes a sponsorship as a three-way relationship: sponsor, property, and consumer.

The Property Need for Revenue

The benefits to the property are obvious upon entering into a sponsorship agreement as it adds another major revenue stream to its business. For example, corporate sponsorship is the IOC's second largest revenue source, generating 45 percent of its revenue, trailing only broadcast revenue which accounts for 47 percent of its revenue (http://www.olympic. org/ioc-financing-revenue-sources-distribution?tab=sources).

In some instances the property is reliant on the economic support of sponsors to the point where the existence of certain events might not be possible without them. Schiller (1989) wrote extensively about the role of the corporation in influencing the types of content and events that remain or what becomes extinct within the culture. He claims that there are two choices for control of ideas or images, either "big government" or "big business." He contends that corporations have emerged as the proliferators of culture and ideas, largely through their advertising support. According to Schiller (1989) through their economic support corporations take on the role of validating agents for certain images, expressions, ideas, and entire entities to have an existence within the culture.

While the role of the sponsor in providing funding is clear, the ultimate validating agent might still be the audience that is participating in these events either through its attendance or through the media. Sponsors use these events as the vehicle to reach an audience that they might not otherwise reach. If an event does not attract a sizable audience it will be difficult to obtain and retain corporate support. It can, therefore, be argued that it is ultimately the audience that is determining which types of content and events continue having a presence within the culture. It must be noted that there does not need to be a majority of the audience participating in that content or event, just merely a large enough audience to garner enough sponsorship support to sustain its existence. Even the Super Bowl, which is clearly the event that the most people in the United States collectively engage in, does not have a majority of the country's population watching the game.

For the organizations whose events are dependent on government subsidies, with government budgets being reduced, sponsorship is playing an increasing role in funding their existence (Schwaiger, Sarstedt, & Taylor, 2010). The United States Olympic Committee (USOC), for example, does not receive any direct government money and relies on corporate support and private donations. Fortunately for the USOC there are many companies that want to contribute to the organization and be a part of the Olympic movement.

Other events are not as fortunate in attracting continued sponsorship support, and due to this lack of funding they cease operations. For example, the annual Blue/Gray College Football All-Star game started in 1939 in Alabama and was played on Christmas Day every year beginning in 1979. The game was discontinued because it could not obtain a corporate sponsor. In August, 2002, Charles "Fats" Jones, executive director of the Blue/ Gray Classic, could not find a sponsor in time to meet a deadline imposed by ABC, the network that televised the game. Jones explained, "It takes about $800,000 to do this game and have a charitable contribution, and we don't have that in reserve" (Washington Post, 2002, p. D2). The game was sponsored for many years by Kelly Tires, which ended its sponsorship after the 2000 game.

The Tour de Georgia cycling event was canceled in 2009 because it could not find a sponsor. The six-day, 600-mile race through Georgia needed approximately $3.5 million to fund the event. Tom Saddlemire, a board member for the Tour de Georgia Foundation, explained, "Putting together a tour at a world-class level takes some pretty significant sponsor money. That kind of money behind something like cycling, where you can't sell tickets, is not for every sponsor in every kind of economy" (Tharpe, 2010, p. 1B). Saddlemire and the Tour de Georgia Foundation were unsuccessful in securing a core sponsor for approximately $500,000 to $1 million that would lead a roster of secondary sponsors that would each pay approximately $150,000. Any prospects of the state government assuming the costs were also dismissed as Saddlemire commented, "The state has its own challenges in terms of how to balance the budget" (Tharpe, 2010, p. 1B).

The Women's United Soccer Association (WUSA) was created after the United States women's soccer team won the 1999 World Cup in Pasadena, California, on Brandi Chastain's penalty kick. In September of 2003 the WUSA was forced to fold. John Hendricks, WUSA founder and chairman, concluded, "The missing ingredient was corporate sponsorship" (Jensen, 2003, p. E1). In 2002 Hendricks tried to recruit eight sponsors to pay $2.5 million per year. He was only able to secure two sponsors, Hyundai and Johnson & Johnson. Hendricks stated, "I was intoxicated by what I witnessed in the World Cup and all the sponsorships surrounding the event and just mistakenly assumed that would flow over into the league" (Jensen, 2003, p. E1).

The WUSA was cancelled five days prior to the beginning of the 2003 World Cup. At the time the players remained hopeful as to the league's viability. Julie Foudy, United States team captain, stated, "the Women's World Cup will provide a platform to generate additional interest in women's soccer that could be the catalyst to more sponsor support" (Ziehm, 2003, p. 105). Mia Hamm, the United States player, male or female, who when she retired scored the most goals in international competition, added, "The players remain hopeful that more sponsors will recognize the value of associating their brands and products with the wholesomeness of the WUSA" (Ziehm, 2003, p. 105).

While the league officials and the players cite a lack of sponsorship support, it must be noted that the WUSA's low television viewership and low stadium attendance were the reasons for the lack of sponsorship support. If the league was drawing a substantial audience there is no reason to believe that it would not have received the support of sponsors. In this scenario it became untenable for sponsors to continue supporting the league without seeing evidence of an audience interest. Perhaps, some companies might have felt so strongly about wanting there to be a women's professional soccer league in the United States, almost in a philanthropic sense, that they paid a fee to become a sponsor even though they knew they would not reach a large audience. There were simply not enough companies of that mindset to pay for a sponsorship that would not deliver an audience and provide achievement of any promotional communication business goals.

Sponsors as Property Promoters

It is clear that securing revenue is the obvious primary role that a property has for its sponsors. Sponsors also play a role in promoting the property. Much of a league's promotion is done by its partners — the television network broadcasting its games, which provides the league with its greatest exposure source (Fortunato, 2001), and the sponsors promoting the league, its teams, and its players in their own promotional communication endeavors. The IOC sees its sponsors as having a role in promoting the Olympic brand and its ideals. The role that sponsors have as a funding source and a promotional entity in the IOC's functions is explicitly detailed in the IOC's listing of the Fundamental Objectives of Olympic Marketing:

- To ensure the independent financial stability of the Olympic Movement, and thereby to assist in the worldwide promotion of Olympism.
- To create and maintain long-term marketing programs, and thereby to ensure the financial security of the Olympic Movement and the Olympic Games.
- To build on the successful activities developed by each Organizing Committee for the Olympic Games (OCOGs) and thereby to eliminate the need to recreate the marketing structure with each Olympic Games.
- To generate revenue to be distributed throughout the entire Olympic Movement — including the OCOGs, the National Olympic Committees (NOCs) and their continental associations, the International Federations (IFs) and other recognized international sports organizations — and to provide financial support for sport in emerging nations.
- To ensure that the Olympic Games can be experienced by the maximum number of people throughout the world principally via broadcast coverage.
- To protect and promote the equity that is inherent in the Olympic image and ideals.
- To control and limit the commercialization of the Olympic Games.
- To enlist the support of Olympic marketing partners in the promotion of the Olympic ideals.

[Olympic Marketing Fact File, 2012, p. 5. http://www.olympic.org/Documents/IOC_Marketing/OLYMPIC-MARKETING-FACT-FILE-2012.pdf].

A property that does not yet have a large audience will want to attract prominent sponsors who can serve this dual function of being a revenue source and a promotional communication partner as the event tries to grow. One group that was successful in this endeavor was the Ultimate Fighting Championship (UFC). Dana White, UFC president, described the sponsorship of the UFC by Anheuser-Busch's Bud Light brand as "a milestone for our organization and our sport" (Anheuser-Busch press release, April 6, 2011). Mark Wright, vice president of sports, media and entertainment marketing for Anheuser-Busch, explained, "Bud Light's first three years with the UFC have focused largely on growing awareness and viewership of the sport at bars, restaurants and all the other places Bud Light is sold across the country" (Anheuser-Busch press release, April 6, 2011)

The methods used by sponsors to promote properties will be discussed in more detail in Chapter Six through the concept of sponsorship activation.

The Sponsorship Negotiation Process

While the property sees the sponsor as a major source of revenue and a promotional communication partner, the key advantageous distinction for a company in utilizing sponsorship as opposed to traditional spot commercial advertising is the ability to negotiate all of the parameters of the deal with the property. Through negotiation of sponsorship agreements anything is possible — it is merely a matter of what the sponsor and the property can agree to (Fortunato & Dunnam, 2004). Cornwell (2008) explains that "sponsorship decision making is thick with negotiation, barter, and deal making" (p. 46).

The primary responsibility upon entering into the negotiation with a property is with the sponsor as the determinant of its own success. Sponsors have to believe that they have some control over the parameters of the agreement. Although constantly being recruited, a company is not forced to sponsor any property that it does not choose. Sponsors can also choose to agree or not agree to how the sponsorship will be implemented. The parameters of a sponsorship are bound only by the creative ideas and willingness to implement these ideas of the people negotiating the deal. Sponsorship can simply be thought of as an "ideas business."

There is a sequence to the sponsorship negotiation process with the challenge of completing the task within budgetary constraints and the time constraints of coordinating the sponsorship with the product being available in the market at the peak of its selling cycle. The process first begins with the company itself investing resources to conduct research about its brand. Karla and Soberman (2010) explain that companies need to research and identify consumer perceptions about the brand, understand their competition, understand which brand is selling in the product market, and formulate all the information that is gathered so that the proper promotional communication business goals will be established and addressed through the sponsorship. Davis (2002) provides a series of brand perception questions that can be asked during the research process, including: When I say the name of our brand, what is the first thing that comes to mind? Why was that response the first thing that came to mind about our brand? What are the strengths and weaknesses or our brand? What factors have contributed to your perceptions of these strengths and weaknesses? What brands did you consider before you bought our brand? Has our brand met your needs and expectations? (p. 59).

This research will help identify the core promotional communication business goals. Establishment of clear corporate goals is an essential part of the sponsorship process. Thjomoe, Olson, and Bronn (2002) contend, "A logical approach to sponsorship decision making would dictate that firms should have clear targets and goals for sponsorship" (p. 6). Chadwick and Thwaites (2005), however, found in their study of personnel who managed corporate sponsorships that only 54 percent of respondents had set goals for their sponsorships.

Within the ultimate goal of persuasion Gwinner (1997) provides a comprehensive list of goals that a sponsorship has the potential to achieve, including increase brand awareness through unique exposure opportunities, increase goodwill through corporate generosity, and establish, enhance, or change brand image by linking the brand with a favorable cause or a sports property. It should be noted that a sponsorship with one property can achieve multiple goals. For example, Visa has sponsored the Olympic Games since 1986 and claims that "it has utilized its sponsorship to increase its global brand leadership, grow Visa transaction volume, expand acceptance in new and emerging markets, and enhance preference for its products and services" (Visa press release, October 27, 2009).

Once goals are established sponsors will research the properties that they believe can best help them achieve their goals. By having clear knowledge of the business goals the sponsor can be more efficient in selecting the property and more explicit in communicating with the property about what it hopes the sponsorship will achieve. Tony Ponturo was the head of media and sports marketing for Anheuser-Busch and is considered one of the leaders in the sponsorship industry. Ponturo explains that the sponsorship process "begins with the basics — understanding the customer that you are trying to reach, understanding the brand's goals, and finding the best properties to accomplish those things" (personal communication, February 21, 2012). Sponsors will proactively seek out and contact these properties to discuss the sponsorship possibilities.

While sponsors will take the initiative and contact properties, simultaneously properties are proactively pursuing sponsors. Larger corporations are pitched sponsorship opportunities as much as they actively seek them. For example, MillerCoors receives more than 1,000 sponsorship solicitations annually (Lefton, 2011a). With the property need for revenue, sponsor recruitment and retention is a constant challenge (Lachowetz, McDonald, Sutton, & Hedrick, 2003).

There is a sequence to the sponsorship process from the property perspective as well. Reaching a sponsorship agreement takes a considerable amount of time, ranging anywhere from one to two years from first thinking about a product category potentially being open to a contract between a property and a sponsor actually being signed. From the property perspective, Keith Wachtel, NHL senior vice president of integrated sales, details that the property has to identify all of the companies that are within that product category that could serve as potential sponsors. Properties then need to spend months researching their potential sponsors to understand the core brand principles and messaging of each of these brands. The property must also identify ways that it can apply its own assets to the sponsor's brand needs.

Wachtel emphasizes that approaching the sponsors at the right time is critical, as once these companies have committed their allocated promotional communication budgets, even if they see the property as a logical business partner, they will not have the capability to afford the sponsorship. The properties have to become aware of which companies will have the budget available to fulfill the sponsorship at the financial level desired by the property.

Lou Imbriano is the president and CEO of TrinityOne, a marketing strategies and business consulting firm, the former vice president and chief marketing officer for the New England Patriots and Gillette Stadium, and the author, along with Elizabeth King, of *Winning the Customer: Turn Customers into Fans and Get Them to Spend More*. Imbriano also explains that the sponsorship process from the property perspective begins with identifying companies that the property thinks might be interested in obtaining a sponsorship. The property must then thoroughly research the company to confirm if there is indeed alignment between the sponsor and the property. If it is determined that there is an opportunity for business, at that point the potential sponsor is approached. Rather than a simple cold call, it is preferable through the vast network of the property's personnel and their many relationships that a personal introduction be made to an executive representing the potential sponsor.

Paul Asencio is the senior vice president of corporate sales and partnerships for the New York Mets. Asencio offers one strategy for identifying potential sponsors is to be aware of a company's current promotional communication strategy in terms of both placement, noticing how and where companies are advertising, and the content of their promotional communication, what is their brand message. By monitoring other sports programming and seeing a company advertising in those locations it can be concluded that a company is already spending money to reach that target audience and finds value in advertising during that type of content. It is important to note that the team's sales departments are the groups selling large amounts of inventory, especially if selling the commercial time during the team's television and radio broadcasts are part of their responsibilities. For example, a Major League Baseball team has to sell stadium-related inventory to 81 home games and broadcast space on television and radio for 162 games, not including spring training games.

Another strategy identified by Asencio is for the property to monitor the promotional communication within the geographic area of a team. For example, if a company placed a billboard on a highway near the team's stadium, a representative from the team could simply call that advertiser and comment that he or she noticed the billboard and was wondering if the company would be interested in learning about promotional communication opportunities with the team. The advertiser could be flattered that the billboard was noticed and that the team, which often holds a special place in the hearts of the community, is seeking it out. That advertiser might have never initiated a call with the team about a sponsorship. The initial fear for the advertiser might have been that a sponsorship with the team would be too expensive for a company that normally only purchases billboard space. The advertiser who purchased the billboard, however, is probably not aware of the several possibilities that could occur from a sponsorship with the team. By the team proactively approaching the advertiser, the next phase of the sponsorship sequence can commence: a meeting between representatives from the property and the sponsor.

In the initial meeting, the property needs to learn the business goals of the sponsor. From the property perspective, Paul Asencio explains his initial inquiries to a sponsor include, "Tell me about your marketing objectives? And, how can we (the New York Mets) help?" (personal communication, January 5, 2012). Lou Imbriano stresses that for the property this first meeting should be "98 percent listening and two percent speaking" (personal communication, January 30, 2012). He believes that a sponsorship package should not be pitched at the initial meeting, with the property waiting until it has a clear understanding of the sponsor's business goals. Imbriano summarizes his overall approach to the initial negotiation meeting as, "We have a property, we think your company is a match, let us sit down with you and learn about your company and your business goals; we think we can help you do business" (personal communication, January 30, 2002).

As the property is learning the sponsor's goals, the sponsor is learning about the assets that the property has to offer and the overall benefits of a sponsorship with the property. The concept of "eduselling" where there is a thorough education of the opportunities prepared for potential sponsors is one approach that researchers encourage properties to adopt (Jowdy & McDonald, 2002; O'Keefe, Titlebaum, & Hill, 2009; Sutton, Lachowetz, & Clark, 2000). Keith Wachtel, NHL senior vice president of integrated sales, contends that in an initial presentation the property should demonstrate that it understands the brand and that the property could present some initial ideas or "thought starters" for how the property can deliver assets that will maximize value for the sponsor (personal communication, February 21, 2012). It is through this type of inquiry and explanation of the properties' assets that a program that addresses the sponsors' goals and the advantageous characteristic of negotiation making anything possible in a sponsorship agreement is beginning to be realized.

It is important for the property to not strictly dictate all of the terms of the agreement or present a standard, cookie-cutter proposal, but rather help devise a program using its multitude of assets in which it can assist the sponsors in achieving their goals. Different sponsorship programs need to be implemented for each specific goal. For example, if the sponsor desires more brand exposure to improve brand awareness and brand recall, perhaps stadium signage that is also visible through the television camera is the appropriate strategy. If the sponsor is focusing on improving its brand image, perhaps partnering with the team in one of its charitable programs is possible. If the sponsor is looking to drive customers to its retail locations, perhaps a program that includes a discount when presenting a game ticket stub, customers visiting the store for a chance to win tickets to the team's games, a store window or in-store display that focuses on the team, or even a visit to the store by the team mascot or a player could be a part of the overall strategy. Every sponsorship program, therefore, must be flexible and customized for each sponsor.

While the property is generating revenue, if negotiated and executed properly the benefits of the sponsorship agreement to the corporation should become apparent through a customized program that achieves promotional communication business goals. Ultimately, the desired outcome is a successful partnership and relationship that benefits both the sponsor and the property. The nature of this sponsorship relationship can thus be better characterized as interdependent. Once the interdependency is realized, the better characterization of partnership can be fostered.

In this negotiation between a sponsor and a property, two aspects that are a part of any negotiation process have to be acknowledged. The first aspect is to understand which group has the leverage in the negotiation. This manifests itself in the number of potential sponsors competing within each product category or the number of potential property partners that the sponsor has available. If many companies are competing for the sponsorship with the property, there is an opportunity for a bidding process that provides a higher fee to the property. If there are not many potential sponsors, obviously the property will have a more difficult time demanding a higher fee. A distinct example might be the insurance industry, which features many national companies, compared to the soft drink industry, which essentially offers a binary choice.

Conversely, sponsors may have several property options to invest their money that would achieve their promotional communication business goals. If the sponsors do have many viable options, they might not give in to the high price demand of one property and invest with another property. If the sponsor feels it must contract with that specific property, it will be more inclined to pay whatever the fee. Each property is, in essence, competing with all other properties for sponsorship dollars.

The work of Schiller (1989) can again be applied to the revenue-generating role that sponsors play. The need for revenue by a property could be a determinant as to who is in a more powerful position in the negotiation. Properties that are desperate for revenue might be more willing to capitulate to the demands of a sponsor, putting the sponsor in a more powerful position in the negotiation. More popular properties that do not have difficulty in recruiting sponsors might not give into any demands of a sponsoring corporation knowing that there is another corporation in that product category probably very willing to take that spot. These popular properties are certainly in a stronger negotiation position with sponsors than properties that are not as popular. If a popular league is not pleased with the arrangement with its current sponsor when the contract expires it could simply offer that sponsorship to a rival company.

The negotiation over determining the cost of the sponsorship can obviously be contentious. Some properties might have a dollar figure in mind that they plan to attain from a product category and then seek the sponsors even if it means contracting with two sponsors to reach that figure. Tony Ponturo explains that in the negotiation the sponsors are buying an asset. The sponsor must ask the property to justify and explain how it determined the value of that asset, while the sponsor has to apply its own logic into determining the value of the property. Gordon Kane, founder of Victory Sports Marketing, a company which specializes in leveraging the benefits of sponsorship for both sponsors and properties, contends that value used to be defined as whatever the sponsor paid for the property, as the property needed the revenue. Through this approach, however, opportunities to foster relationships and better align the brands were missed. Ultimately, the sponsor has to make a determination about how much it values the property.

The second aspect that is part of any negotiation process being applied here is the people doing the actual negotiating. The crafting of these sponsorship programs and their overall success is completely reliant on the talent of the practitioners engaged in the process. Fahy, Farrelly, and Quester (2004) explain that sponsorship effectiveness is attributed to the sponsors' capabilities, such as having experienced sponsorship managers, market orientation capabilities, and organizational routines. The characteristic of capabilities indicates that the practice of sponsorship is very much a skill, one that can be taught and one that can be improved upon with experience. While these practitioners are ideally representing the best interests of their respective brands, it is not the Ford Motor Company per se that is making the sponsorship decisions, but the people who represent Ford.

One byproduct of the cost of sponsorships being so high is that professionals have had to be more precise in their sponsorship planning and execution. Gordon Kane believes the talent of the people creating sponsorship deals and their understanding of the industry has improved. He believes that properties have become better at understanding what sponsors desire. He explains that "driving the professionalism of the sports marketing business is the escalation of values" (personal communication, November 22, 2011). With so much money at stake, sponsors and properties cannot afford to not understand the process or be inefficient in their spending, especially if signing a long-term deal.

Each company will approach the sponsorship decision making process differently. Some companies might provide budgetary guidelines, but then give the marketing departments autonomy in making decisions, as it is the promotional communication or brand specialists that are experts in their understanding of the sponsorship industry. Karla and

Soberman (2010) indicate that marketing decisions are also made by regional managers or mid-level personnel, not necessarily the CEO or the chief marketing executive.

Other companies will make the sponsorship decisions at the executive level. One concern of decisions being made only at the executive level is that these executives' expertise might be in the company's specific industry, but not in promotional communication. These executives could also justify the sponsorship expenditure on any number of variables, including their own personal interest or support of the team, and not necessarily in the best interests of the brand (Chadwick & Thwaites, 2005; Cornwell, 2008; Seguin, Teed, & O'Reilly, 2005). Upper management, at no cost to itself, could invest in and justify using corporate money to purchase tickets or other up-close interactions with a property that are only enjoyed by the people at the very top of the corporation with this investment providing little, if any, return toward achieving the brand's business goals.

The Role of Agencies in the Sponsorship Process

The complexity of the sponsorship industry has led many companies to hire multiple agencies that specialize in the different aspects of the sponsorship process. The specialization of the sponsorship industry and the need for agencies in a variety of areas to support the company continues to grow. In the 2013 IEG and Performance Research survey, 60 percent of respondents reported that their company used public relations agencies, an increase from 52 percent in 2012, 63 percent indicated that they used advertising agencies, up from 51 percent in 2011, 17 percent used an independent sponsorship specialist, and 8 percent used a sponsorship specialist agency, which sold them the rights. Only 23 percent of executives surveyed claimed that they did not use specialized firms and that all aspects of the sponsorship were conducted within their company, a decrease from 34 percent in 2011 and a more pronounced 49 percent in 2009 (IEG Sponsorship Report, April 22, 2013). IEG and Performance Research conduct an annual survey of international sponsorship executives inquiring about their companies' current and planned sponsorship activities. The state of the industry review survey in March 2013 had 110 participants respond to an online questionnaire. The survey features a range of executives from small, medium, and large companies. The sample was comprised of 26 percent of respondents' companies spending up to $500,000 on sponsorship, 9 percent spending between $500,000 and $1 million, 19 percent spending between $1 million and $5 million, 9 percent spending between $5 million and $15 million, 8 percent spending between $15 million and $30 million, and 5 percent spending $30 million or greater on their sponsorships [IEG/Performance Research Survey, www.iegsr.com or www.sponsorship.com].)

The agency role is that of trusted advisor that will consult about all aspects of the sponsorship process: selecting the right property, negotiating the financial terms, negotiating what the sponsorship will entail, executing the sponsorship, and evaluating the sponsorship. The degree of autonomy in sponsorship decision making will be a function of the relationship between the agency and its client. Some agencies have a longtime relationship with a client that will result in the agency having a high degree of autonomy. In many other instances, the agency will continue to need approval from the client before implementing any plans. Gordon Kane describes his responsibility is to help the sponsor and the property understand each others' desires and to build trust between the organizations.

One of the first steps that the agency will do is meet with the sponsor to better understand its promotional communication business goals. The agency will have to learn all aspects of the brand, such as its features, its competition, its selling cycle, or if any new product launches are planned. As the agency learns these goals, it can go seek out the properties that it believes will be able to satisfy the sponsors' needs. An agency, such as the Marketing Arm, whose objective is to "make brands mean something to consumers" (www.themarketingarm.com/whatwedo.html), does extensive research about the various possible sports properties to better align its clients with the best placement location. Mike Singer, consulting director for the Marketing Arm and its client, AT&T, explains that often there are one-, two-, and three-year plans devised for a company that are based on its goals and the audience it is trying to reach. The agency will then consider the company's current sponsorship portfolio as well as other opportunities within the marketplace in finding the properties that can best achieve the company's goals (personal communication, February 7, 2012).

To better illustrate the need and increased role of specialized agencies in the sponsorship process, with universities perhaps not having the expertise needed to properly negotiate and orchestrate their sponsorship programs, companies such as IMG College have filled that void. IMG College is the multimedia rights holder for more than 200 collegiate properties, including the NCAA and its 89 championships, many collegiate conferences, and numerous universities with major sports programs, such as Alabama, Auburn, Connecticut, Duke, Florida, Kentucky, Michigan, Notre Dame, Ohio State, Oregon, and Texas (for a full listing of the universities that IMG College represents see www.imgcollege.com/about-us/imgc-properties.html). Multimedia rights include local television and radio broadcasts of games, ancillary programming such as coach's shows, digital, print, on-site signage and events, and hospitality. The perspective of IMG College is that it "has the expertise and experience to help both our collegiate properties and our corporate sponsors maximize their opportunities, enhance the fan experience, and generate revenue" (www.imgcollege.com/services/imgc-services.html).

The acquisition of a university's media rights by an external company was started by Jim Host. In 1974, Host forever changed the collegiate media business when he contracted with the University of Kentucky to acquire the team's radio rights. Host was able to grow his business by acquiring more media and event rights from the universities as well as expanding the roster of universities that his company represented. In 2007 IMG Worldwide purchased Host Communications as well as the Collegiate Licensing Company to form IMG College as a division of IMG Worldwide (www.imgcollege.com/about-us/imgc-history.html).

IMG College pays a university for its multimedia rights, with most universities receiving a guaranteed dollar amount. One estimate has the universities in the Big Ten earning anywhere from $4 to $7 million per year, with Ohio State commanding a fee of nearly $11 million for its multimedia rights (Smith, 2012a). It is important to point out that some universities have a revenue-sharing agreement with IMG College rather than a only a guaranteed fee. The extent of rights provided by the university is also negotiated. While IMG College might seek to acquire as much of the rights as possible, the universities can decide to retain some of these rights and the revenue that comes from these sponsorships. Many universities retain their lucrative uniform and equipment sponsorships as well as their pouring rights to their stadiums and arenas (it should be noted some pouring-rights agreements cover the entire campus). IMG College does have representatives at many of the larger universities who work more directly with school personnel as well as prospecting clients and creating sponsorship programs on a local and regional level.

From the sponsor's perspective one advantage to negotiating with IMG College is that it acquires the rights to use the logos of all of IMG College's contracted universities in one deal. To illustrate this point, in 2011 UPS reached an agreement with IMG College. In this one agreement UPS received the rights to 68 universities. Ron Rogowski, vice president of global sponsorships and events for UPS, stated, "We looked at the college landscape, and going to individual schools, that becomes a real monster. This deal gave us a new way of looking at the school, and going to the local market is really impactful. You can do a broad-based marketing plan; we have a (sponsorship) with the NCAA. But when you get down to the school level it really is unique from a sponsorship level. It doesn't have every school, but 68 schools is pretty good. That's 68 schools, 68 contracts and 68 conference calls with attorneys we would have had to make" (Thomaselli, 2011, p. 2). Estimates are that it would have cost a company double or even triple if it had to try to contract with every university individually (Thomaselli, 2011).

There are some conditions in which the one agreement with IMG College does not provide access to all of the universities. For example, the university might already have a sponsorship agreement with another company in that product category. If one of IMG's universities had already obtained a sponsorship with a shipping company, that university would not be a part of the UPS agreement. Another possibility where an agreement with IMG College would not provide access to all of the universities is if the university has a policy not to have a sponsor within a particular product category. When IMG College reached an agreement with MillerCoors, some universities did not permit the promotion of an alcoholic beverage brand.

By owning the multimedia rights to so many universities, IMG College has endless ability for flexibility and customization of sponsorship programs. George Pyne, president of IMG Sports and Entertainment, explains that by IMG College "having the rights to Florida, Florida State, Miami, and South Florida, a multimedia sponsorship program that covers the entire state of Florida can be developed" (personal communication, January 27, 2012). With those schools being in different conferences, there would be tremendous difficulty in doing a promotion for the entire state of Florida without being able to form one agreement through IMG College.

The advantageous characteristic of negotiation makes anything possible through sponsorship. Practical execution is the key to a successful sponsorship. Similar to traditional advertising, sponsorship involves a process of decision making that is designed to ultimately achieve the basic goal of persuasion. Just as in the practice of advertising, through sponsorship the company has to make critical decisions that it can control. The first decision needing to be made is the selection of which property to sponsor; promotional communication placement. The second decision is what the sponsorship will entail, referred to as activation; promotional communication message content.

Chapter Three

Sponsorship Selection: Audience Variables, Cost and Exclusivity

Property Selection Overview

For the sponsor, decision making begins with selection of the property. Although constantly being recruited a company is not forced to sponsor any property, and it has complete discretion in choosing the properties it will sponsor. One of the questions that the executives in the annual IEG and Performance Research survey in 2012 responded to was how they went about selecting properties to sponsor. Eighty-four percent of respondents reported that the company sets its strategy and then seeks the right property, 70 percent responded that they were approached directly by the property, 25 percent answered that they received details about a property from a sales agency, and 19 percent claimed that they consulted a sponsorship specialist to determine which properties to sponsor (IEG/Performance Research Survey, http://performanceresearch.com/sponsor-survey.htm).

There are many variables for a sponsor to consider in property selection: the size of the audience, brand exposure opportunities to reach its target audience, the ability to obtain brand exposure in a new geographic market, the timing of the sponsorship, support of a geographic community, cost, exclusivity within a product category, brand image association, activation opportunities, hospitality opportunities, and product sales potential. These selection variables are not mutually exclusive. In fact, proper selection that addresses as many of these variables as possible can lead to a successful sponsorship. For the respondents in the annual IEG and Performance Research survey in 2013, the ability to increase brand loyalty was found to be the most important variable in the evaluation of a property. The opportunity to create brand awareness ranked second, and changing or reinforcing a brand image ranked third (IEG Sponsorship Report, April 22, 2013).

Property Selection: Target Audience

Brand awareness is reliant on opportunities for brand exposure to the target audience. For most companies sponsorship selection of a property will always evaluate the brand exposure opportunities. Exposure of the brand is often the most vital element to the success of the entire sponsorship agreement and has to be the initial achieved objective of the sponsorship. Other sponsorship objectives might not be achieved if the brand is not noticed in that particular location. Without the brand being noticed, any audience reaction or behavior toward the brand is due to some other reason than the promotional communication or any specific sponsorship.

Brand exposure is based on the dimensions of the size of the audience and the demographic profile of the audience. A demographic profile includes variables such as age, income, ethnicity, education level, gender, geography, and common interest. Companies must clearly identify who their target audience is prior to making property selection decisions. Eighty-eight percent of respondents in the annual IEG and Performance Research survey in 2012 identified the demographics of the audience as the primary factor in making sponsorship selection decisions, with fan passion/affinity ranking second at 76 percent, and the size of the event attendance coming in third at 73 percent (IEG/Performance Research Survey, http://performancereserch.com/sponsor-survey.htm).

Advertising and sponsorship with sports properties become desirable for companies because they consistently reach a certain target audience that might not be available through other media content options. Wenner (1989) explains that sport is sold just as any other news or entertainment commodity, stating, "The content per se is not what is being sold; rather it is the audience for that content that is being sold to advertisers" (p. 22). He claims that advertising with sports properties is a good proposition because they offer the desirable, and relatively hard-to-reach, male audience between the ages of 18 and 49. Wenner (1989) points out the sports programming demographic tends to be well educated with considerable disposable income, and "advertisers are willing to pay top dollar for this audience because they tend to make purchase decisions about big-ticket items such as automobiles and computers" (p. 14).

In one specific example, George Pyne, president of IMG Sports and Entertainment, explains that college sports provide an audience that is very attractive because it is large, well educated, a sizeable portion of the audience is affluent, a sizeable portion of the audience is female, and these games deliver the hard-to-reach 18- 24-year-old demographic. Finally, college sports help foster the emotional connection that already exists between a student or alum and his or her university as well as the deep connection between the university and the geographic community in which it is located (personal communication, January 27, 2012).

To further illustrate how brand exposure to a desired target audience is always a factor in sponsorship selection, some practical examples are provided. When United Airlines replaced Delta as the official airline of the PGA Tour, Jeff Jones, United's manager of sponsorship marketing, commented, "The audience the tour attracts aligns perfectly with our current demos and advertising strategy" (Ourand, 2010, p. 43). Kirk Perry, vice president, North America, Procter & Gamble, highlighted the target audience of women, teenagers, and adults ages 18–34 that the Olympics appeal to as a reason for Procter & Gamble's sponsorship of both the IOC and the USOC. Perry explained that the Olympic demographic "encompasses our consumer base. It connects at every income level. It is such an iconic and important event" (Thomas, 2009, p. B16). Antonio Lucio, chief marketing officer for Visa, said of Visa's sponsorship with the Olympics, "The Olympic Games deliver tremendous global exposure and access to virtually every demographic group" (Visa press release, October 27, 2009).

Often property selection is based on multiple demographic variables. In other instances the sponsorship selection is using the property for brand exposure to a very specific target audience. In some instances when there is at least a prioritization of demographic variables, selection of a specific property is influenced by one particular variable. In an example of sponsorship selection based primarily on trying to reach a specific ethnic group, the Hispanic market is a demographic that companies are making extended efforts to reach. In 2011, Anheuser-Busch signed a four-year extension with Major League Soccer that included extensions with the United States and Mexican national soccer teams. Anheuser-Busch will promote its Budweiser and Budweiser Chelada brands at Major League Soccer and United States men's games. The Bud Light brand will be featured for United States women's games and Mexican national team games played in the United States. Mark Wright, vice president of media, sports and entertainment marketing for Anheuser-Busch, commented that the decision was driven by Anheuser-Busch's "significant share in the Latino segment" (Dreier, 2011b, p. 4). MillerCoors has its Coors Light brand as a sponsor of Mexico's Primera Division soccer league. The Miller Lite brand sponsors the CONCACAF Gold Cup and one of Mexico's most popular soccer teams, the Chivas club (Lefton, 2011a).

Some corporations that transcend many demographic variables, such as McDonald's or Coca-Cola, might simply look to sponsor properties that have a large audience (i.e., the Super Bowl, Olympics, FIFA World Cup, or *American Idol*). These large companies might use one of their specific brands in a particular sponsorship to reach a specific target audience. In 2011, Coca-Cola reached a multiyear extension with the NBA. Coca-Cola has been a sponsor of the NBA since 1986 and continues to feature its Sprite brand as the official soft drink of the league as it has done since 1994. Mark Tatum, NBA executive vice president, global marketing partnerships, stated, "Sprite is an exciting and vibrant brand that maintains a meaningful connection to the younger consumers that also make up a valuable segment of our fan-base" (Coca-Cola press release, February 15, 2011). In other examples, Kellogg's cereal uses its Frosted Flakes brand to sponsor the Little League World Series. Pepsi has its Mountain Dew brand sponsor extreme sports. Anheuser-Busch had its Stella Artois brand replace its Bud Select brand as the official beer of Churchill Downs and the Kentucky Derby. Brad Brown, vice president of sports and entertainment marketing for Anheuser-Busch, commented that the Kentucky Derby is a "very social, high end event" with Stella Artois being a more expensive beer than other Anheuser-Busch brands (Mullen, 2012a, p. 3).

Property Selection: Income

Some companies focus on the demographic variable of income for their sponsorship selections. In one example of using sports sponsorships opportunities to reach a target audience with income being the most important variable, Tiffany, the well-known high-end jewelry company, is the official sponsor of the United States Ski and Snowboard Association (USSA). Tom O'Rourke, Tiffany vice president of business sales, explained the reason the company signed with the USSA was "the audience the USSA reaches is not one we traditionally have a way of getting to. From a gut level, you know the recreational skier simply has to be more affluent because of the nature of the sport. The audience aligns well with our consumer" (Mickle, 2011a, p. 6).

The affluent target audience for horse racing is certainly a match for a private jet company. Sentient Jet has been the official private aviation sponsor for the Breeders' Cup since 2008. The Breeders' Cup is horse racing's annual championship and in 2011 featured 15 races held on two days with purses totaling $26 million. Title sponsorships are sold for each race. Sentient Jet was the title sponsor of the $500,000 Juvenile Sprint, the $1 million Filly and Mare Sprint, and the $1.5 million Breeders' Cup Sprint. The announcers recognize Sentient Jet in their call of the race (i.e., the Sentient Jet Breeders' Cup Juvenile Sprint). Sentient Jet also aired commercials during the television coverage of the Breeders' Cup on ESPN. Carter Carnegie, Breeders' Cup senior vice president of sales and business development, stated, "Sentient Jet's is appreciated by the horse racing industry. We are pleased to have a partner in the private aviation category that continues to recognize the importance of the Breeders' Cup as a marketing vehicle to reach our affluent audience" (Sentient Jet press release, July 19, 2011). Grey Goose and Emirates Airline are other companies that each sponsored two Breeders' Cup races in 2011.

In addition to sponsoring the Breeders' Cup in fulfilling the need to reach a very specific affluent target audience, Sentient Jet is the official private jet provider for the PGA Tour and golf's Champions Tour in a contract that runs through 2013. Sentient Jet features a membership program approach to its private aviation service that offers guaranteed availability, one-way pricing, and hourly rates with clients choosing from three jet models, rather than the fractional jet ownership model employed by other private aviation companies. Sentient Jet provides tour members access to its full range of planes to accommodate their travel schedule.

Property Selection: Geographic Scope

Sponsorship selection allows for facilitation of brand exposure into specific geographic markets in an attempt to reach a new target audience. This has certainly been evident in how companies approach their sponsorship opportunities to reach the population of China. Chinese tennis player Li Na became the first player ever from China to win a grand slam tournament when she won the 2011 French Open. Estimates were that 116 million people in China watched her championship match. After her French Open victory, Na quickly reached a deal with Mercedes-Benz for $5.8 million over three years (Kaplan, 2011b). Na would have a Mercedes-Benz patch on her dress as part of the deal by the time the Wimbledon tournament began only a few weeks after the French Open concluded. After reaching the Australian Open final earlier in the 2011 season, Na signed deals with Rolex and Häagen-Dazs. With companies striving to gain a presence into China, Na's earnings could reach an estimated $40 million in endorsements over the next three years (Kaplan, 2011b).

The NBA has partnered with sponsors where both have a desire to reach China. The popularity of the NBA in China has grown with the assistance of Chinese players coming to the NBA, most notably Yao Ming. The NBA has league offices in Beijing, Shanghai, and Hong Kong, with estimates in 2010 being that the NBA produced $150 to $170 million in revenue in China, equating to roughly half of the NBA's international revenue (Lombardo, 2010). NBA China has sponsorships with international companies, including Coca-Cola, Gatorade, Visa, Adidas, and Nike as well as Chinese companies, China Everbright Bank, and footwear company Peak (Lombardo, 2010). Adidas, the official NBA apparel partner, and Nike, the apparel rights holder for USA Basketball, both have nearly 6000 stores in China (Lombardo, 2010). Nike has also supported high school basketball in Taiwan (Lee & Aiken, 2010), while Gatorade and Amway have conducted branded basketball academies and camp events in China (Lombardo, 2010).

Sprite has advertising during international telecasts of NBA games and sponsorship programs in 215 countries and territories in 42 languages. Scott McCune, vice president of global partnerships and experiential marketing for Coca-Cola, commented, "The passion for the NBA continues to grow around the world and through our global partnership we are able to create marketing programs in multiple countries, such as China, where our brand and NBA basketball are both incredibly popular" (Coca-Cola press release, February 15, 2011). Coca-Cola sold more than 1 billion unit cases in China from January through June in 2011, with Sprite ranking as the country's leading selling soft drink (*Newark Star-Ledger*, p. 23). Sprite and the NBA also collaborate on grassroots programs that get kids to play basketball throughout the world, including Mexico and Africa. Scott McCune explained, "We are able to create grassroots programs in markets around the world to encourage young people to play basketball and drink Sprite" (Coca-Cola press release, February 15, 2011).

Federal Express has used badminton as its main sponsorship vehicle in China. Federal Express communicates its sponsorship by having members of the Chinese badminton team appear in television commercials, on product packaging, and in attendance at media events (Ho, 2011). Federal Express has sponsored the Chinese badminton team since 2005, describing, "This hugely successful partnership once again represents the excellent passion of speed, accuracy, and leadership shared by both parties" (Federal Express press release, August 20, 2009).

To bolster its international profile, Federal Express has a sponsorship with the Association of Tennis Professionals (ATP) World Tour that will run through 2013. As a global platinum sponsor and the official carrier of the World Tour, Federal Express receives global marketing rights, sponsors 17 tournaments in 12 different countries on four different continents, has on-court brand exposure, and exposure on the ATPWorldTour.com Web site. A special section of the ATP Web site, referred to as the FedEx Reliability Zone, was created and provides player information and statistics. Adam Helfan, ATP executive chairman and president, stated, "FedEx is a recognized leader in sports marketing and we are proud that it has chosen the ATP World Tour for this major foray into international sports sponsorship" (Federal Express press release, September 8, 2010). Rajesh Subramanian, Federal Express senior vice president of international marketing, added, "The global nature of the ATP World Tour perfectly complements FedEx which serves customers in more than 220 countries and territories worldwide. In addition to the core attribute of reliability, professional tennis and FedEx also share the characteristics of speed and precision" (Federal Express press release, September 8, 2010).

Similarly, foreign companies have used sponsorship as a way to reach consumers in the United States. For Barclays, the British-based global financial services firm, one of its most prominent sponsorships is as the title sponsor of the English Premier League, the world's most prestigious soccer league. Through the agreement, in addition to having the league's naming rights, Barclays receives exclusive world-wide marketing rights, tickets, hospitality, and broadcast advertising for a league that is televised in 211 countries and territories. Robert Diamond, Jr., president of Barclays, explained the Barclays Premier League sponsorship "is a very important element of our marketing mix and provides a cost effective method to market our organization, helping us in our ambition to be one of a handful of banks leading the global financial services industry" (Barclays press release, October 26, 2009). Richard Scudamore, English Premier League executive, added, "The Premier League's strength is that it is an essentially English competition which has gained a huge international following. This clearly resonates with Barclays own business development and aspirations" (Barclays press release, October 26, 2009).

Barclays has used sponsorship specifically to support its entrance and growth in the United States. On a national level, Barclays has an agreement with the NFL for a co-branded credit card. In focusing more specifically on the New York area and its financial influence, Barclays has acquired the naming rights to the arena in Brooklyn that is the home to the NBA's Brooklyn Nets. Barclays is also the title sponsor of an annual golf tournament in the New York area that is the first round of the FedEx Cup playoff series, a sponsorship that will remain through 2016.

Golf is a major part of the Barclays sponsorship portfolio to reach different geographic locations throughout the world. In addition to the golf tournament in New York, Barclays sponsors the Barclays Scottish Open and the Barclays Singapore Open. A Barclays' statement explained that golf "provides an opportunity for the firm to build stronger relationships with clients and increase brand awareness. It also enables Barclays to align itself with a game that has global appeal, strong ethics and which exemplifies quality, confidence, and focus" (Barclays press release, August 25, 2011).

BBVA Compass, a global financial services company originating in Spain, reached a sponsorship agreement with the NBA in 2010. Gregorio Panadero, BBVA Compass global chief communications officer, explained, "This agreement solidifies BBVA's position as the "Bank of Sports" and opens up a new and ambitious pathway to growth in Spain, as well as in the U.S., through the BBVA Compass brand" (BBVA Compass press release, September 13, 2010). Mark Tatum, NBA executive vice president of global marketing partnerships, added, "BBVA is a leading global brand with a successful history of reaching fans and consumers around the world through sports. Basketball is a global game and this new partnership illustrates how the transcending popularity of the NBA, the WNBA, and the NBA D-League provide our partners with unique opportunities to engage our fans and celebrate the game in a variety of cultures" (BBVA Compass press release, September 13, 2010). BBVA Compass was the title sponsor of the Rising Stars Challenge rookie/sophomore game in 2012. The NBA is only one sponsorship in the United States for BBVA as it also has naming rights to the soccer-only stadium in Houston and a college football bowl game in Birmingham, Alabama.

In an example of trying to more forcefully reach new geographic markets within the United States, in 2011 Delta replaced Virgin America as the official airlines of the Los Angeles Lakers. One of the reasons was simply the brand exposure and hopeful brand usage in the Los Angeles market. Tim Mapes, Delta senior vice president of marketing, stated, "From our perspective, when you think about Los Angeles it is one of the world's largest travel markets. It makes total sense that the world's largest airline would be associated with what is arguably one of the world's greatest sports brands" (Mullen, 2011a, p. 5). Delta is also a sponsor of the New York Yankees, New York Mets, and New York Knicks. One of the ventures that Delta will promote through these sponsorships, that now include the Los Angeles Lakers, is Delta Private Jets and its business elite service between New York and Los Angeles. Mapes stated, "The link between our presence in Los Angeles and New York is not coincidental" (Mullen, 2011a, p. 5).

Property Selection: Common Interest

Some sponsors are trying to attract a target audience based on a common interest. Property selection based on the idea of common interest relates to the Elaboration Likelihood Model characteristic of individual involvement with a product category. Companies strive to learn the demographics of the audience as well as its involvement with the product category. Selection of property is, therefore, not always based on attracting the largest audience, but attracting the right audience in terms of its interest in the product category. Certain niche companies have sponsorships that are very niche oriented because of the audience having high involvement, or common interest, toward that product category. For example, a golf equipment manufacturer has a very niche audience, golfers, so that company will be efficient in choosing a golf-oriented sponsorship to reach that group. Miloch and Lambrecht (2006) point out that niche sports, such as bowling, fishing, cycling, and snow sports, "allow sponsors to become involved with the activities that mean the most to their target consumer" (p. 147). They add that the participants and supporters are more passionate about these niche sports, making them more likely than the average consumer to be aware of the sponsors and purchase their products.

In 2011, Nike made a calculated decision to focus more on the sponsorship of action sports, such as skateboarding, snowboarding, and surfing. Action sports represented approximately $390 million in revenue for Nike in 2011, with the hopes of doubling that figure in the next five years. Mark Parker, Nike chief executive and president, told Nike shareholders at a meeting in May, 2011, "When we looked at action sports, we saw a unique consumer segment that was underserved in terms of product innovation" (Vega, 2011). In an extension of its "Just Do It" campaign Nike created a new program called "The Chosen" that featured prominent skateboarder Paul Rodriguez, surfer Laura Enever, and snowboarder Danny Kass. In the past Nike has sponsored the United States Open of Surfing. Nike has also focused on building its brand in action sports through the sponsorship of youth events and creating an online contest in which athletes can submit videos of themselves performing on the Nike action sports Facebook page. Visitors to the page are able to vote for the video that they like the best (Vega, 2011).

This Nike example reveals that because there are so many different audience demographic variables that guide sponsorship selection, companies have to engage in multiple sponsorships. One sponsorship might satisfy one promotional communication business goal while another sponsorship might fulfill a different objective. For example, USAA insurance company sells insurance and other financial services to an audience that consists of only military, retired military, and their families. In terms of common interest USAA sponsors the athletic teams for Army and Navy, including the presenting sponsorship of the Army versus Navy football game. In terms of geography, USAA, headquartered in San Antonio, is a sponsor of the San Antonio Spurs. In combining both the common interest and geographic variables, USAA has sponsorships with the Washington Redskins and San Diego Padres, teams in cities with large military populations. In trying for increased brand exposure, with the assistance of its sports marketing agency, IMG, USAA reached a four-year sponsorship agreement with the NFL in 2011. Don Clark, USAA executive director of marketing, stated, "It is a noisy insurance market, but we like this opportunity to show our eligible universe of sixty million consumers what kind of company we are" (Lefton, 2011d, p. 27). In the first season of its NFL sponsorship, USAA did report a double-digit increase in brand awareness and an increase in brand likeability (Lefton, 2012). USAA refers to itself as the official military sponsor of the NFL.

Sponsorship Timing

Selection of the property should coordinate the sponsorship reaching the desired audience demographic at the appropriate time that coincides with the temporal selling of the product (Fortunato, 2001). One notable example of timing being an important consideration in sponsorship selection is the Macy's Thanksgiving Day Parade. Beginning in 1924, the parade was originally known as the Macy's Christmas Parade and was considered to be the official start of the holiday season. The parade generally has over 3 million people line the streets of New York City and approximately 50 million people watching on television (www.macys.com/parade). Macy's is receiving large amounts of brand exposure and top-of-mind awareness just when people are about to spend money purchasing holiday gifts. The parade has even made Macy's location at Herald Square in New York City a tourist attraction.

Because of these exposure benefits, the parade itself has been able to attract sponsors, which in 2012 included Delta Airlines, GMC Trucks, Toro work and utility vehicles, Timberland, Remo, which manufactures banners for marching bands, and the Affinia Manhattan Hotel in New York City. Remo is getting to advertise its brand for a very specialized product. The Macy's parade sponsorship by Timberland as the official outerwear partner certainly seems to be driven by the timing variable as the cold weather season is just beginning.

There are other examples where property selection seems to be driven by the coordination of timing and product usage. Gatorade has a distinct selling season, warm weather, and therefore sponsoring the NBA with the NBA playoffs from April through June strongly matches the beginning of its peak selling season (Fortunato, 2001). Scotts Lawn company is a sponsor of Major League Baseball. The two occasions during the year when Major League Baseball is prominent in the minds of the audience are during the playoffs and World Series in the autumn and opening day in the spring. These two time periods fit perfectly with Scotts promoting the importance of autumn and spring treatment of one's lawn. Tiffany is the official sponsor of the United States Ski and Snowboard Association (USSA). As part of this sponsorship Tiffany is the official vendor for the USSA

Gold Pass, which allows donors who contribute more than $10,000 annually to the USSA unlimited access to any ski resort in the country. The USSA sells more than 300 Gold Passes annually. Andrew Judelson, USSA's chief revenue and marketing officer categorized the timing of this sponsorship as "perfect because those Gold Passes are delivered in late October (in a Tiffany box), right before the holiday sales season. It's a target audience at a very strategic time" (Mickle, 2011a, p. 6).

Sponsorship Cost

While identifying the target audience and finding a property that offers the ability to reach that audience at the perfect time might be easily learned, having the financial resources to obtain the sponsorship with that property is another matter. Fahy et al. (2004) state, "Financial resources are by far the most important tangible asset to consider when examining sponsorship activity" (p. 1020). Sponsorship selection is always determined by the level of investment the company is willing and able to make — the cost of sponsoring the property. Corporations obviously believe that investing in promotional communication with sports properties is a valuable tool in the marketing mix as evidenced by the enormous spending on television commercials during sports programming alone (see Table One).

Table One: Top 25 Sports Advertisers on Television, 2011

Company	2011 Sports Spending
1. Verizon	$345,438,719
2. Anheuser-Busch	$299,721,969
3. AT&T	$296,940,250
4. Ford	$263,507,645
5. Chevrolet	$249,866,151
6. Toyota	$218,603,617
7. MillerCoors	$203,025,062
8. Sprint	$171,090,500
9. Southwest Airlines	$165,499,688
10. Geico	$163,494,641
11. Nissan	$153,167,485
12. Direct-TV	$137,980,781
13. McDonald's	$127,131,258
14. State Farm	$125,383,266
15. Warner Bros. Ent.	$123,810,031
16. Lexus	$120,587,471
17. Mercedes-Benz	$101,405,853
18. Chrysler	$96,888,814
19. Subway	$96,174,164
20. Apple	$95,068,961
21. Honda	$94,147,979
22. Volkswagen	$93,320,194
23. Hyundai	$88,229,366
24. Coca-Cola	$86,550,656
25. Capital One Bank	$85,617,227

Source: *Street & Smith's Sports Business Journal*, June 4–10, 2012, p. 26.

It is important to note that part of the spending on commercials is required by leagues as a condition of a company being an official league sponsor (this concept is examined in more detail in Chapter Four). Also, a company obviously does not have to be an official league sponsor in order to buy commercial time during the broadcast of a sports event.

In 2011, the top 50 companies in sports advertising on television combined spent approximately $5.68 billion, a dollar figure that represents a decrease of 8.5 percent from what companies spent in 2010, but an increase of 19 percent from what companies spent in 2009. Fourteen of the top 50 companies increased their spending in 2011 in comparison to 2010 (Broughton, 2012a). Forty-six of the top 50 companies had increased their sports spending in 2010 from 2009 (Broughton, 2011). The biggest reason for increased spending in 2010 was that year featured a Winter Olympic Games and the FIFA World Cup. Coca-Cola, for example, increased its 2010 advertising spending by 78 percent in comparison to 2009. In 2011 it decreased its spending by 40 percent in comparison to 2010 (Broughton, 2012a).

For some companies a majority of their total advertising expenditures on television are with sports programs. Southwest Airlines had 68.7 percent of its total $240,861,062 advertising spending on television in sports in 2011. Anheuser-Busch was second in having its total advertising expenditures on television with sports programs at 65.7 percent, and MillerCoors was third with 56.3 percent of its total advertising spending on television in sports (*Street & Smith's Sports Business Journal*, June 4–10, 2012, p. 26).

In terms of sports advertising on television, the car companies continue to be the leading product category with 18 of the top 50 companies being automotive brands. Other prominent product categories are telecommunications, quick-service restaurants, insurance providers, and banking institutions. One sports league made the list as the NFL ranked number 33, spending just over $70 million in advertising on television with sports programs. The $70 million figure represents 78.3 percent of the NFL's total advertising spending on television in 2011 (*Street & Smith's Sports Business Journal*, June 4–10, 2012, p. 26).

The financial investment of promotional communication into sports remains robust. In the first three months of 2012, advertisers spent more than $3 billion on sports telecasts, an increase of 9 percent from the same time period in 2011 (Broughton, 2012a). In its annual sponsorship spending industry review and forecast issued in January 2013, IEG reported that sponsorship spending in North America increased 4.4 percent in 2012 to a total of $18.9 billion. Global sponsorship spending grew 5.1 percent in 2012 to a total of $51.1 billion. IEG projects that sponsorship with sports properties will represent 69 percent of sponsorship spending in 2013, making sports sponsorship by far the largest property sector (IEG press release, January 7, 2013).

It must be pointed out that sponsorship with the more popular sports properties (i.e., NFL, NBA, NHL, Major League Baseball, the World Cup, or the Olympics) is cost prohibitive for many companies, with many agreements also often being long-term commitments (Fortunato & Richards, 2007).

Consider the following:

- MillerCoors pays the NHL $375 million over seven years to be the league's official beer sponsor (Dreier, 2011c).
- For the PGA Tour, title sponsors of tournaments pay approximately $7 to $8 million for events that are on network television, for example the FedEx St. Jude Classic, and $10 to $12 million for title sponsorship of World Golf Classic events, for example the Cadillac World Golf Classic from Doral (Ourand, 2010).

- Adidas agrees to pay the NBA $400 million over 11 years to be the league's official uniform supplier (Lombardo, 2006).
- Corona Extra signs a five-and-a-half-year contract in 2010 to become the main sponsor of the Association of Tennis Professionals (ATP) Men's Tour for $13 million per year (*Street & Smith's Sports Business Journal*, December 20–26, 2010).
- Adidas is the official sponsor and athletic supplier of Major League Soccer in a deal estimated at more than $200 million through 2018 (*Street & Smith's Sports Business Journal*, December 20–26, 2010).
- Anheuser-Busch is the official beer sponsor of Major League Soccer in a four-year contract valued to total more than $10 million (*Street & Smith's Sports Business Journal*, December 19–25, 2011).
- Warrior Sports agrees to a $41.3 million annual contract with English Premier League team, Liverpool FC, the largest kit deal in league history (*Street & Smith's Sports Business Journal*, December 19–25, 2011).
- Sprint pays NASCAR $750 million over ten years to be the title sponsor of its premier racing series, the Sprint Cup Series (*Street & Smith's Sports Business Journal*, November 28–December 4, 2011).
- Pepsi pays Major League Soccer an estimated $3 million annually to be the league's official soft drink. The contract runs through 2014 (*Street & Smith's Sports Business Journal*, December 12–18, 2011).
- BBVA Compass, a Spanish financial firm, reaches a four-year agreement with the NBA in a deal estimated valuing more than $100 million (Belson, 2010c).
- UPS pays IMG College $100 million in a four-year agreement giving UPS access to 68 universities whose multimedia and marketing rights are owned by IMG College (Thomaselli, 2011).
- Federal Express pays an estimated $30 to $35 million per year for the naming rights to the FedEx Cup, the season-ending playoff series of the PGA Tour (*Street & Smith's Sports Business Journal*, January 9–15, 2012).
- Emirates Airlines pays the United States Tennis Association an estimated $90 million over seven years to become the title sponsor of the U.S. Open Series and the official airline of the U.S. Open (*Street & Smith's Sports Business Journal*, February 20–26, 2012).
- Sprint pays the NBA $45 million over four years to be the league's official wireless partner (*Street & Smith's Sports Business Journal*, December 19–25, 2011).
- BMW pays the United States Olympic Committee $4 million per year in a six-year contract that began in 2010 (Mickle, 2012d).
- Visa signs an eight-year deal to sponsor the FIFA World Cup through 2022 in a deal valued at more than $170 million (Mickle, 2013a).
- Microsoft pays the NFL $400 million over five years for a technology sponsorship that will include tablets on the sidelines (Fisher, Lefton, & Kaplan, 2013).

For the Olympics the IOC's The Olympic Partner (TOP) program began in 1985 and provides global marketing rights within a product category for a four-year cycle, referred to as the Olympic Quadrennium, that ensures covering both a Winter and Summer Olympics. TOP sponsors pay an estimated $100 million for the four-year time period

(Bradshaw & Kortekaas, 2011; *Street & Smith's Sports Business Journal*, December 19–25, 2011). For the 2009–2012 Quadrennium that covered the Vancouver Winter and the London Summer Olympics, there were eleven TOP sponsors, generating $957 million in revenue for the IOC. The first TOP Quadrennium from 1985 to 1988, that covered the Calgary Winter and the Seoul Summer Olympics, had nine TOP sponsors and generated $96 million (Olympic Marketing Fact File, 2012, p. 11. http://www.olympic.org/Documents/IOC_Marketing/OLYMPIC-MARKETING-FACT-FILE-2012.pdf).

This exorbitant cost for the high profile sponsorships eliminates many companies that do not have large marketing budgets, helping maintain brand prominence and, therefore, brand dominance. These prominent brands are more likely to be identified as official sponsors of an event even if they are not the official sponsors. For example, if asked which company sponsors the uniforms and equipment for any university, a person without absolute certainty of which brand is the official sponsor might automatically respond "Nike" because of Nike's brand prominence. It provides a challenge to other uniform and equipment companies, such as Under Armour or Adidas, to have their name recalled even if they are indeed the official sponsor. Large companies to some extent probably do not mind the fact that sponsorship costs are very high because these costs do eliminate several companies from even having the opportunity to obtain the sponsorships with high profile properties and accrue their benefits.

Sponsorship expenditures are obviously going to be dictated by the economy. In difficult economic times promotional communication budgets are often an area that gets cut (Maestas, 2009). For example, in the wake of the 2008–2009 economic downturn several companies decided not to renew their sponsorship of PGA Tour events. Tom Wade, PGA Tour marketing executive, explained that "the worst period was 2009, when we had some sponsors that went through bankruptcies and we took a hit" (Smith, 2011b, p. 33). NASCAR went from 2008 until 2013 before adding a new sponsor (NASCAR did have sponsorship renewals) when the Sherwin-Williams paint company agreed to a five-year deal valued at more than $2 million per year (Mickle, 2013b).

In NASCAR primary and secondary sponsors began dissolving that designation by splitting a driver's season. The primary sponsor features the brand prominently on the car through its branded paint scheme. Instead of being the primary sponsor for the entire NASCAR season several sponsors are choosing to be the primary sponsor for only a portion of the season, forcing the race teams to find additional sponsors willing to invest at the primary level. This scenario of companies reducing primary sponsorships obviously creates more sponsorship inventory with less demand, thereby lowering the cost. The price of NASCAR primary sponsorships has dropped significantly from approximately $400,000 per race to $150,000 or less in some circumstances (Ryan, 2011). Jerry Freeze, general manager at Front Row Motorsports, highlights the one positive, that more companies might be able to compete for the sponsorships at the lower price point, stating, "Maybe instead of a Fortune 100 now it's back to Fortune 1000" (Ryan, 2011, p. 9c). With a need for more sponsors to make up for a reduction in revenue from the primary sponsor, more logos have become noticeable on cars, pit crews, and driver uniforms (Broughton, 2010).

Pearsall (2009) cautions that a poor economy raises skepticism on the part of the audience about corporate sponsorship spending. He contends, "Similar to their own feeling of fiscal responsibility, there may be a new concern among consumers to know that sponsors are being fiscally responsible as well" (p. 32). Pearsall (2009) believes the tough economy may lead consumers to think and act more favorably "towards companies that are less brash in their sponsorship presence" (p. 30).

The public skepticism regarding sponsorship spending was amplified toward financial institutions who took money from taxpayers through the United States federal government's Troubled Asset Relief Program (TARP). Taxpayers and government officials questioned how companies that were being bailed out with taxpayers' money could afford and justify their sponsorship spending. For example, Citigroup in 2006 agreed to pay the New York Mets $20 million per year for the then new Mets ballpark to be called Citi Field. The $20 million amount was double what any previous stadium naming rights agreement had earned. As part of the TARP financial bailout, Citigroup received $45 billion. Some members of the United States Congress called on the Treasury Department to direct financial institutions to end their stadium naming rights contracts, such as Citi's contract with the Mets (Sandomir, 2009). Joseph Goode, spokesman for Bank of America, which has the naming rights to the football stadium in Charlotte, North Carolina, explained that the financial institutions were required to pay TARP money back to the government and that sponsorships "are profitable business activities that generate the earnings required to fulfill these obligations" (Sandomir, 2009, p. B12).

The quest for properties to obtain needed revenue has forced leagues and teams to sell sponsorships in previously unsold product categories. For example, in 2010 the NBA became the first major sports league to sell a league-wide sponsorship to a spirits company when it signed a three-year contract with Bacardi. Prior to 2009, liquor companies were able to have agreements with individual NBA teams that allowed for the sponsorship of clubs and suites in arenas so long as the brand names were not visible by television cameras. In March 2009, the NBA lifted the television camera restriction, allowing liquor companies to have sponsorship agreements that included courtside signage. In 2009, 26 NBA teams reached or extended sponsorships with liquor companies, including Absolut, Bacardi, Captain Morgan, and Jack Daniels (Belson, 2010b).

Beginning with the 2010–2011 season the New York Knicks reached an agreement with Proximo Spirits, maker of 1800 Silver Tequila, that included courtside and scoreboard signage during games. Elwyn Gladstone, vice president of marketing at Proximo, described Knicks' games at Madison Square Garden as "a high energy environment with a very iconic team, which is a great environment to show off our brand" (Belson, 2010b, p. 16). Greg Elliott, senior vice president for marketing partnerships at Madison Square Garden, commented on the opportunity presented in the liquor product category, stating, "Many categories rise and fall, but the spirits category is a new area for us to reach out to. There's room for growth" (Belson, 2010b, p. 16). The Knicks also have an agreement with Sobieski, a vodka brand. In competing with the Knicks, the Nets in anticipation of their move to Brooklyn reached a five-year agreement with Russian vodka maker, Stolichnaya, for an estimated $2 million per year (Belson, 2010b).

In 2012 the NFL permitted its teams to sell sponsorships and advertising to casinos. The NFL was the last of the four major sports leagues to accept casino sponsorships and advertising. The NFL did place restrictions on how the casinos can be presented: stadium signage can only be in the upper bowl or concourse of the stadium, restricting the television exposure, advertisements can only be on radio or in print — not television or digital, the casinos that secure the sponsorships cannot have sports gambling, players or coaches cannot appear in the advertisements, the advertisements cannot depict people gambling or include language that implies that gamblers can win big, and finally, the casino must donate 5 percent of the sponsorship and advertising value to the NFL's anti-gambling program. An NFL memo issued to the teams explained, "These policy modifications are designed to ensure that all permitted gambling advertising by NFL clubs is executed in accordance with industry best practices" (Kaplan, 2012, p. 3). The memo adds, the policy restrictions are designed to "minimize any potential negative impact on the NFL brand" (Kaplan, 2012, p. 3).

Sponsorship Exclusivity

Although costs can be exorbitant there are certain characteristics of sponsorship that are unique and advantageous in comparison to other forms of promotional communication. Most noteworthy is the characteristic of exclusivity. Exclusivity is valuable because it simply eliminates any competition that one company might receive from a rival within that product category at the sponsored event or location or with the sponsored league or team (Fortunato & Dunnam, 2004). Exclusivity for the sponsoring company within its particular product category is one of the primary elements of the negotiated agreement. It is incumbent upon the sponsoring company to ensure that exclusivity is indeed part of the negotiated agreement and that another brand of the same product category will not have the opportunity for exposure at that location. The responsibility to protect exclusivity first lies with the sponsoring company because any expectation that a property would turn down additional revenue from another brand is probably unrealistic.

In the annual IEG and Performance Research survey in 2013, 73 percent of executives reported that category exclusivity was the most sought after benefit for their company through the sponsorship (73 percent of executive ranked exclusivity a 9 or 10 on a scale that had a 10 meaning "extremely valuable"). In fact, category exclusivity has been the most sought after sponsorship benefit according to respondents in the survey every year from 2007 through 2013. It should be noted that in 2011, on-site signage was also recognized by 63 percent of respondents as a desired sponsorship benefit. On-site signage ranked the second most valuable desired benefit in the 2013 survey, followed by obtaining the rights to the property marks and logo (IEG Sponsorship Report, April 22, 2013).

The result of exclusivity could be a distinct competitive advantage for the sponsor. Miyazaki and Morgan (2001) note that "the ability to be an exclusive sponsor in one's product category presumably aids in avoiding the competitive interference that typically is experienced in other media contexts" (p. 10). Steve Margosian, NBC Sports senior vice president enterprise sales and marketing, adds that through an exclusive sponsorship there is an opportunity to "position the brand to the consumer in a very unique way that is different from the competition" (personal communication, January 11, 2012).

Papadimitriou and Apostolopoulou (2009) explain that exclusivity acts as a barrier to competitors who might have tried to acquire that same sponsorship or at least diffuses the promotional attempts of competitors during the time that the company is sponsoring the property. Sponsorship decisions, therefore, can be made in relation to the competition within the product category (Johar & Pham, 1999). There could be a fear on the part of a company that if it is not the exclusive sponsor in that location that designation will go to a primary competitor. If Visa does not the secure the sponsorship of a property, American Express, MasterCard, or Discover almost certainly will. Tony Ponturo, former head of media and sports marketing for Anheuser-Busch, cautions about the strategy of purchasing a sponsorship from a defensive position of not letting the competition secure that property, especially considering the high costs of the sponsorship and if there are no brand goals that are going to be achieved. He indicates that the company is probably better served by seeking and investing in another property that can achieve its brand goals.

Companies compete intensely to secure the exclusive sponsorship within their product category to the most prestigious properties. To illustrate the quest for exclusivity no area is as competitive as the soft drink industry due to its largely binary choice: Coca-Cola or Pepsi (it should be noted that the Dr Pepper Snapple Group that features the Dr Pepper, 7 Up, A&W Root Beer, Canada Dry, and Country Time lemonade brands do have sponsorships as well). In terms of soda sales for the first half of 2011 Coca-Cola had a market share of 35 percent, compared to Pepsi's 32.9 percent (Horovitz, 2011). In 2011, Diet Coke surpassed Pepsi as the second most popular soda in the United States, trailing only regular Coke (Sisario, 2011). In 2010, Pepsi spent $136 million in television advertising, compared to Coca-Cola's $203 million (Sisario, 2011). Coca-Cola has also beaten Pepsi in the number of media mentions, with almost three times more than Pepsi in the four years prior to 2011 (Horovitz, 2011).

To illustrate the competition between Coca-Cola and Pepsi, one example plays itself out noticeably on television sets through Coca-Cola's sponsorship of *American Idol* and Pepsi's sponsorship of *The X Factor*. Both shows are televised on Fox with *The X Factor* airing in the autumn and *American Idol* airing in the spring. Coca-Cola has sponsored *American Idol* since the debut of the show in 2001 and has large red cups with the Coca-Cola logo displayed on the judges' table. *American Idol* has two other major sponsors: (1) AT&T, with host of the show, Ryan Seacrest, instructing viewers to use their AT&T phones to cast their votes, and (2) Ford, which has a music video each week featuring one of its vehicles and the contestants.

Pepsi paid $60 million for its sponsorship of *The X Factor* (Sisario, 2011; Steinberg, 2011). The winner of *The X Factor* received a $5 million recording contract and appeared in a Pepsi commercial that debuted during the broadcast of the Super Bowl in 2012 on NBC. During an episode of *The X Factor* Pepsi had commercials that showed clips of previous Pepsi advertisements that featured some of music's top performers of a particular generation, including Michael Jackson, Ray Charles, Britney Spears, and Mariah Carey. The commercial ended with the question "Who's Next?" indicating that the winner of *The X Factor* will be the next music sensation. The commercial featured the tagline "Where there's Pepsi, there's music."

The X Factor and Pepsi teamed together to create an online presence. At the Web site www.pepsisoundoff.com, fans could comment on *The X Factor* with the best remark appearing in a future Pepsi commercial when the comment of the week is highlighted. Simon Cowell, creator of *The X Factor*, said of the show's relationship with Pepsi, "It's been the most collaborative relationship I've ever had with a sponsor. From day one, they just bought into what we'd planned for the show, and almost became like producers. As we developed the show, we consulted with them in all the decisions, and they came and presented to us their own marketing ideas" (Sisario, 2011, p. 2). Frank Cooper, global consumer engagement officer for Pepsi, added, "*The X Factor* relationship is more about what role a brand can play in an entertainment platform beyond simple sponsorship" (Sisario, 2011, p. 2). Pepsi furthered its connection to music in 2013 when it became the sponsor of the Super Bowl halftime show.

Sports properties sell exclusive sponsorships in a variety of product categories, such as soft drink, beer, telecommunications, bank, airlines, credit card, financial institution, and insurance. In terms of sports properties, competition first exists to be the official exclusive sponsor for the major sports leagues in the United States as well as prominent worldwide events (see Table Two).

Table Two: Sports Leagues Official Soft Drink, Beer and Credit Card Sponsors, 2012

League	Soft Drink	Beer	Credit Card
Major League Baseball	Pepsi	Anheuser-Busch	MasterCard
Major League Soccer	Pepsi	Anheuser-Busch	Visa
NASCAR	Coca-Cola	MillerCoors	Visa
NBA	Coca-Cola	Anheuser-Busch	American Express
NCAA	Coca-Cola	none	Capital One
NFL	Pepsi	Anheuser-Busch	Visa
NHL	Pepsi	MillerCoors	Discover/Visa
Olympics	Coca-Cola	Anheuser-Busch	Visa
PGA Tour	Coca-Cola	Anheuser-Busch	MasterCard
World Cup Soccer	Coca-Cola	Anheuser-Busch	Visa

Note: For the NHL, Visa has Canadian marketing rights, while Discover has United States marketing rights.

This exclusive sponsorship at the highest level with the property is, however, only one of the multiple entry points that a sponsor can obtain. There are many entry points for sponsors to engage with a particular sport or event. For example, a company can enter into a sponsorship agreement with a sports league (the NFL), one of the league's teams (Green Bay Packers), the broadcasts of the games (ranging from national television to local radio), or one of the league's players (Green Bay quarterback Aaron Rodgers).

There are some positives for the sponsor in this arrangement of multiple entry points. The first deals with the issue of cost. Although some companies cannot afford the highest level sponsorship with a property, there are opportunities for entry at a lower level that will cost less, but can perhaps be even more efficient in reaching a particular target audience. Sponsorship thus becomes a viable strategy because selection can be tailored to meet not only specific promotional communication business objectives, but budgetary constraints as well (Wakefield et al., 2007). Wakefield, Beeker-Olsen and Cornwell (2007) explain, "Title- or anchor-level sponsorships tend to come with high price tags commensurate with superior visibility and high levels of integration with the event. Less expensive lower-level sponsorships tend to be associated with less visibility and less integration" (p. 61). Wakefield et al. (2007) did find that higher-level sponsorship investments outperformed lower-level sponsorship investments in terms of recall accuracy.

Tony Ponturo does explain that in a negotiation with a league a sponsor might look at its total spending in that sport and have a price limit. With the league not wanting to take money away from its teams, the sponsor could use this fact as leverage in its negotiation with the league. The sponsor might, for example, indicate that if more money has to be paid to the league, it would come out of the budget that was planned for spending with the teams.

The PGA Tour offers sponsorships on two levels: 1) official marketing partner for the Tour and 2) title sponsor of a tournament. According to the PGA Tour Web site, "Official marketing partners have rights to use the PGA Tour marks and build brand association with the PGA Tour and the values of the game of golf" (www.pgatour.com/company/marketing_official_marketing_partnership.html).

The benefits for official marketing partners of the PGA Tour are:

1. Use of PGA Tour marks in advertising campaigns
2. Brand association with winning values of golf
3. Membership to TPC clubs network
4. Multi-channel marketing opportunities
5. Unparalleled relationship building opportunities
6. Substantial public relations coverage
7. VIP access to tournaments
8. Worldwide brand exposure
9. Premium hospitality
10. Local and national promotional opportunities

[www.pgatour.com/company/marketing_official_marketing_partnership.html].

PGA Tour official marketing partners for 2013 include Anheuser-Busch (Michelob Ultra and O'Doul's brands), Bridgestone, Charles Schwab, Coca-Cola, Federal Express, Forbes, General Electric, John Deere, MasterCard, Nature Valley, PricewaterhouseCoopers, Rolex, Sentient Jet, Tiffany & Co., and United Airlines (http://www.pgatour.com/company/partners.html).

According to the PGA Tour Web site, "As a title sponsor, a tournament becomes identified by your company's name and a combined Tour/company logo" (www.pgatour.com/company/marketing_title_sponsor.html). The benefits for title sponsors are:

1. Brand association with winning values of golf
2. Multi-channel marketing opportunities
3. Unparalleled relationship-building opportunities
4. Substantial public relations coverage
5. Positive community impact
6. VIP access to tournaments
7. Worldwide brand exposure
8. Premium hospitality
9. Pro-am spots
10. Local and national promotional opportunities

[www.pgatour.com/company/marketing_title_sponsor.html].

Among the PGA Tour event title sponsors for the 2013 season are AT&T (AT&T Pebble Beach National Pro Am), Honda, Shell, Waste Management, Farmers Insurance,

Hyundai, John Deere, and Federal Express. Of course, these or other companies can enter into a sponsorship agreement with any player as well.

Some league sponsors support the national platform with sponsorships of individual teams. This provides the opportunity to reinforce the sponsorship that has a national profile with a sponsorship in a specific market. So Pepsi sponsors Major League Baseball, and then supports that national sponsorship by sponsoring individual teams. Pepsi has been an official sponsor of Major League Baseball since 1997 and has pouring rights agreements with sixteen teams. Pepsi's national sponsorship is supported in the New York metropolitan area with agreements with both the New York Mets and the New York Yankees. Pepsi has also used Yankees starting pitcher C. C. Sabathia in its television commercials. In 2011, Pepsi spent an estimated $7.6 million in total advertising time during nationally televised baseball games. USAA Insurance, which serves military members and their families has a deal with the NFL, the Washington Redskins, and in 2013 signed Redskins QB Robert Griffin III. Both of Griffin's parents served in the Army (Lefton, 2013c). Don Clark, USAA executive director of marketing, stated. "He was at the top of our list. Obviously, his military ties are strong and impressive, and they're something that will further solidify our relationship with the NFL" (Lefton, 2013c, p. 3).

In other examples, in support of its sponsorship with the NFL, Verizon has an agreement with the Chicago Bears, which includes a smartphone app that provides updates on team activities, in-depth information on players, stadium information, a game center, and merchandise. Even in non-team sports, Coca-Cola has been the official soft drink of NASCAR since 1998 and will continue in that capacity through 2017. To support this larger sponsorship, Coca-Cola is the title sponsor for two races, the Coca-Cola 600 and the Coke Zero 400, and has partnerships with ten Sprint Cup Series drivers.

Keith Wachtel, NHL senior vice president of integrated sales, stresses that it is important that national, league-wide sponsors spend money on the teams as it is often the local team that is the true passion-point for the fan. The NHL has a collaborative approach between the league and its teams where if a team has an available product category, the league could help craft a national sponsorship that includes those teams as well. So when Enterprise rental car became a sponsor of the NHL in 2009, because the product category had not been sold by any individual teams, Enterprise was able to partner with the league and all of its teams. Tony Ponturo, former head of media and sports marketing for Anheuser-Busch, also indicates the real passion in sports is with the teams, but some companies might not have the personnel and resources to negotiate a sponsorship in each market. By signing a league-wide sponsorship, national recognition can be achieved through one singular negotiation.

For the Olympics there are multiple points of entry: the International Olympic Committee (IOC), the national Organizing Committees for the Olympic Games (OCOG's), a national team, such as the United States Olympic Committee (USOC), one of the individual Olympic teams from a country (United States skiing), the broadcast of the Olympics on NBC, or an individual athlete (Olympic swimmer, Michael Phelps). It is important to note that sponsorship at one entry point does not mean there has to be sponsorship at other entry points. A company can just sponsor the IOC or it can choose to only sponsor Michael Phelps.

Again, it is the TOP Olympic program that is the most extensive exclusive, global sponsorship level (see Table Three).

Table Three: TOP Olympic Sponsors, 2009–2012

Company	Product Category
Coca-Cola	Non-alcoholic Beverages
Acer	Computing Technology Equipment
Atos Origin	Information Technology
Dow	Chemistry Company
General Electric	Select Products & Services from GE (Healthcare, Energy)
McDonald's	Retail Food Service
Omega	Timing, Scoring and Venue Results Services
Panasonic	Audio/TV/Video Equipment
Procter & Gamble	Personal Care and Household Products
Samsung	Wireless Communications Equipment
Visa	Consumer Payment Systems

Many of the current TOP sponsors have reached agreements with the IOC beyond the 2012 Quadrennium, including Atos Origin and Samsung through 2016 and Coca-Cola, Dow, McDonald's, Omega, Panasonic, Procter & Gamble, and Visa signed up through 2020.

The national Organizing Committees for the Olympic Games (OCOG's) provide domestic sponsorship programs that grant exclusive marketing rights only within the host country or territory. Domestic OCOG sponsorships are also on different levels: sponsors, suppliers, and providers. OCOG sponsorships generated more than $1.2 billion in revenue for the 2008 Beijing Summer Olympics and $688 million for the Vancouver Winter Olympics (Olympic Marketing Fact File, 2012, p. 17. http://www.olympic.org/Documents/IOC_Marketing/OLYMPIC-MARKETING-FACT-FILE-2012.pdf). It is important to note that not all Olympic sponsorship transactions are only cash-based, with some agreements being for services rendered or a combination of cash and services (Bradshaw & Kortekaas, 2011).

To illustrate the concept of a sponsor being involved with a property at multiple levels, Procter & Gamble has Olympic sponsorships with the IOC, USOC, USA Gymnastics and several Olympic athletes. This multiple sponsorship approach provides many different exposure opportunities for Procter & Gamble's product roster, which features 22 brands that each generates more than $1 billion in sales annually (Procter & Gamble press release, July 28, 2010). Procter & Gamble's roster of brands includes Bounty, Charmin, Crest, Dawn, Downy, Duracell, Febreze, Gillette, Head & Shoulders, Old Spice, Pampers, Pantene, Pepto-Bismol, Pringles, Scope, Tide, and Vicks.

Procter & Gamble had agreements with several Olympic athletes who were featured in the promotion of several Procter & Gamble brands through the 2010 Vancouver Winter Olympics. Among the Olympians were Tanith Belbin, ice dancing; Sasha Cohen, figure skating; Chad Hedrick, speedskating; Lindsey Jacobellis, snowboarding; Julie Mancuso, skiing, Apolo Anton Ohno, short track speedskating; and Lindsey Vonn, skiing. The athletes were used in an array of integrated promotional communication vehicles, such as traditional television commercials, public relations campaigns, in-store displays, mobile and digital technologies, and direct mail. The diverse roster of Procter & Gamble products allowed for matching up specific athletes with specific brands. For example, Julie Mancuso was associated with Crest, Sasha Cohen was affiliated with Pepto-Bismol, and Chad Hedrick partnered with Pampers. Kirk Perry, vice president, North America, Procter & Gamble, stated, "We are so proud to be affiliated with athletes who are achieving their personal best, while P&G products help them and people around the world achieve their personal best every day" (Procter & Gamble press release, January 7, 2010).

Product Category Definition

Because revenue through sponsorship is such a necessity for a property, sports leagues will make determinations about which product categories they will allow their teams to sell, as has been demonstrated in the discussion of the NBA in the liquor product category and the NFL in the casino product category (this issue will be focused on in more detail regarding the uniforms and beer product categories later in the book). The leagues and their teams will create product category segments that invite multiple, although sometimes similar, companies to be associated with that property. The definition of what exclusive product categories that will be sold is initially at the discretion of the property. The sponsors, in purchasing an exclusivity agreement with a property, could further define the category that they are buying in the negotiation process.

In all scenarios it is important for the sponsor to be clear as to what rights are a part of the exclusive product category that it is purchasing, with any ambiguity potentially creating an opening for another company to weave its way into that location. Gordon Kane, founder of Victory Sports Marketing, explains that "definition of category" is vital in the negotiation process (personal communication, November 22, 2011). For example, are sponsorship exclusivity rights within a product category for only a domestic designation and do not cover an imported designation? The Detroit Red Wings have an official sponsor for domestic beer, MillerCoors' Miller Lite brand, and an official sponsor for imported beer, Molson Canadian. Or, in another rights confusion example, for an automobile sponsorship, does it include all types of vehicles or only sport utility vehicle trucks? In some product categories the NHL sells Canadian and United States rights separately. In the credit card product category for the NHL, Visa has Canadian marketing rights, while Discover has United States rights. Some soft drink sponsorships provide for pass-through rights, where the rights extend to the quick service restaurants that exclusively sell that company's soft drink brands. For example, in Coca-Cola's sponsorship with the NCAA, it has pass-through rights to the quick service restaurants that serve the Coca-Cola brand, such as McDonald's, Domino's, and Buffalo Wild Wings. These rights allow for Coca-Cola-branded NCAA promotions at these restaurant locations (Smith, 2012b).

To further illustrate this product category definition dilemma, the PGA Tour has Charles Schwab as its official investment firm sponsor and PricewaterhouseCoopers as its official professional services firm sponsor specializing in tax and advisory. A description by the companies themselves reflects a similarity in their performance functions. Charles Schwab explains that it "offers a complete range of investment services and products including an extensive selection of mutual funds; financial planning and investment advice; retirement plan and equity compensation plan services; referrals to independent fee-based investment advisors; and custodial, operational and trading support for independent, fee-based investment advisors" (Charles Schwab press release, September 20, 2011). PricewaterhouseCoopers describes itself as "committed to delivering quality in assurance, tax, and advisory services" (PricewaterhouseCoopers press release, December 8, 2011).

While the sponsor and the property are sorting through their relationship, the networks broadcasting all of these games and events have a major role in the sponsorship process as well. Television networks too offer exclusive sponsorship opportunities. Sponsors and properties have to coordinate their agreements with the television networks that have the function of being a major revenue stream for sports leagues. It is the televising of games that provides many of the brand exposure opportunities for sponsors.

Chapter Four

Sponsorship Selection: Game/Event Brand Exposure Opportunities Through Media

Through sponsorship with a league, team, or athlete, companies have the opportunity to receive brand exposure during the televising of games or events. Sports sponsorships are desirable because an essential positive attribute of sponsorship, similar to product placement, is that the brand exposure is during the actual game or event — whether the audience is attending the game or experiencing it through the mass media. As noted in Chapter Two that not all brands appearing on the screen are a part of a sponsorship agreement, conversely not every sponsorship agreement has brand exposure through placement as its primary objective. For those brands that do desire exposure in terms of watching a game on television, people might change channels during commercials, but it can be logically concluded that if they tuned in to watch a game that during that time they virtually cannot escape the brand name exposure.

In terms of brand exposure during televised events, the way that people experience sports is relevant to any evaluation of sponsorship selection opportunities involving placement during the game. Experiencing sports continues to be driven by watching a game live on television with, obviously, more people viewing the game on television than are in attendance at the stadium. In some instances usage of the brand product might not even be available in the city of the event, but the company is still a sponsor because of the benefits of the event coverage on television. In one example, Emirates Airlines sponsored a tennis tournament originating from Montreal, Canada, despite not having flights to or from that city, simply because of the television exposure that the company received (Wong, 2009). A national or international sponsorship such as this allows for reaching a geographic area prior to the product being available in that region. If or when the product does eventually become available consumers are already familiar with the brand, having seen it on television. In the sponsorship example provided above, Emirates' exposure to the larger television audience would help assist instant brand recognition if Emirates did begin flying into Montreal (Emirates Airlines does fly to Toronto, Canada).

Understanding sports fans' motivations for behavior is also useful. Wenner and Gantz (1998) claim the unknown outcome of the game is the motivation that generates the most interest and drives the behavior of viewing. They point out that the strongest motivation for watching sports on television deals with resolution of ambiguity. Wenner and Gantz (1998) state, "Concerns with seeing 'who wins' and how one's 'favorite does' are among the strongest individual motivations for sports viewing. These tend to combine with the enjoyment that comes with experiencing the 'drama and tension' and the excitement of 'rooting' for a player or team to win" (p. 236).

For sports, with the outcome unknown, fans can see the unscripted drama unfold live on television. This helps make sports one of the few DVR-proof programs where viewers are compelled to watch the event live. By fans viewing sports programming during the live telecast, not at a later time or another day using a DVR device, the sponsorship is more relevant because the brand is seen at the appropriate time desired by the sponsor. Steve Margosian, NBC Sports senior vice president enterprise sales and marketing, claims that "96 percent of sports is watched live and brand recall is dramatically increased through sports programming as opposed to non-sport advertising because there is less channel-surfing during sports programming" (personal communication, January 11, 2012).

With brand exposure during game broadcasts being such a major desire on the part of sponsors, how sponsors fit into the relationship between sports leagues and television networks is important to examine. Leagues and television networks sign broadcast rights contracts where the network agrees to pay a sports league a certain dollar amount for a certain number of years for the rights to televise that league's games (Fortunato, 2001; Wenner, 1989). Once a contract is signed the league and its television partner work together to create a programming schedule that offers the games with the best teams and best players at the best times in the programming schedule, providing the opportunity for higher audience viewership. While the league receives its money from the networks, these networks that made the investment in the sports league are selling sponsorships and commercial time during these games to advertisers (Fortunato, 2001). It is the size and demographic of the television audience, commonly expressed as television ratings, that will determine the rate that sponsors and advertisers have to pay. Fortunato (2001) summarizes the business relationship between sports leagues, television networks, and advertisers where "the proper exposure and positioning in the program schedule and offering the best product to viewers in the form of teams, players, and matchups are essential to achieve the best television rating, and subsequently to earn the greatest advertising revenue, which would initially benefit the network — and eventually the league — when negotiating its next broadcast rights contract" (p. 73).

It is important to note that traditionally a sponsorship agreement includes the requirement for sponsors to purchase broadcast commercial time during the televising of the league's games (several leagues also require that sponsors spend a certain dollar amount with the individual teams and on activating the sponsorship; both will be discussed in detail later in the book). When Gatorade wanted to be the official sports drink of the NBA and have players drinking out of green cups with the Gatorade logo on them, it was a necessary condition to becoming a league-wide sponsor that Gatorade had to buy commercial time on NBA television broadcasts (Fortunato, 2001).

Leagues differ in how that required media spending by sponsors has to be allocated. The NFL requires sponsors to spend during the live broadcasting of its games, but permits sponsors to spend the requested amount for commercials during game telecasts with any of its four broadcast partners, CBS, NBC, Fox, and ESPN. The NFL also requires its sponsors to purchase media time on the NFL Network and the league's Web site. The NHL has similar requirements for spending with its broadcast partner, NBC, and the league's Web site. The PGA Tour, however, includes its own Web site as part of the media commitment it requires of its sponsors, obviously not as desirable a policy for the television networks that broadcast PGA Tour events.

If the league has multiple broadcast partners, by having the flexibility to choose which network it would like to advertise with, the sponsor could exert some leverage by suggesting that all or a majority of its media-spending commitments could come with one network if it provided a lower advertising rate. If the sponsor has a long-term agreement with the league, and the league has a long-term agreement with multiple networks, in terms of its commercial buys, Tony Ponturo, former head of media and sports marketing for Anheuser-Busch, indicates that he might try to lock in a price for a sponsored element or commercial time over a number of years. This does provide the network with a baseline price for selling its other commercial time. To illustrate this point of multiyear sponsorship and commercial commitments, NBC ended the 2011 NFL season of Sunday Night Football with almost half of its inventory for the 2012 season already sold (Ourand, 2012).

For title sponsors of a golf tournament on the PGA Tour, roughly half of their sponsorship fee goes toward buying commercial time with the network covering the tournament (the other half of the sponsorship fee covers tournament purses and other expenses). The title sponsors of the PGA Tour account for 65 to 75 percent of commercials purchased during a golf tournament's broadcast (Smith, 2011b). In another example, for the broadcast of the Major League Baseball All-Star game in 2011, Fox sold more than 40 percent of its commercials to Major League Baseball sponsors. Fox sold 30-second commercials for as high as $575,000 (Lefton, 2011c). By having sponsors purchase large amounts of advertising space it could allow the network to increase the price for the rest of the available commercial units, as an event with high demand now has a much more limited supply available.

The IOC and the USOC do not require their sponsors to purchase commercial time during NBC's televising of the Olympics. IOC sponsor Acer did not buy time on NBC for the Vancouver or the London Olympics. USOC sponsors Allstate and Hilton did not buy time on NBC for the London Olympics either (Mickle, 2012a). Seth Winter, executive vice president of group sales and marketing for NBC Sports, in explaining NBC's position commented, "We believe firmly that if you're a rings holder you should be investing in the Games. If you're buying the (Olympic) rings and no one knows you own them, then why are you investing in the Games?" (Mickle, 2012a, p. 10). Winter, advocating a system where Olympic sponsors are required to buy advertising time with NBC, added, "Anyone who secures the rings, a TOP sponsor or a domestic sponsor, needs to recognize the investment we (NBC) make in rights (fees)" (Mickle, 2012a, p. 10). NBC was able to sell exclusive commercial deals for the London Olympics in the automotive category with BMW, a USOC sponsor, representing the foreign automotive category and General Motors, a non–USOC sponsor, being the exclusive commercial advertiser in the domestic automotive category (Mickle, 2012a).

There are two ways that sponsors get exposure through television broadcasts within the game, either through a sponsorship agreement with the league or team, or by being the sponsor of an element during the broadcast of a game without being an official sponsor of the league or team. Leagues have worked with sponsors in developing opportunities for guaranteed brand exposure. Companies have their brand in the title of an entire league (i.e., Barclays English Premier League or the Izod Indy Car Racing Series), or the title of a sports event (i.e., Allstate Sugar Bowl or AT&T Pebble Beach National Pro-Am Golf Tournament). Again, the fact that these events are on television increases the value of the sponsorship.

Using the appeal of television and multimedia exposure, properties have become creative in developing sponsored assets. To try to generate excitement at the end of the PGA Tour season after all of the major tournaments have been played, the FedEx Cup was created in 2007. The FedEx Cup has a regular season of tournaments that begin in January and run through August. Through their performance in these regular season tournaments players accumulate points that enable them to qualify for the FedEx Cup Playoffs. In the autumn, four tournaments comprise the FedEx Cup playoffs, with each tournament having its own title sponsor, the Barclays from New York, the Deutsche Bank Championship from Boston, the BMW Championship from Chicago, and the Tour Championship presented by Coca-Cola from Atlanta. After each playoff tournament golfers are eliminated based on their points total, with the winner being crowned the PGA Tour FedEx Cup Champion. Tiger Woods was the inaugural champion in 2007 and was the winner again in 2009. In 2012, Brent Snedeker won the $10 million prize awarded to the FedEx Cup Champion. A special Web site has been established for the FedEx Cup, www.pgatour.com/fedexcup.

In the five years of the FedEx Cup playoffs the PGA Tour claims there has been a 48 percent increase in reach, the number of different households exposed at least once to a program, a 30 percent increase in average minutes viewed, and a 29 percent increase in television ratings for the third and final tournaments of the playoff series in comparison to PGA Tour events in the autumn from 2004 and 2006 before the creation of the FedEx Cup (Smith, 2011c). Ty Votaw, PGA Tour executive vice president of communications and international affairs, commented, "You have to look at the new normal versus the old normal. When you look at the amount of time viewers spend watching golf and the cumulative audience this time of year, those numbers are well up compared to what they used to be. Granted, it's a period of time that's very competitive and we understand that there's a lot of interest in college and pro football, but it's clearly an overall net add to where we were before the playoffs" (Smith, 2011c, p. 41). David Grant, an executive at Team Epic, the agency representing Federal Express added, "People are talking about golf in September. That was one of the driving forces behind the creation of the FedEx Cup and it's working" (Smith, 2011c).

When Notre Dame extended its contract with NBC to televise all of the team's home football games, a prime-time game at a neutral-site was added. In 2009 Notre Dame played Washington State in San Antonio, in 2010 played Army in the first college football game at the new Yankee Stadium, and in 2011 played Maryland at FedEx Field. The neutral-site games are considered home games for Notre Dame giving the university the rights to sell any sponsorship in accordance with NBC as the broadcast rights holder for these games. With the opportunity for a sponsor to obtain brand exposure in a prime-time game on NBC, Notre Dame sold a presenting sponsorship for the neutral site game. Sprint agreed to sponsor the 2011 game against Maryland as well as the 2012 neutral-site game at Soldier Field in Chicago against the University of Miami. Tim Considine, Sprint director of marketing and sports sponsorship, commented, "We're partnering with a national brand that is synonymous with excellence, and this enables us to extend the reach of our exclusive marketing agreement into two major markets, D.C. and Chicago" (Smith, 2011a, p. 4).

Sponsored Elements Within the Broadcast

Television networks sell sponsorships for elements within the broadcast as well. A multimedia company such as NBC has a plethora of communication platforms and programming assets to offer sponsors. Following its merger with Comcast, NBC Sports now has its traditional broadcast network, which has all of the major events for which NBC has obtained broadcast rights, such as the Olympics, golf's United States Open, and the NFL, cable television properties, the NBC Sports Network and the Golf Channel, whose programming delivers a highly targeted, passionate audience, 12 regional sports networks that televise many local teams' games, and its digital platforms.

Stotlar (2001) contends that sponsorship can be more effective than traditional spot advertising by weaving elements of the brand into the actual game or event broadcast. In examining the 2007 college football national championship game, McAllister (2010) reported that more than 80 percent of the game's telecast featured some form of an advertisement on the screen. Any location that offers extended camera coverage is a prime location for brand exposure during the television coverage of the game. These locations include signage placement at prominent locations on or around the field, such as the rotating signs behind home plate for a baseball game, the signs at mid-court or on the court for a basketball game, or center ice for a hockey game. Other recent examples of sponsors using camera placement of sporting events to obtain brand exposure include Allstate Insurance or State Farm Insurance putting its logo and corporate name on the net behind the goal posts at a college football field, making it visible whenever a team attempts a field goal or an extra point, Chase and Mercedes-Benz having their logos on the net during the tennis matches as part of their sponsorship of the U.S. Open tournament, teams having sponsor signage in the dugouts of baseball games and in the bullpens, knowing these areas are frequently shown on camera, and sponsors having their names on the ceilings of arenas so that during a basketball game when a low-angle camera behind the basket is shooting the game, their brand can be seen.

Many of these sponsorships during the televising of the game have the announcer repeatedly giving the name of the sponsor, establishing the audiovisual component that researchers claim can be a determinant of an effective product placement (Gupta & Lord, 1998; Law & Braun, 2000). In these instances the announcer provides the brand name as part of a segment of the broadcast, such as the half-time show (i.e., Visa at the Half) or a sponsored element within the game (i.e., Chevrolet Player of the Game). Each week when a PGA Tour event is part of the FedEx Cup it is mentioned during the televised broadcast. For example, when CBS announcer Jim Nantz welcomed viewers to the AT&T Pebble Beach National Pro-Am, he then stated that the tournament is "part of the season-long race for the FedEx Cup." The FedEx logo appeared on the screen during Nantz's announcement. In one instance, the announcer even made an unplanned reference to the sponsor. In the Bowl Championship Series national championship football game in 2011 sponsored by Tostitos, as Auburn University's Wes Byrum was setting up to kick the game-winning field goal, legendary play-by-play announcer Brent Musburger would exclaim, "This is for all the Tostitos."

Sponsors can even receive brand exposure during the game through virtual advertising with the advertisement being seen by the viewers at home, but not by fans at the stadium (Matuszewski, 2002; Mills, 2011; Yerak, 1999). For the 1999 Rose Bowl presenting sponsor AT&T had its logo virtually appear on the 50-yard line. Virtual advertisements also appeared during the 1999 broadcast of the Rose Bowl for Ford, Federal Express, Nokia, and Tostitos (Yerak, 1999). New York Rangers home games broadcast on the Madison Square Garden Network have virtual advertisements displayed on the glass behind each goal.

For nationally televised games, the leagues take control of the sponsorship space that is visible through the camera. For example, during a New York Rangers home game broadcast on the local cable Madison Square Garden Network, there are a series of sponsors along the boards of the rink that have been sold by the Rangers. When a Rangers game from Madison Square Garden is televised on NBC, some of the NHL's official sponsors get that space along the boards. During a February 12, 2012, game on NBC against the Washington Capitals, league sponsors Bridgestone, Coors Light, Discover, Enterprise, and Verizon had sponsorship space along with Sirius XM, and two signs for the NHL on NBC. None of these companies had sponsorship space for the Rangers game played three days earlier that was televised on the Madison Square Garden Network. Of particular interest is that during the game on the Madison Square Garden Network, Bud Light, a sponsor of the Rangers, had signage on the boards. During the game on NBC, NHL sponsor Coors Light had signage in an arena that sells Bud Light.

When a network has a sponsored element (i.e., a sponsor for the player of the game or scoreboard), often it will coordinate with the league and first offer that opportunity to a league sponsor. If the league sponsors decline, the network has the ability to seek another sponsor, including a competitor within the product category of the league sponsor. If a non-league sponsor does become the sponsor of the television broadcast element the network will be sure to not depict that sponsor as an official sponsor of the league. For example, the player of the game recognition might only be a shot of the player's face along with the sponsor's logo, rather than showing a picture of the player in his team jersey or alongside any league logos. While the NHL's beer sponsor is MillerCoors, after Stanley Cup playoff games, rights holder, NBC, had the "Bud Light Post Game Report" on the NBC Sports Network. For the NFL, any in-game sponsored elements have to be with an official league sponsor. For any sponsored elements that are a part of the pre-game or post-game shows, the television networks can sell that time or space to any companies they desire, including a rival company to a league sponsor within a product category.

Finally, Russell (2011) identifies a key distinction in promotional communication methods as either "purchased media (space in the media is purchased by advertisers) and earned media (space in the media is acquired without payment through journalistic and public relations efforts)" (p. 125). Beyond the game itself, sponsors of a prominent sports team or athlete often have the highlights of their games appear in other media outlets, such as ESPN *SportsCenter*, online vehicles, newspapers, or magazines such as *Sports Illustrated*. These additional earned media offer further opportunities for brand exposure. Corporate brands certainly treat this additional brand exposure through sports media coverage as an extra incentive in their sponsorship selection decisions (Fortunato & Yost, 2006).

In one notable example, Tiger Woods' victory in the 2005 Masters Golf Tournament can be utilized. Woods' victory featured a miraculous chip shot on hole number 16 during the final round of the tournament in which the ball rolling on the green toward the hole momentarily paused, giving viewers a clear image of the Nike logo on his golf ball, before dropping into the cup. The shot would be widely featured and replayed in every media outlet that covered the Masters. Estimates were that Nike received as much as $1 million in equivalent advertising time in media exposure from the shot in the immediate days following Woods' victory (Rovell, 2005). The shot by Woods is still often used in network promotions of the Masters.

Nike would also use the shot, described by Woods as "under the circumstances, it's one of the best (shots) I've ever hit" (Rovell, 2005), to form an entire advertising campaign. Chris Mike, Nike Golf's director of marketing, stated, "We wanted to be able to remind people about how special it was to connect our product to that moment." He also pointed out, "You don't often get natural opportunities like this" (Rovell, 2005). Scott Becher, president of the Sports & Sponsorships sports marketing firm, referred to the opportunity presented to Nike as "a marketing no-brainer." He explained, "Advertising is usually about what a product can conceptually do for you, but this was a real moment that happened in a pressure-packed environment that proved that both Tiger, and by association, Nike, could deliver" (Rovell, 2005).

Any location where there is the potential for additional media coverage after the game is played is being utilized to sell sponsorships or provide added value to a current sponsorship. Another example of this brand exposure through media coverage is the interview backdrop for players and coaches. The backdrop features the company name and logo alongside the team logo. In the NFL, for example, teams have sold a sponsorship for the interview backdrop when the head coach and players speak to the media. In 2012, Verizon had the interview backdrop sponsorship placement for the Atlanta Falcons, Chicago Bears, and Houston Texans. The Washington Redskins have an electronic backdrop where the companies change.

Stadium and Arena Naming Rights Sponsorship

One sponsorship brand exposure strategy that satisfies multiple audience selection variables is to acquire the naming rights to a stadium or arena. Cameron (2009) points out that all brand exposure elements are not equal. The quality of the exposure location is important in achieving product brand recall. Miloch and Lambrecht (2006) studied the impact of the location of sponsors within a venue, finding that sponsors with signage in highly visible or high traffic areas received higher recall rates than sponsors whose signs were not in as prominent locations. In addition to the quality of the exposure, Maxwell and Lough (2009) report that the quantity of games that fans attended influenced brand recall, leading them to argue that because sponsors benefit from higher attendance they need to play a role in helping the team sell tickets.

Certainly no signage opportunity is as significant as the naming rights to a stadium or arena. A stadium being named after a brand obviously has a better chance for brand recall than a small sign within the stadium. Priscilla Brown, senior vice president, head of marketing and strategy for Sun Life Financial, the company that has the naming rights to Sun Life Stadium in Miami, home of the NFL's Dolphins, the University of Miami, and the annual Orange Bowl, provides an overview of the benefits of a naming rights deal. She explains:

> Stadium naming rights sponsorships represent the pinnacle of sports marketing, a rare opportunity to elevate a brand's identity by aligning with the nation's most visible and treasured venues, and the teams they host. After all, the supply is limited given there are only so many venues that serve as homes to pro sports teams. These partnerships are powerful marketing tools that can significantly accelerate brand awareness in an extremely efficient manner while delivering other key business objectives. In terms of sheer exposure, it's hard to find sponsorships that generate as many impressions [Brown, 2011].

For the property (city, team, or university), selling the naming rights to the stadium or arena provides a lucrative revenue source (see Table Four).

Table Four: Top 10 Stadium & Arena Naming Rights Sponsorships (Total $ Value)

Arena	City	# of years	Total $ Value
1. Barclays Center	Brooklyn	20	$400 million
2. American Airlines Center	Dallas	30	$195 million
3. Phillips Arena	Atlanta	20	$185 million
4. TD Garden	Boston	20	$119.1 million
5. Staples Center	Los Angeles	20	$116 million
6. Prudential Center	Newark	20	$105.3 million
7. Toyota Center	Houston	20	$95 million
8. FedEx Forum	Memphis	22	$90 million
9. RBC Center	Raleigh	20	$80 million
10. Xcel Energy Center	St. Paul	25	$75 million

Stadium	City	# of years	Total $ Value
1. Citi Field	New York	20	$400 million
2. Reliant Stadium	Houston	31	$310 million
3. FedEx Field	Landover	27	$205 million
4. Minute Maid Park	Houston	28	$178 million
5. University of Phoenix Stadium	Glendale	20	$154.5 million
6. Bank of America Stadium	Charlotte	20	$140 million
7. Lincoln Financial Field	Philadelphia	20	$139.6 million
8. Lucas Oil Stadium	Indianapolis	20	$121.5 million
9. Gillette Stadium	Foxboro	15	$120 million
10. Sports Authority Field at Mile High	Denver	20	$120 million

Source: *Street & Smith's Sports Business Journal* Annual Resource Guide & Fact Book, 2012.

Note: In August 2011, Sports Authority assumed the last ten years of the naming rights to the stadium in Denver that was previously held by Invesco. The Broncos split the money from the naming rights evenly with the local government (Pankratz, 2011).

Regarding the practice of naming rights Jensen (2007) contends, "if done correctly there seems to be benefits for all partners. The sports organizations receive greatly needed cash and the corporate sponsor achieves any one of several public relations and/or marketing objectives. At the same time, many fans might prefer walking into a ballpark with a corporate name than absorb the sticker shock of higher prices for tickets, parking, concessions, and the like" (p. 107).

Stadium naming rights is not a new concept. Wrigley Field in Chicago has been the home of the Cubs since 1916 and was called Cubs Park from 1920 through the 1926 season. In November 1926 team owner William Wrigley, Jr., changed the name of the ballpark to Wrigley Field. While it is his family name, Wrigley also represents the name of the company's products. Today, stadium naming rights have accelerated to the point where it is more surprising when a stadium or arena does not have a corporate name attached: the Yankees still play in Yankee Stadium.

Hollis (2008) explains that "one of the benefits that companies are looking for when purchasing naming rights is general brand awareness" (p. 393). Gerrard, Parent, and Slack (2007) state, "The fundamental driver of the asset value of stadium naming rights is the size of the potential audience, particularly the number of spectators attending events hosted by the stadium, as well as the number of television viewers and other media-based followers of these events" (p. 11). To demonstrate that naming rights brand exposure is greatly enhanced through media coverage of events and not merely to those in attendance, the Staples Center in Los Angeles is a perfect example. The Staples Center opened in 1999 and has been host to many prominent events, including the 2000 Democratic National Convention and the Grammy Awards, which have taken place at the Staples Center every year but one since 2000, and is the home of the NBA's Los Angeles Lakers, NBA's Los Angeles Clippers, NHL's Los Angeles Kings, and the WNBA's Los Angeles Sparks. Since its opening the Lakers have been to the NBA Finals on seven occasions, and in 2012 the Kings won the Stanley Cup, providing exposure for the Staples brand on television during a highly watched event. In another fortuitous example of brand exposure through arena naming rights, in the 2006 and 2011 NBA Finals, the Miami Heat played the Dallas Mavericks. The arenas in both Miami and Dallas are named for American Airlines, the American Airlines Center in Dallas and the American Airlines Arena in Miami.

In August 2011, MetLife, the largest insurance provider in the United States, reached a 25-year agreement to acquire the naming rights to the Meadowlands Stadium that opened in 2010, home of the NFL's New York Giants and New York Jets. MetLife pays approximately $17 to $18 million per year for the naming rights (Caroom, 2011). This agreement provides the company with brand exposure on most NFL weekends, including several prime-time and nationally televised broadcasts. With the New York Giants winning the Super Bowl in 2012, MetLife Stadium hosted the first prime-time game of the 2012 regular season. MetLife Stadium will also be host to Super Bowl XLVIII in February, 2014. Steven Karndarian, president and CEO of MetLife, stated, "With our status as one of the world's leading life insurers, we wanted to partner with a world-class venue that would extend the reach of our brand to levels unmatched in the industry. I'm confident that this partnership will strengthen our brand and help drive value for shareholders" (MetLife press release, August 23, 2011).

Often, a stadium naming rights agreement includes other elements: signage within the stadium, hospitality opportunities, tickets, media time, and an online presence (Hollis, 2008). In its deal MetLife becomes the official insurance company of the Giants and the Jets, receives 120,000 square feet of branded space at the main west entrance to the stadium, has four illuminated signs on the exterior of the building, has four inner-bowl signs, and receives media opportunities. Beth Hirschhorn, chief marketing officer of MetLife, stated, "Hundreds of millions of people will experience events at MetLife Stadium either in person or via broadcasts from the venue. MetLife Stadium now joins the portfolio of powerful and iconic marketing assets the company has cultivated over the years, including the MetLife blimps and the company's association with the Peanuts characters" (MetLife press release, August 23, 2011).

Prior to the stadium naming rights deal, MetLife had been one of the four cornerstone entrance sponsors at a cost of approximately $7 million per year (Caroom, 2011). The cornerstone entrance concept provides four sponsors their own branded zones at the stadium. As a cornerstone entrance sponsor to the new Meadowlands Stadium in 2010 MetLife was able to sign up over 30,000 fans for contests and promotions (Caroom, 2011).

Companies are using naming rights agreements to try to boost their international brand exposure as well. Mercedes-Benz has the naming rights to the arena in Shanghai. MasterCard has a five-year naming rights agreement paying more than $4 million annually for the arena in Beijing (*Street & Smith's Sports Business Journal*, December 19–25, 2011).

In addition to general brand exposure, there is research that demonstrates that customers develop positive feelings toward a brand due to its naming rights agreement. Bal and Boucher (2011) found that people who were not customers of the O_2 telecommunications company had a higher opinion of the O_2 brand after attending the O_2 Arena in London. At the O_2 Arena, O_2 customers have the ability to receive extra privileges, such as knowledge of ticket information and purchase ability for arena events before the general public, fast-track entrance, and the use of certain bar and lounge locations at the arena. Bal and Boucher (2011) explain, O_2 "positions itself as the friend everyone wants to have, the one who will inform you in advance and help you get into sought-after places" (p. 243). They add, "Non-customers, after witnessing this special treatment, may ask themselves whether or not they receive the same attention from their mobile phone provider" (p. 243).

There have been instances where fans reacted negatively to stadium naming rights agreements (Hollis, 2008; Jensen, 2007; Woisetschlager & Haselhoff, 2009). Jensen (2007) documents how the people in Denver reacted negatively when the Broncos, whose stadium was known as Mile High Stadium, signed a naming rights deal with Invesco. The reaction of the community, which did not want the Mile High phrasing that is emblematic of the city removed, led the stadium to be named Invesco Field at Mile High. In San Francisco, the fans reacted negatively to the change of the name of the stadium from Candlestick Park to 3Com Park (Hollis, 2008; Jensen, 2007). After the expiration of the contract with 3Com, the name of the stadium was changed to Monster Park, for the Monster Cable Company. In 2004, the voters of San Francisco passed an initiative that the name of the stadium would revert back to Candlestick Park permanently after the contract with Monster expired in 2008 (Hollis, 2008). Estimates had the abandoning of the naming rights deals costing the city of San Francisco $1 million per year (Jensen, 2007).

In keeping with the sponsorship concept of anything being possible, there have been some unique ideas put forth in the practice of naming rights. In a first in United States sponsorship, one stadium naming rights deal had the team paying the sponsor. In March 2011, Sporting Kansas City of Major League Soccer agreed to pay $7.5 million over six years to Livestrong, the organization known for its commitment to cancer research, the yellow wristbands that signify the fight against cancer, and its spokesman, Lance Armstrong. The 18,467 seat stadium in Kansas City was known as Livestrong Sporting Park. The Livestrong name was dropped from the stadium name in January, 2013 after Lance Armstrong admitted to using performance enhancing drugs.

In another unique naming rights initiative in December 2012, Qualcomm, the name of the football stadium in San Diego, decided to have the Snapdragon brand be used as the stadium's name for a ten-day period. The idea was to increase consumer awareness for Snapdragon, a mobile processor brand used by Qualcomm, and explain the role that the processors play in how people use their mobile devices. Paul Jacobs, chairman and CEO of Qualcomm, explained, "Mobile is the biggest technology platform in human history, having a transformative impact on billions of people around the world. Naming Snapdragon Stadium will help us drive consumer awareness for Qualcomm's Snapdragon mobile processors and how they enhance the user's experience on hundreds of smartphones worldwide" (*Marketing Weekly News*, 2012, p. 185). All Qualcomm stadium signage would be replaced with red Snapdragon signs and banners. Snapdragon supported the name change with device giveaways and an advertising campaign.

The timing of the name change coincided with three nationally televised football games from the stadium: the San Diego Chargers prime-time game on December 18 against the Baltimore Ravens, the San Diego County Credit Union Poinsettia Bowl on December 21, and the Bridgepoint Education Holiday Bowl on December 28. Dean Spanos, chairman of the board and president of the San Diego Chargers, stated, "This is a first-of-its-kind effort to completely rename a stadium without changing naming rights. We look forward to playing in Snapdragon Stadium and helping Qualcomm bring awareness to the technologies Snapdragon processors enable" (*Marketing Weekly News*, 2012, p. 185). Bruce Binkowski, executive director of the San Diego Bowl Game Association, added that the Bowl Game Association is "excited to be on the leading edge of what could become a new trend in stadium and arena naming rights programs" (*Marketing Weekly News*, 2012, p. 185).

Naming rights are now being sold for professional team practice facilities. JetBlue Airlines is the official airlines of the Boston Red Sox, and as part of its eight-year renewal agreement the Red Sox spring training facility in Fort Myers, Florida, is named JetBlue Park. The New York Giants training facility is the Timex Center, with signage visible from a major highway leading to the Lincoln Tunnel entering New York City. Under Armour has a ten-year agreement with the Baltimore Ravens in which the team's practice facility is called the Under Armour Performance Center.

Stadium and arena naming rights agreements have extended to university facilities, providing these schools with a lucrative revenue source (see Table Five).

Table Five: Top 5 University Naming Rights Agreements

Facility	*University*	*# of years*	*Total $ Value*
Save Mart Center	Fresno State	20	$40 million
TCF Bank Stadium	Minnesota	25	$35 million

Comcast Center	Maryland	25	$25 million
Chevy Chase Bank Field	Maryland	25	$20 million
AT&T Stadium	Texas Tech	25	$20 million

Notes: Save Mart Supermarkets received the naming rights from Pepsi, the original rights holder. Comcast pays an additional $5 million for logo rights to the basketball court.

Source: *Street & Smith's Sports Business Journal* Annual Resource Guide & Fact Book, 2012.

In June 2011, Rutgers University sold the naming rights for its football stadium in a ten-year agreement worth a total of $6.5 million to High Point Solutions, a supplier of technology and online equipment founded and owned by two brothers born in New Jersey. Tim Pernetti, then Rutgers athletic director, stated, "We were picky about a partner. We were trying to find someone who has the same core values and a New Jersey-based company. And in the end, we're thrilled with the results" (Vorkunov & Luicci, 2011, p. 5). Greg Schiano, former head football coach of Rutgers, explained, "It's expensive to run a major college football program. You have assets and if you're not capitalizing on those assets you're really not doing the best you can for your program" (Luicci, 2011, p. 47). Mike Mendiburu, one of the owners of High Point Solutions along with his brother Tom, stated, "This is our first football sponsorship and our first stadium. I think it's a win-win. It's a win for New Jersey, it's a win for Rutgers, it's a win for High Point" (Vorkunov & Luicci, 2011, p. 5). High Point Solutions also has a naming rights agreement for the Quinnipiac University ice hockey arena (Jones, 2011).

Sponsor Role in Stadium Construction and Financing

A company being a part of the financing of a stadium or arena and then becoming the naming rights holder has been done in the past. Cornwell (2008), in fact, claims, "It is almost unimaginable that community development or refurbishment of a major sports arena would be accomplished without corporate sponsorship" (p. 42). Through financing 90 percent of the arena in Columbus, Ohio, Nationwide has indefinite naming rights to the arena. In Denver, Molson Coors was granted naming rights for Coors Field through its contribution to the stadium's construction (*Street & Smith's Sports Business Journal* Annual Resource Guide & Fact Book, 2009, p. F-151).

Naming rights have even been granted for stadiums being constructed or still in the proposal stage. Levi's reached a twenty-year, $220 million deal for the naming rights to the the football stadium that will be the home of the San Francisco 49ers beginning in 2014 (Muret, 2013). Farmers Insurance has acquired the naming rights to a proposed football stadium in Los Angeles, Farmers Field, for a deal valued at $700 million over 30 years. The terms of the deal include an increased fee if the stadium acquires two NFL teams. Bob Woudstra, Farmers Insurance CEO, stated, "This investment will court the NFL, and bring jobs and economic development to downtown Los Angeles. Farmers Insurance was founded in Los Angeles and has been headquartered here for more than 80 years. We have always sought to be net givers, not net takers, in the communities we serve, and we are excited to be a part of this lasting legacy" (Farmers Insurance press release, February 1, 2011). Kevin Kelso, executive vice president and chief marketing officer of Farmers

Insurance, added, "Farmers Field represents a rare opportunity to merge a significant investment in Los Angeles with tremendous exposure for the Farmers brand. But this extends well beyond the Los Angeles market: this showcases the Farmers brand on a national stage" (Farmers Insurance press release, February 1, 2011).

Taxpayers simply look to sponsors as a way to defray the costs of the stadium or arena's construction and continued operations. When Mercedes-Benz reached a ten-year naming rights deal to have the Louisiana Superdome in New Orleans subsequently re-named the Mercedes-Benz Superdome, the people of Louisiana were a major beneficiary. In addition to being the home of the NFL's Saints, the Superdome has hosted numerous Super Bowls, NCAA Final Fours, the annual Sugar Bowl game, and Muhammad Ali winning the heavyweight championship of the world for a third time in defeating Leon Spinks in 1978. The Superdome also became a visual symbol of Hurricane Katrina when it was used as a shelter and the roof of the stadium was torn off.

The taxpayers of Louisiana had been providing subsidies to the Saints, paying the team as much as $23 million in one year (Hogan, 2011). The money from Mercedes-Benz would relieve the state from its financial obligation to the Saints. Bobby Jindal, Louisiana governor, explained, "From the state's perspective this is a very good deal for the state and for taxpayers. This will either significantly reduce or potentially eliminate the state's annual payment to the Saints" (Hogan, 2011). Tom Benson, Saints owner, commented, "We project that the state will no longer have any inducement obligations to the team and that is a benefit to everyone" (Hogan, 2011). The Mercedes-Benz Superdome hosted the Bowl Championship Series college football national championship game in January, 2012, and the Final Four in April, 2012. In 2013, the Mercedes-Benz Superdome hosted the Super Bowl.

New arenas and stadiums are constructed with spaces designed to be sold to sponsors. One of the reasons that teams seek new stadiums or arenas is the revenue-generating possibilities through sponsorship. In 2010, the Pittsburgh Penguins moved into the newly constructed Consol Energy Center. The naming rights agreement is for 21 years and pays the Penguins an estimated $4 to $5 million annually. When the arena opened the featured spaces included the Lexus Club, which provides a pre-game buffet for premium seat holders and other season-ticket holders who pay $500 annually for membership. In the club, actual Lexus automobiles are on display. The Captain Morgan and First Niagara Bank clubs feature seating with an open view of the ice. The suite level is sponsored by PNC Wealth Management.

When it opened, the Consol Energy Center arena entrances were also sponsored. At the Verizon entrance fans can try out the brand's products. The Trib Total Media entrance has touch screen technology where fans can watch Penguins highlights. At the American Eagle Outfitters entrance fans see electronic displays shaped as giant hockey pucks that provide arena information. Because of the new arena and the Penguins providing these additional sponsorship opportunities, the team doubled the number of corporate partners, including having a partnership with 25 of the top 50 companies in the Pittsburgh area. The amount of revenue derived from these sponsorships launched the Penguins from the bottom quarter of the NHL in local sponsorship income to one of the top five teams in the league (Muret, 2010a).

Similarly in Orlando in 2010, the Amway Center opened as the new home of the

Orlando Magic. One of the sponsored areas of the Amway Center is the Kia Motors Terrace, which is designed as a Kia Motors dealership showroom with cars on display and a 30-person space that is available for customers who test drive Kia cars and then receive two free tickets to a Magic game. The Budweiser Baseline Bar, Coors Light Mountain Bar, and the Gentleman Jack Terrace are areas where all fans can visit, regardless of what they paid for the ticket. The Mercedes-Benz Star Lounge and the Ritz-Carlton Destination Chairman's Suite are exclusive to designated premium seat holders (Muret, 2010b).

Another example of a "sub-naming rights" deal beyond branded areas of an arena is Lexus reaching an agreement with the Florida Panthers for the naming rights to the team's ice rink. The official title is Lexus Rink at the Bank Atlantic Center. The Panthers' announcers reference Lexus Rink during the team's broadcasts. In addition to its branded parking lot and multiple car displays in the arena, Michael Yormark, president and chief operating officer for the Panthers parent company, Sunrise Sports & Entertainment, explained that Lexus "challenged me to come up with something new. For us, it created new inventory that we haven't taken advantage of in the past" (Muret, 2011, p. 4). The Lexus deal does not include in-ice exposure, but the company does have a right of first refusal should any of the current Panthers in-ice sponsors, Bud Light, Dex Imaging, Ford, and Gulfstream Park, withdraw their sponsorship. The name of the arena, Bank Atlantic Center, is emblazoned on the ice at the center circle (Muret, 2011).

Leagues do have official policies as to corporate designations on the playing surface. The NHL permits four sponsorship positions on the ice along with the arena naming rights holder having an additional center ice position. The NFL and Major League Baseball do not permit corporate logos on the field of play (Muret, 2011). The NBA used to only allow the company that has the naming rights of the arena to appear on its court, however, beginning with the 2013–14 season teams will be able to sell space in front of the team benches as well as on top of backboards. These decals will be removed during national television broadcasts. Alex Martin, CEO of the Orlando Magic, commented, "This platform to grow inventory of camera-visible signage will allow us all to continue to grow our business for our teams and our players. I applaud the league for opening up this opportunity for our teams and our clients" (Lombardo, 2013). Corporate logos on basketball courts and football fields are certainly common for college athletics, most notably having corporate names on display in the playing of college football bowl games.

College Football Bowl Game Sponsorship

Much as stadium or arena naming rights sponsorships are now the norm, so too is sponsorship of college football bowl games. The idea is that corporate sponsorship of the bowl games provides some benefit to all of the entities involved. Farhi (1988) comments, "While traditionalists may decry the commercial exploitation of what is supposed to be a sport played by amateur student-athletes, proponents argue that sponsor fees provide something for everyone. Companies get to tout their products. Broadcasters wind up paying less for air rights. And the colleges take home fatter purses" (p. A1).

The emergence of corporate sponsorship of bowl games was in response to television networks not wanting to continue paying exorbitant fees to bowl games for what at the time was decreasing audience viewership. In 1984, the Cotton, Orange, Rose, and Sugar Bowls had viewership that combined to reach 70.2 percent of all television households. The viewership dropped to 55.2 percent for these same bowl games in 1988 (Farhi, 1988).

Sunkist became the first sponsor of a bowl game with the Sunkist Fiesta Bowl. The timing could not have been more perfect for Sunkist, as in January 1987 the Fiesta Bowl matched the University of Miami against Penn State for the national championship. The game was even moved from January 1 to January 2 and put in prime-time on NBC to increase its exposure and not compete against the slew of other bowl games slated on the traditional New Year's Day schedule. The Penn State victory over Miami remains the highest rated televised college football game of all time.

As the sponsor of the Fiesta Bowl, for an annual payment of $2.5 million, Sunkist received naming rights to the game, on-field brand exposure, brand exposure on the teams' uniforms, a presence at the Fiesta Bowl parade and other community events, and a reduced rate for 30-second commercials during the game's broadcast on NBC (Farhi, 1988). Ray Cole, marketing executive at Sunkist, explained, "There's no way we could buy this kind of publicity with the kind of advertising budget we have" (Farhi, 1988, p. A1). Bruce Skinner, executive director of the Sunkist Fiesta Bowl, added, "For what Sunkist is paying us, they could buy maybe three spots on the Super Bowl. Sponsoring an event is a far more creative way for a company to spend its money than just picking up the phone and ordering advertising time" (Farhi, 1988, p. A1).

Some corporate sponsors have made their brand name the only part of the bowl game name. In 1989 John Hancock dropped "Sun" from the Sun Bowl, making the annual game played in El Paso, Texas, the John Hancock Bowl. The John Hancock Bowl name would last five years before returning to have "Sun" as part of the game's name. Other companies followed the strategy of John Hancock. Quick service restaurant Chick-fil-A became the sponsor of the Peach Bowl game played in Atlanta before eventually dropping "Peach" from the game's title (McMurphy, 2006). In 1996 Outback Steakhouse became the sole name of the Outback Bowl, a change from the previous name, the Hall of Fame Bowl. Jim McVay, Outback Bowl CEO, explained, "This is a business. The College Football Hall of Fame didn't want to lose its name on the game, but schools want more money and you have to find it somewhere" (Matuszewski, 2002, p. 1).

Beyond exposure during the televised broadcast of the game, the mere mentioning of the game provides additional media exposure. For example, in 2005 with the University of South Florida as a participant, the Meineke Car Care Bowl was mentioned 156 times in the *Tampa Tribune*. The next season with South Florida appearing in the PapaJohns.com Bowl, it would be the Papa John's brand name with numerous mentions in the *Tampa Tribune* (McMurphy, 2006). Teams upon winning games that clinch their trip to the bowl games might even celebrate with the brand's products. While it was customary to see players holding a rose, knowing their team had just earned a trip to the Rose Bowl, a team might simply have bags of Tostitos on its sideline after winning a game that secures a birth in the Tostitos Fiesta Bowl.

The Rose Bowl was the last of the bowl games to have a corporate sponsor when the game in 1999 was referred to as "the Rose Bowl presented by AT&T" (rather than the corporate name getting the first mention, such as the Discover Orange Bowl). The economics of the bowl game were certainly a factor in forcing the Rose Bowl to accept a corporate partner. Harrimon Cronk, Rose Bowl chairman, admitted it was necessary to "bring somebody to the table like AT&T from a financial standpoint" (Rogers, 1998, p. 7E). A few years later, Mitch Dorger, Rose Bowl CEO, recalled, "It was a necessity to enhance the payouts. We didn't have much of a choice in the matter, though (the sponsorship agreement) wasn't going to be with just any company that came along. It had to be the right fit" (Matuszewski, 2002, p. 1). In the first year of the agreement with the Rose Bowl, AT&T did not have any images of its logo permitted in the stadium. Corporate logos were, however, digitally inserted into the television broadcast (Matuszewski, 2002; Yerak, 1999). All Rose Bowl games after 1999 did feature AT&T as part of the Rose Bowl logo, and the company did have an on-field presence.

Bowl games often change corporate affiliations. After AT&T, Citi was the presenting sponsor of the Rose Bowl for seven years through the conclusion of the 2010 game (Wharton, 2010). In October, 2010, Vizio, a consumer electronics maker, became the presenting sponsor in a four-year agreement that will include the Rose Bowl's centennial game in 2014 as well as the 2014 Bowl Championship Series national championship football game. Randy Waynick, chief sales officer at Vizio, stated, "Sports fans, particularly football fans, are a critically important audience for our brand as it continues to grow and expand. Serving as presenting sponsor of the 'granddaddy of all Bowl Games' provides a rare opportunity to reach a captive audience on New Year's Day. It also provides tremendous marketing potential leading up to the game during the critical holiday buying season" (McClellan, 2010).

As has been demonstrated in the example of the Rose Bowl, the need for revenue certainly plays a significant role in the discussion of the time and space that the property is going to sell. Truthfully, the property can sell sponsorships for an unlimited number of items or space. The fact that the Yankees play in Yankee Stadium is largely because the Yankees have other very lucrative revenue streams, most notably the ownership of the local cable television network that broadcasts their games. The IOC, which has the lucrative revenue source of television broadcast rights and its TOP sponsorship program, does not sell what would be a fruitful sponsorship opportunity by eliminating stadium signage during the Olympics. The position of the IOC is "to ensure that no advertising or other commercial message in or near the Olympic venues is visible to the Olympic Games venue spectators or to the Olympic Games broadcast audience. No advertising or commercial messages are permitted in the Olympic stadia, on the person of venue spectators, or on the uniforms of the Olympic athletes, coaches, officials, or judges" (Olympic Marketing Fact File, 2012, p. 36. http://www.olympic.org/Documents/ IOC_Marketing/ OLYMPIC-MARKETING-FACT-FILE-2012.pdf).

Audience Reaction to Sponsorship

The other factor underlying the sponsorship process is the reaction of the audience. Kinney and McDaniel (1996, 2004) extend the concept of attitude-toward-the-ad into assessing attitude-toward-the-sponsorship. Kinney and McDaniel (2004) concede that "event organizers and sponsoring companies may perceive the sponsorship as helping stage the event and contributing to the sporting experience," but simply pose the questions if sponsorship is "welcomed by fans" and if consumers "appreciate sponsors contributions" to sports events? (p. 212). Real (1996), for example, cautions against the overcommercialization of sports, while McAllister (1998) expresses the overcommercialization concern particularly in relation to college sports.

In studying the Olympic Games, Kinney and McDaniel (1996) found that attitude-toward-the-sponsorship did have a positive influence on consumers' attitude-toward-the-brand and purchase intention. In their study of general sports sponsorship, Kinney and McDaniel (2004) reported that the majority of American consumers are more comfortable with sponsorships of professional sports than collegiate sports, almost 36 percent do not believe ticket prices are reduced, the majority does not believe sponsoring brands are superior, and the majority does not seek out sponsor's brands.

For the most part the sports fans have become desensitized to the number of advertising messages that they are going to receive during the course of a game. Perhaps the first time that people heard that the bowl game will be called the Sunkist Fiesta Bowl or that the Washington Redskins would no longer play in Robert F. Kennedy Stadium, but in a stadium called FedEx Field, they might have been surprised or found it intrusive. Now, the bombardment of sponsors is expected. The fans know the game will be played in a branded stadium and many elements of the game will be sponsored.

Fans might not find the amount of sponsorship problematic if they believe that these sponsors help defray the costs involved with experiencing sports, such as the cost of the ticket. Kinney and McDaniel (2004) did have 40 percent of their sample agree or strongly agree that sponsorship helps keep ticket prices down, with another 20 percent of respondents neither agreeing or disagreeing (p. 218). If not a direct reduction in ticket costs, sponsorship money can provide added value to the experience of attending a game, such as a promotional giveaway. For most teams, every giveaway is sponsored (this will be discussed in greater detail in Chapter Six, that focuses on sponsorship activation). Sponsorship revenue can help a team increase its payroll, giving it a greater ability to acquire more talented players. Woisetschlager, Eiting, Haselhoff, and Michaelis (2010) argue that ideally the sponsor should be publicly credited with helping a team sign a key free agent player.

Of course, it is also the sponsors' willingness to buy commercial time and pay for sponsored elements during a broadcast that still provide many sports games to be available on free, over-the-air television and radio. It should be noted that many prominent sports events are now moving to cable television networks because they have the dual revenue source of advertising income and monthly subscription fees. ESPN is the most expensive cable network. Cable providers pay more than an estimated $5.54 per month per subscriber to have ESPN as part of the package of channels that they offer to customers (Deitsch, 2013).

Finally, sports fans are often looking for more ways to connect with the properties, especially the teams that they love. Sponsors can play a role in enhancing that emotional connection. Beyond the opportunity for mere brand exposure, through sponsorship companies are creating an association between the brands and the property. It is this association with the property that can facilitate a more meaningful connection between the brand and its consumers.

Chapter Five

Sponsorship Selection: Brand Association

In addition to brand exposure opportunities based on audience demographic variables, selection of the sponsorship property very much involves creating and communicating a brand association between the sponsor and the property. Gordon Kane, founder of Victory of Sports Marketing, highlights that through sponsorship selection there is a relationship between brand building and property alignment. He explains that "sponsors are buying physical assets as well as emotional assets." Kane contends that because of this association characteristic, there is an opportunity to "change the way an organization is perceived through sponsorship" (personal communication, November 22, 2011).

Many authors indicate that developing and communicating a brand association between the sponsoring brand and the sponsored property is an objective that can be achieved through a sponsorship (Cornwell & Maignan, 1998; Dean, 2002; Gwinner, 1997; Gwinner & Eaton, 1999; Irwin, Lachowetz, Cornwell, & Clark, 2003; Meenaghan, 2001; Olson, 2010; Olson & Thjomoe, 2011; Pedersen et al., 2007; Shank, 2008; Till & Shimp, 1998; Walliser, 2003). Dean (2002) explains that "for the payment of a fee (or other value) to the sponsee, the sponsor receives the right to associate itself with the sponsee or event" (p. 78). He adds that "by associating itself with the sponsee, the sponsoring firm/brand shares in the image of the sponsee" (p. 78). Grohs and Reisinger (2005) point out that "the aim is to evoke positive feelings and attitudes toward the sponsor, by closely linking the sponsor to an event the recipient values highly" (p. 44). Stipp and Schiavone (1996) claim the sponsorship goals assume that the target audience for the sponsorship will transfer their loyalty from the sponsored property or event to the sponsor itself. Shaw and Amis (2001) conclude that sponsorships are an effective communication tool that can alter and enhance a company's image and reputation. Other researchers have found that sponsorship could be a source of differentiating a company from its competition, thereby making it a source of competitive advantage for a company (Amis, 2003; Amis, Slack, & Berrett, 1999; Cornwell, Roy, & Steinard, 2001; Fahy et al., 2004; Gwinner & Eaton, 1999; Irwin et al., 2003; Papadimitriou & Apostolopoulou, 2009; Stipp & Schiavone, 1996).

As noted previously, through a sponsorship agreement the sponsor has the ability to place its logo at agreed upon locations at the stadium or arena so that it receives the needed brand exposure. Being an official, exclusive sponsor provides the sponsor the right to use the league and team brand trademarks and logos as well. Sports leagues and teams have developed iconic logos (i.e., the NFL shield, the New York Yankees interlocking N-Y, the Dallas Cowboys star, or the University of Texas Longhorn). This use of logos on product packaging or in advertisements helps to clearly communicate the brand association between the sponsor and the property and helps achieve the desired brand transfer. For example, a Pepsi case, or even an individual can or bottle, can have the image of the New York Mets logo. Or, McDonald's can have the Olympic rings logo on its bags and use the Olympic logo in its television commercials that might also communicate to the viewer that McDonald's is a "Proud Partner" of the Olympic Games (Fortunato, 2008). The ideal outcome for the sponsor is that the popularity and the positive image of these sports leagues, teams, and events can precipitate a similar favorable feeling by fans and consumers toward its brand. New York Met fans might think favorably about Pepsi because that company supports their favorite team. This advantageous communication characteristic leads Finch, O'Reilly, Varella, and Wolf (2009) to state that the emotional connection of a sponsorship "is purported to deepen the relationship between a firm and its consumers in ways that asymmetrical 30-second spots simply cannot" (p. 62).

It is incumbent upon the sponsor to explicitly communicate its brand association with a property. Fortunato (2008) points out that some of the television commercials of Olympic sponsors during the broadcast of the Olympics games featured nothing more than communicating their association with the Olympics rather than speaking to any specific brand characteristics. For example, one Coca-Cola commercial during the winter Olympics from Torino, Italy, in 2006 featured people sitting on a couch as if it were a bobsled. Other Coca-Cola commercials invited viewers to "Drink Coke, live Olympic." For the Winter Olympics from Vancouver, Canada, in 2010 Coca-Cola ran a commercial celebrating its 80-year partnership with the Olympics. The commercial featured footage of generations of Olympic athletes receiving their medals. The commercial had a voice-over which stated, "If you've had a Coke in the last eighty years, you've had a hand in making every Olympic dream come true" (*Street & Smith's Sports Business Journal*, March 15–21, 2010).

In other Olympic examples, some McDonald's commercials during the Olympics broadcast have featured its Ronald McDonald character participating in events such as figure skating and ski jumping. Home Depot has used commercials that featured both United States Olympic and Paralympic athletes with an announcer voice-over talking about the characteristics of a superhero. It was stated in one television commercial that "the Home Depot is proud to employ more Olympic and Paralympic superheroes than any other company." One commercial featured Tony Benshoff, a Paralympic athlete, in one scene wearing his competitive uniform, then in the next scene wearing a Home Depot apron. Samsung has used in its Olympic commercials the image of a person running with the Olympic torch into a stadium with the people in attendance using their Samsung cellular phones to take a picture of the scene. The advertisement ended with the announced statement, "The Samsung salute to the Olympic games." Finally, Visa had Olympics commercials with the announced slogan, "Visa salutes America's Olympic athletes because no matter what it takes to live your dreams, life takes Visa" (Fortunato, 2008).

The rights to use league trademarks can be done in ways beyond broadcast commercials and product packaging. In September 2011, Marriott International signed a multiyear deal with the NFL using its Courtyard by Marriott brand as the official hotel sponsor of the NFL. For the 2012 Super Bowl the JW Marriott located in downtown Indianapolis would have the image of the Super Bowl trophy adorn the hotel. The image was seen in several aerial views of Indianapolis during Super Bowl week.

As noted in Chapter Two, this use of the sport in the sponsors' commercials serves to further promote the league, team, or event. So leagues are not only receiving an upfront fee from the sponsors for an association and usage rights to content and logos, the leagues are then receiving further promotion through the sponsors' advertisements (i.e., Bud Light as a sponsor of the NFL using NFL jerseys in its advertisements). Sponsors are often encouraged and assisted by the property to use the property logo in their promotional communication. Properties often present sponsors with specific ideas about how they could be using their logos or event imagery. NBC Sports even has its own agency that helps produce commercials for league sponsors that will better integrate the sponsor with the property.

Brand Congruence

In terms of property selection, enhanced brand association relies on the concept of brand fit, or brand congruence, between the sponsor and the property (Aaker, 1997; Becker-Olson, 2003; Keller, 2003; Prendergast, Poon, & West, 2010; Simmons & Becker-Olsen, 2006; Speed & Thompson, 2000; Woisetschlager et al., 2010). As individuals perceive a relevant connection between a sponsor and a property, they are more likely to perceive the sponsor in a positive manner, and their ability to identify and recall the correct sponsors of the property increases (Cornwell & Coote, 2005; Gwinner & Eaton, 1999; Gwinner & Swanson, 2003; Johar & Pham, 1999; Johar, Pham, & Wakefield, 2006; Madrigal, 2000; Pham & Johar, 2001; Roy & Cornwell, 2004; Speed & Thompson, 2000). Some researchers even contend that the sponsorship may be harmful to the company if there is not an adequate brand fit (Keller & Aaker, 1992; Speed & Thompson, 2000).

Although it is argued to be extremely important, the investment in evaluating fit between the brand and a property prior to sponsorship selection appears to be lacking. In the annual IEG and Performance Research survey in 2012, 45 percent of respondents reported that their company does not spend any money on preselection research to evaluate fit. Less than 1 percent of respondents claimed that their company spends more than 5 percent of the sponsorship's total budget to evaluate fit prior to property selection (IEG/Performance Research Survey, http://performanceresearch.com/sponsor-survey.htm).

Prendergast, Poon, and West (2010) explain that congruence occurs on two parameters: (1) self-congruence: congruence between the individual and the property, and (2) sponsor congruence: congruence between the sponsor and the property. In this characterization it is clear that the property is the connective element between the sponsor and the individual. Prendergast et al. (2010) contend that both forms of congruence can have a positive influence on consumers' relation to the brand. The ideal scenario for the sponsor might be when the property assists in articulating the congruence between the sponsor and the individual.

Individual (Self) Congruence

Sirgy, Lee, Johar, and Tidwell (2008) point out that individual, or self, congruence with a property has a positive influence on consumer brand loyalty. The characteristics of the sports audience and its passion toward the leagues and teams is a meaningful example of congruence between the individual and the property, thus creating another important reason for choosing to sponsor a sports property. Sloan (1989) contends the term *fan*, short for fanatic, is more descriptive for people who watch sports, rather than describing them as merely spectators or viewers. For fans, experiencing sports has been shown to provide emotional satisfaction (Gwinner & Swanson, 2003; Madrigal, 2000; Mullin et al., 2007; Shank, 2008; Tutko, 1989; Underwood, Bond, & Baer, 2001; Wann, Royalty, & Roberts, 2000; Zillmann, Bryant, & Sapolsky, 1989). Tutko (1989) speaks to the emotional characteristic of being a sports fan, claiming that

> there can be little doubt that the athletic area has become a center for taking care of our emotional needs. We participate in and are spectators of the emotional charge. If athletics did not provide excitement it would be gone in a short period. We look forward to indulging in the joys of victory but all too often steep in the agony of defeat. Without the occasional emotional charge, life would be a little bit duller — a little bit less alive and perhaps even have less meaning [p. 113].

Raney (2006) describes the emotional attachment that fans have toward sports is through a desire to be entertained by watching athletes perform in the sport at a level significantly higher than the average individual, bolstering self-esteem and pride through companionship and group affiliation, and the need for escape.

Because experiencing sports can satisfy emotional needs, the sports audience has been described as very loyal in its behavior (Madrigal, 2000; Mullin et al., 2007; Underwood et al., 2001; Wann et al., 2000). Funk and James (2001) indicate that the emotional and loyalty characteristics of the sports fan can result in consistent and enduring behaviors, including attendance, watching games on television, and behavior in other media forms such as print publication purchases, sports talk radio, and Internet or other digital media use to experience sports content. The hope for sponsors is that this audience characteristic of loyalty transfers to the behavior of purchasing the brand. Maxwell and Lough (2009), for example, did in fact find that the higher the fans' identification with the team, the more they correctly identified sponsors.

A major part of the experience and the congruence that is fostered between the individual and the sports property is through a group association. Parsimoniously stated, people want to have some form of group association. Cialdini, Borden, Thorne, Walker, Freeman, and Sloan (1976) presented the concept of basking-in-reflected-glory where fans behavior celebrated the success of their favorite team through referring to the team as "we" and wearing clothing that promoted their association with the team following a victory. Dalakas, Madrigal, and Anderson (2004) contend that sponsors should seek to further their brand association and capitalize on the fans propensity of basking-in-reflected-glory behavior. They suggest, for example, that sponsors can try to have their name on merchandise commemorating a team victory.

The concept of group association and its importance is best explained through social identity theory, which posits that people value group membership of a social category and that this association even helps them define themselves (Hickmank, Lawrence, 2010; Kahle, 1996; Mael & Ashforth, 2001; Stryker, 1980; Tajfel, 1982). Tajfel (1982) defines social identity as "the individual's knowledge that he (or she) belongs to certain social groups together with some emotional and value significance to him (or her) of the group membership" (p. 31).

Sherif (2001) provides an important variable to consider in this group association dynamic, pointing out that people tend to view positively groups with which they can identify. If the individual can identify with a sport, a team, and the players there will be more of a desire on his or her part to associate with that entity. Researchers consistently identify that the critical variable in reaching out to and building a relationship with the sports audience is personal experience (James, Kolbe, & Trail, 2002; Mullin et al., 2007). The sports experience at a young age largely comes through playing the game, attendance of games, and experiencing the sport through the mass media, particularly for sports watching games live on television (Bee & Kahle, 2006; Fortunato, 2001).

Sponsors and sports properties try to tap into this group membership desire and can develop strategies that enhance this emotional connection. The concept of relationship marketing is described as activities directed toward establishing, developing, and maintaining successful relationship exchanges (Arnold & Bianchi, 2001; Morgan & Hunt, 1994; Peterson, 1995). Sheth and Parvatiyar (2000) explain relationship marketing entails ongoing cooperative behavior between the marketer and the consumer. In speaking specifically in the context of sports, Bee and Kahle (2006) claim all sports marketing transactions involve some form of relationship marketing. They comment, "Teams, leagues, athletes, marketing corporations, and fans have relationships with one another that depend on successful relationship enactment" (p. 102) and that "relationship marketing is characterized by the attraction, development, and retention of customers" (p. 103). As these identities and group memberships are established, individuals seek opportunities for them to be reinforced (Arnett & Laverie, 2000; Jones, Suter, & Koch, 2006).

Sponsors can play a role in this reinforcement of a group dynamic. Jackson (2010) emphasizes the importance of sponsors understanding the characteristics of fans. He claims that often "sponsors failed to recognize the fact that sponsoring something is an honor, and something which should engender no small amount of pride" (p. 217). Jackson (2010) contends that the sponsorship platform is not owned by the property or the sponsor, but rather the fans, as it is their space the sponsor is essentially moving into. He explains, "Attendance at an event becomes an act of faith, and demonstrates a belief in something greater. This sense of faith is particularly important because it means that people do not require any additional enticements or encouragements to be a part of something. All they are looking for is empathy and understanding about how it feels to lose oneself in the moment and commit fully to the experience" (p. 217). Something as simple as a sponsored rally towel that fans wave at the game, for example, helps perpetuate the group association and starts to meld the congruence between the individual and the property along with the sponsor and the property. A theoretical progression can be established where relationship marketing helps produce and reinforce the social identity, which could help produce the participation behavior, including potentially the support of sponsors.

Sponsor Congruence

In defining congruence between the sponsor and the property, Prendergast et al. (2010) highlight that two components of congruence emerge: 1) image congruence, when the sponsor and the property have similar brand images, and 2) functional congruence, when the sponsor's product is aligned with the event or more explicitly and relevantly has a participatory role in the event. Prendergast et al. (2010) emphasize that image congruence and functional congruence are not mutually exclusive, and both types can be factored into selection decision making and communicated to the consumer through the sponsorship.

The ideal scenario is that the sponsor has both image and functional congruence with the property. That scenario, however, is simply not possible in every sponsorship selection situation. A sponsor's products do not always have a participatory role in the sponsored event. This obviously does not disqualify a sponsor from establishing brand congruence on only one variable. Indeed, more sponsorship foundations are based on only the image congruence component. While it is ideal for Chevrolet to sponsor NASCAR drivers who will use its cars and the brand is prominently on display in a race, the lack of functional congruence does not negate Chevrolet's desire to sponsor Major League Baseball on an image congruence basis, expressed through the slogan Chevrolet introduced in 1975, "Baseball, hot dogs, apple pie, and Chevrolet" (Chevrolet, *Street & Sports Business Journal*, November 28–December 4, 2011).

Sponsor Congruence: Image

Gwinner and Eaton (1999) emphasize brand congruence on the variable of image, defining image congruence as "the consistency between the event image and the brand image" (p. 53). They claim that brand image transfer will be stronger between brands and properties that have a relevant image-based connection. Keller (1993) brings the consumer into the evaluation of brand image congruence, defining brand image as the "perceptions about a brand as reflected by brand associations held in memory" (p. 3). Sponsorship selection projects an image of the companies' values with selection, even being thought of as a way to improve the companies' image (Cunningham, Cornwell, & Coote, 2009). Again, sports properties become desirable; as Kaynak, Salman, and Tatoglu (2007) state, "Organizations use sport as a medium of creating a distinctive image in the eyes of consumers and may in turn distinguish their brand from those of their competitors" (p. 336).

The Olympics certainly has an appeal on an image congruence component. Paul Deighton, chief executive of the London Organizing Committee for the Olympic Games, referred to the Olympics as "the ultimate feel-good association" (Bradshaw & Kortekaas, 2011, p. 12). Timo Lumme, IOC director of television and marketing, added, "You're buying an overall association to a brand that has a set of ideals" (Bradshaw & Kortekaas, 2011, p. 12). Catherine Ladousse, executive director of corporate marketing and communications for Lenovo, explained that Lenovo's sponsorship of the Olympics was a strong brand fit because the Olympic "values of sportsmanship, performance and international brotherhood are close to the corporate and brand values Lenovo has embraced both internally and externally" (Ladousse, 2009, p. 202).

Through selection corporations have the ability to only sponsor the properties that they believe share their brand image. For example, Disney would probably choose not to sponsor and create an association with the Ultimate Fighting Championship because it does not match Disney's image. Conversely, properties in their recruitment and selection of sponsors only have to choose companies who also share their brand image. NASCAR received criticism when it allowed the Texas Motor Speedway have its Sprint Cup race sponsored by the National Rifle Association only a few months after a shooting occurred at a grammar school in Newtown, Connecticut (Rosner, 2013). Most properties are consciously making decisions as to which companies they will allow to be their sponsors. The NCAA purposely does not sell an official sponsorship in the beer category. The IOC is selective about which types of product categories it is willing to offer sponsorships. The position of the IOC is "to control sponsorship programs to ensure that partnerships are compatible with the Olympic ideals. The IOC does not accept commercial associations with tobacco products, alcoholic beverages (other than beer and wine), or other products that may conflict with or be considered inappropriate to the mission of the IOC or to the spirit of Olympism" (Olympic Marketing Fact File, 2012, p. 36. http://www.olympic. org/Documents/IOC_Marketing/OLYMPIC-MARKETING-FACT-FILE-2012.pdf).

On some occasions, a property can be pressured into dropping a sponsor because there is concern about the sponsor's products and image. The Orange Bowl football game dropped Camacho Cigars as one of its sponsors after a letter was sent by Senators Dick Durbin, Frank Lautenberg, and Richard Blumenthal to Mark Emmert, president of the NCAA, and Jeffrey Roberts, president and chairman of the Orange Bowl. The letter stated, "Tobacco has no place in sports, and the promotion of cigars at the Orange Bowl sends the wrong message to young fans." (www.durbin.senate.gov, December 22, 2011). The letter continued, "This sponsorship uses a high-profile and prestigious sporting event to promote tobacco use and undermines the long fight to end sport and entertainment sponsorships that promote tobacco products, particularly to youth" (www.durbin.senate. gov, December 22, 2011).

In referring to the Family Smoking Prevention and Tobacco Control Act of 2009, which bans sponsorship of sporting and entertainment events by cigarette and smokeless tobacco brands, the letter concluded, "A tobacco company's sponsorship of the Orange Bowl undermines a premier collegiate sporting event and promotes tobacco use to young fans, putting them at risk of developing an addictive and dangerous habit. Furthermore, Camacho Cigars' sponsorship is at odds with the NCAA rules prohibiting tobacco use by student athletes and all game personnel in any form at practice and in competitions. We commend the NCAA for its internal policy forbidding tobacco use and urge the NCAA and Orange Bowl Committee to protect the health of their fans by reconsidering Camacho Cigars' sponsorship of the Discover Orange Bowl" (www.durbin.senate.gov, December 22, 2011). Under the three-year sponsorship agreement with the Orange Bowl that would have included a Bowl Championship Series national championship football game, Camacho Cigars would have had a significant presence at the Orange Bowl, including cigar lounges open to fans, a lounge at the largest pre-game event, and the Camacho Cigars' logo on the official Orange Bowl Web site.

Sponsor Congruence: Functional

The opportunity for functional congruence can clearly and meaningfully demonstrate a brand association. Olson and Thjomoe (2011) claim overall fit is enhanced by the participants of the event using the products of the sponsor. For some companies their sponsorship can feature athletes using their brand during competition. The advantage for these companies is that the viewers not only see these athletes sponsoring the product in commercials, they see that athlete wearing or using their product in a real-life situation, the actual game. When Nike sponsored Michael Jordan, the viewer not only saw Jordan in Nike commercials, but then when the game resumed Jordan was playing in his Nike sneakers. Multiple grand slam tennis tournament champion Serena Williams is not only sponsored by Wilson, it is a Wilson tennis racket that she uses in competition. These brands' products are actually helping these athletes perform their jobs at the highest level. For the brands that have this advantageous characteristic of functional congruence and their products being actually used during the game or event, consumers can have greater brand recall, can more easily make the brand association, and may eventually purchase the brand after seeing a star athlete use the product.

The battle between Coca-Cola and Pepsi for sponsorships includes the sports drink brands of each company, Powerade from Coca-Cola and Gatorade from Pepsi. The sports drink sponsorship is attractive because of the functional characteristics of the product appearing on the sidelines and being used during competition. Gatorade has been a sponsor of the NFL since 1983, making Gatorade the league's longest active sponsorship partner. When Gatorade renewed with the NFL in 2004, Tom Fox, former senior vice president for sports marketing for Gatorade, commented, "This is the most valuable real estate in sports. Our product was founded on the football field so this is critically important to our business" (Rovell, 2004). Gatorade, which is owned by PepsiCo, was part of Pepsi's ten-year renewal with the NFL that was agreed to in September of 2011 and commenced with the 2012 NFL season.

While Gatorade dominates in terms of market share, Coca-Cola has secured some prominent sponsorships for its Powerade brand, including the FIFA World Cup and all 88 NCAA Championship competitions. Through the deal with the NCAA which began in 2002 and is an eleven-year, $135 million contract (*Street & Smith's Sports Business Journal*, March 11–17, 2013), Powerade is deemed the "Official Sports Drink of the NCAA," and its products are available to players, coaches, and event employees. During these NCAA events Powerade will have a sideline branding presence through coolers, cups, and squeeze bottles (Coca-Cola press release, November 9, 2010).

There are numerous other examples that illustrate the concept of functional congruence between a sponsor and a property. The most prolific example might be automobile racing drivers using a particular brand of car. Chevrolet vehicles have won the Indianapolis 500 dating back to 1920, and its small-block V-8 powered engine, introduced in 1955, dominated the NASCAR circuit that year with multiple wins and seven of the top ten finishers in the Southern 500 driving the Chevrolet V-8 (Chevrolet, *Street & Sports Business Journal*, November 28–December 4, 2011). More recently, Chevrolet is the manufacturer for Earnhardt Ganassi Racing, Hendrick Motorsports, Richard Childress Racing, and Stewart-Hass Racing, four of NASCAR's most successful racing teams. Chevrolet cars are driven by five-time consecutive NASCAR champion, Jimmie Johnson. Finally, Chevrolet became the first brand to have its vehicles win the Indianapolis 500, the Daytona 500, and the Brickyard 400 in the same year (Chevrolet, *Street & Sports Business Journal*, November 28–December 4, 2011).

The largest sports relationship for the Scotts Miracle-Gro Company, which specializes in lawn care products, is with Major League Baseball. Certainly the green grass of the baseball field makes a relationship with a lawn care company a logical and functional brand fit. Tim Brosnan, executive vice president, business for Major League Baseball, stated, "The grass on the field of play is part of the very foundation of baseball, so this deal with Scotts, the worldwide leader in lawn care, is a natural fit for Major League Baseball. Now with the help of Scotts, our fans can challenge their local clubs for the title of who has the 'best lawn in the neighborhood'" (Scotts press release, January 20, 2010). John Price, senior brand manager of sports marketing and sponsorship for Scotts Miracle-Gro, commented, "This is a partnership between two great American brands. The overlap between baseball fans and home owners is immense. Now fans can use the same Scotts technology and seed varieties used on Major League Baseball fields to achieve premium results on their home lawns" (Scotts press release, January 20, 2010). One example used to clearly communicate the functional brand fit between the Scotts brand and a baseball field is at the Ballpark at Arlington, home of the Texas Rangers, where one of the signs on the right field wall states, "Scotts Used Here."

Tiffany has the function of providing the winning trophy for many sports events, including the Super Bowl, the World Series, and the Rose Bowl. As a sponsor of the Rose Bowl, Tiffany has brand exposure at the game, the Tournament of Roses Parade, tickets and hospitality, and has access to the Rose Bowl President's Ball. Tiffany does have a store located in Pasadena, California, site of the game. In making the Rose Bowl trophy Tiffany has a functional congruence to the game. Again, these sponsorships where a functional congruence is apparent can be simultaneously tapping into a brand image association. Tiffany believes there is strong brand image congruence between its brand and the Rose Bowl. Tom O'Rourke, Tiffany vice president of business sales, commented, "We're both symbolic of great American tradition, and we want to be a part of every important celebration" (Lefton, 2010b, p. 11).

Ritchie (2011) explains that there are many business-to-business opportunities available through a sponsorship because of recognizable functional congruence characteristics. She cites examples of technology companies having their products provide all of the communication data and infrastructure support during major sports events, such as IBM products used at Wimbledon or Avaya products being used during the Olympics. Ritchie (2011) points out that beyond reaching the individual consumer, this demonstration of the brand serving the technology needs of a major sporting event indicates to other businesses that the technology company would be able to handle their organization's communication data and infrastructure needs as well.

The IOC explains how its sponsors from a functional congruence perspective assist in the production of the Olympic Games, describing, "Sponsors provide support for the staging of the Olympic Games and the operations of the Olympic Movement in the form of products, services, technology, expertise, and staff deployment," and "Sponsors provide essential products and services for broadcasters, journalists, photographers, and other media" (Olympic Marketing Fact File, 2012, p. 10. http://www.olympic.org/Documents/IOC_Marketing/OLYMPIC-MARKETING-FACT-FILE-2012.pdf). In Olympic examples of functional congruence, as part of its sponsorship Lenovo provided more than 30,000 pieces of equipment for the 2008 Summer Olympics in Beijing, including the technological infrastructure for all 302 medal ceremonies (Ladousse, 2009). In regard to its Olympic sponsorship, Patrick Adiba, head of major events for Atos Origin, claimed the Olympics allow others to see the capabilities of Atos Origin. He stated, "We (Atos Origin) showcase to our clients what we do to prepare for the games, how we manage the technology and information systems" (Bradshaw & Kortekaas, 2011, p. 12).

These examples document when the sponsors' products and services are instrumental in the functional support of an event. In other instances when this is not possible, properties might be contractually required to use sponsors' products or services (i.e., the sponsor's hotels or shipping service). Even if not contractually obligated, the league will make every effort to support its sponsor and not alienate a partner. This aspect of the sponsorship does allow the sponsor to recoup some of its initial sponsorship fee.

The opportunity for explicit functional congruence that is visible for all fans to witness is not available for all types of products. Cornwell, Humphreys, Maguire, Weeks, and Tellegen (2006) suggest that if brand congruence is not overtly apparent, it needs to be explained to consumers in an attempt to increase recall accuracy. Even if the business-to-business functional congruence is apparent and recognizable, companies can still take advantage of opportunities to more explicitly communicate how their brand helps support an event.

In October 2011, United Parcel Service (UPS) signed a multiyear agreement with NASCAR to be its official logistics partner. UPS has been a sponsor of NASCAR since 2000 when it signed on as its official express delivery company. Through this sponsorship, UPS offers trackside service, which "provides members of the NASCAR family exclusive access to UPS shipping services during race week. For those with garage access, the UPS Trackside Services Center will be able to handle all shipments to and from the track" (www.racing.ups.com/trackside/services/). Ron Rogowski, UPS vice president of sponsorship and events for UPS, commented, "UPS has enjoyed a great relationship with NASCAR and our official status allows us to continue providing logistics solutions for other great NASCAR partners both at and away from the racetrack" (UPS press release, October 27, 2011). Jim O'Connell, chief sales officer for NASCAR, added, "NASCAR works for business because our fans are among the most brand loyal in all sports. UPS is a world-class company and one that we are proud to call our partner" (UPS press release, October 27, 2011).

For a company with a business-to-business focus, such as UPS, there is the opportunity through sponsorship to generate direct revenue as well as to tell the story of the UPS brand by demonstrating its ability to provide answers to complex business problems. In one example, in 2011 the Pacific 12 Conference held its inaugural conference championship football game at the university that earned the home field advantage by having the best record in the conference. This location was not determined until six days prior to the game, when Oregon defeated Oregon State, making it the host school. UPS would provide all logistical support in helping play the game.

Communication technology has facilitated the ability of a company to tell the story of the brand itself through the distribution vehicle of the Internet. UPS produced three one-minute vignettes that detailed how it provided logistical support for the Pac-12 conference football championship game. All three vignettes began the same way; with a football being placed on a conveyer belt along with boxed packages. This video was followed by a still shot of the UPS logo with the vignette title "Logistics of the Game, delivered by UPS." At the bottom of the screen was the wording "Official logistics partner of the Pac-12."

Two of the vignettes featured Jim Steeg, director of the Pac-12 football championship game, explaining the logistical support that UPS provided, such as transportation of the team equipment, broadcast equipment, merchandise, and tickets. One vignette concluded with Steeg stating, "Logistics is the game and we play to win. I love logistics." The third vignette featured Archie Held, the artist who designed the Pac-12 football championship trophy. Held described how UPS was instrumental in assisting his production of the trophy. In the vignette, Held explained, "All materials had to be there when I needed them, and that's logistics." Held added that "from the very first sketch to the finished product this is a story of passion and logistics." The vignette ended with Held detailing that the Pac-12 championship trophy was shipped using carbon neutral shipping from UPS.

UPS also ran a commercial during the television broadcast of the Pac-12 football championship game on Fox explaining its logistical support of the event. UPS received one other unexpected promotion — after winning the Pac-12 championship game, Chip Kelly, then Oregon head coach, when being interviewed on the field would state, "We're just so excited that we get to represent this university in the Rose Bowl. And we're going to drink some Dr Pepper and mail our Christmas presents with UPS."

Geographic Congruence

Congruence does not have to be only on parameters of image or functionality. Another prominent type of congruence often conveyed is a geographic association. Woisetschlager, et al. (2010) emphasize the regional brand association as a representation of congruence between a sponsor and a property. They state, "A sponsor should raise the awareness of the benefits that the sponsee receives from their partnership and emphasize that it is regionally embedded" (p. 176).

In 2011, the NHL reached a seven-year agreement with Molson Coors in Canada and MillerCoors in the United States to make the Molson Canadian brand the official sponsor of the NHL. Dave Perkins, president and CEO of Molson Coors Canada, stated, "Molson Canadian is synonymous with the game of hockey and was the brand that helped build the tradition of 'Hockey Night' across Canada. Partnering with the NHL reinforces Molson Canadian's 'Made from Canada' brand position, and also reflects our company's desire to help Canadians connect over shared passions and great beer" (MillerCoors press release, February 22, 2011). The Coors Light brand will also be promoted through the sponsorship with the NHL. Andy England, executive vice president, chief marketing officer of MillerCoors, commented, "Coors Light, the brand that's all about 'cold refreshment,' will use the NHL partnership to strengthen its presence in NHL markets, especially in regions such as the Northeast and Great Lakes" (MillerCoors press release, February 22, 2011).

Hollis (2008) highlights that a stadium or arena naming rights agreement can demonstrate a connection to the geographical community. In acquiring naming rights, the sponsor receives brand exposure and a brand association with what might be one of the most recognizable buildings in that city. For example, among the prominent attractions in Chicago are the Willis Tower (formerly known as the Sears Tower) and Wrigley Field.

There are many instances where the naming rights sponsor of a stadium or arena is a major employer within that city. Woisetschlager et al. (2010) contend sponsors that employ many people should make that fact known. Federal Express has its headquarters in Memphis and has the naming rights to the city's arena, the FedEx Forum. The Bridgestone tire company, headquartered in Nashville, has the naming rights to that city's arena. In commenting on Prudential acquiring the naming rights to the arena in Newark in a $105.3 million deal over 30 years, Bob DeFillippo, Prudential spokesman, explained, "We're very happy with the naming rights deal we have. A lot of it goes back to Prudential being here in Newark and our 135-year history here" (Jones, 2011).

In other examples, the Sherwin-Williams Paint Company, based in Cleveland, has sponsorships with the Browns, Cavaliers and Indians. In addition to its sponsorships of the Breeders' Cup and PGA Tour aimed at an affluent target audience, Sentient Jet, a Boston-based company, is the official private jet partner of the Boston Celtics. As part of this sponsorship, Sentient Jet supports the Boston Celtics Shamrock Foundation in its charity work and sponsors the concierge desk within the Boston Celtics Courtside Club of the TD Garden (named for TD Bank), where guests have the opportunity to book a flight while attending a Celtics game. Marty Guinoo, Sentient Jet CEO, stated, "We always appreciate the opportunity to be a part of a winning team and as a Boston-based company, without question this partnership has special meaning because it allows us to support the local community and fans" (Sentient Jet press release, October 25, 2010).

Golf tournament title sponsorships often have a geographic congruence. Federal Express, with its headquarters in Memphis, is title sponsor of the PGA Tour event originating from that city, the FedEx St. Jude Classic. Coca-Cola has title sponsorship of the PGA Tour event in Atlanta. Bowl games also often have a title sponsor from the geographic region. For example, the Little Caesars Pizza Bowl takes place in Detroit, hometown of Little Caesars corporate headquarters, and the AutoZone Liberty Bowl takes place in Memphis, the city where AutoZone is headquartered.

Multiple-Sponsor Congruence

In terms of selection based on brand congruence, researchers point out that there are multiple, or concurrent sponsors, for the same event. They claim that in addition to evaluating their own brand congruence with a property, sponsors consider which other companies are sponsoring the same event and how their own brand fits with these other companies in their selection decisions (Carrillat, Harris, & Lafferty, 2010; Carrillat, et al., 2005). Ruth and Simonin (2003, 2006) point out that sponsoring brands are presented together simultaneously at the same event. They argue that some companies will not sponsor at a location or with a property if another controversial company is on the sponsorship roster.

Keller (2003) explains that this evaluation of what is being referred to here as multiple-sponsor congruence allows for a brand to not only create an image association with the event, but the other sponsors as well. Carrillat, Harris, and Lafferty (2010) claim that sponsorships can have concurrent sponsorship side effects where "brands are affected not only by the perceived image of the sponsored event, but also by the perceived images of other brands concurrently sponsoring the event" (p. 109). In a positive aspect of concurrent sponsorship they conclude that because these sponsors can share images, there are opportunities for sponsors that do not compete in the same category to cooperate with each other.

The roster of sponsors for a property may offer an opportunity for business collaboration. Such is the case with Samsung and Visa through their sponsorship of the Olympics. Starting with the 2012 London Olympics customers are able to make payments through Visa using a Samsung mobile handset. All customers have to do for a faster and more convenient transaction is use the Visa mobile contactless application, select pay and hold the phone in front of a contactless reader at the point of purchase. Peter Ayliffe, CEO of Visa Europe, explained, "Visa, like Samsung, shares the vision of leveraging our Olympic and Paralympic Games sponsorship to leave a lasting legacy in the market for banks, retailers, mobile operators, and consumers. We are not only breaking new ground for Olympic partnerships, we are committed to enabling consumers to connect with mobile and contactless payments technology for 2012 and beyond" (Visa press release, March 31, 2011). Gyehyun Kwon, vice president and head of worldwide sports marketing for Samsung Electronics, stated, "This marks the very first partnership between two worldwide Olympic partners of the London 2012 Olympic Games. We are delighted to be joining forces with Visa to make the Olympic Games more accessible and convenient for everyone. This fits extremely well with our ambition to enable more people to participate in the Games through our smart technology" (Visa press release, March 31, 2011).

Carrillat, Lafferty, and Harris (2005) contend that the evaluation of other sponsors at that location can be a very viable strategy for lesser known brands, with these lesser known brands potentially benefiting from sponsoring a property that has more familiar brands as the other sponsors. To some extent, the lesser known brand is elevated to a level of equality with the more familiar brands through the sponsorship. Carrillat et al. (2005) state lesser known brands may "decide about their sponsorship agreement based not only on the association with the event, but also on the association with the other sponsoring brands" (p. 61).

Consumer Behavior

Brand awareness, brand recall, and brand congruence are obviously important business objectives, but merely steps in the process for the sponsoring company that eventually needs achievement of the ultimate goal of the promotional communication campaign, the consumer behavior of purchasing its products — a point noted in Chapter One. Cornwell and Maignan (1998) describe the objectives of sponsorship to include development of goodwill, image, awareness, and *increased sales* (emphasis added here). Jackie Woodward, vice president of media and marketing strategies for MillerCoors, in the context of being recruited for sponsorship deals, commented, "What you'd like to hear is someone at the other end of the line saying, 'I have a solution that will help you sell more beer.' That just doesn't happen often enough" (Lefton, 2011a, p. 19).

Achieving sales through sponsorship is an attainable goal. Several researchers have indicated that developing a brand association transfer through sponsorship strategies could result in an increase in purchasing the products of the sponsoring brand (Cornwell & Maignan, 1998; Cornwell et al., 2001; Dean, 2002; Harvey, 2001; Madrigal, 2000; Meenaghan, 2001; Miyazaki & Morgan, 2001). In examining college football fans, Madrigal (2000) found that fan behavior did extend from support of a team to support of companies that sponsor and are associated with that team. He states, "Loyalty toward a preferred team may have beneficial consequences for corporate sponsors. Consistent with the idea of in-group favoritism, higher levels of team identification among attendees of a sporting event appear to be positively related to intentions to purchase a sponsor's products" (p. 21). Harvey (2001) adds, "Sponsorship changes the consumer's perception of a specific sponsor — which can rub off positively on brands that sponsor in terms of willingness to purchase those brands" (p. 64).

The success of NASCAR sponsorships in terms of sales has been well documented. Lapio and Speter (2000) found that NASCAR fans are three times more likely to purchase sponsor brands. Amato, Peters, and Shao (2005) also found that NASCAR fans consciously decide to purchase the products of its sponsors. More recently, the results of a survey by Degaris, West, and Dodds (2009) showed that nearly two-thirds of fans responded that they bought products from companies because they were NASCAR sponsors. Fans that were identified as more passionate about NASCAR showed an even higher rate of purchasing sponsors' products.

Purchase Congruence

While Prendergast et al. (2010) offered that sponsorship congruence with a property can be based on image congruence or functional congruence, an important third type of congruence needs to be included in selection determinations, what is being referred to as "purchase congruence." The idea of "purchase congruence" being introduced here is when sponsors have the ability for their products to be bought at the sponsored location. For some industries, most notably soft drink companies, the characteristic of exclusivity provides them not only with brand exposure and a brand association, but the additional advantage of stadium point-of-purchase of their brands to an audience without competition.

Through an exclusive sponsorship agreement with a team, a trip to the stadium will provide the consumer with only one brand option, depending on who is the team's sponsor. With some stadiums attracting millions of customers each year, these exclusive sponsorships are an extremely valuable commodity because of the opportunity to sell product (Fortunato & Richards, 2007). In 2011, more than 6 million people attended Major League Baseball games in New York. With both the Yankees and the Mets sponsored by Pepsi, the result is more than 6 million people only having the ability to purchase Pepsi products during their approximately three-hour stay at the ballpark. On an emotional level, these pouring rights also provide the soft drink company a chance to be a part of an amazing experience, a day at the ballpark.

Sensing a purchase congruence opportunity, many leagues have reached an agreement with a telecommunications company to provide exclusive content to its customers. It should be noted that Major League Baseball has chosen to create its own mobile service application rather than offer exclusive content for any singular wireless provider (Futterman & Ante, 2013). Major League Baseball does have an official wireless telecommunications sponsor, T-Mobile, which includes the brand being integrated into the game through the use of wireless dugout and bullpen phones. The contract is for three-years with T-Mobile paying approximately $125 million (Fisher & Lefton, 2013).

The NFL is sponsored by Verizon. Through this sponsorship agreement the available programming through select mobile phones that Verizon customers receive includes live streaming of Sunday, Thursday, and Monday night football games, the NFL Network, and the NFL Red Zone Channel, which airs live look-ins of every key play and touchdown from Sunday afternoon games. Other features of NFL Mobile on Verizon Wireless include live streaming of the NFL Draft, live audio broadcasts of every regular season and playoff game, game highlights, an extensive collection of on-demand video featuring analysis, and inside access from NFL Network and NFL Films. NFL Mobile from Verizon also allows for personalization and customization of content, including team or player alerts, ringtones, graphics, and fantasy information and statistics (NFL press release, March 22, 2010). Upon reaching the sponsorship deal, John Stratton, executive vice president and chief marketing officer for Verizon Wireless, stated, "This is an agreement that has, at its core, a mutual desire by both the NFL and Verizon Wireless to provide consumers with what they want on and off the field." Brian Rolapp, NFL senior vice president of media strategy, commented, "Our fans have an insatiable appetite for football, and we will be able to keep them connected wherever they are on game day, but also throughout the year" (NFL press release, March 22, 2010). In 2012, for the first time NFL playoff games and the Super Bowl were available on handheld devices.

Verizon renewed its sponsorship with the NFL in 2013, paying the league $1 billion over four years, a forty-percent increase, in a deal scheduled to begin in 2014. In the latest agreement Verizon will expand its NFL offerings with all home-market games played on Sunday also being available to customers on their mobile phones. Brian Angiolet, Verizon vice president of marketing and communications, explained, "We look for these deals to drive switching, loyalty, and subscription fees" (Futterman & Ante, 2013).

Similarly in the wireless content provider category, in 2012 Verizon reached a three-year extension with the NHL. In the agreement the NHL created a system where Verizon customers received exclusive content, including a live feed of the weekly game on NBC with bonus camera angles and on-demand plays of the week. So as not to eliminate other mobile customers, the NHL GameCenter that provides scores, standings, and photo galleries is available to everyone (Fisher, 2012). Sprint has a contract with the NBA valued at more than $55 million per year where unlimited data customers can watch 97 live NBA games for no additional charge on mobile devices (Futterman & Ante, 2013). Also, the Sprint NBA Mobile application offers fans live NBA games on Sprint TV's ESPN channel, live home and away radio broadcasts of games, in-game video highlights, and real-time scores, statistics, and alerts. As an official sponsor of the Masters Golf Tournament, AT&T provides exclusive content offerings to its customers, such as coverage of the action taking place live at Amen Corner, the famed 11th, 12th, and 13th holes of Augusta National. Dan York, AT&T Entertainment Services head of content and programming, commented, "Consumers today crave connectivity. They want to be able to access great content no matter where they are. Through our agreement with the Masters, we're able to deliver even more iconic footage to more people in more places than ever before" (AT&T Press Release, April 2, 2008).

Uniform/Apparel Sponsorship

As property selection is designed to satisfy multiple brand exposure and audience variables, some sponsorships satisfy multiple brand congruence variables. One notable example is a uniform sponsorship. Glenn (2011) contends that league or team uniform sponsorship is more closely aligned with fan exposure during the game than stadium or arena naming rights. He argues, "Although the stadium sponsor may appear on the field of play, brands on jerseys are the focus of fans throughout the event, whether viewed live or televised. Given the active focus of fans on the players — and the jersey — one might expect more effective brand recall and association from the jersey sponsor" (p. 22). There are two types of uniform sponsorships: 1) the manufacturer of the uniform which brings congruence on function, image, and purchase dimensions, or 2) a sponsor having its name or logo placed on the uniform.

Competition in the apparel, uniform, and shoe industry has been altered throughout the past couple of decades and now remains dominated by a few brands: Nike, Adidas/Reebok, and the continued emergence of Under Armour. Nike bolstered its portfolio in 2003 when it purchased Converse for approximately $305 million. Previously Converse was the dominant company in the basketball sneaker market with its Chuck Taylor All-Star sneakers and sponsorship endorsement contracts with Larry Bird, Julius Erving, and Magic Johnson (McCarthy, 2003). In 2007, Nike continued with its strategy by purchasing British based Umbro, giving Nike a pronounced presence in soccer and the English Premier League (Chiesa, 2007). In 2005, to combat Nike, Reebok and Adidas merged.

For the companies with the capability to manufacture the uniforms, becoming the official sponsor in that product category for a league is a major desire because they will not only receive brand exposure but their branded product will be used in the actual game, and these uniforms are widely purchased by fans. Uniform manufacturer sponsorships are sold on a league-wide basis for the NBA, NFL, NHL, and Major League Baseball with only one manufacturing company supplying all of the league's team uniforms.

Nike, which had been a supplier for the NFL in the mid–1990's, replaced Reebok as the uniform supplier for the NFL starting in April, 2012. The five-year contract with the NFL is reported to be valued at a total of $175 million (Kaplan, 2011a). Through the agreement Nike becomes responsible to produce all on-field apparel, including game uniforms and sideline personnel apparel (Diaz, 2010). Charlie Denson, Nike brand president, stated, "With this relationship, Nike's position in our largest market in the world will be stronger than ever. We believe the agreement with the NFL enhances the Nike brand,

and provides a significant opportunity to drive growth across the business" (Belson, 2010a, p. B14).

The NFL reached agreements with different companies that specialize in other aspects of the apparel business. Hat manufacturer New Era obtained the rights to sideline caps. New Era is the on-field rights holder for Major League Baseball caps. Outerstuff will make youth-sized clothing, '47 Brand will manufacture hats for fans, Gill will make outerwear and lifestyle apparel, VF obtained the license to produce T-shirts and fleece apparel, and Under Armour will provide gear and sponsor the NFL Scouting Combine, an annual gathering in Indianapolis where future NFL draft picks showcase their talents in front of scouts from every team (Belson, 2010a; Pyle, 2010). Income from apparel and headwear represents nearly half of the NFL's income from licensed products (Belson, 2010a). Eric Grubman, NFL executive vice president of NFL ventures and business operations, explained, "The new framework will provide fans with a wider breadth of merchandise from global category leaders in the sports licensed apparel industry" (Diaz, 2010, p. B7).

One of the byproducts of changing uniform manufacturers is the availability of the product during the time of the transition. With Reebok ending its sponsorship of the NFL after the 2012 Super Bowl, supplies became limited for Giants fans who wanted to purchase jerseys before the Super Bowl. Fans would have a difficult time finding jerseys for Giants players Victor Cruz and Jason Pierre-Paul, who emerged as stars during the season. Tyler Reed, district manager for Sports Authority, explained that Reebok orders "blanks from overseas and they put the screen print on them with the names and numbers. Once their blanks were done, they're not going to go and buy more" (Caroom, 2012, p. 1).

The complications during the transition from one sponsorship rights holder to another were further demonstrated in the uniform/apparel product category during the NFL off-season when the very popular Tim Tebow was traded from the Denver Broncos to the New York Jets. With the trade occurring in March 2012 and Nike scheduled to become the uniform supplier for the NFL on April 1, Reebok saw this as one final opportunity to capitalize on its partnership with the NFL. Immediately after the trade Reebok manufactured Jets jerseys and T-shirts with Tebow's name and number. Even the NFL's official merchandise Web site, nflshop.com, was selling Tebow Jets jerseys produced by Reebok (Gearty, 2012).

Nike countered with a lawsuit against Reebok, arguing that Reebok was illegally trying to meet the "vociferous demand for Tebow Jets products" and that "the opportunity to see the first Tebow-identified Jets apparel is a unique and short-lived opportunity" (Golding, 2012). Nike further claimed that "it is unlikely that a consumer who purchases an unauthorized Tebow-identified NFL jersey or t-shirt from Reebok will purchase an authorized Tebow jersey or t-shirt from Nike the following week" (Golding, 2012). The suit sought to block further sales of Reebok's Tebow merchandise and compensate Nike unspecified damages (Gearty, 2012).

In late March, United States District Judge Kevin Castel temporarily blocked Reebok from selling Tebow Jets jerseys. In arguing to lift the ban, Reebok attorney Julian Friedman claimed that in its contract with the NFL Reebok is permitted to sell leftover apparel for two months after its contract expired and, therefore, should be permitted to sell the Tebow Jets jerseys until the end of May. Castel, however, countered that the termination window for merchandise sales "is not your termination bonus; it's so you don't get stuck with unsold merchandise" (Neumeister, 2012). Reebok would eventually be ordered to buy back all of the jerseys it manufactured with Tebow's name. Reebok would not pay Nike any damages (Belson, 2012).

The placement of a sponsor's logo or a brand name on a uniform is a function of what the league permits its teams to sell. Major League Soccer has allowed its teams to sell uniform sponsorships since 2007, with most teams earning approximately between $2 and $4 million per year. The Los Angeles Galaxy signed the longest and most lucrative jersey deal in the MLS in March 2012, reaching a ten-year, $44 million agreement with Herbalife (*Street & Smith's Sports Business Journal*, December 17–23, 2012, p. 20). Uniform sponsorship in soccer is not unique, with European leagues having the sponsor being the predominant visual on the uniform and the team identified through a logo relegated to a smaller location on the uniform chest. In the English Premier League, Liverpool earns $31.5 million annually to have Standard Chartered as its uniform sponsor, Manchester United earns $31.5 million annually to have Aon Corporation as its uniform sponsor, and Manchester City earns $31.5 million annually to have Etihad Airways as its uniform sponsor. The 20 teams of the English Premier League in 2012 combined to earn more than $193 million in uniform sponsorships (*Street & Smith's Sports Business Journal*, July 30–August 5, 2012, p. 18).

In 2011, the WNBA partnered with Boost Mobile, a prepaid wireless service provider owned by Sprint, allowing Boost Mobile to put its logo on most of the teams' uniforms. In a four-year contract, the Boost Mobile logo will appear on 11 of the league's 12 teams' uniforms with a patch that is located on the front of the uniforms below the numbers. The San Antonio Silver Stars, which have a sponsorship deal with AT&T, do not have to comply with the agreement so as to not conflict with the team's sponsorship deal with a wireless provider that was already in place. The Boost Mobile agreement with the WNBA does not preclude teams from securing other uniform sponsorships on a local basis. Several teams have sponsors that are the predominant visual on the uniform with the brand name appearing above the numbers on the front of the uniforms. For example, the Los Angeles Sparks have Farmers Insurance as their uniform sponsor and the New York Liberty have Foxwoods Hotel and Casino in Connecticut as their uniform sponsor.

For Boost Mobile, the uniform brand exposure is one aspect of its sponsorship agreement with the WNBA. Boost Mobile is the title sponsor of the WNBA All-Star Game, presenting sponsor of the 2011 WNBA playoffs and finals, presenting sponsor of the WNBA opening season, presenting sponsor of the WNBA's Top 15 Moments program, a partner in the WNBA Draft, and has courtside exposure including pole pads and floor signage. Steve Gaffney, Sprint vice president of corporate marketing, commented, "When we looked at all the assets of the deal, from the jersey visibility to the overall stature of the Boost Mobile brand, it is great alignment" (Lombardo, 2011b, p. 33).

In 2013, the ATP provided greater economic opportunity for its players by allowing them to wear more corporate logos, increasing the size of these branded logos, and allowing players to wear logos of gambling establishments, if those companies do not accept wagers on tennis. Prior to 2013, tennis players could only wear the logo for their apparel or racket company on their headwear, which must be on the side of the cap. The new available location on the back of the shirt by the collar, however, must be occupied by an ATP sponsor. The shirt sleeve logos will increase from four to six inches, with the front of the shirt logo limited to four inches. These guidelines apply to the 61 ATP tournaments and do not apply to the major tournaments (Kaplan, 2013).

Players are interviewed before and after practice, and footage and pictures from practice are often used in media reports, providing another sponsorship opportunity for brand exposure through uniform placement. Sports leagues allow teams to sell sponsorships for their practice uniforms. In 2009, the New Jersey Nets became the first team in the NBA to sell a practice uniform sponsorship, signing with PNY Technologies, a flash drive manufacturer headquartered in New Jersey (Lombardo, 2009). In addition to its $31.5 million contract with Aon for its game uniform, Manchester United became the first English Premier League team to sign a deal for its practice uniform. DHL pays Manchester United $16.5 million per season for its logo to appear on the team's practice uniform.

University Uniform and Equipment Sponsorship

With there only being a few major sports leagues in which a company can secure uniform manufacturing rights, being the official uniform and equipment sponsor for a university is a major desire. The strategy of sponsoring many prominent sports universities' equipment and uniforms seems to be logical for many reasons. Uniform manufacturers that serve as official sponsors receive considerable brand exposure with many universities' football and basketball teams' games often on television, with the logo that appears on the team uniforms and equipment being seen during the game when people are less apt to change channels. These companies can capitalize on the fact that there is a strong brand image association created with the university, a functional congruence element that these companies' products are being used in an actual game, and that collegiate team uniforms are a major seller, creating an opportunity for purchase congruence. These characteristics make university sponsorship a very competitive product category for brands such as Nike, Under Armour, and Adidas (see Table Six).

Table Six: University Uniform Football Sponsors, 2012

ACC		Big Ten	
University	*Sponsor*	*University*	*Sponsor*
Boston College	Under Armour	Illinois	Nike
Clemson	Nike	Indiana	Adidas
Duke	Nike	Iowa	Nike
Florida St.	Nike	Michigan	Adidas
Georgia Tech	Russell	Michigan St.	Nike
Maryland	Under Armour	Minnesota	Nike
Miami	Nike	Nebraska	Adidas
North Carolina	Nike	Northwestern	Under Armour
North Carolina St.	Adidas	Ohio St.	Nike
Virginia	Nike	Penn St.	Nike
Virginia Tech	Nike	Purdue	Nike
Wake Forest	Nike	Wisconsin	Adidas

Big 12		Big East	
University	*Sponsor*	*University*	*Sponsor*
Baylor	Nike	Cincinnati	Adidas
Iowa St.	Nike	Connecticut	Nike

Kansas	Adidas	Louisville	Adidas
Kansas St.	Nike	Pittsburgh	Nike
Oklahoma	Nike	Rutgers	Nike
Oklahoma St.	Nike	South Florida	Under Armour
Texas	Nike	Syracuse	Nike
Texas Christian	Nike	Temple	Under Armour
Texas Tech	Under Armour		
West Virginia	Nike		

Pac 12		*SEC*	
University	*Sponsor*	*University*	*Sponsor*
Arizona	Nike	Alabama	Nike
Arizona St.	Nike	Arkansas	Nike
California	Nike	Auburn	Under Armour
Colorado	Nike	Florida	Nike
Oregon	Nike	Georgia	Nike
Oregon St.	Nike	Kentucky	Nike
Stanford	Nike	LSU	Nike
UCLA	Adidas	Mississippi	Nike
USC	Nike	Mississippi St.	Adidas
Utah	Under Armour	Missouri	Nike
Washington	Nike	South Carolina	Under Armour
Washington St.	Nike	Tennessee	Adidas
		Texas A&M	Adidas
		Vanderbilt	Nike

Other prominent sports universities sponsored by Nike are: Boise State, Butler, and Brigham Young. Nike also sponsors the sports teams for Army, Navy, and the Air Force. Notre Dame is sponsored by Adidas. While some universities have one supplier for all of their teams, it is important to note that some universities have different uniform and equipment sponsors for each of their sports teams. For example, for the 2012–2013 collegiate sports season, Baylor University had Nike as the sponsor for its football, women's basketball, and track & field teams, but Adidas was the sponsor for the Baylor men's basketball team, and Under Armour sponsored the Baylor baseball team.

Sponsorship of universities has been a major part of the Under Armour strategy in trying to grow the brand in a very competitive marketplace against the more established Nike and Adidas/Reebok. The sponsorship of universities became an entry point for the younger company to obtain brand exposure and have consumers see its brand being used in competition.

Under Armour was started in 1996 by Kevin Plank, a former University of Maryland football player. Plank was "tired of repeatedly changing the cotton t-shirt under his jersey as it became wet and heavy during the course of a game" (http://investor.underarmour. com/company/managementTeam.cfm). Plank's idea was to develop a T-shirt that helped regulate an athlete's body temperature and enhance performance by having perspiration be eliminated rather than absorbed. The apparel is designed specifically for cold or warm weather. Under Armour's aim "is to provide the world with technically advanced products engineered with our superior fabric construction, exclusive moisture management, and proven innovation. Every Under Armour product is doing something for you; it's making you better" (http://investor.underarmour.com/company/about.cfm).

Under Armour first used sponsorship as one of its promotional communicational methods to obtain brand exposure in movies and television programs. In 1999, Under Armour was prominently displayed on the football uniforms in Oliver Stone's *Any Given Sunday*, a movie that featured a star-studded cast of Al Pacino, Jamie Foxx, Cameron Diaz, Charlton Heston, James Woods, and Dennis Quaid along with NFL Hall of Famers Jim Brown and Lawrence Taylor. Under Armour was featured in other football-themed movies, *The Replacements* and *Gridiron Gang*, and was displayed on the uniforms of the Dillon Panthers and the East Dillon Lions, the fictional high school football teams that were the focus of the television series *Friday Night Lights* (Walker, 2008). In one episode of *Friday Night Lights*, head football coach Eric Taylor, played by Emmy Award–winning actor Kyle Chandler, meets with a representative from Under Armour about getting new uniforms for the team in which the Under Armour representative thanks the coach for being a great friend to Under Armour.

One of the major university sponsorships for the Baltimore-based Under Armour is with Plank's alma mater, the University of Maryland, where the football team has worn Under Armour uniforms since 2004. In 2009, Under Armour began a five-year, $17.5 million contract with the University of Maryland to provide uniforms for all of its varsity teams (Tanier, 2011). The contract has Under Armour providing the University of Maryland with $2 million in equipment and paying $1.5 million in cash annually (Stevens, 2008). Kevin Plank commented about Under Armour's relationship with the University of Maryland, stating, "This is our flagship. This is thirty miles from our office. We have people on campus here probably three, four times a week, testing, prototyping and trying new things. That's how we're really going to use this partnership. We want to make ourselves better" (Stevens, 2008, p. C8).

Under Armour has used some university sponsorships as a way to promote its brand into geographic markets where professional sports league sponsorships have not yet been secured. Slater and Lloyd (2004) similarly describe how Reebok was able to secure a sponsorship with Xavier University because Nike was already involved with the University of Cincinnati in that market. Under Armour's sponsorships with Boston College, Temple University, and Northwestern are specifically designed to reach consumers in Boston, Philadelphia, and Chicago. Of its sponsorship with Boston College, Plank stated, "BC has maintained a loyal and fervent fan base in a city that demands excellence from all of its teams, and this partnership will have an immediate, positive impact for our brand and this elite athletic program and institution" (Under Armour press release, December 1, 2009). Matt Mirchin, senior vice president of sports marketing for Under Armour, said of its sponsorship with Temple University, "As one of the top athletic programs of the Northeast, Temple University is an ideal match for the Under Armour brand." Mirchin added, "In a pro sports city, Temple has been able to grow and maintain a loyal and fervent fan base" (Temple University Athletics press release, July 14, 2010).

The competition between Under Armour and Nike was on full display during the Bowl Championship Series national championship football game in January 2011, between Oregon, closely associated with Nike and its founder and Oregon alum Phil Knight, and Auburn University, the first university in the Southeastern Conference to sign with Under Armour, which agreed to a five-year, $10.6 million contract with Auburn in 2006 (Stevens, 2008). Not only did Under Armour's Auburn University defeat Oregon on the scoreboard, but estimates were that Under Armour received $1.8 million worth of advertising for its logo on Auburn head coach Gene Chizik, with Nike receiving $1.4 million in advertising value in exposure through Oregon head coach Chip Kelly (Hiestand, 2011).

These uniform manufacturers have been at the forefront of designing new uniforms for their university teams with the aim to at least draw attention, if not explicitly sell product (Tanier, 2011). Oregon, with its close relationship to Nike, has worn multiple uniform designs featuring different helmets, jerseys, and pants. For the 2011 college football season Nike developed new football uniform ensembles for Arizona State and Oklahoma State. Nike has also developed what it calls Pro Combat uniforms for many university football teams. In the past when Army and Navy played in their annual game, Nike has designed uniforms with Navy having a gold anchor on its helmet and Army uniforms resembling battle fatigues. Adidas has gotten into the act, with more traditional schools such as Michigan and Notre Dame wearing retro-inspired uniforms when they played in a nationally televised game on ABC in 2011.

Under Armour embraced the uniform-design craze in a pronounced way when the University of Maryland would debut uniforms intended to evoke Maryland Pride in a nationally televised game on ESPN on Labor Day night in 2011 against the University of Miami. The Maryland Pride uniforms featured the right side of the helmet covered in a black and gold checkerboard pattern and the left side of the helmet displaying a red and white cross, resembling the state flag. The jerseys extended the helmet design. The jerseys were not for sale, but Under Armour designed four additional jerseys for Maryland which were available to the public. Maryland team captains would choose the uniform design the team wore for each specific game, which included four different pant styles and two different helmets. Shawn Nestor, University of Maryland spokesman, commented, "They're trying to increase their visibility and so are we" (Tanier, 2011, p. 1). Paul Lukas, athletic uniform reporter for ESPN and editor of Uni-Watch.com, however, was critical of the University of Maryland look for the Labor Day game, stating, "the trend in uniform design is more toward making costumes for superheroes than uniforms for athletes. Last night (the Maryland versus Miami game) a very foolish school and a very foolish company showed just how desperate for attention they are" (Tanier, 2011, p. 1). (These alternate university uniforms are often criticized. In an analysis of the camouflage-style Louisville uniforms and the lime green Notre Dame uniforms created by Adidas for the men's basketball teams heading into the Big East and NCAA tournaments, Haney [2013] commented, "This matchup was great for the supplier, but did little to benefit the school's presentation" [p. 23].)

Under Armour has been able to secure a sponsorship with one major professional sports league. In February 2011, Under Armour became the official performance footwear supplier for Major League Baseball. Under Armour obtained the rights to include the Major League Baseball logo and team trademarks for in-store, digital, and print advertising for baseball footwear. In communicating a functional congruence through this sponsorship Under Armour is now able to promote its new cleats, which feature a rotational traction cleat configuration that is designed to maximize acceleration and power. Howard Smith, Major League Baseball senior vice president for licensing, stated, "Under Armour brings a unique attitude and energy to everything it does." He added, "Its commitment to performance is respected throughout the industry, and we have no doubt our players and fans will be excited about its baseball footwear" (Under Armour press release, February

14, 2011). In trying to grow internationally, in March 2011, Under Armour reached a five-year kit agreement with Tottenham Hotspur of the English Premier League.

The desire on the part of sponsors to reach the audience has certainly led to creative brand exposure locations and brand association connections on many levels of congruence beginning with image or geographic congruence, but when possible tapping into functional congruence and purchase congruence possibilities. Property selection will always be based on target audience, cost, and brand association variables. Mere brand exposure, however, is often not enough to produce a desired behavior effect by the consumer. Therefore, activation of the sponsorship is necessary.

Chapter Six

Sponsorship Activation

The sponsorship attribute of negotiation making anything possible and sponsorship being an industry that is built on creative and constructive ideas that can illuminate a brand association is most evident in documenting how companies activate, or leverage, their sponsorships (Papadimitriou & Apostolopoulou, 2009, use the terms activation, implementation, sponsorship leveraging, and exploitation interchangeably). Activation can simply be thought of as the methods used by sponsors to communicate and clearly associate their brand to the property and to consumers. Cornwell, Weeks, and Roy (2005) formally define activation as "collateral communication of a brand's relationship with a property" (p. 36).

Acquiring rights is only one part of the financial investment that companies need to make. Gordon Kane, founder of Victory Sports Marketing, describes the acquisition of rights as "the ticket to the prom" with money for all of the other aspects of the event still required (buying the clothes and renting the limousine — personal communication, November 22, 2011). Such is the case with sponsorship activation — an additional expenditure beyond the acquisition of rights is required for a successful sponsorship (Cameron, 2009; Cornwell, 1995; Fahy et al., 2004; Farrelly, Quester, & Burton, 1997; Meenaghan, 1991; Papadimitriou & Apostolopoulou, 2009).

Activation Spending

There is no consistent guideline as to what should be spent on activating a sponsorship, with researchers and practitioners estimating $1 to $5 be spent on activation for every dollar spent in the acquisition of rights. Cameron (2009) specifically calls for every $1 spent in acquiring rights, an additional $3 should be spent on activation programs. Ultimately it is the judgment of the sponsor to determine how much of an additional financial investment needs to be made in activating the sponsorship to accomplish the desired promotional communication business goals. Gordon Kane suggests that it is best that the money needed for activation be built into the sponsor's overall budget at the beginning of the negotiation process so that the client is clear on the total expenditure required to execute the sponsorship.

In their study which interviewed personnel who managed corporate sponsorships, Chadwick and Thwaites (2005) found that 24 percent of respondents had no additional money for activation activities, and 58 percent of respondents stated they spent only 25 percent of the value of the sponsorship on activation. More recently, in the annual IEG and Performance Research survey in 2013 executives reported that their companies spent an average of $1.50 toward activating the sponsorship for every $1 the company spent in rights fees, a decrease from the $1.70 to $1 ratio reported in 2012 and the first decrease since 2009. One reason cited for the decrease in activation spending is the increased use of social media which costs less than other promotional communication vehicles. The largest majority of respondents, 52 percent, spent at a $1 to $1 ratio. Twenty-two percent of respondents spent even less, a rate of between zero and $1 in activation to every $1 spent in rights fees. Twelve percent of respondents spent over $2 in activation to $1 in rights fees, and 7 percent of respondents did report spending over $3 and $4 respectively in activation to every $1 spent in rights fees. Seventy-three percent of respondents claimed they would spend even less on activation in the next year (IEG Sponsorship Report, April 22, 2013).

Researchers are clear in reporting that the amount of activation investment is a factor in the success of a sponsorship. Meenaghan (1991) plainly states, "The success of the sponsorship program will be dependent to a large extent of how it is implemented" (p. 43). Cornwell et al. (2005) claim, "Both the weight and the nature of leveraging activities are central to the communication effects achieved in sponsorship" (p. 36). Roy and Cornwell (2004) emphasize that for a lesser-known brand it is more imperative to activate the sponsorship in meaningful ways that ensure brand exposure and foster brand associations, as these brands have to aggressively confront the concept of brand prominence, the notion that well-known brands that already spend large amounts of money in promotional communication have an advantage in being recalled even if they are not the official sponsor.

Still despite the evidence strongly suggesting a need for investing in activation, not all companies are maximizing these opportunities. Papadimitriou and Apostolopoulou (2009) emphasize the importance of companies recognizing the activation possibilities with a property. In studying the sponsorship of companies within Greece that had a sponsorship with the 2004 Summer Olympics in Athens, they claim that the companies that contributed the necessary resources in activation derived more significant returns. They summarized, "Obtaining access to a unique sponsorship resource of the magnitude of the Olympic Games is of limited value if a company is not ready to place the additional resources for exploitation and has not developed a full understanding of the opportunities attached with, and the capabilities required, for creating competitive advantage" (p. 114). Papadimitriou and Apostolopoulou (2009) correctly note that the amount spent on activating a sponsorship *does not guarantee* (emphasis added here) achievement of promotional communication goals or definitively lead to a competitive advantage. They, however, unequivocally state, "Sponsorship activation is necessary if the sponsor is to receive returns on its investment" (p. 95). They characterized the companies who were sponsors but did not extensively activate their sponsorship as missing an opportunity.

Several leagues require that their sponsors spend a certain amount of money on activation programs. Activation is centered on the leagues' variety of assets. Sponsors used to simply be buying the intellectual property, the trademarks of the league. Now these sponsors have a list of assets around which to activate. The NFL, for example, has its own media platforms, in-season activities such as Kickoff Weekend, its charitable weekends that focus on breast cancer and the NFL's Play 60 initiative, and obviously the Super

Bowl, as well as off-season activities such as the NFL Draft and Combine. Leagues hope that their sponsors activate around all of these assets. Each company, however, will activate around the league's assets as it chooses.

In terms of activation, Tony Ponturo, former head of media and sports marketing for Anheuser-Busch, stresses that the sponsor "cannot put the asset on the shelf." He adds that activation "needs to be relatable to the product and the market" (personal communication, February 21, 2012). Therefore, a company should not engage in sponsorship just for the sake of engaging in sponsorship, and it should not activate the sponsorship just for the sake of activating the sponsorship — both should be part of a larger promotional communication strategy designed to achieve the brand's goals.

Some properties are offering financial flexibility for their sponsors to more readily allocate money for activation efforts. In 2011, Goodyear extended its sponsorship as the official tire company of NASCAR in a deal estimated between $12 and $15 million per year that will run through 2016. In the previous contract Goodyear was required to provide a financial investment beyond the rights fee with a specified amount used for purchasing commercial time during NASCAR broadcasts and a specified amount used for activation at the race track. In this contract extension, Goodyear is permitted to spend the additional money beyond the rights fee in the manner it chooses. Jim O'Connell, NASCAR's chief sales officer, commented "It's key to give flexibility to our partners so they can get the maximum (return on investment). We want to support our broadcast media partners, but at the same time give our marketing partners flexibility" (Mickle, 2011c, p. 3).

Activation: Planning and Customization

Activation is only limited by the creativity and imagination of the people representing the sponsor and the property with ideas originating from either party. Sponsorship activation ideas include additional brand exposure, sales promotions, stadium give-aways, fan experiences at the stadium or in the city of the event, online or digital media fan interactions, fan contests, in-store displays, tickets, bringing a ticket-stub to a store to receive a discount, corporate social responsibility endeavors, appearances with athletes, ticket discounts for sponsors' employees, hospitality for employees or clients, and product sampling (Arthur, Scott, Woods, & Booker, 1998; Farrelly et al., 1997; Fortunato, 2011; Polonsky & Speed, 2001; Pope & Voges, 2000).

The proper approach to activation program development is for it to be part of the negotiation process. Gordon Kane, founder of Victory Sports Marketing, believes that "really good activation starts before you sign the deal" (personal communication, November 22, 2011). Activation ideas need to be thought out at the earliest stages of the sponsorship process, with sponsors having a clear idea of how they want to use the assets of the property to achieve their business goals rather than signing a contract and then developing an activation plan.

Activation programs need to be customized to address the sponsor's promotional communication business goals. Mike Singer, consulting director for the Marketing Arm, identifies coming up with activation ideas and recommending a comprehensive activation program as a major function of a sponsorship agency. He describes that he is developing activation ideas and presenting them to the property, who, based on understanding its own assets, its demographic audience variables, or a specific team or geographic angle, will offer suggestions to make the program more unique and customizable (personal communication, February 7, 2012).

To illustrate the important point of customization, for the companies that need increased brand awareness, stadium signage makes sense as part of the activation program. For other companies activation must go far beyond brand exposure and simply placing a company logo in various locations. Jackson (2010) comments, "For too long, marketers and brands have acted as though it was sufficient merely to stick a badge or logo onto something" (p. 216). Seiferheld (2013) plainly states, "Expecting a logo to drive anything beyond recall is somewhat unfair" (p. 15). If, for example, the brand goal is to increase product trial, signage is not overly effective. That brand might develop an activation program such as a sweepstakes with a desirable prize where customers have to try the product in order to enter.

The activation programs must also be flexible to adjust to changing brand goals. With many sponsorships being long-term agreements the partnership between the sponsor and the property can have more strategic development and allow for activation programs to evolve (Chadwick & Thwaites, 2005). Antonio Lucio, chief marketing officer for Visa, for example, explained the changing nature of Visa's sponsorship with the Olympics, stating, "During the early days of our Olympic sponsorship, we (Visa) focused on promoting our exclusive acceptance at the Games. Today, we utilize the sponsorship platform to promote the advantages of using Visa instead of cash and checks and to facilitate the development and advancement of the payment infrastructure in Olympic host countries" (Visa press release, October 27, 2009).

Speed and Thompson (2000) also explain that a long-term sponsorship contract helps demonstrate a commitment and sincerity on the part of the sponsor toward the team, its fans, and the community in which it plays. For a beer company, Tony Ponturo, former head of media and sports marketing for Anheuser-Busch, points out that he was often seeking a long-term deal of three to five years so that the product distribution systems had time to properly develop the sponsorship. He explained that beer wholesalers needed time to develop retail aspects of the sponsorship, and they needed to know that the sponsor and the property will have a partnership that will build equity (personal communication, February 21, 2012).

Activation: Brand Association

Companies use activation to explicitly communicate a brand association between the sponsor and the property and potential consumers (Cameron, 2009). Savary (2008) stresses the importance of fostering a brand association, particularly in confronting challenges in the current promotional communication environment. She states, "Brands must now forge an emotional connection with the consumer. Marketing messages must show how a product is relevant to a consumer. Campaigns need to evoke affinity and create a 'that brand is like me' sentiment. Brands need to show future customers not just how a product meets their needs, but how the product integrates into their life and how the brand reflects their values and reinforces their self-image" (p. 212). Savary (2008) adds, "The discipline of sponsorship and engagement marketing is ideally and perhaps uniquely suited to this challenge. Engagement marketing professionals know that this discipline surpasses other forms of marketing in inspiring passion and loyalty, creating a sense of shared values and turning fans into brand advocates" (p. 212).

Jim Biegalski, senior vice president of consulting for the Marketing Arm, explains that "activation involves aligning a brand with a passion point in an engaging and entertaining way that has a high degree of authenticity." He adds that "through sponsorship there is an opportunity for a sponsor to have a more meaningful role in the relationship that customers have with their passion point" (personal communication, February 8, 2012). Biegalski also indicates, because the audience can be segmented, multiple tailored brand-activation plans can be developed.

Papadimitriou and Apostolopoulou (2009) emphasize the importance of using a variety of promotional communication methods to activate the sponsorship. Digital media certainly offer countless possibilities. In terms of digital media, just as sponsoring any team or league allows for the use of their logo on product packaging, the sponsorship allows for the sponsor's logo to appear on that league or team Web site. In many instances it is more than the appearance of the logo, but rather some interactive feature that is presented to online visitors. Two other promotional opportunities present themselves for sponsors through the Internet: the ability to produce a longer form advertisement on the Web site using that league or team imagery to better communicate the brand association between the company and the property and the ability for the user to visit the sponsor's Web site simply by clicking on the corporate logo. From the property perspective, its logo in all probability will have a presence on the sponsoring brand's Web site as well.

Activation: Brand Theme

It is incumbent upon the sponsor to creatively activate the sponsorship in a way that uses the property and its assets to help communicate a brand theme. Dan Donnelly is an executive vice president and managing director with Starcom MediaVest, an agency that defines its purpose as "to grow our clients businesses by transforming human behavior through uplifting, meaningful human experiences." Donnelly explains that sponsorship needs to move beyond awareness and address the critical question of "what does the brand stand for?" (personal communication, December 19, 2011). Through a customized sponsorship activation program there is the ability for a company to portray and communicate its brand themes in a creative way that picks up on characteristics of the property as well. For example, the idea of having a no-calorie beverage that tastes like Coca-Cola is the objective of Coke Zero. Through its sponsorship of the NCAA and the men's college basketball tournament, a brand theme of "Making the impossible, possible" is one that aligns with the incredible, seemingly impossible moments of the NCAA Tournament and what Coca-Cola has created with its Coke Zero product.

In other examples of trying to activate a sponsorship in a manner that communicates a brand theme, Allstate insurance company has as its tag-line, "You're in good hands with Allstate." In amplifying this brand theme, through its sponsorship of Major League Soccer, a four-year agreement reached in February, 2011, Allstate presents the league's Goalkeeper of the Year award. Buffalo Wild Wings, a corporate partner of the NCAA, refers to itself as "the official hangout" of March Madness. For college football, ESPN's College Gameday program is built by the Home Depot, while for college basketball, ESPN's College Gameday program is covered by State Farm.

Activation: Fan Experiences

Beyond communication of similarly associated themes, sponsorship activation offers the opportunity to provide the customer with an experience that he or she will remember and credit the brand for providing. Collett (2008) describes these sponsorship activation opportunities as "money can't buy" experiences. These experiences could precipitate a positive feeling toward the brand that will hopefully lead to the tangible reward of consumer purchase behavior. For example, for the 2012 Summer Olympics, IOC sponsor McDonald's arranged to bring over 200 children to London where they would have the opportunity to stand on the deck of the Olympic swimming pool, play beach volleyball and shoot archery at the Olympic venues, and get to meet Olympic athletes (Mickle, 2012b).

Some studies have examined the impact of activation programs compared to only brand exposure elements. Keller (1993) claims that "anything that causes the consumer to 'experience' or be exposed to the brand has the potential to increase familiarity and awareness" (p. 10). Joachimsthaler and Aaker (1997) argue that "these experiences create a relationship that goes beyond the loyalty generated by any objective assessment of a brand's value" (p. 45). Cameron (2009) found that seeing a billboard does not have the same value as a well-designed brand experience. Maxwell and Lough (2009) report that activation programs produce better brand recall than in-arena signage only. In studying NASCAR fans, Degaris et al. (2009) claim that activation "is particularly useful if the goal is to build a long-term relationship with a targeted audience" (p. 97). They found an increase in fans' purchase of sponsor's products if they participated in a sponsor's promotion, such as a contest or sweepstakes, a rewards program, or received free NASCAR merchandise. They conclude, "The greatest barrier to increased promotional participation among NASCAR fans is a lack of awareness" (p. 96). It is thus essential to promote awareness of the activation program.

Experiences allow consumers an opportunity to connect to the event and have the perception that the experience essentially would not have occurred without the support of the sponsor. Dan Donnelly explains that for too many companies "sponsorship signifies buying what already exists instead of creating something that without the sponsor being there would not be possible" (personal communication, December 19, 2011). He adds, "There are opportunities to be a part of an event or a television show in a major way that can be created for the consumer" (personal communication, December 19, 2011). When fans get to go online and vote or create a commercial they can connect with a property through a customized opportunity created for them by the sponsor. All of these activation programs do have to reflect the brand's goals.

An agency such as the Marketing Arm is constantly searching for ways to activate their clients' sponsorship programs in a way that allows for fan participation. Darin David, account director for the Marketing Arm, suggests that "sponsorship allows for brand messaging to transition into a space in a way that makes sense to fans" (personal communication, February 7, 2012). He adds, "The challenge is to develop creative ways that engage the customer while using the event or team they love" (personal communication, February 7, 2012).

Mike Singer, consulting director for the Marketing Arm, describes one engagement activation program that the Marketing Arm's client, AT&T, was able to develop through the company's sponsorship of NHL teams. In this activation program a contest was initiated where a fan would get to create the design of goaltender's mask. Fans were able to enter through a Web site or by visiting an AT&T store via an AT&T smartphone or tablet. In some instances the team's goaltender would visit store locations to promote the contest. In this AT&T example with the goal to increase customer product trial, the activation program has a component at its stores where customers have to try the product to enter the contest.

In another fan participation activation contest developed by the Marketing Arm, as an official sponsor of the NFL, Frito Lay's Doritos brand was able to name its activation program "Crash the Super Bowl" contest. In this contest fans develop their own television commercial for Doritos with a chance that it will air during the Super Bowl. Fans simply have to upload a 30-second commercial that featured the fans showing their love for Doritos to a special Web site. The Web site featured Doritos logos, product shots, music, and animations for fans to download and use. Five finalists' commercials were selected from which fans voted for their favorite commercial online to determine the winning Doritos spot. Each of the five finalists won $25,000 and a trip to Indianapolis to attend Super Bowl XLVI in a private luxury suite. Among the prizes for the contestants was a $1 million payment if the commercial ranked number one in the *USA Today* Super Bowl Ad Meter, which tracks the second-by-second responses of a panel of viewers to commercials during the national broadcast of the Super Bowl and ranks them favorite to least favorite. Since the promotion began in 2007, consumer-created Doritos advertisements have consistently ranked in the top five spots of the *USA Today* Ad Meter. In 2012, for the third time in four years, it was a consumer-created Doritos commercial that ranked number one on the *USA Today* Ad Meter. Darin David, account director for the Marketing Arm, exclaims, "Without question, the 'Crash the Super Bowl' campaign that we created for the Doritos brand continues to be held up as a model of genuine consumer engagement" (personal communication, February 7, 2011).

Activation in Practice

To illustrate how companies are activating their sponsorships using multiple communication methods simultaneously, communicating a brand association, communicating their own brand themes, and having fans participate in different sponsor driven experiences, several examples are provided. These examples demonstrate the concept of "anything is possible," that sponsorship is indeed an ideas business, and that there needs to be a customizable activation program based on a sponsor's promotional communication business goals.

The Scotts Lawn Company sponsorship with Major League Baseball is one example where the promotional communication business goal is not brand exposure. John Price, senior brand manager of sports marketing and sponsorship for Scotts, commented, "We have almost universal brand recognition, so increased awareness is almost a moot point" (Lefton, 2011b). Scotts activates its sponsorship with Major League Baseball in a myriad of ways that encourage fan participation. Scotts sponsored in-store balloting for the 2012 All-Star Game at Lowe's stores and Chevrolet dealerships, had a presence at the All-Star Game Fan Fest, produced Major League Baseball-themed commercials, produced a feature called Grass Clippings on the MLB Network, which showed lawn-stained defensive plays from major league games, created a "Take the Field" program during opening week that reinforced the connection between the start of the baseball season and seeing a lush lawn, and sponsored the "Beat the Streak" contest on the mlb.com Web site where fans select a player they believe will get a hit in that day's game with the objective of selecting a player on enough consecutive days to break Joe Dimaggio's 56-game hit streak. The nature of the "Beat the Streak" contest has fans constantly returning to the Web site to play.

On the mlb.com Web site Scotts also has "Fields of Play" videos which feature major league ballpark groundskeepers giving watering, seeding, and mowing tips for a quality lawn. John Price explained, "Lawn care is a category that's confusing to most consumers, so our strategy is to connect, educate, and demystify. We want to be the brand that connects homeowners with nature. If we can amplify that experience in an endemic way, then we're doing the right thing — and that should increase sales" (Lefton, 2011b).

In 2012, Scotts' national sponsorship of Major League Baseball was supported with sponsorships of eight individual teams. Activation occurs at the team sponsorship level as well. Scotts has created team-branded grass available for purchase by consumers with the Boston Red Sox, Chicago Cubs, Cincinnati Reds, New York Yankees, Philadelphia Phillies, and St. Louis Cardinals (the other teams that have sponsorships with Scotts are the Atlanta Braves, and Texas Rangers). The Yankees even had a Scotts-sponsored Yankees grass seed planter night giveaway at one of their home games.

In using the available assets and platforms, upon becoming the official and exclusive beer sponsor of the NFL in 2011, the first opportunity that Bud Light had to activate this sponsorship was the NFL Draft. The main element of Bud Light's NFL Draft activation was the "Best Round Ever" contest, where if a fan predicted the entire first round of the NFL Draft correctly he or she would win $10 million. In another contest created for the NFL Draft, Bud Light provided an opportunity for a fan to join a legendary NFL player on stage to announce his or her favorite team's second round draft pick. Fans could also enter a sweepstakes for the "Bud Light NFL Draft VIP Experience" in which the winners received a trip for two to New York City for the NFL Draft, including having access to an exclusive pre-draft party that is attended by several NFL Hall of Famers.

To support the sponsorship through the television broadcast, Bud Light was the exclusive presenting sponsor of ESPN's coverage of all seven rounds of the NFL Draft. Bud Light had purchased commercial time during the NFL Network's Draft coverage as well. At the draft location, New York City's Radio City Music Hall, Bud Light turned part of the mezzanine into the Bud Light Fan Zone, an exclusive hospitality area for 700 fans. Bud Light even developed a commemorative NFL Draft aluminum bottle. Mike

Sundet, senior director for Bud Light, commented, "The NFL Draft has become an unofficial holiday for fans — something they begin looking forward to almost as soon as the previous season ends. It's also a highly social event, which makes it a perfect fit for Bud Light (Anheuser-Busch press release, April 1, 2011).

The Draft was only the first activation initiative of Bud Light and its NFL sponsorship. In the autumn of 2011 Bud Light launched its Bud Light Fan Camp mobile experience, which visited 60 cities over 15 weeks. Fans who registered at www.facebook.com/BudLight formed teams consisting of two males and two females that competed against each other in football drills, such as kicking a field goal, precision passing, and relay races, as well as competed in playing EA Sports Madden NFL. Teams earned points during each event. The team with the most points won a trip to the 2012 Pro Bowl in Honolulu and represented its city in the Bud Light Fan Camp Finals at Aloha Stadium the day after the Pro Bowl. The Fan Camp promotion was incorporated into an episode of *Jimmy Kimmel Live!* with Kimmel challenging fans to compete in the skills. Mike Sundet, senior director for Bud Light, explained, "Fans are looking for new ways to immerse themselves into the NFL, and as the official beer sponsor of the league, we're bringing them once-in-a-lifetime experiences all season as only Bud Light can. Fan camp is our spin on an NFL training camp — we've kept the competition and football skills challenges, but combined it with the social spirit of Bud Light" (Anheuser-Busch press release, August 4, 2011).

In another activation program Bud Light is making fans purchase the brand as the means to competing in the Ultimate Fan Experience. Through NFL-themed tags on specially marked Bud Light 12-pack bottle cases and point-of-sale materials, fans could enter through www.BudLight.com/UltimateFan to win trips to the Super Bowl, Pro Bowl, and NFL Draft and season tickets for the team of the winner's choice.

Finally, Bud Light created an online community for NFL fans, the Bud Light Huddle. This Web site offers fans unique content and the ability to interact with other fans. Bud Light Huddle participants are identified through a customizable avatar made by superimposing their picture on a three-dimensional Bud Light bobble head. Mike Sundet summarized the overall Bud Light activation program, stating, "We're going to be the friend most NFL fans dream of — the one with tickets, connections and access to everything. We're going to bring fans up close and personal with the league's marquee events, and we're going to do it all year long. Unless you're wearing a uniform, you won't be able to get any closer to the NFL than Bud Light can take you" (Anheuser-Busch press release, September 7, 2011).

Federal Express' relationship with the NFL is activated through multiple initiatives as well. The FedEx Air and Ground Player of the Year are given to an NFL quarterback and running back respectively. The air and ground concepts fit synergistically with the Federal Express delivery systems. Each week during the NFL season, three quarterback and running back nominees are identified. On the main page of the NFL's Web site, www.nfl.com, there is a link where fans can watch highlights from the previous weekend's games for each of the nominees and vote for who should be that week's Federal Express air and ground winners. Based on the season-long fan voting, three finalists are chosen in each category by a panel of NFL experts. Of the three finalists fans vote online to select the winner. In honor of the winner, Federal Express makes a donation to a charity in that player's city. Pepsi and General Motors also sponsor weekly voting contests on the NFL

Web site. Pepsi sponsors the Rookie of the Week and the Rookie of the Year, while General Motors sponsors the "Never say Never Moment of the Week" and the "Never say Never Moment of the Year."

Federal Express has created two other activation elements in conjunction with the NFL and its fans' voting for the air and ground winners. There is a series of videos entitled, "Inside the Huddle: Small Business Solutions delivered by FedEx" that appear at the Web site location where fans vote for the air and ground winners. These videos feature executives with a connection to football, such as San Diego Chargers president, Dean Spanos, speaking about how they run their business with topics ranging from hiring employees and treating customers to being involved in the community. The videos end with the slogan on the screen, "FedEx: Solutions That Matter," accompanied by both the NFL and FedEx logos.

There is also a contest on the Web site in which fans can enter their own business to be the "FedEx Small Business of the Week." To have your small business be placed in consideration a representative of the company has to fill out a form that includes a response of 500 characters or less to the question, "What is the one solution that has helped you grow your business?" Three small-business nominees are selected each week, and fans can read their small-business solutions prior to voting for a winner. The winning small business receives $5,000. The purpose of the contest is stated on the Web site: "Making the right plays on the field takes talent, perseverance, focus and a whole lot of hard work. At FedEx, we know the same skills that make the FedEx Air & Ground nominees and winners successful on the football field are what delivers success in every field. That's why we're proud to recognize three small businesses each week that have what it takes to play and win. Just like the FedEx Air & Ground NFL Players of the Week, each of these businesses delivers when the pressure is on" (www.nfl.com). At this location on the NFL Web site, there is a link to the FedEx Small Business Solutions Center Web site.

In another activation between Federal Express and the NFL, players spend time working in Federal Express shipping centers as part of the "Pack and Ship with the Pros" promotion which coincides with the beginning of the holiday season. Through this promotion, customers could see NFL players at a Federal Express shipping center behind the counter for a brief time helping customers pack and ship their packages. Fans that sign up and ship items have the opportunity to win season tickets, autographed merchandise, and other prizes. In a Federal Express press release, DeMarcus Ware, Dallas Cowboys All-Pro linebacker, was quoted as saying, "Instead of pass rushing, I'll be packing and shipping with the pros at FedEx Office. I'll have some fun with my fans in a new environment" (Federal Express press release, November 1, 2010). Kim Dixon, Federal Express executive vice president and COO commented, "At FedEx, our goal is always to deliver an outstanding customer experience, and we want people to know they can count on us to get their packages where they need to be this holiday season 'safely and on-time'" (Federal Express press release, November 1, 2010).

Procter & Gamble is a sponsor of the NFL and has certainly used phrasing to better communicate its brand theme and its association with the NFL by creating a unique sponsorship product category. Procter & Gamble refers to itself as the "official locker room products of the NFL" (Procter & Gamble press release, August 3, 2010). One television commercial for Procter & Gamble's Febreze brand showed a houseful of guests wearing NFL jerseys watching the NFL and then having someone spray the house with Febreze at the end of the day. Other commercials feature Drew Brees, New Orleans Saints quarterback, or Lovie Smith, former Chicago Bears head coach, promoting the Vicks Nyquil and Dayquil brands and how these products help them quickly recover if sick and allow them to get back on the field.

In 2009, Procter & Gamble began its "Take it to the House" campaign, using phrasing that describes scoring a touchdown, but "also signifies the goal of bringing P&G products into the homes of football fans and consumers across the country" (Procter & Gamble press release, August 3, 2010). The campaign featured Jerry Rice, the NFL's all-time leader in receptions and touchdowns, as its national spokesman. The campaign was promoted through a social media component on Facebook, www.facebook.com/TakeIt ToTheHouse, which featured tips for in-home game day preparation, tips for fantasy football, a photo contest in which prizes included an at-home meet-and-greet with retired NFL legends, annual supplies of Procter & Gamble products, a series of donations to local health and wellness organizations, and a grand prize trip to the Pro Bowl in Hawaii. Kirk Perry, vice president, North America, Procter & Gamble, commented, "P&G's corporate mission is to touch and improve the lives of more people, more completely and this program fulfills that purpose by reaching NFL fans in a way that is relevant and meaningful to them" (Procter & Gamble press release, August 3, 2010).

Procter & Gamble is a sponsor of the IOC and the USOC. For the 2010 Winter Olympics from Vancouver, Canada, Procter & Gamble created the "Thank You, Mom" campaign to recognize the difficulties and sacrifices of the mothers of Olympic athletes in helping their children make the Olympic team. The parents of all United States Olympic and Paralympic athletes were given a $3,000 Visa card courtesy of Proctor & Gamble to defray travel costs and expenses while attending the games (Dreier, 2010). Visa is, of course, another TOP Olympic sponsor. The Procter & Gamble "Thank You, Mom" campaign was promoted through a one-minute commercial that showed children dressed as athletes competing at the Olympics. The commercial ends showing moms in the crowd cheering on their children with the on-screen graphic, "To their moms, they'll always be kids."

In Vancouver, the Procter & Gamble Family Home was created for the more than 300 athletes and coaches who were part of the United States Olympic team and their families where they could meet in a non-crowded environment, watch Olympic coverage, obtain Internet access, and have food provided free of charge. At the Family Home Procter & Gamble promoted 18 different brands with complimentary amenities such as the Tide laundry center, the Pringles entertainment lounge, the Pampers children's play area, and pampering ranging from quick refreshers to complete makeovers at the Procter & Gamble Beauty and Grooming Salon and Spa, which promoted the Covergirl, Pantene, Secret, and Venus brands.

The Procter & Gamble Family Home was promoted with the parents of Olympians appearing on the *Today Show* the day prior to the opening ceremony (it should be noted that NBC is the rights holder for the Olympics), television, print, and online advertising, as well as a Web site for the house where fans could see Olympic family photos and videos. At the Web site fans could also submit short stories of how their parents supported them in their life (Dreier, 2010). Lisa Baird, USOC chief marketing officer, explained, "At the Olympic Winter Games, our athletes are deeply focused on being performance-ready and podium-prepared. The P&G Family Home will allow them to have peace of mind and spend stress-free, invaluable time with their families. In addition to providing a centralized location for the families of U.S. Olympians, the program gives Team USA a place to interact and celebrate their achievements" (Procter & Gamble press release, January 21, 2010). Procter & Gamble hosted a similar Family Home for the 2012 Summer Olympics in London.

After the Vancouver Olympics, Procter & Gamble continued with its "Thank You, Mom" program through the IOC's inaugural Youth Olympic Games held in Singapore in August of 2010. Procter & Gamble assisted 25 mothers of Youth Olympic athletes, including three mothers of United States athletes, with travel and lodging costs in Singapore. Procter & Gamble also partnered with the mothers of six high-profile Olympic athletes from across the world, including Debbie Phelps, mother of swimmer Michael Phelps, and Jennifer Bolt, mother of sprinter Usain Bolt, to provide their experience. Procter & Gamble produced a documentary video series entitled "Raising an Olympian, The P&G Momumentary Project" that provided the stories of Olympians through the eyes of their mothers. The documentary series attempted to answer the question "What does it take to raise an Olympian?" and aired leading up to and during the 2012 London Summer Olympics (Procter & Gamble press release, July 28, 2010).

Mark Pritchard, Procter & Gamble global marketing and brand building officer, commented on the "Thank You, Mom" campaign, "We know from our successful results in Vancouver that this is about much more than a sponsorship. For P&G, it's about partnering with the IOC to make life better for athletes, moms and their families as we take the Olympic Movement to our four billion consumers around the world that our brands already serve" (Procter & Gamble press release, July 28, 2010). Pritchard estimated that Procter & Gamble should reach its target of $500 million in additional sales from the London Olympics. He explained, "it all starts with convincing retailers to put up more displays on their floors: then you'll get more sales. They not only did more displays, they did multiple brand displays in different parts of the store (*Street & Smith's Sports Business Journal*, October 29–November 4, 2012, p. 8).

In another event-driven example, Mexican brewer Tecate is a major sponsor of boxing. Tecate uses traditional brand exposure methods such as having its name on the ring mat as it did for the Manny Pacquiao against Juan Manuel Marquez championship fight in 2011. To encourage product trial Tecate offers a rebate for the cost of a pay-per-view fight for people who order the fight and purchase a Tecate product. Rebate offers are promoted on television and through in-store displays in largely Hispanic areas, such as Southern California, a geographic region that accounts for 35 percent of Tecate's United States business (King, 2011).

For the 2011 championship fight between Floyd Mayweather and Victor Ortiz, which occurred during Mexican Independence Week, although the fight was in Las Vegas, Tecate created an event in Southern California. The original plan was to hold a concert at a five- to six-thousand-seat venue in Los Angeles and then show the fight to the audience. Richard Schaefer, Golden Boy Promotions CEO, instead organized a fight to be held at the Staples Center in Los Angeles with Mexican boxer, Saul "Canelo" Alvarez. The Staples Center crowd would see the live fight, then watch the Mayweather/Ortiz bout on the arena's video screens. With HBO covering both fights as part of its pay-per-view telecast, the fans attending the Mayweather/Ortiz fight in Las Vegas would see the Alvarez fight, originating from Los Angeles, on the arena screens. A festival featuring two well-known Mexican musical acts would also be a part of the event in Los Angeles sponsored by Tecate (King, 2011). Richard Schaefer commented, "With Los Angeles now more than half Hispanic, this is an important date here (Mexican Independence). Having that date, having the right fighter, having the right sponsor partners, led by Tecate, which are going to put together a Southern California activation which is unheard of" (King, 2011, p. 4). Felix Palau, vice president of marketing for Tecate, explained that the attraction of a fight in Los Angeles "increases the ability to promote a bigger concept locally. We're taking that and putting it on top of what we already do nationally to make a really big event" (King, 2011, p. 4). Tecate supported the event with more than $800,000 in radio, television, and outdoor advertising in Southern California.

Chevrolet, an official Major League Baseball sponsor, activated around the All-Star Game in 2012 with a track where fans could test-drive the Camaro ZL1 and Corvette. The game's MVP, Melky Cabrera, San Francisco Giants outfielder, also won a Camaro ZL1 for his performance. Chris Perry, Chevrolet vice president of global marketing, explained, "We're just showing people our passion for baseball, and getting fans here exposed to our product lineup, which has turned over almost completely in the last two years. We use the attraction of baseball to generate leads and change consumer opinion about the brand" (Fisher & Lefton, 2012, p. 39).

Activation In-Stadium/In-Arena

Many sponsors include in their activation programs an in-stadium or in-arena element. For sponsorship activation at the stadium or arena there needs to be coordination between the sponsor and the team. Jowdy and McDonald (2002) claim, "Sports properties/organizers are not only charged with producing unique products for consumers, they must offer unique marketing platforms that attract corporate sponsors" (p. 248). James, Kolbe, and Trail (2002) point out that "a team's financial success is predicated, in large part, on the creation of an adequate income stream. This necessitates that sport teams attract, develop, and maintain a relationship with a substantial number of sports consumers" (p. 215). The term *sports consumers* can be applied in a general sense and includes fans and sponsors that make a significant contribution to the revenue stream of a sports team.

One of the prominent in-stadium or in-arena game day sponsorship activation promotions is fan giveaways. Miloch and Lambrecht (2006) found that companies that activated their sponsorship through providing a souvenir or product sampling received higher brand recall. In this endeavor a potential conflict could emerge with the team desiring to use the promotion to increase attendance, while the sponsor is, perhaps, hoping for a game that is guaranteed a strong attendance to boost brand exposure and connect with the fans by giving them an item or experience courtesy of the sponsor (Boyd & Krehbiel, 2003; Fortunato, 2006). In 2012, Major League Baseball teams had 767 giveaway dates, a four percent drop from 2011, but a two percent increase from 2010. The teams had an additional 1,505 non-giveaway promotions, such as fireworks, concerts, discounted parking, college nights, or discounted food, a decrease of twenty percent from 2011, but an increase of five percent from the 2010 season. Most, if not all, of these promotional dates have a sponsor attached. The New York Yankees had the most giveaway dates in 2011 with 44. Twenty six teams had bobblehead giveaways on 94 different dates and twenty two teams had fireworks nights on 186 different dates in 2012 (Broughton, 2012b).

Several sponsors' promotions throughout Major League Baseball involve branding a specific night with an added value component. For example, in 2013, the Baltimore Orioles had every Tuesday home game as Ollie's Bargain Night in which fans could purchase upper reserve seats for $9, courtesy of Ollie's Bargain Outlet. Every Friday Orioles home game was AT&T student night, in which any student presenting a valid school identification card could purchase left field, upper reserve tickets for $6.

Sponsors can be incorporated into ticket offerings in a way that has a purchase congruence element. During the 2012–13 season, for all Saturday and Sunday Miami Heat home games fans could purchase the Papa John's Heat Family Meal Deal for $150. The deal included four upper-level tickets, a voucher for four small drinks and four Papa John's arena pizzas, and a coupon for a free large Papa John's pizza at one of its restaurant locations. In the NHL in the 2011–12 season, the New Jersey Devils sold Pepsi Family Packs where fans received four tickets, four Pepsis, and four hot dogs, with pricing based on the arena seat location and if the game was played on a weekend or a weekday. Upper-deck Pepsi Family Packs sold for $164 regardless of the day of the week. For lower level seats in rows six through ten, the Pepsi Family Packs were $320 for weekday games and $364 for weekend games. For lower level seats further from the ice, the prices ranged from $220 on weekdays to $264 on weekends.

Beyond giveaway items there are multiple opportunities for companies to activate their sponsorship at the stadium or arena in a way that communicates a brand theme. Hugo Boss activates its sponsorship with the New York Knicks through an in-arena promotion. In the third quarter of Knicks games well-dressed fans appear on the Madison Square Garden video screens, with the fan receiving the loudest applause from the crowd winning a $500 Hugo Boss gift certificate. Video of Knicks players entering the arena before the game is also put on the video screens with fans' applause indicating the best-dressed player. Hugo Boss has courtside signage during Knicks games and signage outside Madison Square Garden during Fashion Week in New York City (Lombardo, 2011a). Hugo Boss has stores at four locations in Manhattan and two additional stores located at terminals inside John F. Kennedy Airport.

Non-Stadium/Arena Activation

In the autumn of 2011, Deloitte LLP, an audit, financial, tax, and consulting firm, as part of its sponsorship with the USOC created a tour that visited 17 universities with the "It's Your Race, Take the Lead" events. The tour featured lectures by Olympic and Paralympic athletes who discussed the concepts of passion and leadership in telling the stories of their own struggles and triumphs in achieving Olympic success. The tour was designed to motivate and inspire students in building their careers as well as introduce them to the Deloitte culture. Apolo Anton Ohno, eight-time Olympic medalist and one of the tour's speakers, explained, "Whether we are talking about a career on the playing field or in a business, our message to students is the same: pursue your goals with commitment and determination, and share your successes with others" (Deloitte press release, October 18, 2011). Ohno was also involved in the Deloitte National Leadership Conference in the summer of 2011, an interactive career development workshop designed to teach undergraduate students leadership skills.

The university tour is a method for Deloitte to recruit its future workforce, a major objective for the accounting and financial consulting firm. At the events featuring Olympic athletes, students have the opportunity to meet recruiters from Deloitte and learn of career opportunities with the firm. The university events are designed to provide students "a glimpse into Deloitte's high-performance culture and commitment to fostering leadership in its professionals. Deloitte's relationship with non-profit organizations such as the United States Olympic Committee and ongoing commitment to skills-based volunteering and pro-bono service demonstrate to potential recruits that they can make a difference while developing important leadership skills" (Deloitte press release, October 18, 2011). Diane Borhani, Deloitte's national director of campus recruiting, commented, "The Olympic and Paralympic athletes motivate young people to recognize their full potential, and they exemplify our culture of extraordinary performance, integrity, community service, and leadership. Alongside these inspirational figures at campus events, we have the opportunity to meet potential future talent and reinforce our organization's value and bold vision to be a place where leaders thrive" (Deloitte press release, October 18, 2011).

As part of its Web site, Deloitte has a section that describes its sponsorship with the USOC (www.deloitte.com/view/en_US/About/olympics/index.html). On the Web site Deloitte explains, "The Olympic Games give athletes from around the world the opportunity to push limits and break record. Relentless in our own pursuit of excellence, Deloitte is proud to sponsor the United States Olympic Committee and the United States Olympic and Paralympic athletes and hopefuls. Committed to our community and our people, Deloitte's sponsorship provides our professionals with the opportunity to put their experience and passion to work for the benefit of the USOC." (www.deloitte.com/view/en_US/About/olympics/index.html).

On the Web site there is a video by Apolo Anton Ohno talking about achieving his Olympic success. At one point Ohno asks questions of students listening to his lecture. Ohno asks one student what is his major, with the student responding, "Accounting." Another point in the video shows a student majoring in "finance with an international focus, who started a recycling program on campus, with a 3.8 grade point average." The video portion ends with Ohno stating, "There has to be a vision, a dream, and a plan. You have to chase it with zero regrets and everything you've got. Now, who's ready to work?" The approximately two-minute video ends with three different message screens. The first has the statement "The starting line for a high-performance career" with the Web address: facebook.com/yourfutureatdeloitte. The next screen has the Deloitte name along with the Olympic rings logo and the statement "Official Professional Services Sponsor." The final screen has the saying "It's your future, how far will you take it?"

From that page there is a link to the university tour page. On the university tour page there are links that include a listing of the athletes who participated in the university tour with their biographical information, videos that document the athletes' journeys to the Olympics, a tour schedule, photos from events, and video clips of students commenting about their enjoyment of the Deloitte-sponsored events.

In 2011, Deloitte was also the presenting sponsor for the 2011 Warrior Games, an event hosted by the USOC's Paralympic Military Program. In 2011, 220 wounded, ill, and injured members of the military competed in an Olympic-style competition in seven different sports. The event had the support of several Deloitte employee volunteers (www.deloitte.com/view/en_US/us?About/olympics/warrior-games/index.htm).

Anheuser-Busch along with Major League Soccer, which it also sponsors, created the Budweiser Cup, an amateur soccer tournament. The 2011 Budweiser Cup had teams compete in six-a-side matches throughout Southern California, Arizona, and Las Vegas. The Budweiser Cup had tournaments in 19 cities beginning in Santa Ana, California, on April 30 and concluding in Las Vegas on May 29. Each local tournament hosted as many as 64 teams with each team paying $100 to enter. All players received an Adidas soccer jersey. Adidas is also a sponsor of Major League Soccer. The two team finalists from each city received a cash reward, $1,000 for the first-place team and $500 for the second-place team, and a spot in the championship round which was played on June 11 at the Home Depot Center in Carson, California, prior to the Major League Soccer game between the Los Angeles Galaxy and Toronto FC.

The winning team of the championship round received a trip to Argentina to represent the United States and play against teams from around the world in the Global Beer Champions Tournament held at the legendary La Bombonera Stadium. Courtesy of Budweiser and Major League Soccer, winners had all first-class accommodations paid for and received tickets to two matches of South America's largest soccer tournament. Mark Wright, vice-president of media, sports, and entertainment marketing for Anheuser-Busch, explained, "By partnering with Major League Soccer to present the Budweiser Cup, we have the opportunity to provide soccer's passionate fans and amateur players a chance to compete in and experience one of the world's premier soccer events in person. The tournament also reinforces Budweiser's commitment to advancing the sport of soccer by bringing the nation's top amateur players to the global stage to compete against teams from across the world" (Anheuser-Busch press release, May 3, 2011). Anheuser-Busch is the sponsor of the FIFA World Cup and FIFA Confederations Cup through the 2022 tournaments.

Hospitality

Another aspect of a sponsorship activation program is hospitality. The IOC identifies hospitality opportunities as one of the benefits of being an official Olympic sponsor (http://www.olympic.org/sponsorship?tab=1). As part of its Olympic sponsorship activation Lenovo was a sponsor of the Olympic Torch Relay for the 2008 Summer Olympics in Beijing, had a Lenovo Showcase at the Olympic Green and Internet lounges in the Olympic Village and media center provided athletes with Lenovo equipment to better enable their ability to connect with fans, and hospitality initiatives that included hosting key stakeholders at sporting events as well as other gala events (Ladousee, 2009).

Hospitality events could be arranged for sponsors' clients, employees, or any other important stakeholders. Dan Donnelly, executive vice president and managing director with Starcom MediaVest, explains that companies have many constituency groups beyond consumers that they have to interact with, such as retailers, distributors, employees, and the local community. Sponsorship provides opportunities for engagement with each of these groups. He contends that a different sponsorship activation can "excite all of these constituency groups" (personal communication, December 19, 2011). For example, an end-of-aisle display might help excite distributors and sales forces, while a hospitality event might engage another key constituency group.

Hospitality is obviously done on the executive level. A hospitality event could be having high-level executives flown into the city of a major sports event. At that location the executives and perhaps even their families might participate in a structured event, such as a golf tournament, and interact with former players and coaches associated with the event before attending the event as a guest of the sponsor.

Some teams hold a hospitality luncheon where representatives from their sponsors are invited to watch a portion of the team's practice before attending a luncheon where there is an autograph session with the players and coaches. At the luncheon one team member or coach is seated at every table with the representatives from the various sponsors. The star players are seated with the companies that are spending the most money with the team. In this system, a hierarchy is established, and it becomes apparent which are the top sponsors with the team. The team is implicitly communicating to other sponsors there are probably opportunities to further their investment in the team (Fortunato, 2001).

Other examples of hospitality at the executive level can be provided. Since 2004 NASCAR has invited top executives from approximately 40 of its largest sponsors to comprise NASCAR's Fuel for Business Council. At their meetings executives interact with one another in hospitality settings designed to create business-to-business opportunities. In the past, NASCAR has had the executives compete in a go-kart race, while at another event NASCAR set up a speed-meeting gathering where company representatives quickly went from meeting-to-meeting to introduce themselves to executives from the other companies in attendance and briefly highlight their company's brand strategy (Newman, 2009). Jeff Charney, chief marketing officer for Aflac, described the events as "a wonderful way to do business away from the boardroom. I don't have my business suit on, but I have my business mind-set and I'm ready to do business" (Newman, 2009, p. B4).

According to NASCAR, through meeting with executives from other sponsors at these gatherings, the Best Western hotel chain was able to generate over $16 million in revenue. Best Western also began patronizing other NASCAR sponsors, including buying its office supplies from Office Depot and using UPS as its shipping carrier. In turn, these companies used Best Western for work-related travel. Similarly, Ford which also switched to using Office Depot and UPS through the interactions coordinated by NASCAR, set up a program where those companies offered Ford vehicles to their employees at a discounted rate. In 2008, approximately 1,800 UPS employees and 100 Office Depot employees purchased Ford cars through the program. In 2000, UPS conducted business with 40 percent of NASCAR sponsors; in 2009 the number had increased to 90 percent (Newman, 2009).

In another example, BMW brought some of its cars to the headquarters of other United States Olympic Committee sponsors such as Nike and AT&T where those companies employees were allowed to test drive the cars (Mickle, 2012d). These business deal-ings relate to the importance of the multi-sponsor congruence and the purchase congruence concepts introduced in Chapter Five. The fact that business is being conducted between sponsors can help a company feel that it is receiving value through the sponsorship and can be a major impetus in the sponsor renewing with the property.

The other group that hospitality is aimed at is the sponsor's employees. The benefits that might be obtained from corporate involvement with events through sponsorship could be thought of as a way to increase employee morale (Farrelly & Greyser, 2007; Hickman et al., 2005; Mitchell, 2002; Rogan, 2008; Rucci, Kirn, & Quinn, 1998). Rogan (2008) contends the sponsorship could help produce lower employee turnover, increase productivity and profitability, and gain higher customer loyalty. He points out that some level of employee involvement in the sponsorship can be negotiated with the property. For example, employees of a sponsor might be able to purchase tickets to the sponsored team's games at a discount. Rogan (2008) suggests that internal communication of the sponsorship should begin immediately when the sponsorship partnership is formed, and employee-related initiatives should continue throughout the sponsorship.

Several examples of employee benefits through a company's sponsorship can be pro-vided. Ho (2011) describes that through its sponsorship of the Olympic Torch Relay for the Beijing Summer Olympics Volkswagen was able to appoint 320 torchbearers both internally and externally. McDonald's has used its sponsorship with the Olympics as a way to reward employees by giving them the opportunity to work at the McDonald's restaurants and serve the athletes at the Olympic village (Mickle, 2011d). In creating com-petition among its dealerships, BMW invited its top forty dealerships to the London Olympics where employees were taken to several events (Mickle, 2012d). Discover through its sponsorship of the NHL was able to bring the Stanley Cup to its Riverwoods, Illinois, headquarters the year that the Chicago Blackhawks won the Stanley Cup, allowing employees to take pictures with the iconic trophy. Through its sponsorship with the uni-versities represented through IMG College, UPS has created an employee reward where one of its drivers hands the game ball to the referee (Spanberg, 2012b).

In another activation example to increase employee morale, sponsors have had their NASCAR drivers visit employees at the company's headquarters. Matt Kenseth, winner of the 2009 Daytona 500 and sponsored by DeWalt toolmaker, visited the company's headquarters in Towson, Maryland. Jon Howland, DeWalt marketing director, stated, "What Matt Kenseth was able to do for us internally in a down economy when we're going through a lot of challenging times is bring a lot of energy and passion back to the employees of DeWalt and to the brand itself" (Newman, 2009, B4). The DeWalt head-quarters featured an actual race car in its lobby, and employees often dressed in DeWalt racing shirts (Newman, 2009).

This level of employee involvement as a source of motivation and satisfaction can be an impetus for sponsor retention, with employees becoming dissatisfied with management if it does not renew a sponsorship that brought them some tangible benefits or entertaining experiences. David Grant, an executive at the consulting firm Team Epic summarized, "In this day and age, most companies will tell you that their workforce is one of their most critical assets. So if you have a sponsorship in your portfolio and you can make that work to your advantage with internal constituencies, I think that's critical" (Spanberg, 2012b, p. 13).

Hospitality could even be conducted for participants of the event. One form of executive hospitality activation for Sentient Jet in its sponsorship of the Breeders' Cup is the "Perfect Trip" award, which is based on the 68 Breeders' Cup Challenge qualifying races. From a panel of horse racing experts, the horse that personifies the "Perfect Trip" is chosen as the winner. Sentient Jet then provides that horse's owner and six guests complimentary round-trip service to the Breeders' Cup on one of its planes. Marty Guinoo, Sentient Jet CEO, explained that the company is excited to be "sponsoring the 'Sentient Perfect Trip' award and to give this year's winner the opportunity to experience what all Sentient clients receive: a perfect trip of their own" (Sentient Jet press release, July 19, 2011).

As part of its sponsorship of golf's FedEx Cup playoff series, BMW, which also sponsors the third tournament of the playoff series — the BMW Championship, provides the players in the FedEx Cup playoffs a BMW to drive for the week. There were 156 BMW vehicles provided for players and tournament officials at the Barclays Tournament in August, 2011. All vehicles were equipped with GPS systems that were pre-programmed with directions to the golf course, hotel, restaurants, and other places of interest. The Barclays logo was placed on all of the BMW vehicles (Prunty, 2011).

Credit Card Industry

To further demonstrate how the concepts of brand exposure, exclusivity, brand association, purchase congruence, and sponsorship activation work in synchronicity, the credit card industry provides an ideal product category to examine. Similar to pouring rights in the soft drink industry, there is an opportunity for point-of-purchase at the stadium through the opportunity to sign up customers for the team's sponsor's credit card. The major incentive to be an official exclusive sponsor for a credit card company is the opportunity to develop league- and team-branded cards, referred to as affinity marketing cards (Jones et al., 2006; Woo, Fock, & Hui, 2006). Macciette and Roy (1992) define affinity marketing as "a strategy used by vendors of goods and services to offer special incentives to association members in return for the endorsement [and to] capitalize on people's goodwill toward the group to which they belong" (p. 48). Affinity marketing campaigns can certainly capitalize on the group association dynamic as articulated in social identity theory. Affinity membership can be categorized by the members' participation with the entity, length of time as a member, level of social interaction within the group, commitment by the members to the central mission of the organization, and if payment for membership is a condition of joining the group (Gruen, 2000; Woo et al., 2006).

Jones, Suter, and Koch (2006) describe an affinity credit card as a unique type of relationship because it involves the consumer, the credit card company, and the property. Swaminathan and Reddy (2000) explain the benefit to the individual is the psychological satisfaction of benefiting the affinity group. Woo, Fock, and Hui (2006) contend, "An affinity partnering program represents a 'win-win-win' arrangement for individual cardholders to derive psychological satisfaction from supporting their affinity group, for the financial institution to solicit additional business, and for the affinity group to raise funds" (p. 110). Varadarajan and Menon (1988) explain that affinity marketing can particularly be effective for product categories in which there is little product differentiation, such as the credit card industry, reflecting the peripheral route idea of persuasion articulated by Petty and Cacioppo (1979, 1981, 1984). Passionate and loyal sports fans might choose a Visa or MasterCard credit card simply because the card will have an association with their favorite team and that team's logo is on the front of the card.

A major part of the sponsorship activation for affinity credit cards are the perks that are provided for cardholders. In its relationship with Major League Baseball, MasterCard has its Priceless Perks, a program which through a special online portal, www.mlb.com/mastercard, offers cardholders benefits that include savings on game tickets, message alerts to upcoming ticket deals, exclusive ticket offers only for MasterCard customers, a 20 percent discount off Major League Baseball Shop merchandise purchased with the card, and a 20 percent discount on MLB.TV (MasterCard press release, July 15, 2010).

These affinity credit card perks often include the opportunity for fan experiences that are otherwise unobtainable. For example, through MasterCard's sponsorship of the PGA Tour, one of the perks is for cardholders to receive exclusive "play like the pros" access to some of the golf courses that host PGA tournaments, such as TPC Sawgrass and TPC Blue Monster at Doral. If eligible, for their round of golf cardholders have a professional caddie, access to the players' locker room, and eat in the players' dining room (MasterCard press release, May 16, 2011).

For other credit card companies, the incentive to be a league sponsor might be the ability to offer their customers hard-to-get tickets to events. In December 2010, American Express became the official credit card of the NBA in a three-year agreement that includes USA Basketball, the WNBA, and the NBA Development League. The main perk for cardholders is the opportunity for tickets to the NBA All-Star Game or Draft. Courtney Kelso, vice president for global media and sponsorship marketing for American Express, indicated the request for tickets by cardholders was the impetus for the company to obtain a league sponsorship (Belson, 2010c).

Visa is the NFL's exclusive payment services sponsor. In 2009, Visa, a sponsor of the NFL since 1995, extended its relationship with the league through the 2014 season. All NFL events, such as the Super Bowl or the Pro Bowl, will only accept Visa as the payment option for either tickets to the games or the purchase of merchandise at the games and their associated events (i.e., fan festivals). Antonio Lucio, chief marketing officer for Visa, stated, "The NFL is the premier professional sports league in the United States, and its popularity delivers an unprecedented passionate audience, and a wide range of events that appeal to virtually every demographic. The NFL's numbers speak for themselves in terms of interest, viewership, and attendance. We know from our own research that this sponsorship generates transactions, builds our brand, and allows us to deliver our key messages of superior convenience, acceptance, and security. Furthermore, the NFL partnership provides a powerful platform for us to emphasize to millions of fans the benefits of making everyday purchases with a Visa card over cash or checks" (Visa press release, September 22, 2009).

In terms of media promotion of its sponsorship of the NFL, Visa for the ninth consecutive season in 2012 was the presenting sponsor for the Visa Halftime Report on Fox NFL broadcasts. Visa has also been a sponsor of Yahoo! Sports Fantasy Football. In support of its league-wide sponsorship, Visa had sponsorship agreements with 15 NFL teams.

Visa offers its own set of perks and opportunities for its cardholders. A major activation program for Visa through its relationship with the NFL is the Visa You & 10 Super Bowl Sweepstakes. From mid–September through December 27, 2011, when Visa cardholders used their card they were automatically entered for a chance for them and ten guests to receive tickets to the Super Bowl, round-trip airfare, ground transportation, hotel accommodations, admission to an NFL party, a meal with an NFL player, and a Visa gift card. Alex Craddock, Visa's head of North America marketing, explained, "Fans experience the NFL in a variety of different ways throughout the season, but one constant we've observed is that they enjoy it most when sharing it with other fans. This campaign and promotion aim to celebrate the social aspect of being an NFL fan and reward our cardholders who enjoy their NFL experience even more when they are surrounded by friends and family" (Visa press release, September 15, 2011). The Visa You & 10 Super Bowl Sweepstakes was promoted extensively through national television commercials (Visa runs a similar contest through its sponsorship of the NHL in Canada with the opportunity to attend the Stanley Cup).

In 2012, Visa developed the "Make It Epic" campaign in which fans could win epic experiences, such as Super Bowl tickets, watching the Pro Bowl from the sidelines, watching football with NFL Hall of Fame head coach and legendary announcer John Madden, and hearing an NFL coach's game day speech in person in an NFL locker room. Fans who used their card more often, increased their opportunities to win one of these experiences (www.visa.com/makeitepic).

Started in 2005, another activation program by Visa through its relationship with the NFL is the creation of *Financial Football*, a free interactive game that teaches players financial literacy and improves their money management skills. Visa has partnered with 29 state governments to distribute the game to high schools as well as created an online version, www.practicalmoneyskills.com/football (Visa press release, September 15, 2011). Visa has also released the game as a free iPhone application, and a version is available for the iPad. The financial literacy program has been supported with NFL players visiting local high schools to promote the initiative (Visa press release, November 9, 2010).

The *Financial Football* game tests students' financial knowledge in a simulation that combines the structure and rules of an NFL game with financial questions. By properly answering questions players advance the ball down the field and score a touchdown. The game is set in an NFL stadium-like setting and opens with the well-known Monday Night Football theme music. Participants can play an individual game or in a head-to-head matchup. The game is available in English and Spanish. There are three levels of game difficulty: the rookie level is designed for kids 11–14, the pro level for kids 14–18, and the Hall of Fame level for players age 18 and older. Players select the NFL matchup that they desire and which will be the home team with uniforms reflecting the NFL teams. Players select the offensive and defensive play. They then receive a financial question with multiple choice responses. If they correctly answer the question a green check appears and they watch the play unfold based on the correct response. A correct response on offense will result in a positive yardage gain. A correct response on defense might result in an incomplete pass or a loss of yardage for the offense.

Prior to playing, fans can visit the lessons section, which is designed to be a financial literacy training camp. In this section there are tutorials in four categories: (1) saving, (2) budgets take balance, (3) credit, debit, and prepaid cards, and 4) how credit worthy are you? There are tutorials on these four topics for each of the age levels. The tutorials are a multi-page explanation of the financial concepts within that category.

In the credit card industry consumers can be affected when a property switches the sponsor of the bank that issues the credit card. If fans want to continue having a credit card with the property represented, they too have to switch. Such was the case in 2010 when Barclaycard, a part of Barclays Global Retail Banking division that creates customized co-branded credit card programs, reached an exclusive, multiyear agreement with the NFL to market credit cards using the NFL and team logos. The previous sponsor, Bank of America, had an estimated 1 million holders of an NFL credit card that had to switch their credit card provider. Cardholders who wanted Bank of America to remain their card provider had to switch the type of affinity card they used (Armstrong, 2010). Among the ways that fans would be able to sign up for the NFL credit card issued by Barclaycard were at the stadium and through the NFL's Web site.

Barclaycard too offers customers benefits for its NFL-themed credit cards. Cardholders are able to earn points that could be redeemed for tickets, memorabilia, merchandise, or team experiences, and they get a 20 percent discount on purchases through NFL.com. Scott Young, general manager-partnerships for Barclaycard U.S., explained, "We've worked closely with the NFL to create a brand new credit card program with a collection of benefits and rewards that will appeal to the many fans of this thrilling game. With all the exciting new NFL extra points redemption choices, cardholders will have plenty of reasons to use the card" (Barclaycard press release, September 1, 2010).

Sponsorship Retention and Renewal

Professional sports leagues and collegiate conferences are no longer entities that just develop a schedule of games, establish the game's rules, legislate player conduct, or negotiate contracts with television networks and sponsors. They are now media companies owning their own television networks and Web sites. They are also marketing agencies developing ideas for all aspects of the sponsorship, especially activation. As demonstrated, it is clear that additional money beyond the rights fee is needed to implement activation programs. It is also clear that anything is possible, with activation ideas only limited by the creativity of the people developing and executing the sponsorship, that activation should focus on communicating and demonstrating a brand association and on communicating and demonstrating a brand theme, that there is rarely only one form of activation being used with sponsors implementing several elements, and that, ultimately, these activation programs are flexible and customized to enhance the effectiveness of the sponsorship and achieve promotional communication business goals.

Even effective sponsorships will try to be improved. From the sponsor perspective improvement means to develop better opportunities that address and satisfy the brand's goals. From the property perspective improvement means to better apply the property's assets in a way that will help the sponsors achieve their brand goals while at the same time increasing revenue for the property. Representatives from the sponsor and the property will continuously discuss ways to improve the sponsorship. The cultivation of the sponsorship relationship is, thus, an endless endeavor with the structure of a sponsorship being built over time.

It is the creation of a successful activation program that facilitates the sponsor renewing with the property. Lou Imbriano, president and CEO of TrinityOne, stresses that building an activation program that addresses the sponsor's goals and helps it improve its business is the best way to retain clients. It must be noted that all of the negotiation aspects mentioned in Chapter Two, property selection based on a target audience, the ability to achieve promotional communication business goals, and budget allocations, will continue to be factors as well in the decision making process regarding sponsorship renewal.

The renewal process is enhanced if during the sponsorship there was on-going dialogue between the sponsor and the property. To illustrate, the sponsor might evaluate if there were opportunities presented to it beyond the requirements specified in the contract. The concept of "under-promise and over-deliver" can easily be employed where the property has assets that it could provide to sponsors that serve as bonuses or added value. The added value could include something appealing to the sponsor's executives and employees. For example, through a sponsorship of a baseball team executives or employees could get a chance to watch batting practice from the field or a visit to the dugout that might include a meet-and-greet with a player or coach. Many of these added elements can be provided to the sponsor at almost no cost to the team.

More importantly, the added value could be something that provides additional brand recognition, such as having a promotional giveaway at the stadium in which the team might ask the sponsor to only cover the costs of executing the promotion with no additional rights fee (i.e., only purchasing the giveaway item). An added value element of this nature might only be a one-time bonus, but through this sampling of what the team can do the sponsor gets a much stronger sense of what else is possible through the sponsorship. The sponsor might see this concept being implemented and decide it was of great value and that it should be a permanent part of the sponsor's overall activation program with the team.

Keith Wachtel, NHL senior vice president of integrated sales, states, "There must be persistence in building and maintaining a relationship" (personal communication, February 21, 2012). He stresses it is not enough to just contact the sponsor at renewal time, but continue to prospect sponsors with strategic opportunities that assist in their brand messaging and brand goals. As leagues continue to develop assets that are available to sponsors, they must be in contact with them to see if they are interested in these new activation opportunities.

The NHL has been at the forefront of creating assets that might entice sponsors, such as the Winter Classic, an NHL game played outdoors generally on New Year's Day that has Bridgestone as its sponsor, and the Thanksgiving Showdown, played the day after Thanksgiving. Both of these games are broadcast on national television on NBC. The NHL uses these assets to prospect sponsors. In the process of trying to renew a contract with Discover as the official credit card sponsor of the NHL, the NHL was able to apply one of its newly created assets, the inaugural Thanksgiving Showdown. Discover would become the game's title sponsor, naming the game the "Discover NHL Thanksgiving Showdown." The timing of the game being on customarily one of the busiest shopping days of the year certainly fit well with the timing of the use of the Discover card.

To further enhance the renewal and promote the game on Thanksgiving Friday, the NHL and Discover placed a co-branded float in the Macy's Thanksgiving Day Parade. The float featured a singing performance by Cee Lo Green, a musical artist who also appears as a judge on NBC's *The Voice*, past NHL stars, a synthetic ice rink, and a 12-foot turkey that served as the hockey goal. With the parade being televised on NBC, this offered an easy opportunity to promote the next day's hockey game. Keith Wachtel explains the sponsorship renewal process is the best opportunity in terms of business development and significant monetary increases. He cites that product categories are often filled with a sponsor and rarely are new product categories even developed.

In the renewal process, non-rights holders might inquire if the sponsorship within the product category might become available. The cultivating of relationships could include companies that are not official sponsors, knowing that having more companies interested in the property will only drive up the price of the sponsorship. If, for example, a product category is coming up for renewal after the league's season ends in another year, the league might be speaking with other potential sponsors prior to and throughout the season to demonstrate the league's assets and showcase why a sponsorship for that company would work with the league. From the sponsor perspective, in terms of renewals, Tony Ponturo, former head of media and sports marketing for Anheuser-Busch, suggests the sponsor with a year or so left should be proactive and show a willingness to negotiate an extension of the sponsorship.

Finally, because of the time needed to research and understand the potential sponsors' brands and that their sponsorship dollars get committed so quickly, Keith Wachtel stresses the importance of staggering when sponsorships end so that not many of the league's most lucrative sponsorships are ending in the same year. Ideally, there should only be one or at most two of the league's most lucrative sponsorships ending in a given year so that there is no major risk to the revenue structure of the property. The property can then more efficiently deploy its personnel to the important product category renewal process.

Chapter Seven

Hindrances to a Successful Sponsorship

While the importance of the proper selection of the property and implementing creative and constructive activation ideas to achieve an effective sponsorship are clear, as has been indicated, no degree of success is guaranteed. In fact, there are several hindrances to a sponsorship that both the sponsor and the property need to recognize and be prepared to address. It is important for the sponsor and the property to identify and work together to curtail, rectify, and, if possible, eliminate any potential threats to achieving a successful partnership.

Many of the hindrances to the success of a sponsorship deal with improper brand recognition of official sponsors by the audience. For a company to capitalize on the advantages of the sponsorship promotional communication strategy, proper brand recognition as an official sponsor of the property by the audience is essential. As has been demonstrated, it is this brand recognition and brand association that can drive achievement of promotional communication business goals, including consumer behavior. Recognition of a competing brand as the official sponsor for a property negates the positives that can be obtained through a sponsorship. Any consumer confusion as to who is the official sponsor hinders the desired brand association and essentially devalues the sponsorship.

Improper recognition is not only a problem for the sponsors, but considering that they are a major revenue source, the problem needs to be confronted by the property as well. As Johar, Pham, and Wakefield (2006) state, "If much of the audience is unable to correctly identify the sponsor of an event or, worse, identify companies who did not pay the sponsorship fees (including competitors!), the value of the sponsorship becomes highly questionable. This affects not only the sponsors themselves, but also the various properties that seek sponsorship fees" (p. 183). They add, "Should sponsor misidentification remain widespread, it will become increasingly difficult for the properties to justify the sponsorship fees that they seek" (p. 195).

For each sports league as well as NASCAR, the PGA Tour, and the Olympics, *Street & Smith's Sports Business Journal* publishes survey results conducted by Turnkey Intelligence, a research and consulting firm for leagues, teams, and sports brands, that measures if fans can correctly recognize the league's official sponsors. The surveys segment the leagues' fans into two categories. Avid fans are defined as responding with a four or a five on a five-point scale to the question of how big a fan are you (of the league)? These avid fans report to "look up news, scores, and standings several times a week or more often," they "watch/listen/attend at least eleven games per season," and they "have a favorite team." Casual fans are defined as responding with a three on a five-point scale to the question of how big a fan are you (of the league)? These casual fans report to "look up news, scores, and standings several times a month or more often," they "watch/listen/attend at least three games per season," and they "have a favorite team" (Broughton, 2012c, p. 17).

The survey for fan recognition of Major League Baseball sponsors for 2012 was conducted from October 24 through November 1, 2012. The sample respondents reported recognition on several product categories in which there is an official Major League Baseball sponsor: quick-service restaurants, soft drink, automobile, hotel, sports drink, beer, bank, insurance, tire, and credit card. Anheuser-Busch, Major League Baseball's official beer sponsor since 1980, had the highest level of recognition for all companies by both avid fans, 51.7 percent, and casual fans, 47.4 percent. Anheuser-Busch also had the largest recognition gap in any product category. In the survey, Miller was recognized as the official Major League Baseball sponsor in the beer category by only nine percent of avid fans and 9.8 percent of casual fans in 2012. Anheuser-Busch has agreements with 23 teams producing 22 team specific Budweiser cans, (for the 2013 season, Budweiser produced 130 million, twelve-ounce cans with its sponsored team logos. In cities where Budweiser was not the sponsor of the team, Budweiser used the Major League Baseball logo on its can — Lefton, 2013a), the naming rights to the stadium of the St. Louis Cardinals, and in 2012 was the presenting sponsor of Major League Baseball's inaugural single-elimination, wild card games. Anheuser-Busch also had the highest increase in recognition as an official Major League Baseball sponsor in comparison to the 2011 results among avid fans with an 11.8 percentage point increase. In August of 2012, Anheuser-Busch announced it will continue as Major League Baseball's official beer sponsor through 2018.

Gatorade, an official Major League Baseball sponsor since 1990, had similar brand dominance in its product category. Gatorade was recognized as the official sponsor of Major League Baseball in the sports drink category by 50.2 percent of avid fans and 38.1 percent of casual fans. In the survey, Powerade was recognized as the official Major League Baseball sponsor in the sports drink category by only 9.5 percent of avid fans and 8.2 percent of casual fans in 2012. In addition to its league sponsorship, Gatorade has sponsorship deals with eighteen teams, and Derek Jeter of the New York Yankees and Joe Mauer of the Minnesota Twins serve as spokesmen.

Some official Major League Baseball sponsors were not as fortunate in having their brand as overwhelmingly recognized with that association. MasterCard is the official sponsor for Major League Baseball in the credit card product category, but its recognition by avid fans of 24.4 percent was slightly less than non-sponsor Visa having 24.9 percent declare it as an official Major League Baseball sponsor. MasterCard was more recognized as an official sponsor by casual fans, 22.2 percent, compared to Visa's 20.1 percent. The 2012 survey also marked the first year that Taco Bell surpassed McDonald's in recognition among avid fans in the quick service restaurant product category (Broughton, 2012c).

In another research report trying to measure fan recognition of official sponsors, Echo Research surveyed 1,002 adults in Britain about correct recognition of FIFA World Cup sponsors in 2010 (O'Reilly, 2010). The results revealed that no official World Cup sponsor was identified as such by greater than half of the respondents, with Coca-Cola and McDonald's being the most recognized at 48 percent and 40 percent respectively. Hyundai, an official sponsor, was identified as an official World Cup sponsor by only 15 percent of respondents. Nike was identified as an official sponsor of the World Cup by 20 percent of respondents, despite Adidas having that designation (O'Reilly, 2010).

Advertising Clutter

One of the major hindrances to proper brand recognition and a successful sponsorship is advertising clutter (Brown & Rothschild, 1993; Elliot & Speck, 1998; Johnson & Cobb-Walgren, 1994; McAllister, 1996). Simply as more companies are a sponsor of the same property, the more difficult it is to have consumers notice one brand from all of the others. Elliot and Speck (1998) define advertising clutter as "the level of advertising or promotion in a medium" (p. 29). However, one certainly has to factor in that often people are exposed to many mediums at one particular time. For example, a person might have a television turned on while at the same time reading a magazine or looking at various Web sites on his or her iPad, exacerbating the cluttered promotional communication environment. Even in 1979, long before the Internet, Webb and Ray (1979) found that advertising clutter was a hindrance to brand recall.

Proper brand recall can become almost impossible if other brands from the same product category are consistently mentioned. In relation to advertising clutter McAllister (1996) claims that companies would like to control what other ads run near their advertisements, or in the case of sponsorship what other companies might be associated with the property. Clearly the sponsor would most be concerned with competing brands from the same product category. Obviously if Coca-Cola was an official sponsor, it would not want Pepsi obtaining exposure in that same location; thus the importance of having product category exclusivity be a part of any sponsorship agreement. Kent and Allen (1994) did find that familiar brands are less susceptible to advertising clutter hindrances than unfamiliar brands.

Because of its loyal audience and because games are somewhat DVR-proof, sports properties and programs remain a popular option in confronting advertising clutter. Speaking specifically of televised sports, Bellamy (1998) explains that "with a seemingly endless proliferation of television channels, sport is seen as the programming that can best break through the clutter of channels and advertising and consistently produce a desirable audience for sale to advertisers" (p. 73). There are, however, certain events, such as the ice and boards during an NHL game or a NASCAR race, where there are many sponsors at that one location. The Masters Golf Tournament on the other hand consciously only has three sponsors to avoid clutter and make its sponsorships more attractive. The Masters sponsors are recognized by one of the executives from the Augusta National Golf Club in an announcement thanking them for their support during the early portion of the television broadcast on each day of the tournament.

The IOC also tries to limit the numbers of partners it contracts with in an attempt to reduce advertising clutter. In its Olympic Marketing Fact File, the IOC states that it "constructs and manages programs in which only a small number of corporations participate. Each partner participating in the Worldwide TOP Program has global category exclusivity. OCOG programs are also designed to maximize support for the Games through the minimum number of partnerships" (Olympic Marketing Fact File, 2012, p. 36. http://www.olympic.org/Documents/IOC_Marketing/OLYMPIC-MARKETING-FACT-FILE-2012.pdf).

Some teams take a similar approach of having fewer sponsors, but allowing them to have a bigger role in their involvement with the team. John Knebel, vice president and managing director of corporate partnerships and business development for the Washington Nationals, explains that the teams could make it so that there is only one dominant brand being seen at one time. For example, instead of having all of the electronic boards in the stadium or an arena display different brands at the same time producing advertising clutter (i.e., Coca-Cola on one sign, McDonald's on another sign, and UPS on another sign), all of the electronic boards throughout the stadium or arena could display the same brand at one time (i.e., all Coca-Cola signs) then switch all signs to another brand (i.e., switch all Coca-Cola signs to all UPS signs). What this also does is change the background lighting, especially in an arena. Even if looking down at the ice or the court, the background lighting of the entire arena changing from Coca-Cola red to UPS brown might be more noticeable to fans.

Ambush Marketing

Advertising clutter's challenge of being noticed because there are many sponsors at that location is only one hindrance to a successful sponsorship. Another major hindrance is trying to protect against other companies attempting to have their brand noticed at a location and recognized as an official sponsor without having purchased rights for the property. This hindrance to proper brand recognition and a successful sponsorship without payment for an official designation is a practice referred to as ambush marketing. Meenaghan (1996) defines ambush marketing as a "corporate sponsorship practice in which a company, often an event sponsor's competitor, attempts to deflect the audience's attention to itself and away from the sponsor" (p. 103). Burton and Chadwick (2009) describe ambush marketing as a "form of associative marketing, utilized by an organization to capitalize upon the awareness, attention, goodwill, and other benefits, generated by having an association with an event or property, without that organization having an official or direct connection to that event or property" (p. 305).

In their seminal study Sandler and Shani (1989) claim the goal of ambush marketing is to create confusion as to who is the official sponsor. McKelvey (2003) explains that through ambush marketing "companies create the impression of an affiliation with a sports event without 'official' sanctioning from the property itself" (p. 23). Farrelly, Quester, and Greyser (2005) point out that "ambushers have aimed to enhance their own brand equity, at the expense of official sponsors, by illegitimately associating their name with the positive brand equity of the target sport or event" (p. 340). Burton and Chadwick (2009) conclude that ambush marketing campaigns are "positioned strategically to reinforce an intended mis-association and link a brand to an event or property in the absence of an official relationship" (p. 304).

Meenaghan (1994, 1996) explains that ambush marketing threatens the integrity of an event and undermines its financial viability because sponsorships are being devalued. Duke (2001) importantly addresses that a major financial investment is made through a sponsorship and in ambush marketing practices "companies that didn't pay for event sponsorship show up at the event anyway" (p. 43). Elliot (2002) states, "When an organization tries to gain the benefits of such an association without paying out these significant sums of money, corporate angst among those who have done so is understandable" (p. 14). Elliot (2002) concludes that "ambush marketing has a negative effect on everyone involved with an event and, in the end on sport itself" (p. 14).

Several scholarly studies have examined if ambush marketing practices are effective by measuring if consumers can recognize which companies are the official sponsors of an event or if consumers attached that designation to an un-official sponsor (Lee, Shani, & Sandler, 1997; Lyberger & McCarthy, 2001; Robinson & Bauman, 2008; Sandler & Shani, 1989). Duke (2001) claims that "few would deny that the unofficial presence of brands has an impact on the profile that the official sponsors receive. Indeed, sponsorship awareness surveys frequently reveal non-associated companies as being more closely identified with an event than those who have invested millions to be there" (p. 43). Other researchers add that it is easier for ambushers to be a well-recognized brand that fits the audience profile of a brand they would view as a typical sponsor for that property (Farrelly et al., 2005; Lardinois & Quester, 2001).

Ambush Marketing Practices

One common ambush marketing practice is to place advertisements and develop customer participatory experiences in the geographic region of an event at locations where the rights have not been secured through the official sponsorship. Often the ambush marketers use imagery or phrasing that is vague or misleading and is not protected in the official sponsorship. The practice of ambush marketing gained notoriety in 1984 when Converse, the official sponsor of the Summer Olympics, was ambushed by Nike, who developed murals of Nike-sponsored track athletes visible near the Los Angeles Coliseum. The ambush marketing by Nike resulted in 42 percent of consumers believing that Nike was an official sponsor of the Olympics (Burton & Chadwick, 2009).

In a more recent example, Heineken has been a sponsor of the United States Open tennis tournament since 1992 and in 2011 extended its contract for another four years. The geographic footprint of the United States Open sponsorship in New York City includes all nearby parkland, the Citi Field parking lot, and the boardwalk stretching from the subway station to the National Tennis Center. It does not include the train platform of the Long Island Rail Road, the property of the New York City Metropolitan Transit Authority, from which the National Tennis Center is visible and is the mode of transportation for several fans. In 2011, Stella Artois, a Belgian brand owned by Anheuser-Busch, placed 15 advertisements along the Long Island Rail Road platform using tennis-themed language, such as "The Top-Seeded Belgian" and "A Perfect Match." The United States Tennis Association demanded that Stella Artois remove the advertisements. Chris Widmaier, a United States Tennis Association spokesman commented, "We have many people who would like to capitalize on the power of the U.S. Open without going through proper channels" (Kaplan, 2011c, p. 8). Stella Artois declined to remove the advertisements.

Major events such as the Olympics and the FIFA World Cup are prime locations for ambush marketing attempts. In the 1992 Summer Olympics from Barcelona, Visa was upset over an American Express commercial that stated, "And remember, to visit Spain you don't need a visa." Coca-Cola was angered over a Pepsi commercial that saluted USA Basketball star Magic Johnson (Myerson, 1996). Burton and Chadwick (2009) provide numerous examples of ambush marketing campaigns involving the Olympics, such as during the 2002 Winter Olympics in Salt Lake City, Schirf Brewery, a local brand, put on its delivery trucks "the Unofficial Beer of the 2002 Winter Games" in an attempt to ambush official sponsor, Anheuser-Busch.

During the 2006 World Cup soccer tournament in Germany, there were 3,300 reports of sponsor-rights infringements (Palomba, 2011). One official sponsor, Budweiser, was ambushed by Dutch brewery Bavaria, when Bavaria enticed fans to wear its company's promotional clothing in the stadium. Stadium officials forced over 1,000 Dutch fans to watch the game in their underwear. The brewery received so much media coverage from the incident that at the 2010 World Cup in South Africa 36 women were sent to a stadium wearing orange dresses with the Bavaria logo. The women were escorted out of the stadium (Palomba, 2011).

In another ambush marketing example at the World Cup, in 2010 Nike ambushed official sponsor, Adidas, by starting a grass-roots soccer campaign throughout South Africa to simply capitalize on the enthusiasm of soccer. Nike used online and social media in its World Cup promotional campaign. Nike created a "Write the Future" campaign with an advertisement that was a three-minute video showing soccer superstars, such as Wayne Rooney, Didier Drogba, and Cristiano Ronaldo, controlling their fate with their play. The video, which also featured Kobe Bryant and Roger Federer, set records for the most views in a debut week for a viral advertisement with 7.8 million. From its debut on May 17, 2011, through the middle of June, the Nike "Write the Future" video had over 16.3 million hits on YouTube (Artsitas, 2010). Adidas tried to combat the Nike video with one of its own featuring David Beckham and Snoop Dogg, but it only attracted 3.5 million views from its debut on June 4 through the middle of June.

In a measurement of online buzz for the month before the World Cup, Nike received a 30.2 percent share, doubling that of Adidas. Even when the World Cup was under way, Google searches that involved the words Nike and World Cup together nearly doubled that of Adidas (Artsitas, 2010). To further its efforts, Nike set up an LED screen 30 stories high at the South Africa Life Center, with fans having the opportunity for their messages sent in from Twitter and Facebook displayed as part of the "Write the Headline" component to the "Write the Future" campaign. Not being an official sponsor did not prevent Derek Kent, Nike spokesman, from stating "(the World Cup) is a tremendous opportunity to amplify the sport, and Nike wants be the center of it" (Artsitas, 2010).

Another strategy that can be characterized as ambush marketing because of its potential for the same result of improper identification of official sponsors is for non-official sponsors to purchase commercial time during the broadcasting of games and events. Again, imagery or phrasing that is vague or misleading is often used in these commercial advertisements. Chevrolet is the official sponsor of Major League Baseball, but during Fox's broadcasting of the 2011 World Series, the trivia question was sponsored by Volkswagen. Preventing non-official sponsors from buying commercial time is difficult if the broadcast network cannot sell all of its commercial time during the event, and the official sponsors are not willing to purchase more time. One company could enter into an exclusive contract for the commercial space during the event's broadcast. General Motors did reach an exclusive deal with NBC so that General Motors was the exclusive domestic automotive advertiser during the 2012 London Summer Olympics.

Ambush Marketing Remedies

Elliot (2002) claims that while it is virtually impossible to stop companies from ambush marketing, there are things that both official sponsors and properties can do to control the communication environment in which the brand name will be exposed to the audience. Burton and Chadwick (2009) declare that remedies to ambush marketing can be either proactive or reactive. Norcross (2011) stresses the need for sponsors and properties to be proactive in confronting ambush marketing, claiming, "Unless organizations adopt a proactive strategy for dealing with ambushers, we will continue to see more and more unwelcome ambush campaigns and unhappy sponsors as a result" (p. 15).

Farrelly et al. (2005) provide a series of potential remedies to ambush marketing based on the sponsor being proactive in promoting its association to the property. They explain that official sponsors need to have the mindset that ambush marketing will in fact be tried and attempts should be made to "out ambush the ambusher" (p. 346). The main strategy in combating ambush marketing identified by Farrelly et al. (2005) is for the official sponsor to explicitly communicate the connection between the brand and the property. This can be achieved through the content of the official sponsors' commercials and other activation programs. Farrelly et al. (2005) state, "When a sponsor's advertising content clearly relates to the spirit of the sponsored property, this signals official sponsorship" (p. 346).

Farrelly et al. (2005) stress activating the sponsorship so that the official sponsor is seen on multiple occasions. They state, "The best protection against ambushers is to allocate more money for direct communication of the sponsorship to consumers" (p. 344). They add, "Ultimately, a multilayered activation strategy leaving little doubt as to who is the official sponsor (and what the property means to the sponsor's brand) is the best defense (and offense) in the fight against ambushers to secure optimal benefit for the legitimate sponsor" (p. 346). Farrelly et al. (2005) conclude that official sponsors "have no excuse if usurped by ambushers because they have all the tools in hand to maximize (and thus safeguard) their investment, including the opportunity to build images associated with legitimacy and to leverage these images" (p. 346). So while it may cost more in the short-term, the benefits of proper official sponsor recognition will be obtained in the long-term.

Burton and Chadwick (2009) claim the responsibility to protect sponsors from ambush marketing lies more with the property. Properties certainly need to be protective of their major revenue source. Papadimitriou and Apostolopoulou (2009) state that "increased efforts to protect official sponsors from ambush marketing campaigns contribute to the efforts of ensuring sponsors' benefit from their partnerships" (p. 94). Gordon Kane, founder of Victory Sports Marketing, specifically cites trust as a characteristic that is vital to the success of a sponsorship. He explains the need for trust is amplified in situations of ambush marketing in that sponsors have to trust that the property will protect their rights. On the team level, for example, if the team is sponsored by a retail store that sells multiple brands, such as Best Buy, if Best Buy and Panasonic are both sponsors of a team, the team will make sure its logo when used in Best Buy advertisements is not placed next to a Sony product.

Burton and Chadwick (2009) suggest another proactive strategy of companies identified as ambush marketers is to prevent them from bidding for the official sponsorship designation for future events. This remedy is problematic because properties need to have multiple bidders for their sponsorships as a way to drive up the cost of being the official sponsor. If, for example, Pepsi was eliminated from bidding on a property, without any competition within the product category Coca-Cola would then obtain a strong bargaining advantage in negotiating the fee to be the official sponsor of that property.

Norcross (2011) identifies two other potential remedies that can be proactively implemented by the property to combat ambush marketing. The first is for the property to communicate with nonsponsors prior to major events to inform them that ambush marketing attempts will be monitored. The second suggested remedy is for the property to broaden as much as possible the rights that the official sponsor can secure, forcing any ambush marketing attempts to be done in more remote locations. Nikki Hart, assistant council for the NFL, commented, "The bigger circle of rights we can carve out, the further back we can [push] ambushers" (Norcross, 2011). In that light, Burton and Chadwick (2009) recommend securing the rights to all advertising in the geographic area of the event, including billboards. Again, this level of exclusivity might result in a higher cost, but clearly one that the sponsor should invest in to try to prevent ambush marketing attempts.

As companies have become creative in implementing ambush marketing campaigns, properties are becoming equally creative in trying to derail these efforts. Some properties do work extensively to negate ambush marketing efforts. The IOC identifies one of the benefits of being an official sponsor is that it will provide ambush marketing protection (http://www.olympic.org/sponsorship?tab=1). Gerhard Heiberg, chairman of the IOC Marketing Commission commented on ambush practices, stating, "Ultimately, companies which try to create the false impression that they are an official partner of the Olympic Games, or create a false association with the Olympic Games, are cheating Olympic athletes. It is important that the public is made aware of these organizations and how they are depriving the Olympic Games and sport development around the world of essential support" (Shipley, 2010, p. D8).

Organizations such as the IOC and FIFA are now forcing the countries that are holding the Olympics or the World Cup to pass legislation to address ambush marketing concerns (Burton & Chadwick, 2009; Grady, McKelvey, & Bernthal, 2010). Researchers have provided an overview of Olympic sponsorship legislation (Ellis, Gauthier, & Seguin, 2011; Grady et al., 2010; Palomba, 2011). Grady, McKelvey, and Bernthal (2010) document that since the 2000 Summer Olympics in Sydney, Australia, in the bidding process for the Olympics the IOC requires that a host country and city enact legislation to protect "the commercial interests of the Olympic movement and its official sponsors" (pp. 146–147). These protections include trademark, advertising, services, and sales. The legislation for the London 2012 Summer Olympics created two groups of banned words. In the first group were: "games," "two thousand and twelve," "2012," and "twenty twelve." In the second group were: "gold," "silver," "bronze," "London," "medals," " sponsor," and "summer." The law was violated if non-sponsors use any of the words from the first group in combination with any of the words from the second group (Grady et al., 2010; Palomba, 2011). The London Organizing Committee for the Olympic Games did not permit a local real estate agency from having a window display that featured the Olympic rings made from plastic gym ropes and Olympic torches from "for sale" signs. The London Committee also stopped a butcher from displaying sausages in the shape of Olympic rings (Grady & McKelvey, 2012). In another example of trying to limit connotative language, the NFL has tried to trademark the term "The Big Game" as a way to prevent non-official sponsors from trying to link their brand to the Super Bowl (Burton & Chadwick, 2009).

Finally, there are reactive strategies, such as a "name and shame" campaign that publicly identifies that the ambush marketing company is not an official sponsor of the property. Burton and Chadwick (2009), however, question if consumers were able to notice the ambush marketer's attempts, pointing out that any "name and shame" efforts provide further brand exposure and attention to the ambush marketer. For the Atlanta 1996 Summer Olympics, the Atlanta Committee for the Olympic Games budgeted $10 million for policing ambush marketing. The committee announced prior to the Olympics that if an ambush marketing practice was identified that it would start a "name and shame" campaign against the company with advertisements that would feature headlines such as "Every Time a Company Runs an Ad Like This, Our U.S. Olympic Team Loses" (Myerson, 1996) or "How do you feel about cheating in the Olympics" (Hiestand, 1996). The advertisements would include the name, address, and phone number of the ambush marketing company's CEO, and the company would be listed on the Atlanta Committee for the Olympic Games Web site.

To further illustrate that the Olympic governing bodies publicly support their sponsors in confronting ambush marketing, official sponsor McDonald's was upset when it considered a commercial broadcast on NBC during the 2010 Vancouver Winter Olympics by Subway that featured swimmer Michael Phelps an ambush attempt on its sponsorship with the Olympics (Mickle, 2011). The Subway commercial featured Phelps swimming through the wall of an indoor pool and down a street past a Subway restaurant "so he can get to where the action is this winter." A map flashed on the screen to demonstrate Phelps' route and his apparent destination of Vancouver. Lisa Baird, chief marketing officer of the USOC, argued, "There's clearly a right way to use (Olympic athletes) and a way that associates with the Olympics that is not OK. We're watching it very vigilantly" (Mickle, 2010, p. 4). She added, "The fundamental issues is, we want to protect our sponsors' rights, because it's only through the financial generosity of our sponsors and donors that our athletes can compete" (Shipley, 2010, p. D8).

Subway issued a statement, retorting, "Subway disagrees with the USOC's perspective and the conclusions being drawn from it. We are well within our rights of utilizing our marketing assets, which include Michael Phelps who has been a fan of Subway for many years. Since late 2008, Phelps has been part of several Subway marketing campaigns and we are looking forward to continuing to work him throughout 2010 and beyond" (Mickle, 2010, p. 4). Phelps' agent, Peter Carlisle, added, "Subway's been a great supporter of Michael and we abide by the rules. We try to make the most we can within the space left for athletes. Through deals we generate in that space, these athletes get the funding necessary to compete" (Mickle, 2010, p. 4).

The USOC also took umbrage in 2010 with Verizon for an advertisement it used during the Olympics. Verizon reached an agreement with United States speedskating that lasted only four months, but allowed the company to use a United States speedskater in a commercial that had the speedskater using Verizon's 3G network to achieve victory. In the commercial, USOC official telecommunications partner, AT&T, is seen as slowing down a competing speedskater (Mickle, 2010).

A final reactive strategy is a lawsuit against the company that is engaging in the ambush marketing campaign. In one legal example, the New Zealand Olympic Association brought suit against telecommunications ambusher, Telecom New Zealand, which used the word "ring" in the context of Olympic rings in its advertisements. In claiming consumers did not make the link, the judge ruled against the New Zealand Olympic Association (Burton & Chadwick, 2009; Hoek & Gendall, 2002).

Overall, Seguin and O'Reilly (2008) found that Olympic sponsors are more concerned with advertising clutter than ambush marketing. Brand exposure, awareness, and image transfer, however, are results that might not occur if either advertising clutter or ambush marketing are not controlled for, thus hindering the sponsorship strategy. With brand image transfer from the team or athlete that the fans love to the sponsor who is supporting that team or athlete as an objective, any confusion as to who is the official sponsor is problematic.

League and Team Conflict: The Legal Battles

Another potential hindrance to a successful sponsorship is that while leagues are selling exclusive sponsorships in a variety of product categories, their teams are permitted to sell sponsorships within the same product category to different companies than those that entered into a sponsorship agreement with the league. So Major League Baseball can have Pepsi as its official soft drink sponsor, but the Boston Red Sox can have Coca-Cola as their official sponsor. The multiple entry points highlight the complexity of the sports sponsorship industry. As noted in Chapter Four, there are positives for sponsors in the system that allows for multiple entry points with a property, most notably the ability for the sponsor to be more efficient in terms of cost and placement for a specific target audience. Having multiple sponsors within the same product category, however, creates a communication conflict that could potentially result in consumer confusion as to which company is the official sponsor of which property (Fortunato & Melzer, 2008; Graham, 1997; Shani & Sandler, 1998). Recognizing the wrong brand as an official sponsor negates some of the positive attributes of the sponsorship strategy. O'Keefe and Zawadzka (2011) argue that being a team sponsor may be more valuable than a sponsorship at the league level, as the league level does not invoke the same level of passion as sponsoring an individual team. They point out that fans often wear apparel of their favorite teams rather than the league.

Conflict occurs when a league-sanctioned event, such as the All-Star Game, is played at an arena where the team is sponsored by a different company from the league's official sponsor in the same product category. In 2000, Coca-Cola was the official soft drink sponsor of the NHL when the league awarded its All-Star Game in 2001 to be played at the arena in Denver—the Pepsi Center (Kiszla, 2001; Dater, 2000). Coca-Cola would force the Pepsi name to be removed from the All-Star tickets and league officials would refer to the arena in generic terms, such as "the home of the Colorado Avalanche" (Kiszla, 2001, p. D1). It would be Pepsi that retained the pouring rights for the game.

The ability for teams to sell their own exclusive sponsorships was notably challenged by Jerry Jones, the owner of the Dallas Cowboys. In 1993 Coca-Cola signed a five-year, $250 million deal with the NFL to be the league's official soft drink sponsor (Roush, 1995). Through this agreement for the 1994 NFL season, Coca-Cola had the pouring rights to all 30 teams' stadiums. Everything changed in August 1995 when the Dallas Cowboys reached an agreement with Pepsi for the pouring rights to Texas Stadium for an estimated $20 million over ten years (Barboza, 1995; Winters, 1995). Jones would tell those gathered at the press conference announcing the deal that he would be "drinking Pepsi, selling Pepsi, and promoting Pepsi" (Barboza, 1995, p. D8). In addition to pouring rights, Pepsi received stadium signage. Pepsi could not, however, use the NFL or Dallas Cowboys logos on cups or in advertisements. All Pepsi promotional material had to make reference to being the official soft drink of Texas Stadium (Roush, 1995). Within weeks of the Cowboys completing their deal with Pepsi, the New England Patriots also reached an agreement to have Pepsi become the pouring rights holder for their stadium (Winters, 1995).

What the Cowboys' contract did was start an assault on the sponsorship arrangement that the NFL had with its teams. NFL Properties had been established to sell the rights to the NFL shield as well as all team logos. The money derived from those agreements would then be split equally amongst all teams. Each team earned approximately $3.5 million from NFL Properties in 1995 (Weisman, 1995). Jerry Jones was arguing that the Cowboys, who led the NFL in merchandise sales with 24.5 percent, deserved a larger share of revenue rather than the equitable distribution (Bell, 1995). Jones was clearly challenging the NFL system and fought for each team to control its local sponsorship deals. Jones stated, "Teams can handle their marketing and sponsorships so much more effectively and can give so much more value than for that to be handled out of the NFL New York office. It's a simple issue: If you want to be a partner with this organization, you've got to come to Dallas, not Park Avenue" (Bell, 1995, p. 12c).

In September of 1995 Jones escalated the battle with the league when he reached a seven-year sponsorship agreement with Nike (Rhoden, 1995). The deal was announced prior to the season's opening Monday night football game, in which the Cowboys were playing in New York against the Giants. At one point during the game, Jones would stand alongside Phil Knight, Nike owner, who was wearing a Cowboys cap on the Dallas sideline. Jones told the press after the game about the timing of the announcement, "We knew the nation would be looking" (Rhoden, 1995, p. B15). Nike, which did not have any apparel agreement with the NFL, was to supply the Cowboys team uniforms and their coaches' jackets, shirts, and pants (Rhoden, 1995). Nike would soon have stadium signage at Texas Stadium and have locations in the stadium that sold Nike-branded Cowboys merchandise (Weisman, 1995). Jones continued to hold the position, "Ultimately, all logos, the helmet and star associated with the Cowboys will be handled by the Dallas Cowboys and not the marketing arm of the NFL" (Myers, 1995, p. 48).

The NFL countered the team-level sponsorship agreements by Jones with a $300 million lawsuit. The lawsuit asked the court "to order the defendants to stop violating their agreements with NFL Properties regarding club marks and logos," and "to prevent the defendants from signing any additional deals that undermine existing NFL sponsorship or licensing contracts" (Myers, 1995, p. 48). At the time Roger Headrick, president of the Minnesota Vikings and chairman of NFL Properties, argued, "The Cowboys have made it clear through their recent actions and statements that they want to change the basic manner in which NFL Properties does business" (Myers, 1995, p. 48). Paul Tagliabue, then commissioner of the NFL, pointed out that the league's sponsors were telling the league "that it was intolerable to have the company being ambushed in this way" (Brennan, 1995, p. D1). Tagliabue added, "the NFL has set some very clear-cut ways of doing business which have distinguished it from all other leagues and made it as great as it is. It's a philosophy and a commitment to do business in a certain way which has been very successful" (Brennan, 1995, p. D1).

With the lawsuit pending, developments would alter the situation: Jones would reach agreements with Kentucky Fried Chicken, Pizza Hut, Taco Bell, and AT&T, Nike would sign on as an official NFL sponsor, and several teams would enter into agreements for their own sponsorship deals (Heath, 1996; Sandomir, 1996). The lawsuit was settled out of court with the Cowboys, and subsequently all teams, being permitted to sell their own individual sponsorships.

In another recent legal battle that highlighted the concept of exclusivity, the conflict between league and team sponsors was challenged in court in the American Needle lawsuit against the NFL. In 2000, NFL Properties entered into an agreement with Reebok on a ten-year, $250 million contract to be the league's exclusive licensee for uniforms and the manufacturer of trademark headgear for all 32 NFL teams. The exclusive contract with Reebok prohibited NFL teams from contracting with their own headwear manufacturers. The NFL, thus, did not renew its contract with American Needle, a suburban Chicago clothing company that had been manufacturing and selling headgear with NFL team logos for more than 20 years. American Needle filed suit against the NFL, claiming that the league violated antitrust laws, which are designed to protect against monopolies or restraints of trade (Kinter, 1973; LaBletta, 2001; Petty, 1992; Wright, 1999).

According to American Needle, the NFL hindered competition by acting as and creating a monopoly in its exclusive agreement with Reebok. The NFL countered that it should be permitted to protect and generate revenue from its logos and trademarks. In a brief submitted to the Court, Reebok pointed out that American Needle could have won the bid for the NFL contract. Reebok claimed in its brief, "The antitrust laws are designed to protect competition — not individual competitors. Having failed to win its license renewal in the marketplace, American Needle cannot now use the antitrust laws to compel a different result" (Brief of Respondent, Reebok Int'l Ltd., *Am. Needle v. NFL*, 538 F.3d 736, 7th Cir. 2008). The case was ultimately heard in the United States Supreme

Court on the question of whether the NFL could stand trial under antitrust laws. The Supreme Court unanimously ruled on the side of American Needle and the case was sent back to the lower court where a trial can proceed (for a detailed account of the *American Needle* case and its implications see Fortunato & Martin, 2010; LeBlanc, 2010; Schwartz, 2011).

The final important variable in teams selling their own sponsorships is that while league-wide sponsorship revenue is shared equally among all teams, individual team sponsorship revenue is not shared and remains with the team. Certainly sponsorships sold by the New York Yankees, the Dallas Cowboys, or the Los Angeles Lakers will generate more revenue than sponsorships sold by the Kansas City Royals, Jacksonville Jaguars, or Memphis Grizzlies. The disparity in revenue from local sponsorships has implications on the league's competitive balance (Fortunato, 2001; Reese & Nagel, 2001).

League and Team Conflict in Practice

In the NFL, league sponsors acquire the rights to the NFL shield and the collective use of all 32 team logos. So, for example, an official sponsor can do a retail display that features all 32 team logos. These league-wide official sponsors cannot pick and choose individual team logos in their promotions. It is important to note that a league-wide sponsor can also sponsor any team it chooses, but it requires reaching an agreement with that team. The official league sponsors can use selective team logos if the sponsor has reached an agreement with that individual team as well. To demonstrate the league and team sponsorship exclusivity conflict in more detail, the beer sponsorship market within the NFL is examined. The NFL beer market is of particular interest because the league previously had a system of one sponsor representing the league and all of its teams. Anheuser-Busch and Miller were national sponsors giving them the ability to use individual team trademarks in their promotions. In 2002, the NFL changed to a system in which the league would pursue a league-wide beer sponsor, but the teams could pursue their own beer sponsors in their local markets.

In 2002, Molson Coors became the official beer sponsor for the NFL, agreeing to a four-year contract valued at $240 million. Coors continued in its role as official sponsor of the NFL when it extended its contract through 2010 in a deal worth over $500 million (Kaplan & Lefton, 2005). As the official beer sponsor of the NFL and the Super Bowl, Coors aired commercials during the regular season and playoffs games, had in-game billboards, and had game program advertisements using the trademark logos of the NFL and Super Bowl. Coors was also recognized as the presenting sponsor of the NFL's "Opening Kickoff Weekend," the NFL Draft, and Super Bowl week on the NFL Network, which included customized opening and closing, presenting sponsor billboards, and on-set logo exposure during the broadcast of *NFL Total Access*, the NFL Network's flagship show. Through its sponsorship of the Super Bowl Coors had "The Road to the Super Bowl" contest, which featured several fan-driven promotions where fans through text messaging or by logging onto the Coors Light Web site entered a promotional code that appeared on product packaging. Coors Light then randomly drew entries with fans winning NFL merchandise or trip packages and tickets to an NFL regular season game, a Monday Night

Football game, a Thanksgiving Day game, a playoff game, the Pro Bowl, the NFL Draft, or the Super Bowl (Fortunato & Melzer, 2008).

The ability to be associated with the NFL through its individual teams still remained. The teams' beer sponsors obtain the use of the team logo on product packaging and in other promotional communication materials and have point-of-purchase pouring rights at the stadium. Some teams have multiple beer sponsors. While Coors was the official beer of the NFL and the Super Bowl, other beer companies had sponsorships with the majority of teams. Anheuser-Busch had agreements with 28 teams. Miller Brewing sponsored four teams: the Chicago Bears, Dallas Cowboys, Green Bay Packers, and Minnesota Vikings. In making a distinction between league and team trademark use, Tony Ponturo, then vice-president of global media and sports marketing for Anheuser-Busch, commented, "If you are telling me I've got to make a choice between the league and club marks, I am taking the clubs" (Kaplan & Lefton, 2005, p. 59).

Through its 28 team sponsorships, Anheuser-Busch used the logos of those teams to produce 78 different team-specific packaging combinations on 12 million cases of Budweiser and Bud Light (Lefton, 2006). Anheuser-Busch also hosted tailgate parties and party zones outside the stadiums where visitors could enter sweepstakes to win game tickets or team merchandise. Non-NFL sponsors such as Anheuser-Busch and Miller were permitted to buy commercial time during NFL games as well. Ponturo explained the Anheuser-Busch strategy: "We (Anheuser-Busch) are confident that this local team sponsorship strategy, supported by national advertising, resonates with fans and helps them make the connection between our brands, their favorite team, and professional football" (Kaplan & Lefton, 2005, p. 59).

To exacerbate the league and team conflict, the broadcast networks carrying the games sell exclusive sponsorships as well. Anheuser-Busch has been the exclusive sponsor of the Super Bowl television broadcast since 1989. Since these are exclusive agreements with the networks, even when Coors was the official beer sponsor of the NFL and the Super Bowl it was unable to advertise during the broadcast of the most watched television program of the year. Anheuser-Busch was, therefore, able to reach more consumers during the Super Bowl than the actual official sponsor of the game. With that type of exposure Anheuser-Busch was also able to capture the last impression of the NFL football season. Confusion may have been the result for many consumers watching the telecast who mistakenly thought that Budweiser was the official beer sponsor of the NFL, meaning that people were likely to associate Anheuser-Busch's brands with the NFL (Fortunato & Melzer, 2008; McCarthy, 2005).

Beginning in 2011, Anheuser-Busch secured the official beer sponsorship to the NFL in a six-year contract valued at $1.2 billion, paying double what MillerCoors had been paying (Lefton, 2010a). Anheuser-Busch uses its Bud Light brand as the official beer sponsor of the NFL, obtaining rights to all NFL trademarks, such as the NFL shield, and the collective use of all 32 team logos. Dave Peacock, president of Anheuser-Busch, stated, "The NFL is the biggest, most watched sport in North America, and we are proud of Bud Light, the world's largest selling beer, to be the league's official beer sponsor" (Anheuser-Busch, press release, May 4, 2010). He added, "We continue to invest in the things that support our brands, and our efforts to manage costs enable us to seize opportunities like this one. We look forward to leveraging this investment to connect our Bud

Light brand more deeply with NFL fans" (Anheuser-Busch, press release, May 4, 2010). In losing out on the NFL beer sponsorship contract, Jackie Woodward, vice president of marketing for MillerCoors, explained, "We decided that the money that would have been required to renew could be better used elsewhere. The investment needed to be at a level that made sense" (Lefton, 2010a, p. 32). MillerCoors had sponsorships with 21 NFL teams in 2011.

For Anheuser-Busch the agreement with the league bolstered its 28 team contracts and Super Bowl television commercial exclusivity. For the start of the 2011 season Bud Light introduced limited-edition 24-pack, 12-ounce cans in the 28 cities, featuring the local team's logos. In the four cities in which Bud Light is not the official team sponsor, special 2011 NFL Kickoff packaging was created, the first beer package to celebrate the start of the NFL season (Anheuser-Busch press release, September 7, 2011). A commemorative Bud Light Super Bowl bottle was also created.

Bud Light commercials during NFL game telecasts in 2011 featured fans in several team jerseys and apparel in stadium settings. The team jerseys used in these commercials were those of teams that were also sponsored by Bud Light. Even though Bud Light is the official sponsor of the NFL, NFL game telecasts are littered with commercials for both Miller Lite and Coors Light. The Coors Light commercials during 2011 NFL game telecasts featured former NFL head coaches Mike Ditka, Herman Edwards, Dennis Green, and Jim Mora and ended with Coors being referred to as "the game's most refreshing beer." In the soft-drink category, Pepsi has a goal of reaching a marketing deal with an NFL player in every city so that it can run some local advertisements and promotions related to the sport even if the team in that city is not sponsored by Pepsi (Lefton, 2013b).

Anheuser-Busch will continue as the exclusive sponsor of the television broadcast of the Super Bowl through 2014. In the 2011 Super Bowl, Anheuser-Busch had one 60-second commercial for its Stella Artois brand, one 60-second commercial for Budweiser, and three 30-second commercials for Bud Light. Estimates are that beer sales during the week of the Super Bowl increase as much as 20 percent above a typical week in January or February (*Buffalo News*, 2011). Dave Peacock, Anheuser-Busch president, commented on the overall NFL strategy, stating, "We wouldn't have done it if the payoff wasn't there" (*Buffalo News*, 2011, p. C6).

This conflict between league-wide sponsors and team sponsors occurs in every sport. The conflict between leagues and teams is again a function of what the league and the sponsor allow as a result of the negotiation process. In its sponsorship with Major League Soccer, Anheuser-Busch signed a four-year extension in 2011 that for the first time in the league's 15-year history provides the teams with the ability to also sell pouring rights to local brewers (Dreier, 2011b). For example, the Portland Timbers have a contract with local brewer, Widmer Brothers, which produces a Timbers-themed seasonal ale with the bottle label having the team's logo. Anheuser-Busch does have agreements with ten Major League Soccer teams for the 2012 season (Spanberg, 2012a). Kathy Carter, president of Soccer United Marketing, a firm that assisted in the negotiation between Anheuser-Busch and Major League Soccer, explained, "Our clubs were really clamoring for the ability to go deeper in negotiations with local beer companies because they want to grow the young adult fan base. Anheuser-Busch recognized this and allowed (MLS) to do that" (Dreier, 2011b, p. 4).

In 2012 in several product categories non–Major League Baseball sponsors were able to use their team sponsorships to activate through stadium giveaway item promotions. Coca-Cola had the most activation dates in 2012 of any brand, with 69 dates through its sponsorship with seven teams. Pepsi, the official Major League Baseball sponsor, had 44 activation dates with nine of the sixteen teams that it sponsors. In the beer category, Major League Baseball sponsor, Anheuser-Busch, had 28 promotional dates with eight different teams, but MillerCoors activated on 38 different dates with seven teams (Broughton, 2012b).

Beyond stadium promotions, team sponsors certainly try to develop unique and engaging activation programs. MasterCard has been a sponsor of Major League Baseball since 1997 and in 2011 extended its agreement for an additional five years. Visa, however, has a partnership with only one Major League Baseball team, the San Francisco Giants. When the Giants won the 2010 World Series, Visa was able to capitalize on their success by becoming the presenting sponsor of a five-month tour of the Giants World Series trophy.

Sports leagues are structured economically to depend on the revenue generated through the selling of sponsorships. The teams are also reliant on the sponsorship revenue stream. The broadcast networks that are paying the leagues exorbitant rights fees to televise that league's games also need to sell sponsored elements within the game telecasts to recoup some of their investment. Sponsorship rights originate with the league. For the sports league there are basically two options: having league, team, and broadcast sponsorships being sold to different companies within the same product category or a sponsorship system of collectively pooling and selling all of the league, team, and broadcast rights to only one sponsor. Leagues will ultimately choose the option that is in their financial interest. The thinking of the league on behalf of the teams in allowing them to sell their own individual sponsorships could be that if a company loses out on the league sponsorship it might be apt to pay more to secure a sponsorship with a team, or the broadcast network, so as to still be associated with the league. For the most part, the leagues do not interfere with their teams' selling of sponsorships. If the team could make more money from a sponsorship by selling it to a particular company, it does not matter if that company is an official league sponsor or a competitor within that product category.

In terms of leagues allowing teams to sell their own sponsorships, a distinction based on the product category and how the audience consumes the product has emerged. To illustrate this point, in the NFL teams sell their own beer sponsorships, but the activation with the team is limited by geography. The NFL, however, places restrictions on teams and grants an exclusive league contract with an apparel manufacturer, the issue addressed in the *American Needle* court case. The distinction here is that in the apparel product category technology has eliminated the concept of geographical markets with consumers easily able to purchase apparel of any team through numerous Web sites, including nfl.com.

A company, of course, always has the option to purchase all of the rights: league, team, and broadcast (nothing other than cost precludes a league-wide sponsor from obtaining the rights to all teams and in all communication vehicles). For the sponsors it could even be argued that through this system of multiple sponsorships being sold they can better choose the specific property (league, team, or broadcast) that best fits the company's promotional communication needs and their sponsorship budget. If the leagues and their teams continue to have a full roster of sponsors and generate higher revenues by selling sponsorships to different companies within the same product category, there will not be a change in how sponsorships are offered. Selling sponsorships to different companies within the same product category only becomes a problem for the league if the confusion on the part of the consumer negatively affects sponsors so much so that the league starts to lose some of its sponsors. Therefore, sports leagues have to continuously evaluate how the system of selling sponsorships to different companies within the same product category compares with the possibility of alienating a current or prospective sponsor and jeopardizing a partnership.

Non-Rights Holder Media Conflict

Beyond the network that is a rights holder and televising the actual game or event in which elements can be sold to companies other than league sponsors as articulated in Chapter Four, popular broadcast or Internet locations sell sponsorships for elements surrounding their media content. There are many media outlets, and so many ways that a brand can associate itself with an event and reach the sports audience without having to pay the high sponsorship-rights fee to the league or team. Keith Turner, NFL senior vice president of sponsorship and media sales, calls the opportunity to purchase sponsorship through media without paying any rights "the biggest challenge" that the leagues contend with in selling sponsorships (personal communication, February 15, 2012).

ESPN *SportsCenter*, for example, provides numerous opportunities. To counter Anheuser-Busch's sponsorship of the NFL, during the NFL season in 2011 Miller Lite sponsored the Monday evening 6:00 P.M., eastern, ESPN *SportsCenter* prior to the network showing that evening's Monday Night Football game. On Monday the *SportsCenter* show was referred to as "Monday Kickoff presented by Miller Lite." During *SportsCenter* there was a Miller Lite "Taste greatness" segment in which statistics of great NFL performances were provided. Miller Lite also had several commercial bumpers coming in and out of commercials in which the company logo appeared with an announcer voice-over.

A Web site such as Yahoo.com is a location where fans consume sports-related content, creating an opportunity for a brand to not have to pay any sponsorship-rights fee, but still receive brand exposure to the sports audience. Although the companies advertising on these Web sites cannot use league or team imagery or logos, a connection in the minds of the audience might still be fostered. Dan Donnelly, executive vice president and managing director with Starcom MediaVest, explains that in the technological environment when "digital did not exist, exclusivity on broadcast truly meant exclusivity." Donnelly explains the sponsorship dilemma of the current environment being "it is harder to maintain exclusivity and it is much easier to activate without exclusivity" (personal communication, December 19, 2011).

For the 2012 Summer Olympics several media companies, such as FoxSports.com, Sports Illustrated, Yahoo!, and USA Today Sports Media Group, would debut Olympic-themed Web sites and dedicated pages. These Web sites offer companies a plausible alternative to television rights holder, NBC. NBC required advertisers to purchase television commercial time if they wanted to purchase digital advertising on NBCOlympics.com, forcing the companies that did not want to purchase television time to go to other media companies' Web sites. Some IOC and USOC sponsors also made purchases on alternate Web sites in addition to their promotional communication purchases on NBC. IOC and USOC sponsor Procter & Gamble purchased time on Yahoo!, whose Web site had customized content for 25 countries in multiple languages. USOC sponsors Citi and DeVry purchased time on FoxSports.com (Mickle & Ourand, 2012).

These additional online opportunities have forced the leagues to extensively promote their own Web sites. With sponsors having to buy time on the league's Web sites, there is certainly an incentive to drive visitors to those Web sites. One of the major reasons for visiting sports Web sites has been the explosion in popularity of fantasy sports. Leagues promote the fantasy games that they provide on their Web sites as a way of helping their sponsors and diluting the potential effect that non-league sponsors might be gaining from advertising on Web sites such as Yahoo!.

In using print media opportunities, prior to the 1996 Atlanta Summer Olympics, non-sponsor Nike purchased an eight-page fold-out insert in *Sports Illustrated* and *Rolling Stone* that featured the slogan "We don't sell dreams, we sell shoes" (Myerson, 1996, p. D1). Dave Fogelson, a Reebok spokesman, criticized Nike, stating "Shame on them. They're undercutting people and companies and products and services that will go to make the ultimate success of their own athletes, if they thought about it." Donna L. Gibbs, a Nike spokeswoman, countered, "We don't rent an event every two years. We stand by our athletes 365 days a year" (Myerson, 1996, p. D1).

Company Scandal

Another important hindrance to consider is if either the property or the sponsoring brand is involved in a scandal, putting the other entity in an uncomfortable position. Jensen (2007) chronicles the story of the Houston Astros and Enron. In 2000, the Astros entered into a 30-year, $100 million deal with Enron to have their ballpark named Enron Field. In December, 2001, Enron declared bankruptcy, and company officials were indicted on charges of bank fraud, money laundering, and insider trading. The allegations included that Enron officials were aware of the company's impending collapse and sold their shares of stock at a profit without issuing a warning to employees and shareholders, whose shares of the stock became worthless. After legal action in bankruptcy court, the Astros were able to remove the Enron name and seek another naming rights partner. In 2002, the Astros reached a 30-year, $170 million deal with Minute Maid, a subsidiary of Coca-Cola, for the ballpark to be named Minute Maid Park (Jensen, 2007). Jensen (2007) provides other examples of corporate bankruptcy causing complications for teams and their stadium naming rights partners, such as Trans-World Airlines and the dome in St. Louis that is the home of the NFL's Rams.

Basinger (2004) found that athletic scandal can lead to an economic loss for a university. In the wake of the Penn State University sexual abuse scandal that led to the dismissal of legendary head football coach Joe Paterno, Cars.com cancelled its presenting sponsorship of Saturday afternoon college football on ESPN for the subsequent two weeks, in which Penn State was scheduled to appear. As a result of the Penn State scandal, Sherwin-Williams paint company, which had put its logo on the backdrop during press conferences, did not have its logo appear in that location after the incident became public. Penn State also removed the sponsors' page from its athletic Web site (Smith, 2011d). For the 2012 football season, State Farm decided it would not directly support Penn State and pulled its advertising for home football games (Torre, 2012).

Fans of Rivals

Because sports fans are so passionate and loyal toward their teams there could be one final concern for sponsors—while the sponsor of a team will endear itself to that team's fans, that sponsorship might turn away customers who are not fans of or strongly dislike that particular team. While evidence has been provided that fans emotions could translate to supporting their favorite teams and players' sponsors, another potential hindrance could be the purposeful behavior of not buying the products of the teams' and players' sponsors that fans dislike. Would a fan of Jimmie Johnson purposely not purchase a brand that sponsors Tony Stewart? Would a fan of the New York Yankees purposely not purchase an item that has a Boston Red Sox logo? Or, in the same geographic region with their schools a mere ten miles from each other and competing in the same conference, would a fan of the University of North Carolina purposely not purchase an item that has a Duke University logo? When Seattle-based Alaska Airlines became the jersey sponsor of Seattle's Major League Soccer rival, the Portland Timbers, the company received hate mail (Botta, 2012b).

Hickman and Lawrence (2010) explain, "While sponsorship can win support from one team's fans, it can also repel the fans of the team's rivals" (p. 265). In what they refer to as the pitchfork effect, they claim that alienating fans of rival teams has the potential to occur. They contend, "This unintended outcome of corporate sponsorship—scorn from rival fans—could translate into a loss of sales if not clearly understood and managed well" (p. 266). In their study of fans of teams in the Big Ten Conference, Hickman and Lawrence (2010) found that "fans tend to evaluate their team's sponsoring brands favorably and the rival team's sponsors unfavorably" (p. 273).

Zillmann, Bryant, and Sapolsky (1989) recognize the sports fans' prominent characteristic of having favorite teams or players in their description of a disposition theory of sportsfanship. Their disposition theory claims that enjoyment of sports and athletic excellence "depends to some extent at least, on the particular person displaying such excellence, and on the particular team to which this person belongs. People applaud great play on the part of their favorite athletes and teams. The same excellence, the same mastery of skills, seems to be far less appreciated, possibly even deplored, when it is exhibited by disliked athletes or resented teams" (p. 256).

The disposition theory presents another characteristic of a sports fan: love of one team means hatred for others. Zillmann et al. (1989) point out, "Spectators are known 'to root' for players and teams, hoping and wishing that their party will succeed in defeating the opposition. By the same token, spectators appear to wish that the players and teams they dislike be defeated, and they seem to take pleasure in seeing the opposition humiliated and 'destroyed'" (p. 256). The disposition theory being applied to fan behavior has been conducted, with the love of a favorite team causing an interest in the games of rivals, leading to the behavior of watching the rivals' games on television (Fortunato, 2004). With the disposition theory leading to behavior being demonstrated, the theory might easily translate to behavior toward sponsors of disliked teams, in this case purposely not buying their products.

Finally, the performance of the team can potentially impact the perception of the sponsoring brand. Pope, Voges, and Brown (2009) state, "In contrast to advertising, wherein the marketer has a controlled message to convey, sponsorship includes the possibility of winning and losing, over which there is no control" (p. 7). They go so far as to recommend, "Managers who wish to change consumer's preexisting perceptions of brand quality should seriously consider team sponsorship, with the caveat that for team sponsorships, underperformance can negatively impact such assessments. It would appear that team sponsorship should be primarily considered for successful teams only" (p. 16). Gatorade has circumvented the need for one particular team or individual to win while capitalizing on the brand visibility and association of winning by creating Gatorade Victory Lane. Through a sponsorship agreement with the International Speedway Corporation for NASCAR races at its twelve tracks, including Daytona which hosts the Daytona 500, all winners of the races will receive their trophy in Gatorade Victory Lane (Mickle, 2012c).

From a team perspective, winning is certainly one element that assists in selling sponsorships. When the University of Connecticut men's basketball team won the national championship in 2011, sponsorship renewal was close to 100 percent, and sponsorship revenue increased by 20 percent (Lefton, 2011e). The New Jersey Devils playoff run to the Stanley Cup in 2012 produced more than $1 million in additional sponsorship revenue (Botta, 2012a). Of course, if the team is winning it is generally having higher stadium attendance, higher television viewership, more radio listeners, and more visits to its Web site as well. Staples' naming rights of the arena in Los Angeles has value not only because of the size of the Los Angeles market, but because the Lakers have been a championship-level franchise and constantly appear on national television. American Airlines sponsorship of the arena in Miami certainly received a boost when Lebron James signed with the Miami Heat, as the team has reached the NBA Finals in his first three seasons with the Heat, winning the championship in 2012 and 2013.

Chapter Eight

Sponsorship of Individuals

Beyond leagues, teams, and popular events, sponsors select individuals to promote and represent their brands. The use of athlete and celebrity endorsers for promotional communication purposes has been well discussed in the academic literature (Atkin & Block, 1983; Boyd & Shank, 2004; Erdogan, 1999; Erdogan, Baker, & Tagg, 2001; Friedman & Friedman, 1979; Jones & Schumann, 2004; Kamins, 1990; Ohanian, 1990, 1991; Till & Busler, 2000). McCracken (1989) simply defines a celebrity endorser as "any individual who enjoys public recognition and who uses this recognition on behalf of a consumer good by appearing with it in an advertisement" (p. 310). The selection of individual sponsors is along similar criteria to the decision making processes for the selection of other properties with variables such as reaching a target audience, cost, and brand association having to be considered. The hope is that the endorser will assist in brand exposure and brand recall and that the image of the endorser will be transferred to the sponsoring brand, thus having a positive influence on consumers' attitudes and ultimately their behavior.

Popular leagues and teams command high dollar amounts for their sponsorships; so do top athletes. Consider the following:

- Maria Sharapova signs an eight-year extension with Nike in 2010 valued at a total of $70 million (*Street & Smith's Sports Business Journal*, December 20–26, 2010).
- John Wall, NBA number one draft pick in 2010, signs a five-year, $25 million contract with Reebok (*Street & Smith's Sports Business Journal*, September 20–26, 2010).
- Usain Bolt, Olympic sprinter from Jamaica, has a four-year contract with Puma for $40 million (*Street & Smith's Sports Business Journal*, December 20–26, 2010).
- Derrick Rose, NBA All-Star with the Chicago Bulls, signs a fourteen-year, $225 million contract with Adidas in February, 2012 (*Sports Illustrated*, March 5, 2012).
- In November 2012, golfer Rory McIlroy reaches a contract worth at least a reported $200 with Nike (http://www.cbssports.com/golf/blog/eye-on-golf/20796847/report-rory-mcilroy-signs-deal-with-nike).

Researchers have commented on the effectiveness of using celebrity endorsers to achieve promotional communication business goals. Researchers have argued that the basic goal of promotional communication of increased brand awareness can be achieved through the use of endorsers (Carison & Donavan, 2008; Friedman & Friedman, 1979;

Kamins, 1990). For the assistance of brand awareness, Atkin and Block (1983) claim that consumers have a preconceived image of the endorser, and this image can be transferred to the endorsed brand. They found products that were endorsed by celebrities gained greater intent to purchase than non-celebrity endorsements. In other studies, Till (2001) claims that athlete endorsements influence the way consumers view the image of the sponsored brand. Stone, Joseph, and Jones (2003) found that through the use of an athlete endorser an emotional tie can be created between the athlete and the consumer, improving both brand awareness and the image of a company.

Again, similar to league or team sponsorship, the attributes of the person receiving the message must be taken into account in assessing how any promotional communication with an endorser will be received (Atkin & Block, 1983; Kahle & Homer, 1985; Petty et al., 1983). The Elaboration Likelihood Model can be applied in trying to articulate the effectiveness of an individual sponsorship. If the individual consumer has high involvement with the product category, he or she will still focus on the quality of the argument being presented and less on the endorser. However, if the individual has low involvement with the product, he or she may be more swayed by the attractiveness of the endorser. Petty et al. (1983) did report evidence that celebrity endorsers influence brand recall.

Endorser Characteristics

As for the characteristics of the endorser, the concepts of image congruence and functional congruence are certainly applied in the selection of individual sponsors by companies. The ideal scenario would be that there is both an image and functional congruence between the athlete and the brand. Michael Jordan's endorsements with Gatorade and Nike fit with this idea. However, similar to the sponsorship of league and team properties, having both an image and functional congruence is not always possible. This does not preclude sponsorships from being formed only on image congruence. Michael Jordan has endorsed brands such as Hanes and Ballpark hot dogs. In fact, again similar to league or team sponsorships, most individual endorsement sponsorships are solely on an image congruence basis.

Theories that focus on the concept of congruence between the individual endorsers and the sponsor have been proffered. One prominent theory of congruence is the match-up hypothesis, which suggests that endorsers are more effective if there is a fit between the individual and the brand that they are endorsing (Fink, Cunningham, & Kensicki, 2004; Kahle & Homer, 1985; Kamins, 1990; Till & Busler, 2000). The match-up hypothesis by definition also posits that an endorser will not be as beneficial if there is not a perceived fit. Such is the case if, for example, an athlete endorses a non-sports-related product.

The match-up hypothesis has been studied in multiple contexts (Koernig & Boyd, 2009; Till & Busler, 2000). In the evaluation of endorser and sponsor fit, congruency has largely focused on his or her attributes, such as expertise, trustworthiness, and attractiveness (Kamins, 1990; Ohanian, 1990; Till & Busler, 2000). It is important to note that these three variables are not mutually exclusive, and it would seem the opportunity exists for sponsors to strive for congruence on all of these variables if possible when selecting an endorser.

Expertise

The concept of expertise closely aligns with that of functional congruence in that the endorser actually uses the product. The functional congruence through an expert endorser can assist in elevating the sponsor as a quality brand by making the promotional communication seem more believable (Bush, Martin, & Bush, 2004; Kamins, Brand, Hoeke, & Moe, 1989; Till, 2001). Having the endorser be thought of as an expert by the audience has positively influenced their views of the brand (Kamins & Gupta, 1994; Till, Stanley, & Priluxk, 2008). Ohanian (1991) even found that perceived endorser expertise had a significant influence on consumers' intent to purchase the endorsed brand.

Expertise might, in fact, be the most important characteristic for an endorser to possess. Biswas, Biswas, and Das (2006) found in their study using high technology products, the endorsement using a perceived expert was more effective than a celebrity who was not considered an expert. This effect was exacerbated if the individual witnessing the message had a high knowledge of the technology product category.

Athletes offer an obvious congruence based on their expertise if they are endorsing a product that helps them play their sport. The real-life quality of sports and the ease with which the consumers can view these performances through the media enhance the communication of this functional congruence. Koernig and Boyd (2009) comment on the authenticity of athlete endorsers, stating, "Athletes present a special case as endorsers because our attitudes and knowledge about them derive not only from seeing them in contrived situations (e.g., movies or events), but also how they behave and perform in spontaneous situations on the field of play" (p. 26). Irwin, Sutton, and McCarthy (2002) claim that when a sports personality endorses a product, fans identify with the sport, the athlete, and the sponsor.

In one example of the athlete expertise characteristic, Till and Busler (2000) demonstrated that when an energy bar was promoted by an athlete rather than a celebrity, brand attitudes were more positive. They claim the fit that was derived through the expertise characteristic between the endorser and the product was the most important variable in influencing brand attitudes and purchase intent. In a more specific, practical example, Drane, Phillips, Williams, and Crow (2005) found the brand recall of Tiger Woods endorsed brands increased from 2000 through 2004. There was an overall increase in the intent to purchase products due to his endorsement over that same time period. Fans who play golf and watch golf demonstrated an even greater awareness and intent to purchase these brands because of Woods. Other researchers found higher purchase intentions for sports-related products even if the athlete was not very famous (Boyd & Shank, 2004; Yoon & Choi, 2005). Koernig and Boyd (2009) do, however, suggest informing consumers of a lesser known athlete's achievements in an attempt to evoke a more positive response for the brand and the endorser.

Individual Sponsors Activation

Activation of a sponsorship occurs for individual endorsers as well. Sponsors develop creative ways that an individual can further communicate about the brand and connect with consumers. In addition to its sponsorship of many universities, another strategy of Under Armour to gain prominence has been to have individual athletes represent the brand. Under Armour has activated these individual sponsorships in a way that shows the technology of its products and fulfills its brand mission of making "all athletes better through passion, design, and the relentless pursuit of innovation" (http://investor.under-armour.com/company/mission.cfm). Kevin Plank, the founder and CEO, often calls the athletes to personally persuade them to join Under Armour (Walker, 2011). As a new company, Under Armour's first endorsement deal was with the unknown Eric Ogbogu, a teammate of Plank at the University of Maryland who had a brief career with the Dallas Cowboys. Ogbogu would become the face of the brand in Under Armour's advertisements, delivering the slogan "We must protect this house."

Under Armour specifically targets first-year players. Often rookies are signed to their shoe and apparel contracts before they are even drafted into their respective leagues. Cam Newton, 2010 Heisman Trophy winner and quarterback of the undefeated national champion Auburn Tigers, reached his agreement with Under Armour in February 2011, two months prior to the NFL Draft. The fact that Newton had been using Under Armour products while in college was referred to in a statement by Newton upon his signing the agreement. Newton stated, "I have had great experience with Under Armour products during some very important events in my career, and I am looking forward to continuing my relationship with the Under Armour team as I prepare for the NFL" (Under Armour press release, February 23, 2011).

Under Armour is the official sponsor of the NFL Scouting Combine. By signing in February, Newton, along with Julio Jones, wide receiver from Alabama, would debut Under Armour's E39 compression shirt fitted with electronic touchpoints that send information to a device in the front of the shirt, referred to as the Bug, that holds the performance information. The E39 technology has the capability to measure speed, g-force, horsepower, heart rate, and breathing rate (Under Armour press release, February 25, 2011).

Under Armour takes a similar approach with players in the NBA, signing players as they are about to enter the league. From the NBA Under Armour reached agreements with the second pick in the 2011 Draft, Derrick Williams from the University of Arizona, and the ninth pick, Kemba Walker, leading scorer from the 2011 NCAA Champion University of Connecticut Huskies. Matt Mirchin, Under Armour senior vice-president of sports marketing, explained, "We have positioned ourselves as a brand for the next generation of athletes" (Walker, 2011, p. C1).

Under Armour does have a relationship with some more established and accomplished athletes, notably three-time Super Bowl champion quarterback Tom Brady and multiple–Olympic Gold Medal-winning swimmer Michael Phelps. Brady reached an agreement in November 2010 and appeared in various in-store and promotional communication campaigns. Of the Brady signing, Kevin Plank commented, "Tom Brady represents a lot of what Under Armour is all about. He's humble and hungry and continues to be focused on winning and getting better every single day. We're proud to have him in our brand" (Under Armour press release, November 8, 2010). Brady explained, "It was important for me to align with a brand that shares my values and helps me perform at my best. Under Armour makes cutting-edge products for the next generation and for athletes who compete at the highest level" (Under Armour press release, November 8, 2010).

Just as there are multiple reasons for sponsoring multiple properties, there are multiple congruence associations that are created when signing individual endorsers. For Michael Phelps, there was a geographical connection between the Baltimore native and the Baltimore-based Under Armour. Peter Carlisle, Phelps' agent, stated, "For Michael, this was really all about finding a way to work with a brand he loves. Michael and Under Armour both hail from Baltimore, which makes it a natural fit; but what really drives it is his affinity for Under Armour, its brand, products, and people" (Walker, 2011, p. C1).

One individual sponsorship activation program focuses not only on the athlete's playing ability, but his physical attributes. Similar to its Olympics sponsorship as a sponsor of the NFL, Procter & Gamble can matchup any of its brands with an NFL player. While Pittsburgh Steelers safety Troy Polamalu is an All-Pro player, it is his long hair flowing from his helmet that made him an ideal fit as an endorser for Procter & Gamble's Head & Shoulders brand shampoo.

The major activation of the sponsorship using Polamalu was the Polamalooza Mane Event, which was a weekly bracket-style tournament that featured eight NFL players competing for the title of most iconic NFL hairstyle of all time. Fans visited the created Web site, troyshair.com, to cast their vote. April Anslinger, North American Head & Shoulders brand manager, commented, "Our goal was to engage customers each week and have them come back and visit our site" (Bruell, 2011, p. 15). The sponsorship of Polamalu was supported through national advertising, and the contest specifically was promoted with paid integrations on ESPN's *Mike & Mike in the Morning* and ABC's *Jimmy Kimmel Live!* (Bruell, 2011). On the Web site fans could play interactive games as well as upload pictures of themselves where they could see how they would look with Polamalu's hair (Sciullo, 2010). Anslinger described, "The whole ad campaign is all so tongue-in-cheek. After all, why in the world would Mr. Polamalu, with that magnificent Samoan hairstyle, need one of the Head & Shoulders products called 'Hair Endurance,' that promotes 'fuller, thicker' hair? Clearly, Troy does not need to be using the product, but he does" (Sciullo, 2010, p. A1).

Procter & Gamble even paid for a $1 million Lloyd's of London insurance policy on Polamalu's hair (Sciullo, 2010). Polamalu had to submit hair samples and undergo an exam by a hair and scalp specialist. Polamalu would have had to lose at least 60 percent of his hair for the insurance policy to take effect, and his hair was only insured against on-field incidents. Jonathan Thomas, accident and health underwriter for the Watkins Syndicate at Lloyd's of London, explained, "In this case, he (Polamalu) has an income stream that comes from one particular part of his body that is clearly identifying, and thus can be justified (to insure)" (Sciullo, 2010, p. A1). April Anslinger described Procter & Gamble's paying for the insurance policy as "a brilliant idea, because at the end of the day we know hair, and we want to protect our (spokesman's) best asset" (Sciullo, 2010, p. A1).

To provide another example of an individual endorser activation program, the relationship between a NASCAR driver and a brand can be used. In NASCAR, the sponsor is very much identified with the car, as it is not uncommon for an announcer to put the driver, car number, and corporate sponsor in his or her description: Jimmie Johnson driving the number 48 Lowe's car. Jimmie Johnson is the five-time NASCAR Sprint Cup series champion. Through the success of Johnson, Lowe's received an estimated $130 million in media exposure from the 2007 through 2010 NASCAR Sprint Cup seasons. Johnson was first signed by Lowe's for the 2002 season, with Lowe's being his primary sponsor. The signing of Johnson was for a race team that would be co-owned by champion NASCAR driver, Jeff Gordon. Lowe's, thus, became an associate sponsor for Gordon and immediately was able to use the well-known Gordon in its retail campaigns and have him make appearances at Lowe's employee events while Johnson was establishing himself as a star (Mickle, 2011b). As an incentive for the then little-known Johnson, Lowe's offered to pay each pit crew member $480 (to match Johnson's number 48) every time Johnson won a race and $480 each time the pit crew completed a pit stop under a specified time.

In activating the Johnson sponsorship, the Team Lowe's Racing Fan Club was formed and amassed more than 1 million members who received a quarterly publication. A Lowe's racing credit card was established, with customers getting in-store discounts when they used the card after a Johnson victory. Lowe's changed the title of its hospitality event locations from the "Lowe's Zone" to "Jimmie Jams." The Jimmie Jams events often feature a musical concert and give employees and customers the chance to attend the event with Johnson (Mickle, 2011b). The Web site, www.lowesracing.com, provides the latest news and video updates for the Jimmie Johnson team. At the Web site there is a team store which sells model cars, apparel, and tailgating items. There is also a link to the Jimmie Jams event schedule. Finally, Lowe's is able to promote some of the brands sold at its stores, such as Valspar Paints and Kobalt Tools, by having those brand names recognized on Johnson's car. Lowe's signed a two-year extension with Johnson to be the primary sponsor for races through 2015.

Athlete and League/Team Conflict

Similar to how there can be a conflict between a league and a team having different official sponsors as documented in the previous chapter, there can be a conflict between the team sponsor and the sponsor of an individual athlete. To demonstrate how the rights are designated, Wise Foods Incorporated, a producer of potato chips, cheese doodles, and an assortment of other snack foods, is an official sponsor of the New York Mets and has signage on the outfield wall at Citi Field. Wise Foods had a sponsorship agreement with Jose Reyes, former Mets All-Star shortstop, when he played in New York. As an official sponsor of both the team and the player in this specific example, Reyes could appear on Wise product packaging in the Mets uniform. Similarly in the example used previously of Procter & Gamble and Troy Polamalu, as an official sponsor of the NFL as well, Procter & Gamble is able to feature Polamalu in his Steelers uniform in all of its promotional communication to better articulate the brand's association with the NFL and Polamalu. By contrast, while Pepsi, with its Aquafina bottled water brand, is an official sponsor of the New York Mets, David Wright, Mets All-Star third baseman, has his own sponsorship deal with Aquafina competitor, Vitamin Water. In any advertisements for Vitamin Water, Wright cannot be seen wearing a Mets hat or uniform, but rather a generic baseball uniform (Fortunato, 2011).

One of the most infamous instances of a conflict between an athlete associated with one sponsor and the property associated with another sponsor occurred during the 1992 Summer Olympics in Barcelona, Spain. Reebok had reached an agreement with the USOC where all athletes would appear on the medal stand wearing a Reebok warm-up suit. Members of the men's basketball "Dream Team" that were associated with Nike did not want to wear the Reebok warm-up suit. On the agreement that Michael Jordan signed with the USOC he even crossed out and initialed the clause that indicated he had to wear the Reebok warm-up suit. Jordan, out of loyalty to Nike, said to the press that there was "no way I'm wearing Reebok" (Katz, 1993, p. 57). Fellow Nike athlete Charles Barkley was quoted saying that he had "two million reasons not to wear Reebok" (Katz, 1993, p. 54). As it was determined that the athletes had to wear the Reebok warm-up suit if they were to accept their medals and stories began circulating that the All-Star players might not appear, Jordan and his agent, David Falk, finally arrived at a solution where the players would roll back their collars so the Reebok name would not be seen. To cover the Reebok emblem on the chest of the warm-up suit, Jordan would drape a large American flag over that side of his body (Katz, 1993).

In other examples of conflict between an athlete and an event sponsor, when Tony Stewart won the Pepsi 400 in July 2006, he told the television audience that Coca-Cola, a sponsor of Stewart's, "tastes a hell of a lot better" (Johnson, 2006). Upon winning the Acura Classic tennis tournament in 2007, Maria Sharapova was awarded a 2007 Acura. Sharapova, laughing, told the crowd, "I don't know what I can do with the car, because Range Rover is my sponsor. Maybe I'll have to put it in the garage and leave it so Range Rover doesn't get mad" (Johnson, 2006). NFL player Reggie Bush was fined $10,000 for a dress code violation in his rookie season when he wore Adidas cleats in his first preseason game, a cleat at the time not permitted by the NFL. Adidas soon after reached an agreement with the NFL allowing Bush and other players to wear the Adidas brand (Johnson, 2006). More recently, Brazilian soccer star Ronaldinho, sponsored by Coca-Cola, was released from his deal when he took a sip from a Pepsi can at a press conference. The sip cost Ronaldinho $760,000 (Kerr, 2012).

Wearing the wrong brand could be cause for termination of an endorsement deal. Such was the case when Under Armour dropped Dez Bryant, Dallas Cowboys wide receiver, from its roster of athletes when Bryant showed up to Cowboys training camp wearing Nike shoes (*Street & Smith's Sports Business Journal*, September 20–26, 2010). In one unique controversy, Marcus Jordan, Michael Jordan's son, wore his father's brand Nike shoes in a game while playing basketball for the University of Central Florida, an Adidas-sponsored school. Adidas subsequently canceled its six-year, $3 million agreement that was to run until 2015, claiming that the University of Central Florida, "has chosen not to deliver on its contractual commitment" (St. Petersburg Times, 2009).

To combat the dilemma of teams and players having different sponsors one trend in the NFL is for the teams to put into their rookie players' contracts language where the player has to first make a good-faith effort to sign with one of the team's sponsors before signing an agreement with a rival sponsor. Mullen (2012b) explains that one NFL player agent "thought such clauses could help clubs secure more lucrative sponsorships with companies if there were more favorable terms for the companies to sign the athlete to a deal, as well" (p. 8). Language was placed into the contract for 2012 NFL rookie quarterbacks Andrew Luck, Robert Griffin III, and Ryan Tannehill. The determination of what constitutes a good faith effort can be ambiguous and who ultimately makes that determination and any repercussions from a dispute remain unclear. Pat Dye, the agent for Tannehill, commented, "there is some obligation to use best efforts to work with team sponsors, but there is nothing preventing him from working with a company that is not a team sponsor" (Mullen, 2012b, p. 8).

Athlete Misbehavior

Athletes putting sponsors in precarious situations due to their misbehavior is another major concern. Researchers caution the influence that can come through the use of athlete endorsements can be both positive and negative (Koernig & Boyd, 2009; Louie & Obermiller, 2002; Miller & Laczniak, 2011; Till, 2001; Till & Shimp, 1998). Money, Shimp, and Sakano (2006) point out that "advertisers cannot control the personal lives of endorsers, and negative publicity surfaces on occasion" (p. 113). Miller and Laczniak (2011) add, "Using an athlete to promote a brand can have unanticipated negative effects on that brand given the unpredictable nature of their off-the-field behavior" (p. 508).

To counter the potential transgressions of athletes Solomon (2011) emphasizes proper selection, including the suggestion to use retired athletes. He explains, "Retired athletes can offer a brand or company a tie to sports and sports nostalgia but without the risk of losing focus on message points because of current performance on the field" (p. 11). He adds, "Brands also face fewer conduct issues when dealing with retired players" (p. 11). Overall, similar to sponsorship with all other properties, the importance for a company to wisely select the individual that it wants to associate its brand with prior to making a major financial investment cannot be understated.

Because many of the individuals who are product sponsors are well-known personalities, their indiscretions will always be a media story. Ito, Larsen, Smith, and Cacioppo (1998) claim that negative stories tend to be evaluated more critically than positive stories. When these negative events occur, pressure mounts for the sponsor to immediately drop the individual as a spokesperson. Groups often call for a boycott of the sponsor's products as a way for the for the public to demonstrate its anger toward the actions of the individual sponsor. These transgressions force the sponsor to make a quick decision as to whether to retain the individual, let the individual go, or not use the person in any of the company's promotional communication until the issue is resolved. Any decision made by the sponsor can be scrutinized. If the individual is not let go, the perception is that the sponsor is condoning the individual's actions. If the individual is dismissed, there could be concerns about a lack of due process being afforded the individual. Miller and Laczniak (2011) suggest that companies have a clearly planned exit strategy that details their actions in the event of a negative story and that they need to act quickly in distancing themselves from the endorser. Endorsers are asked to sign morality clauses, which provide clarity and allow the sponsor to drop the individual for his or her transgressions.

There are countless stories of companies dropping athletes as endorsers because of inappropriate behavior. Some recent examples include:

- Adidas dropping NBA All-Star Gilbert Arenas after he pled guilty to a felony gun charge (*Street & Smith's Sports Business Journal*, September 20–26, 2010)

- AT&T and Reebok dropping boxer Floyd Mayweather Jr. after he released an Internet video in which he made racist and homophobic comments against fellow boxer, Manny Pacquiao (*Street & Smith's Sports Business Journal*, September 20–26, 2010)
- Nutrisystem dropping NFL Hall of Famer Lawrence Taylor following his arrest on rape charges (*Street & Smith's Sports Business Journal*, September 20–26, 2010)
- McDonald's, Nutella, and Sprite did not retain Kobe Bryant after an allegation of rape emerged (Miller & Laczniak, 2011).
- Kellogg's did not renew the contract of Michael Phelps when a video of him smoking marijuana was uncovered (Miller & Laczniak, 2011).
- After a series of off-the-track incidents, which included driving 128 miles per hour in a 45 mph zone in May 2011, and on-the-track incidents including being placed on probation for a pit-road incident and intentionally wrecking another driver during a truck series race in November 2011, Mars Incorporated removed Kyle Busch from driving its M&M's car for the final two races of the 2011 NASCAR Sprint Cup season. Debra Sandler, chief consumer officer of Mars Chocolate North America, stated, "As a proud member of the racing community, Mars and the M&M's brand strongly support the partnership we have with Joe Gibbs Racing and are committed to NASCAR. Yet, Kyle's recent actions are unacceptable and do not reflect the values of Mars" (Mars press release, November 10, 2011).

One of the most covered scandals that forced a decision to be made by sponsors was the behavior of Tiger Woods. After news of his marital indiscretions surfaced, Tiger Woods was dropped by Accenture, AT&T, Gatorade, Gillette, and Tag Heuer. Woods was in the middle of a five-year contract he signed with Gatorade in 2007 worth an estimated $100 million. Gatorade had even developed a Woods-branded drink, Tiger Woods Focus. In a statement by Gatorade the company concluded, "We no longer see a role for Tiger in our marketing efforts and have ended our relationship. We wish him all the best" (McShane, 2010, p. 16). Estimates were that Woods lost between $23 and $30 million in annual sponsorship income, which was estimated at the time to be $100 million annually (Tharp, 2010).

In one dilemma that further demonstrates the potential conflict between event sponsors and individual sponsors, AT&T still sponsored a golf tournament that Tiger Woods served as host and had the Tiger Woods Foundation as one of the tournament's beneficiaries. Woods would not be designated as "host," and his name was removed from the tournament's promotional literature. To highlight the confusion, a CBS television press release which stated "Tiger Woods Hosts and Aims to Defend Title at AT&T National" was quickly changed to eliminate Woods' host designation (Dorman, 2010). Woods was still permitted to meet with corporate executives and children's groups at the event. Woods commented, "I'll still be a big part of the event and working hard behind the scenes as always. This is a great event for our foundation. We're very lucky and very excited that AT&T wanted to still be a part of this event, which is great" (Dorman, 2010, p. B14). When asked specifically about the decision by AT&T to continue its sponsorship of the tournament after dropping him personally as an endorser, Woods commented, "If you're going to have one over the other, you choose it this way. Because we're trying to help as many kids as we possibly can, and this is the way to do it, to bring awareness to the foundation" (Dorman, 2010, p. B14).

To compound his marital problems, Woods was suffering from a losing streak that would extend more than two years before his next tournament victory. The result was that the Tiger Woods apparel brand from Nike suffered a major decline in sales. Golfsmith's 76 stores in the United States in the first half of 2010 had a 7.5 percent drop in sales from the previous year for the Tiger Woods product line. The decline came at a time when over the same period total golf apparel sales rose 11 percent (Sherman, 2010).

Nike, which signed Woods in 1996, elected to retain Woods as its endorser. Shortly after the incident, Phil Knight, Nike chairman, stated of the company's decision to continue its relationship with Woods, "When his career is over, you'll look back on these indiscretions as a minor blip" (Weaver, 2009, p. 19). Coinciding with his return to playing competitive golf at the Masters in April of 2010, Nike produced a 30-second commercial that used the voice of Woods' deceased father, Earl, speaking about responsibility.

There could have been a fear on the part of Nike that if it didn't continue to support Woods, a competitor in that product category would step into that role. Such was the case with Rolex replacing Tag Heuer. When Tag Heuer dropped Woods in 2011, two months later Woods had a new endorsement contract with Rolex (Donegan, 2011). The press release from Rolex announcing the signing of Woods stated:

> This association pays tribute to the exceptional stature of Tiger Woods and the leading role he plays in forging the sport's global appeal. It also constitutes a joint commitment to the future. Rolex is convinced that Tiger Woods still has a long career ahead of him and that he has all the qualities required to continue to mark the history of golf. The brand is committed to accompanying him in his new challenges. Tiger Woods is joining the family of Rolex ambassadors, who are chosen for their talent, their perseverance, and their ability to communicate their passion for their sport [Rolex press release, October 5, 2011].

Earlier in the year Woods had reached an endorsement agreement with a Japanese brand, Kowa, to sponsor its heat rub used to relieve muscles and joint pain (Weigley, 2011). In 2011, Woods also reached a sponsorship agreement with Fuse Science, a sports nutrition start-up company. Fuse Science would have its name on Woods' golf bag during the Chevron World Challenge in December, 2011, a tournament won by Woods on a putt on the 18th hole — his first tournament victory since the 2009 incident. Woods explained about Fuse Science that its brand awareness "is not quite there yet, but that's where I can explain it to people" (Belson, 2011, p. 9B). Andrew Stroth, the attorney hired to negotiate the agreement between Fuse Science and Woods, added, "We purposely went after Tiger. He's one of the most iconic names in sports, and he is going to have a comeback" (Belson, 2011, p. 9B). As part of the endorsement Woods received a stake in Fuse Science. Athletes being given a stake in the company as part of their sponsorships has been previously done, such as Tom Brady with Under Armour and David Wright with Vitamin Water (Belson, 2011).

Conflict Repair Strategies

Wilson, Stavros, and Westberg (2008) provide some guidance for sponsors when dealing with an athlete in crisis, suggesting that at the time of signing a contract there should be a proactive development of programs designed to prevent a crisis, and there should be the development of a strategic plan of how a scandal will be handled. For example, Solomon (2011) stresses the awareness of social media and having endorsers who are media savvy and good citizens, stating, "The last thing you want is to have an athlete spokesperson be a loose cannon and tweet comments that can cause discomfort for your client" (p. 11).

Several scholars have put forth strategies for crisis management that can be applied to endorser transgressions. Benson (1988) points out that during times of crisis there is much at stake for an organization or individual and that the communication could drastically diminish the harm if managed properly or significantly increase the harm if mismanaged. When a crisis occurs restoration strategies are necessary because some responsibility for the offensive act is being attributed to the organization or individual (Benoit, 1995, 2000; Brinson & Benoit, 1999). In these occurrences communication strategies are necessary and heightened to explain not only what are the facts of the situation, but provide a feeling that steps are being taken to help ensure that the situation is being addressed and will not occur again.

Benoit (1995, 2000) presented the theory of image restoration that posits communication is goal driven and designed to maintain a positive reputation and repair a tattered image. Among the general defense strategies that organizations or individuals can implement are to apologize; to take corrective action, where the organization or individual implements steps to solve the problem and prevent a repeat of the crisis, and ingratiation, where the organization or individual reminds its stakeholders of its past good acts and helps create a broader context with which the organization or individual can be evaluated. Coombs (2006) characterizes crisis response strategies by their level of acceptance by critical stakeholders. He identifies apology as having very high acceptance, corrective action as having high acceptance, and ingratiation as having mild acceptance by stakeholders. It is important to note that these strategies are not mutually exclusive and that all can be employed in response to a crisis.

For athletes, there appears to be one other important corrective action: can they play well. For crisis management within a sports context, the ability to contribute to the team winning becomes, in essence, a crisis restoration strategy. If an athlete who has been embroiled in a crisis can return to the field and perform at a high level, there is the opportunity to once again be appreciated by fans and be an endorser of brands. When participation in dog fighting landed Michael Vick in prison, at the time of the indictment Reebok and the NFL immediately halted the sale of his jersey, Coca-Cola and Rawlings dropped him as an endorser, and Nike suspended his contract without pay and did not release the specially designed Michael Vick sneaker, the Air Zoom Vick V (Casey, 2007; Perone, 2007; Sandomir, 2007). In July, 2007, a Nike statement read, "Nike is concerned by the serious and highly disturbing allegations made against Michael Vick, and we consider any cruelty to animals inhumane and abhorrent" (Nike press release, July 19, 2007). Denise Kaigler, Reebok spokeswoman, commented, "We respect the legal process, but we've made a decision to take this step prior to (it) coming to a conclusion. We find the allegations against Mr. Vick too disturbing to ignore" (Perone, 2007, p. 8).

After serving time in jail, in May 2009 Vick returned to the NFL, signing a contract with the Philadelphia Eagles. While Vick became proactive in working with the Humane

Society of the United States (Rhoden, 2009), in the 2010 season Vick would again have a huge impact on the field. Vick started in 12 games, led the Eagles to the playoffs, and posted career highs in touchdown passes, completion percentage, and passing yards (Vick surpassed his season total for passing yards in 2011 as well). For that season, Vick's Eagles' jersey would be the sixth highest selling jersey in the league (Weigley, 2011).

In January 2011, Vick signed his first endorsement deal, a two-year agreement with Unequal Technologies, a sports-accessory provider. In March 2011, a second sports-accessory company, Core Synergy, signed Vick as an endorser. In July 2011, Vick reached an endorsement deal with MusclePharm Corporation, a nutritional supplement company. Brad Pyatt, MusclePharm CEO, explained, "I have four dogs and have been a dog lover for a long time, but with that said we also live in a country that allows for second chances. We truly believe Mike Vick has paid his time for his past mistakes and this is why we are excited to have him on board with the MusclePharm team. For us to agree to this deal and have Mike come on board with MusclePharm, we had to be confident that he has rehabilitated himself and we are convinced that he has" (MusclePharm press release, July 20, 2011). Finally, in July 2011, Vick re-signed with Nike. In a statement Nike explained its position, stating, "Michael acknowledges his past mistakes. We do not condone those actions, but we support the positive changes he has made to better himself off the field" (Weigley, 2011).

All a player needs is one team willing to provide the opportunity for image restoration. History indicates that the opportunity will indeed be there if the team has the belief that the individual can contribute to winning. Michael Vick's best opportunity for image restoration was being signed by the Philadelphia Eagles. His best image restoration behavior is playing well and winning games.

Athlete Injury

Athletes whose sponsors have invested tremendous amounts of time and money with them can also get injured. In the late 1980s and into the early 1990s Nike was paying football and baseball star Bo Jackson an estimated $2 to $3 million per year to promote its cross-training shoes. The "Bo Knows" campaign used Jackson's multi-sport talent as its theme and featured in its advertisements Jackson playing golf, tennis, auto racing, hockey with Wayne Gretzky, and even guitar with Bo Diddley. In the first commercial with Bo Diddley the legendary guitar player would exclaim, "Bo, you don't know Diddley." In a subsequent commercial in which Jackson would then be able to play the guitar well, Diddley would tell him, "You do know Diddley." The "Bo Knows" theme extended into other endorsements, for example in an advertisement for AT&T, Jackson stated that "Bo Knows Long Distance" (Foltz, 1991; Grimm, 1991).

In a January, 1991, NFL playoff game as a running back for the Los Angeles Raiders, Jackson suffered an injury that required him to have a hip replacement surgery. Jackson never played football again. In March 1991, Jackson was also released by Major League Baseball's Kansas City Royals. At the time sports-marketing professionals commented on the endorsement repercussions for Jackson. Marty Blackman, a partner at a sports-marketing and promotions consulting firm commented, "Bo's advantage came from playing in two sports and appearing in sports stories most of the year. With a lot of glitter gone, his fee would certainly be reduced" (Foltz, 1991, p. 1). David Burns, the president of a consulting service for advertising agencies seeking athlete endorsers added, "It certainly does not make sense for sporting goods companies to use an injured sports celebrity" (Foltz, 1991, p. 1).

Nike would rely on its roster of other sports endorsers, which included Michael Jordan, David Robinson, Jerry Rice, and John McEnroe. At the time, Nike spokeswoman, Liz Dolan, stated, "We're a sports company. A lot of companies use athletes interchangeably. Our ads are unique to the person, and we know injuries happen to people like this" (Grimm, 1991, p. 5). Jackson returned to play baseball with the Chicago White Sox in 1991. He sat out the entire 1992 season before returning in 1993. His career ended in 1994.

More recently, Reebok signed NHL star, Sydney Crosby, to a deal that pays him $1.4 million per year to represent the company (*Street & Smith's Sports Business Journal*, September 20–26, 2010). Crosby also has sponsorship agreements with Gatorade, Upper Deck, and Canada Bread. Due to severe concussions Crosby missed 41 games in the 2010–2011 season. Gatorade extended its contract with Crosby through 2015 and filmed new 30-second commercials in anticipation to his return to playing hockey in the 2011–2012 season (Mullen, 2011b). Crosby returned in November 2011, but only played in eight games before complications from concussions forced him to miss more time. Crosby would return to play another 14 games of the 2011–2012 NHL regular season. In June 2012, Crosby did sign a 12-year, $104.4 million contract with the Pittsburgh Penguins.

Injury is not the only performance-related concern for sponsors. For individual sports, if the athlete does not perform well, the sponsor can lose valuable brand exposure. If, for example, a NASCAR driver crashes early in the race and no longer participates, the sponsor does not have its brand receive the desired exposure nor have the opportunity to make all of the positive brand associations that can be a part of that sponsorship. A similar negative outcome would occur if a tennis player loses early in a tournament or a golfer is not high on the leaderboard.

To counter some of the negative events that can occur, many companies are creating a more positive aspect to their sponsorships by developing and implementing corporate social responsibility components. The thinking is that if the public sees that the company is engaged in activities that benefit society, if a negative event occurs there is a positive story that can create a more complete context in which the public can evaluate the brand.

Chapter Nine

Sponsorship and Corporate
Social Responsibility

The sponsorship characteristics of placement selection, negotiation of the parameters of an agreement, communication of a brand association, and creative ideas to activate the sponsorship can help achieve the most basic promotional communication goal, to persuade. In this light, sponsorship has simply been thought of as a logical extension of commercial advertising and a strategy to counter the challenging media use environment of a splintered audience. As has been described sponsorship can also be instrumental in helping a company obtain brand exposure through media coverage, enhance its brand image, and develop and enhance relationships with internal and external stakeholder groups. These activities are three of the main goals of public relations endeavors (Coombs, 2006; Seitel, 2004). Therefore, sponsorship should be thought of as a form of public relations as much as it is considered a form of advertising.

Dean (2002) explains, "Management objectives for sponsorship may be both economic (increased revenues and profits, increased brand awareness, increased channel member interest in the brand) and noneconomic (creation of goodwill with the community, improvement of corporate image, boosting employee morale, recruiting new employees, pure altruism)" (p. 78). For sponsorship to fulfill these public relations goals, there has to be a mindset in negotiating the parameters of the sponsorship. On the need for inclusion of public relations in conjunction with advertising and sponsorship initiatives Sherry (1998) claims that "there can be a number of missed opportunities when public relations is practiced totally independent of promotions, advertising, and other marketing functions" (p. 24).

The key distinction between advertising and public relations endeavors is if the promotional communication is paid. Advertising or sponsorship is clearly defined as paid communication. As noted in Chapter One, although it is a costly endeavor, the advertiser or sponsor controls two vital elements: the placement and the content of the message. Public relations is considered "free media" or "earned media." In these endeavors the organization does not control the placement or the ultimate message content of what appears on the air, in print, or online. The organization is at the discretion of the media gatekeepers (reporters, producers, editors) who will make the final determination. Despite this negative characteristic of a lack of message control, Seitel (2004) claims that free media "is eminently more powerful than advertising" (p. 221).

The Functions of Public Relations

There are two main functions of public relations often characterized in the academic literature: the concept of advocacy and the concept of relationship management. Some researchers view the public relations function from the premise that practitioners act in a communication role of advocacy on behalf of the organization they represent (Benoit, 1995; Phau & Wan, 2006). In this advocacy role public relations professionals are entrusted with the responsibility to proactively communicate about the organization or the individual that they represent in the most positive manner to various stakeholders. The idea of proactive advocacy emanates from a larger philosophy that the actions of the organization and the communication of these actions done through public relations can persuade media coverage and ultimately positively influence public opinion (Berger & Park, 2003; Cameron et al., 1997; Kiousis, Mitrook, Wu, & Seltzer, 2006). Berger and Park (2003) explain, "Public relations programs are carried out to attempt to influence stakeholder attitudes, opinions, perceptions, interpretations, ideologies, and choices to achieve outcomes favorable to the organization" (p. 79). Phau and Wan (2006) add, "Persuasion continues to be an essential function of contemporary public relations, especially in campaigns designed to establish, change, and/or reinforce an organization's image" (p. 102).

Others view the public relations function as the responsibility of building and maintaining mutually beneficial relationships between the organization and the key stakeholder groups on whom its success or failure depends (Cropp & Pincus, 2001; Cutlip, Center, & Broom, 2006; Fearn-Banks, 2001; Grunig & Grunig, 1992; Ledingham, 2006; Ledingham & Bruning, 2000). This relationship management perspective focuses on shared interests and continuous two-way dialogue to help foster understanding between organizations. Fearn-Banks (2001) points out that organizations need to identify stakeholders and should segment them to facilitate communication to those groups. It is important to point out that different relevant facts could be communicated to different stakeholder groups (Coombs, 2006; Fearn-Banks, 2001; Lundy, 2006). Grunig and Grunig (1992) summarize the relationship management perspective stating, "Understanding is the principal objective of public relations rather than persuasion" (p. 289).

Researchers have pointed out that public relations need not be examined from a dichotomous perspective of either being a function of advocacy or relationship management, but rather an assimilation of both philosophies (Cropp & Pincus, 2001; Phau & Wan, 2006). Cancel, Cameron, Sallot, and Mitrook (1997) claim that the public relations practitioner is foremost a problem solver who "must typically choose, either consciously or by default, a stance somewhere between pure advocacy and pure accommodation" (p. 37). Because an assimilation of both public relations functions has value, the role of both advocacy and relationship management contribute to the understanding of sponsorship.

Sponsorship certainly fits within the public relations frameworks of both advocacy and relationship management. Much like public relations practitioners, sponsorship practitioners are relationship management specialists with constant communication occurring between the sponsor and the property in an effort to improve the relationship. In this communication sponsorship practitioners are certainly performing as advocates for their organization in the sponsorship negotiation process to ensure that the brand is positively represented.

Corporate Social Responsibility

Schwaiger (2004) contends that sponsorship can play a role in improving a company's reputation. He explains that a company's reputation consists of two dimensions: competence and likeability. Competence is driven by its quality and performance. Likeability is driven by its attractiveness and corporate social responsibility. Sponsorship clearly offers an opportunity for some companies to demonstrate firm competence as previously explained in documenting the variable of functional congruence. Sponsorship also easily provides an opportunity for a company to demonstrate its likeability by negotiating a corporate social responsibility component as part of the sponsorship agreement.

Although corporate social responsibility can include a multitude of activities, and therefore is difficult to define, researchers have identified the general objective of companies is to operate beyond financial and legal responsibilities and engage in ethical and philanthropic efforts that impact the social good (Brown & Dacin, 1997; Demetriou, Papasolomou, & Vrontis, 2010; Werther & Chandler, 2006). Elkington (1994) explains that companies operate from an awareness of a "triple bottom-line" that includes financial, social, and environmental performance. More recently, Bradish and Cronin (2009) define corporate social responsibility as "a holistic business mindset, much like a corporate culture, where the 'socially responsible' obligations of the firm could and indeed, should incorporate both social and economic interests" (p. 692).

Scholars argue that engaging in corporate social responsibility is not an option, but rather a necessity for companies. Sen and Bhattacharya (2001) claim that corporate social responsibility activities are "an economic imperative" in business (p. 225). Scholars contend that consumers pay close attention to a company's corporate social responsibility initiatives (Dawkins, 2004; Sen & Bhattacharya, 2001). The pressure to engage in corporate social responsibility is, therefore, due to societal or, more appropriately defined, consumer expectations (Basil & Erlandson, 2008; Daugherty, 2001; Sen & Bhattacharya, 2001). Daugherty (2001) points out that "corporations and nonprofits are social institutions that depend on society's acceptance of their roles and activities to survive and grow" (p. 390). He adds, "Corporations have an obligation to solve some of society's most pressing social problems and to devote some of their resources to the solution of these societal problems" (p. 392). Coombs and Holladay (2010) simply conclude that consumers "demand evidence of how a corporation benefits and harms society" (p. 261).

Researchers do, however, point out that companies with bad reputations could have their social responsibility motives questioned in how consumers perceive their activities (Bae & Cameron, 2006; Szykman, Bloom, & Blazing, 2004; Yoon, Gurhan-Canli, & Schwarz, 2006). Harris (2005) explains the initiative "could be perceived as purely philanthropic and a benefit to society as a whole. On the other hand, it could be seen as a manipulation of a dependent constituency for the purposes of whitewashing the image of a company" (p. 486). Companies that were scrutinized for their sponsorship spending during the economic crisis of 2008–2009, for example, turned to emphasizing the social responsibility activation components of their sponsorship. Pearsall (2009) claims, "The harsh economy may be moving the hearts of consumers towards favoring sponsorship with a 'goodwill' component" (p. 30).

The opportunity seems clear for companies; select properties that reflect well on the brand and negotiate a social responsibility component as part of the sponsorship. This comprehensive approach makes the sponsorship more complete. Some companies are certainly taking advantage of this opportunity. Pope (2010) points out that "brands are now developing social sponsorship campaigns to be proof points for brand trust and opportunities to engage customers directly" (p. 243).

Sponsorship Selection: A Corporate Social Responsibility Initiative

Researchers have identified the components of a corporate social responsibility initiative that will make the campaign more effective. Again, proper selection of the property is a vital first step of the process. The fact that sponsors have the obvious ability to choose to associate with properties that have good reputations and fit with their own brand image should make success on this element easily achievable. As stated previously, companies simply do not have to sponsor any property with even the slightest bit of controversy.

Selection of properties that reflect well on the company image can alone be viewed as an act of corporate social responsibility and have a positive effect in the minds of stakeholder groups. Phau and Wan (2006) state that organizations associate themselves with popular or special events because "these linkages function as image enhancers for sponsors, which boost public perception of a corporation or its products/services" (p. 116). Wang (2007) adds corporate social responsibility "rests heavily on a corporation's ability to create in publics' consciousness linkages between a corporation's CSR practices and its corporate image" (p. 125). There is evidence specifically pertaining to sponsorship having a positive impact on consumers' perceptions of brands involved in corporate social responsibility efforts (Dean, 2002; Yoon et al., 2006). Schwaiger, Sarstedt, and Taylor (2010) found that sponsorship of the arts and cultural events has benefits to the sponsor's image. Several researchers point out that there is value in an Olympic sponsorship because the event generates goodwill on behalf of its corporate partners (Meenaghan & Shipley, 1999; Papadimitriou & Apostolopoulou, 2009; Stipp, 1998; Stotlar, 1993). In another example, sponsoring a university could have some intrinsic value as a social responsibility initiative, as even if the school is in a scandal the sponsor could make an argument that it is helping in the educational mission of the university.

In a practical example, Priscilla Brown, senior vice president, head of marketing and strategy for Sun Life Financial, explained the selection philosophy of the company acquiring the naming rights to the Miami Dolphins football stadium. She stated, "As important as exposure and profile are to Sun Life Financial, commitment to the communities we serve is a cornerstone of our philosophical approach, so we had to make sure we found the right market and partnered with the right organization. That was one of the things that really sealed the deal for Sun Life Stadium: that Sun Life and the Miami Dolphins share the same philosophy about giving back to the community" (Brown, 2011). In South Florida, the Dolphins have joined with Sun Life Financial to implement Sun Life's signature corporate responsibility program, Sun Life Rising Star Awards, which provides students in major metropolitan areas with financial resources and access to educational opportunities.

Aaker and Joachimsthaler (2000) explain that distinctions can be made between what the brand is or what the brand does for consumers. They contend that the aspect of what the brand does for consumers touches on more of an emotional benefit and "relates to the ability of the brand to make the buyer or user of a brand feel something during the purchase process or use experience" (p. 49). Polonsky and Wood (2001) claim that through corporate social responsibility "the consumer purchases from product categories that are most probably already in the normal shopping routine. The only major decision relates to brand switching" (p. 13). For product categories that might be designated through the Elaboration Likelihood Model as having low involvement, a corporate social responsibility initiative might be a determinant factor in consumer decision making. Harris (1998) simply argues, "Consumers want to do business with companies that support the causes they care about" (p. 210).

If the intention of corporate social responsibility is to engender some positive response by consumers toward the company, these consumers obviously need to be made aware of its activities. It is necessary for organizations to communicate and promote their corporate social responsibility initiatives if they are to obtain any benefit from these efforts (Basil & Erlandson, 2008; David, Kline & Dai, 2005; Golob & Barlett, 2007; Harris, 1998; Schwaiger et al., 2010). Golob and Bartlett (2007) comment, "Communication of an organization's social impact is important, and disclosing true and relevant information about corporate behavior can have benefits for stakeholders, organizations, and society" (p. 2).

The credibility of corporate social responsibility efforts can be enhanced if companies support causes that fit with their brand (Dawkins, 2004; Geue & Plewa, 2010). Simmons and Becker-Olsen (2006) claim perceived high fit between the sponsor and the cause can increase the brand's equity, with perceived low fit between the sponsor and the cause diluting brand equity. They point out that perceptions of low fit can be reduced through communication efforts that demonstrate fit, such as altering the message to clarify the fit between the sponsor and the cause and having the communication of the fit emanate from the cause and not the sponsor. Szkyman, Bloom, and Blazing (2004) identify that the source of the communication impacts how the message is received, citing an example of a message about the dangers of drunk driving as being more effective if it is coming from Mothers Against Drunk Driving rather than an alcoholic beverage company. The credibility of corporate social responsibility efforts can also be enhanced through third-party endorsements (Coombs & Holladay, 2010). If, for example, a league makes a certain cause its main charity initiative, the recruitment of an organization with the expertise in that cause will enhance its efforts.

Ideas to make the communication of the corporate social responsibility efforts more effective include tailoring messages to specific target audiences (Dawkins 2004), using spokespeople that have trustworthiness and expertise on the topic to enhance credibility (Pornpitakpan, 2003; Till & Busler, 2000), and making effective use of a Web site to communicate the organization's corporate social responsibility initiatives (Basil & Erlandson, 2008; Dawkins, 2004; Maignan & Ralston, 2002).

Corporate Social Responsibility Outcomes

McWilliams, Siegel, and Wright (2006) simply describe corporate social responsibility as a strategic investment. Companies continue to make strategic investments in corporate social responsibility initiatives with the hope of contributing to the social good, while at the same time potentially enhancing their own reputation and financial standing (Coombs & Holladay, 2010; Dawkins, 2004; Demetriou et al., 2010; Drumwright, 1994; Larson, Flaherty, Zablah, Brown, & Wiener, 2008; McWilliams et al., 2006; Murray & Vogel, 1997). The impact of these strategic social responsibility investments has been debated. David et al. (2005) point out the key outcome of the communication and promotion of corporate social responsibility efforts is familiarity or top-of-mind brand awareness on the part of stakeholders.

Many scholars firmly believe that engaging in corporate social responsibility initiatives can help organizations increase their standing in society (Brown & Dacin, 1997; Carroll, 1999; David et al., 2005; Davies, Chun, da Silva, & Roper, 2003; Dawkins, 2004; Harris, 1998; McWilliams et al., 2006; Quester & Thompson, 2001; Schwaiger et al., 2010; Simmons & Becker-Olsen, 2006; Whitehouse, 2006). Schwaiger et al. (2010) claim that through communication press reports, even the attitudes of those who didn't attend an event can be positively influenced. Thus, if properties truly need the contribution of sponsorship dollars to survive, the properties themselves should engage in substantial efforts to publicize the sponsors' support to consumers (Schwaiger et al., 2010). Some researchers have importantly documented that in certain instances corporate social responsibility initiatives and communication of these efforts can indeed have a positive influence on consumer behavior (Dawkins, 2004; Sen & Bhattacharya, 2001).

Other scholars have tried to evaluate if corporate social responsibility efforts can, in fact, contribute to the financial performance of a company (Husted & Salazar, 2006; Pava & Krausz, 1996; Stanwick & Stanwick, 1998; Waddock & Graves, 1997). While Pava and Krausz (1996) reported mixed results, Waddock and Graves (1997) found corporate community involvement can positively correlate with financial returns. Stanwick and Stanwick (1998) claim there is a positive relationship between corporate social responsibility initiatives and financial performance, but the association is weak. Demetriou, Papasolomou, and Vrontis (2010) contend that both financial and reputation objectives can be achieved through corporate social responsibility objectives. They state, "In principle, CSR can be used to strengthen corporate reputation and profitability by signaling to the various stakeholders with whom the organization interacts that it is committed to meeting its moral obligations and expectations beyond common regulatory requirements" (p. 267). Overall, the results of academic studies have not produced a consistent, cause-and-effect relationship, as the corporate social responsibility initiatives of a company are only one of the many variables that determine its financial position.

Corporate Social Responsibility and Sports Sponsorship

Studies applying theoretical concepts of corporate social responsibility to the sports industry have been conducted (Bradish & Cronin, 2009; Godfrey, 2009; Sheth & Babiak, 2010; Smith & Westerbeek, 2007; Walker & Kent, 2009). Some researchers have specifically dealt with the importance of sports teams or leagues engaging in corporate social responsibility activities (Fortunato, 2009; Godfrey, 2009; Hopwood, 2007; L'Etang, 2006; Sheth & Babiak, 2010; Smith & Westerbeek, 2007). Walker and Kent (2009) claim the pressure to produce economically and behave in a socially acceptable manner extends to sports organizations. In a quantitative study of fans of two NFL teams, they found a strong predictive relation with organizational reputation and patronage intentions. Godfrey (2009) indicates it is even more important for sports organizations to engage in corporate social responsibility efforts because these leagues are often in scandal.

From the sponsor's perspective, Watt (2010) explains that "consumers want to know that companies care about what they care about, not only supporting the same team or adding value to events that they attend" (p. 222). He adds, "More than an inanimate sponsorship banner or poster, every point of contact provides an opportunity to live out the company's values and principles while making a meaningful contribution to social development" (p. 223).

Because of a large and loyal audience, activating the sponsorship of a sports property with a corporate social responsibility initiative can serve as an ideal communication vehicle for a company to simultaneously achieve advertising and public relations objectives. Being an official sponsor of a league or team provides a perfect entry point for the sponsor to participate in the corporate social responsibility initiatives that the league or team is involved in. The sponsor can tap into an already established infrastructure to engage in a corporate social responsibility initiative.

In 2007, the NFL began its PLAY 60 program, which is designed to combat childhood obesity through the simple goal of getting kids to be physically active for 60 minutes every day. The concept of play easily fits with a sports league whose main function is obviously to play games. The mission statement of the NFL PLAY 60 program reads:

> NFL PLAY 60 is the NFL Movement for an Active and Healthy Generation, encouraging kids to play for 60 minutes every day in order to tackle childhood obesity. Through in-school, after school, and team-based programs and partnerships with like-minded organizations, the NFL wants fans to join the NFL PLAY 60 Movement. PLAY 60 appears throughout NFLRUSH.com, the NFL's official website for kids, so kids can do what they love — play games and follow their favorite NFL teams — while being reminded to get active every day! [http://www.nflrush.com/play60/parents].

Roger Goodell, NFL Commissioner, stated, "We are taking a leadership role in the movement to get youngsters fit. Our players know the importance of staying healthy and it's important that young fans also understand the value of exercise. PLAY 60 is an important tool in ensuring children get their necessary daily physical activity as recommended by health and fitness experts" (http://www.nflrush.com/play60/parents). Kathleen Sebelius, United States Department of Health and Human Services Secretary, commented, "Curbing the obesity epidemic requires committed people and organizations across the nation working together to take action. We outline a vision for the nation that requires parents, neighborhoods, the medical community, employers, schools, and individuals to take a coordinated and comprehensive approach to combating overweight and obesity" (Health and Human Services press release, January 28, 2010).

The PLAY 60 Web site, www.nflrush.com/play60/, serves as a communication center for all the facets of the PLAY 60 program, including ideas for kids, parents, and educators to stay physically active. On the Web site there are tips for kids to engage in physical activity, such as not having to do all 60 minutes of physical activity at one time, trying different physical fitness activities, and involving friends (http://www.nflrush.com/play60/wmuplanner).

The NFL has produced public service announcements, which are televised during NFL games and on the NFL Network. The NFL has used its more than three-decade partnership with the United Way and its "Kids Get Fit!" initiative to communicate the importance of being physically active (http://www.nflrush.com/play60/parents). The public service announcements speak of the commitment by the the NFL and the United Way to do something about childhood obesity by "encouraging every kid to get in their daily requirement of play" (http://liveunited.org/nfl/). The NFL also has each team designate a home game as an "NFL PLAY 60" game featuring "PLAY 60" on-field displays, sideline banners, goal post wraps, and "NFL PLAY 60" youth ambassadors who run onto the field and stand alongside the players during the National Anthem (http://www.nfl.com/news; November 23, 2009).

Much of the implementation of the PLAY 60 program involves getting schools to participate. The NFL has partnered with the American Heart Association to create the NFL PLAY 60 Challenge, which is a series of curriculum ideas that educators can download to help implement the NFL PLAY 60 Challenge. The curriculum resources include a teacher's guide that offers creative ideas to incorporate physical fitness into the classroom, a 33-page day planner that allows students to record their activities, a classroom scoreboard where all students' activities can be displayed, and certificates that recognize students' achievement in physical activity (http://www.americanheart.org/presenter.jhtml?identifier=3061814).

In another scholastic endeavor the NFL has created the Keep Gym in School program, which is designed to increase access to in-school physical activity and to teach skills needed to establish and sustain healthy lifestyles (http://www.keepgyminschool.com/about-the-program.aspx). The program delivers daily physical education opportunities to school students by funding facility upgrades, physical education instructors, and equipment for physical education classes (http://www.nflrush.com/play60/parents).

In keeping with the educational focus of the PLAY 60 program, the NFL has created its Back to Football Friday Contest, in which schools throughout the United States are asked to show their NFL team pride on a particular day and submit three essays and three to six photos to nflrush.com. The 34 winning schools (32 in NFL markets and two general markets) are named NFL PLAY 60 Super Schools. These schools get a visit from an NFL player and receive a $10,000 NFL PLAY 60 health and wellness grant (http://www.nflrush.com/footballfriday).

Procter & Gamble, an official NFL sponsor, has made significant contributions to the NFL's PLAY 60 program. In 2011, Procter & Gamble showed support for the Back to Football Friday Contest by seeking to find "the ultimate P&G Super Parent," described as "an individual who takes a proactive approach in helping children of the school/community achieve and maintain an active lifestyle" (Procter & Gamble press release, October 31, 2011). In November and December during visits to the 34 Super Schools, a parental figure or spouse of an NFL player presented the school with a $1,000 check for its athletic department as well as honored a Procter & Gamble Super Parent. After all 34 school visits were completed, fans voted for the Ultimate P&G Super Parent on the Procter & Gamble Take it to the House Facebook page. The winner got to attend the 2012 Pro Bowl and was a part of the NFL's PLAY 60 activities for the week. Anne Westbrook, corporate communications leader of United States sports marketing for Procter & Gamble, commented,

"With this program, we invite parents to join us in this effort to empower all parents to take a proactive approach in helping their children achieve and maintain an active lifestyle" (Procter & Gamble press release, October 31, 2011).

Procter & Gamble was also the lead sponsor of the NFL PLAY 60 Community Blitz during Pro Bowl week in Hawaii in 2011. One of the Community Blitz events included having NFL Pro Bowl players Drew Brees, New Orleans Saints quarterback, and Jason Witten, Dallas Cowboys tight end, help in the construction of a new playground at a YMCA in Honolulu. Other Community Blitz events took place throughout Hawaii.

Another aspect of the Procter & Gamble sponsorship activation through the NFL PLAY 60 program and the Pro Bowl was the Touchdown for Kids charitable donation. Procter & Gamble donated $5,000 for every touchdown scored during the 2011 Pro Bowl game to the local United Way of each scoring player's NFL city. The 13 touchdowns led to Procter & Gamble donating $65,000 to United Way chapters. Procter & Gamble then made a donation to the other NFL markets, to bring the total to an estimated $100,000. Anne Westbrook, corporate communications leader of United States sports marketing for Procter & Gamble, explained, "P&G is proud to have provided season-long support of NFL PLAY 60 to help thousands of kids lead happier, healthier lives. P&G's mission is to touch and improve the lives of our consumers, which is why fighting childhood obesity, which affects one-third of our nation's children, is so important to us" (Procter & Gamble press release, February 2, 2011).

Chevrolet incorporates corporate social responsibility initiatives into its sponsorship with Major League Baseball. Through its sponsorship with Major League Baseball Chevrolet has created a promotional communication strategy that simultaneously achieves advertising objectives of obtaining brand exposure and assisting in brand recall and public relations objectives of obtaining media coverage and enhancing the brand's image. For Chevrolet, brand exposure and a brand association with Major League Baseball is obtained and communicated through its being the presenting sponsor of the Most Valuable Player award for the World Series and the All-Star Game, two ceremonies that are part of those games' television broadcasts. Beyond this brand exposure public relations objectives are achieved through the corporate social responsibility initiative of being the presenting sponsor of the Roberto Clemente Award, which recognizes the player who best exemplifies sportsmanship, community involvement, and the individual's contribution to his team. The Roberto Clemente Award honors the 12-time All-Star and Hall of Famer who died in a plane crash on New Year's Eve in 1972, delivering supplies to earthquake victims in Nicaragua.

A representative from each Major League Baseball team is selected to be a finalist for the Clemente award for that season, and from the 30 team nominees, a winner is chosen. Major League Baseball designates a day near the end of the season as Roberto Clemente Day, with home team nominees for the Clemente Award being recognized in an on-the-field ceremony prior to that day's games. At this ceremony the team's nominated player is presented with a donation for his favorite charity by a representative from Chevrolet.

In 2007, fans became a part of the selection process, as from early September through early October fans could visit www.mlb.com/chevy21 to vote for one of the 30 team nominees. The fans' vote winner is tallied as one single vote cast among the votes of other selection committee members that include the wife of Roberto Clemente, Vera Clemente, and Major League Baseball Commissioner Bud Selig. Fans who voted were automatically entered into a contest in which the winner receives a trip to a World Series game where the Clemente Award winner is recognized courtesy of Chevrolet and Major League Baseball. Chevrolet makes a donation to the national winner's charity of choice. An additional donation by Chevrolet goes to the Roberto Clemente Sports City, a non-profit organization that provides sports activities for children in Carolina, Puerto Rico (Fortunato, 2009).

If Chevrolet had its sponsorship with Major League Baseball without any public relations component, it would be losing out on valuable social responsibility recognitions that the company receives. The additional exposure and the fact that Chevrolet's corporate responsibility initiatives are being communicated help build the brand image and speak of a caring company. The characteristic of negotiation allowed for in any sponsorship agreement permits the opportunity to engage in corporate responsibility initiatives that can further a brand's image and, perhaps, influence consumer behavior.

Major League Baseball is but one of Chevrolet's sponsorships in the world of sports that is designed to demonstrate it as a socially responsible company. For example, since 1971 Chevrolet has been awarding scholarships to universities in recognition of the player of the game from each team in college football and basketball games that are on television. This award is mentioned at the end of the broadcast of each game, providing brand exposure, creating an implicit brand association with the universities, enhancing the brand image, and engaging in a corporate social responsibility initiative in a way that is communicated to the audience. This one initiative of awarding scholarships and the use of televised games as the promotional vehicle simultaneously achieves advertising and public relations goals.

Sponsorship activation can involve fan participation, leading to the support of a charity. State Farm Insurance activates its sponsorship with Major League Baseball through a corporate social responsibility initiative that achieves promotional communication goals while emphasizing its brand themes. State Farm has promotional communication goals of top-of-mind awareness and brand consideration in an attempt to generate new policies, especially in auto insurance. State Farm has a brand theme of "Get to a better state" and has used its well-known slogan, "Like a good neighbor, State Farm is there," to promote the company's ideals of service, caring, reliability, and community. The hope is that the communication of these brand themes will appeal to consumers as well as businesses in choosing an insurance provider.

One of the marketing challenges for State Farm is the nature of the product use by the customer, in that insurance is an intangible product that people do not want to purchase, but need to purchase. There are not many interactions between a consumer and an insurance company, and on the occasions that they do interact, it is coming in the form of paying a bill or after an accident in the case of an auto insurance provider. So the ability to communicate brand themes that a caring, reliable company will make these difficult times less stressful is something that State Farm looks to achieve.

State Farm uses its sponsorship activation programs to create a positive experience between itself and its customers. State Farm has been the official insurance sponsor of Major League Baseball since 2007. The audience for Major League Baseball is a fit for State Farm because of the brand exposure opportunities, the demographic audience variable of younger families, the emotional theme of community, and associating with America's national pastime. State Farm is the sponsor of the annual Major League Baseball Home Run Derby that takes place the day before the All-Star Game and is televised on a night when there is practically no competition for the sports viewers' attention. Through the Home Run Derby, State Farm makes a donation to the Boys & Girls Club of America, with the amount determined by the number of home runs hit in the contest. State Farm provides an additional donation if the player hits one of the specially marked gold baseballs for a home run.

As a way to extend the charitable component of its sponsorship with Major League Baseball beyond this one day event, in 2010 State Farm developed the "Go to Bat" campaign. The program occurs for the last ten weeks of the Major League Baseball season, and State Farm uses the Major League Baseball Home Run Derby to help launch and promote the initiative. Fans participate by visiting a specially created Web site, www.statefarm.com/gotobat, where they register and select a preferred charity from the one of the designated charities provided by State Farm. At the Web site fans can learn the missions of the various charities prior to making a selection. By having the fans select from a slew of charities, the multi-faceted interests of many consumers can be recognized, rather than State Farm dictating only a single charity. Fans would then "Go to Bat" for their selected charity in an online mini–State Farm Home Run Derby game where they would try to increase their charity's weekly batting average.

Over the ten-week period of the contest, each week the charity with the highest batting average received an $18,000 donation, and one of the participants who was playing for that charity would be selected to win a trip to the World Series. In 2011, State Farm had over 50,000 people play the "Go to Bat" game, and $205,000 was donated. Population Services International received a $25,000 donation for having the highest "Go to Bat" game batting average. The contest winners of the State Farm program were recognized in an on-the-field ceremony before Game Three of the 2011 World Series. Contest winners and their designated charities were posted on the www.statefarm.com/gotobat Web site.

At the Web site, there are also links for fans to "get a quote" on auto insurance and to "find an agent." The "Go to Bat" campaign helps State Farm communicate the theme of State Farm agents going to bat for their customers. State Farm also had sponsorships with 24 Major League Baseball teams in 2011, which included signage in each stadium. At the team level, State Farm has the "Good Neighbor Award," a monthly award for a local agent. The agent is recognized in an on-the-field ceremony.

MasterCard uses its sponsorship with Major League Baseball and the exposure that the sport provides to launch and promote a program in which it makes a donation to Stand Up to Cancer when people use their MasterCard when eating at a restaurant. In July 2011, MasterCard introduced the "Eat, Drink, and Be Generous" campaign in which every time customers used their MasterCard when dining from July 12 through September 1, 2011, MasterCard made a one-penny donation, up to a total of $4 million, to Stand Up to Cancer. Rusty Robertson, Stand Up to Cancer co-founder, commented, "every penny counts in the fight against cancer. Choosing to use a MasterCard to pay for a meal will be an easy way for consumers to contribute to the progress in cutting-edge research" (MasterCard press release, July 12, 2011).

MasterCard prominently uses the assets of Major League Baseball to communicate its initiative. Through its sponsorship with Major League Baseball MasterCard launched the campaign on the night of the Major League Baseball All-Star Game when actor Terrence Howard appeared during the game's broadcast on Fox to make the initial dining purchase using a MasterCard. The commercial featuring Howard was re-run in major league stadiums and aired on the Major League Baseball Network throughout the rest of the season. Additional commercials featuring actor Ray Romano and actress Reese Witherspoon promoting the campaign also aired during Fox's broadcast of the All-Star Game. On September 27, 2011, MasterCard announced that its $4 million fundraising goal had been reached.

To complete the campaign again using the assets of Major League Baseball prior to the start of Game Four of the 2011 World Series MasterCard made its donation to Stand Up to Cancer in an on-field presentation. During the broadcast of the World Series game on Fox, MasterCard would also debut its "Thank You" commercial to acknowledge the card users for their contribution to the donation. The commercial featured Major League Baseball players "standing up" for the people in their lives who were battling cancer. Among the players were John Kruk, former Philadelphia Phillies' first baseman, who stood up for himself as a cancer survivor, Mitch Williams, former Philadelphia Phillies' pitcher stood up for his parents, Andy Petitte, New York Yankees' pitcher, stood up for his mother-in-law, and Ron Darling, former New York Mets' pitcher, stood up for his former teammate, Hall of Fame catcher, Gary Carter (Carter died in 2012 of a cancerous brain tumor). Craig Vosburg, MasterCard Group executive for United States market development, explained, "our cardholders proved that every penny counts in the fight against cancer through the Eat, Drink and Be Generous campaign whose results exceeded our expectations." He added, "our cardholders and restaurant partners truly came together to stand up for such a wonderful cause, and it shows in the funds we were able to raise for Stand Up to Cancer. The spot airing during tonight's game is just our small way of saying thank you to everyone who used their MasterCard while dining out" (MasterCard press release, October 19, 2011).

In 2012, MasterCard once again in coordination with its sponsorship of Major League Baseball began a campaign to benefit Stand Up to Cancer during the All-Star Game. In its "Dine and Be Generous" campaign MasterCard announced that between July 10 and September 28, 2012, when cardholders spent more than $10 on a meal using their MasterCard, a one-penny donation, up to a total of $4 million, would be made to Stand Up to Cancer. To launch the program R.A. Dickey, All-Star pitcher of the New York Mets, participated in the ceremonial first "swipe" that aired during the Fox broadcast of the All-Star Game.

On September 20, 2012, MasterCard announced that it had reached its $4 million goal. Sue Schwartz, co-founder of Stand Up to Cancer, stated, "we are incredibly grateful for the ongoing support of MasterCard, which has made supporting cancer research as simple as going out to dinner. Our effort to get new and better treatments to patients as quickly as possible could not happen without the company's dedication, passion and generosity. Each year, MasterCard and its cardholders have proven that every precious penny counts in the fight against cancer" (MasterCard press release, September 20, 2012).

To once again complete the campaign using the assets of Major League Baseball prior to the start of Game One of the 2012 World Series MasterCard made its donation to

Stand Up to Cancer in an on-field presentation. A highlight of the presentation was shown on the Fox broadcast of the game during the bottom of the third inning. Before the top of the sixth inning, Fox would show more than two minutes of players, umpires, fans, and its announcers holding up signs with the names of the people who they were "standing up" for in their fight against cancer. The Stand Up to Cancer logo also appeared on the backstop, visible throughout the game's television broadcast.

MasterCard produced another "thank you" commercial that began airing on Fox during the 2012 National League Championship Series. The commercial featured John Lester, Boston Red Sox pitcher who has battled non–Hodgkin's lymphoma, and a nine-year-old cancer patient named Justin who is battling neuroblastoma, a cancerous tumor that develops from nerve tissue in infants and children. MasterCard describes the commercial:

> The spot, titled "Bat on the Ball," uses the simplicity of a pitcher and a batter to symbolize the shared focus, determination and community support that are crucial elements in the fight against cancer. The characters in the spot are meant to illustrate that all involved in the movement to hasten an end to cancer — patients, their families, the support of major donors such as MasterCard and Major League Baseball, and importantly, those who choose to give in their everyday lives through opportunities like MasterCard's Dine And Be Generous program — are heroes [MasterCard press release, October 17, 2012].

The commercial begins with the phrase, "MasterCard, together with Major League Baseball, wants to thank everyone who stood up and helped to raise $4 million for Stand Up to Cancer just by using your MasterCard." The commercial includes the phrase "standing up for those in the fight against cancer: priceless." The visual and the end of the commercial features the MasterCard, Major League Baseball, and Stand Up to Cancer logos with the address for the Stand Up to Cancer Web site, www.standup2cancer.org. Bud Selig, Major League Baseball commissioner, commented, "many of those within our baseball family, like Red Sox pitcher Jon Lester and our great fans across the country have been affected by cancer. Along with our partners at MasterCard, Major League Baseball is committed to supporting Stand Up to Cancer and its tireless work toward eradicating this disease" (Stand Up to Cancer press release, October 17, 2012).

The commercial would run on several occasions during the broadcast of Game One of the World Series on Fox. The commercial also appears on the Stand Up to Cancer Web site as well as the MasterCard Facebook page, www.facebook.com/mastercard/app. On the MasterCard Facebook page under the video is a statement that amplifies its "priceless" brand theme, "there are moments to be celebrated in our everyday lives, moments that provide personal meaning for us and our families, moments that are priceless."

NASCAR has been a launch point for many sponsorship social responsibility initiatives. Federal Express initiated a corporate social responsibility component to its sponsorship portfolio when in May, 2011, for the first time it sponsored a NASCAR Sprint Cup Series race: the FedEx 400, benefiting Autism Speaks from the Dover International Speedway in Delaware. Autism is a complex neurobiological disorder that typically lasts throughout a person's lifetime. Autism is characterized as a spectrum disorder with varying degrees of impairment in communication skills, social abilities, and repetitive behaviors. According to the Centers for Disease Control, autism affects as many as one in every 110 children in the United States (www.autismspeaks.org/what-autism/faq).

A big part of the Federal Express sponsorship of the race was to assist in raising money and awareness for autism. Special ticket packages for the race were created, with the proceeds going to Autism Speaks. An auction was also established in which the winning bidder would wave the green flag to begin the race, receive passes to pit road, and receive a flag signed by all of the drivers. Federal Express, which sponsored the #11 car driven by Denny Hamlin, would have donated an additional $100,000 to Autism Speaks had Hamlin won the race. T. Michael Glenn, executive vice president of market development at Federal Express, stated, "FedEx has the unique opportunity to help support the mission of Autism Speaks as the official sponsor of the FedEx 400. Joining forces for a great cause is a win for both racing fans and supporters of the important work of Autism Speaks." He added that Federal Express is "incredibly proud of the commitment to charity that is a hallmark of FedEx and our team members worldwide" (Federal Express press release, April 21, 2011).

In another example of a company using NASCAR to engage in a socially responsible endeavor, after the terrorist attacks of September 11, 2001, Lowe's and Jimmie Johnson started the "Power of Pride" campaign to raise money for organizations that support the United States military, firefighters, and police officers. The campaign was promoted with an American Flag paint scheme on Johnson's car. One aspect of the campaign offered fans a "Power of Pride" bumper sticker and raised over $6 million (Mickle, 2011b).

In a final example involving NASCAR, rapper 50 Cent's company introduced an energy drink, Street King, in which a portion of the proceeds from sales went toward a global initiative to provide meals to 1 billion people in Africa. To promote the brand and the initiative, NASCAR driver Mike Bliss had his number 32 car feature an image of 50 Cent on its quarter panels (Carp, 2011).

Support of education through college scholarships has been an often used initiative by sponsors. Dr Pepper has a presence in college football through its sponsorship with the ACC, SEC, Big 10, and Pac-12 conferences as well as the Cotton Bowl Classic played in Dallas, Texas. Dr Pepper activates these sponsorships through a corporate responsibility initiative that seems perfectly targeted for the college football audience and plays itself out on national television. In its Dr Pepper Million Dollar Tuition Giveaway more than $1 million in tuition money is distributed to students who submit videos online explaining why they deserve the tuition money. Videos are judged "on the inclusion of Dr Pepper, a college football and tuition theme, the impact of free tuition on the student's life, and overall presentation quality" (Dr Pepper press release, September 21, 2011). The ten fans whose videos are selected then compete during the halftime of the conferences' respective championship games and the Cotton Bowl game. The finalists have to throw footballs from the five-yard line into a two-foot hole in an oversized Dr Pepper can replica. The contestant who completes the most throws in 30 seconds wins a $100,000 scholarship. The runner-up receives a $23,000 scholarship. Sixty other videos are selected to receive a $2,500 scholarship. Contest winners are featured online and on select cans of Dr Pepper (Dr Pepper press release, September 21, 2011).

The necessity for corporate social responsibility activities is heightened when a company has to deal with the usage of its products being thought of as a behavior risk. Such is the situation for a company in the liquor industry. In the sponsorship between Bacardi and the NBA, the main activation program is a scholarship fund established to benefit the Thurgood Marshall College Fund and the Hispanic Scholarship Fund. Barcardi and the NBA's Gold Standard Scholarship Program will award more than $100,000 annually to minority students in select NBA markets who are 21 years of age or older and pursuing undergraduate or graduate degrees.

Through the program, the Thurgood Marshall College Fund and the Hispanic Scholarship Fund select 24 minority students to receive a $10,000 scholarship. From this group of 24, fans go online to select the four students, one male and one female from each organization, who will win an additional scholarship of $30,000. Margaret McDonald, brand director for Bacardi, explained, "We are excited to partner with an organization like the NBA that shares our commitment to giving back to local communities and providing individuals with the resources they need to reach their goals. This collaboration between Bacardi and the NBA is a perfect way to showcase our brand values and establish programs that give back to those in need" (Bacardi press release, April 23, 2010). Mark Tatum, NBA executive vice president of global marketing partnerships, added, "Both of our organizations share a deep-seated commitment to corporate responsibility, and the Gold Standard Scholarship Program will be an important centerpiece of our partnership that will provide a significant amount of aid to young adult leaders in the community" (Bacardi press release, April 23, 2010).

It is even more important for companies in risk behavior industries to directly confront and show a measure of responsibility toward the risk activity. Bacardi has developed an integrated campaign designed to spread the message of drinking responsibly. Bacardi has partnered with tennis champion Rafael Nadal, naming him the Bacardi Limited Global Social Responsibility Ambassador. The Bacardi "Champions Drink Responsibly" campaign began in 2008 with race car champion Michael Schumacher as the first global ambassador. Seamus McBride, Bacardi Limited president and CEO, stated, "Bacardi Limited is dedicated to continue its strong history of educating legal drinking age consumers about responsible drinking. Drinking responsibly is an enjoyable part of one's social life and we expect legal drinking age consumers will continue to engage with the campaign's important message and become champions for responsible drinking themselves" (Bacardi press release, March 22, 2011). To activate this program, Bacardi developed the "Champions Drink Responsibly" campaign using the tennis theme of knowing "where to draw the line" when it comes to drinking. Nadal was featured in a commercial in which he held a tennis racket over a cocktail glass with the slogan, "I'd always tell my friends where the line is" (Bacardi press release, March 22, 2011).

As part of the campaign Bacardi set up an online game that provided an opportunity to meet Nadal. A virtual reality game was created by Bacardi that allowed legal-drinking-age fans the opportunity to "Ace Rafa." The online game featured a real-life version of Nadal reacting to the fans' serve as if he were playing an actual game of tennis. If the fan playing the game aced Nadal, he or she would go into a drawing, with the selected finalist having the opportunity to meet Nadal and try to serve an ace against him in person. In a Bacardi press release, Nadal stated, "I hope my fans enjoy this unique chance to play against me. Drinking responsibly is a serious message and I believe we will reach and influence more people with this important message by expressing it in a more light-hearted and interactive way. 'Knowing where the line is' is vital in tennis and in life" (Bacardi press release, November 11, 2011). Seamus McBride added, "The 'Ace Rafa' promotion is all about connecting with consumers in a dynamic and engaging way to reinforce the important message of responsible drinking" (Bacardi press release, November 11, 2011).

Finally, corporate social responsibility could involve support of the athletes themselves if they are involved in an activity that fans care about, such as the Olympics. As part of its sponsorship with the United States Olympic Committee, Procter & Gamble donated $50,000 to help defray training and expenses for United States athletes. Kirk Perry, vice president, North America, Procter & Gamble, stated, "We are thrilled to continue our commitment to the global Olympic Movement with our new global Olympic partnership, but also by showing the families of all U.S. Olympians, Paralympians and hopefuls that we appreciate their dedication to Team USA. We are proud to help the USOC with this new, additional donation and continue to value our partnership with this organization whose purpose of improving lives through sport so closely matches our own of touching and improving more lives, more completely" (Procter & Gamble press release, July 28, 2010).

Examining the literature that describes the objectives of advertising and the functions of public relations provides a more complete understanding of what can be accomplished through a sponsorship. Much can be achieved through a sponsorship, but similar emphasis needs to be placed on sponsorship selection and activation being designed to achieve public relations goals as much as traditional advertising goals. It is important to note that public relations objectives do not have to replace advertising goals and that the proper approach to a sponsorship can simultaneously achieve both advertising business communication objectives and public relations image goals. To not include a corporate social responsibility initiative as part of a sponsorship appears to be a missed opportunity.

Chapter Ten

Sponsorship Evaluation

While the goals of sponsorship and the numerous strategies designed to achieve these goals can be articulated, determining if these goals are achieved because of a sponsorship is a challenge. Direct causality of consumer behavior because of any promotional communication strategy is difficult to argue. As has been stated, there are numerous variables that can serve as the reason for consumer behavior. That being said, any piece of evidence that can be obtained as to the effectiveness of any form of promotional communication would be extremely valuable to ascertain. Therefore, developing the measurement systems that can gather the needed evaluative data is another essential task of the sponsorship process for both the company making the promotional communication investment and the property selling the promotional communication time and space. Evaluation is one of the most difficult aspects of the sponsorship process, although its importance cannot be understated. Crompton (2004) declares that evaluation is the most important challenge facing the sponsorship industry.

Steyn (2009) simply asks, "How does a marketer know whether the money invested in the sponsorship was worth it?" (p. 318). Several scholars write of the great difficulty in evaluating promotional communication campaigns in general (Burns, 2011; Cornwell & Maignan, 1998; Davis, 2002; Nelson & Katz, 2011; Phillips & Moutinho, 1998; Russell, 2011; Walliser, 2003) and evaluating sponsorship specifically (Collett, 2008; Cornwell, 1995; Crompton, 2004; Farelly et al., 1997; Harvey, 2001; Miyazaki & Morgan, 2001; O'Reilly & Madill, 2009; Thjomoe et al., 2002). Evaluation of sponsorship alone in determining causality is particularly difficult because it is rarely the only form of promotional communication being used. As many companies use an integrated marketing approach, it is easier to point to the success of the entire promotional communication campaign rather than identify a singular specific strategy (Keller, 2001; Maestas, 2009).

Because of its difficulty and the inability to clearly and undeniably link promotional communication efforts to consumer behavior, many companies simply choose to not invest the resources of money, time, and personnel to properly conduct the evaluation (O'Reilly & Madill, 2009; Pearsall, 2010). Quester (1997) reported that only 30 to 50 percent of companies engage in evaluation. Crompton (2004) found that 40 percent of the 200 companies sampled spent no money to evaluate their sponsorship, and an additional 35 percent of the companies sampled spent 1 percent or less of their budget on evaluation. Maestas (2009) advocates a company investing 3 to 5 percent of the sponsorship's value in evaluating the sponsorship. In the annual IEG and Performance Research survey in

2013, 72 percent of respondents reported that their companies spent nothing or less than one percent on measurement in comparison to the amount they spend on right fees. Only two percent or more reported spending more than five percent on measurement in comparison to their companies rights fees expenditure (IEG Sponsorship Report, April 22, 2013).

O'Reilly and Madill (2009) point out that the resources available for measurement are a factor in choosing the evaluation method, but they add that evaluation should not simply be based on the available methodology. In the IEG and Performance Research survey in 2012, only 45 percent of respondents claimed that they had a standardized measurement process. The general questions of measurement are: What to measure? When should the measurement occur? What method of measurement to employ? Who should measure? What questions need to be asked? What does the sample size need to be to deliver meaningful results?

Methods of Evaluation: Brand Exposure Metrics

Miyazaki and Morgan (2001) contend that evaluation methods for a sponsorship are similar to other advertising endeavors. They state, "Methods commonly used to evaluate general advertising effectiveness on brand awareness or image do not differentiate between the value of a sponsorship per se and the value of general advertising and exposure that would accompany a similar nonsponsorship campaign" (p. 10).

Traditional promotional communication measurements include media impressions, the number of actual times the brand appears on the air, in print, or online, recall surveys (both on-site and through follow-up methods), economic measures such as sales or stock price, and qualitative methodologies, such as interviews or focus groups. The evaluation methodologies must be specifically designed to measure success of any brand goals. For example, brand exposure evaluations are truly less important if the brand's goals were not related to exposure (Li & Leckenby, 2007; Savary, 2008).

Crimmins and Horn (1996) claim the most common way of quantifying consumer impact of sponsorship is through measures of visibility and simple brand exposure. Counting the amount of media impressions that a corporation receives and then comparing that number to the advertising cost for that time and space is one method where some estimated value of a sponsorship can be assigned. Fortunato and Yost (2006) examined the number of impressions that Nike received through its sponsorship of major universities in *Sports Illustrated* during the magazine's coverage of the 2004 college football season and then compared that number to the advertising cost for that space. They counted a total of 131 Nike impressions in the six-month sample of pictures of college football coverage in *Sports Illustrated*. By using the cheapest advertising cost, $127,305, provided in the *Sports Illustrated* rate card of January 2005, it was argued that Nike received at least $16,676,955 in exposure value for its sponsorship with universities through this one medium outlet. In this sample Nike was even able to showcase its logo in spaces in the magazine that are not offered for purchase to advertisers. Nike logos were found on three covers and four table-of-contents sections. While Nike receives much greater exposure in their sponsorship of universities during the live broadcasting of their games, this added exposure through an outlet such as *Sports Illustrated* provides an extra, measurable benefit for the company.

In another evaluation using media exposure, *Street & Smith's Sports Business Journal* published a study by Repucom, a sports marketing research firm, that measured the total value of brand impressions for the 41 races of the 2012 NASCAR Sprint Cup series. The total value of $1.21 billion in 2012 represented a 6.6 percent increase from the value measured in 2011. The increase in total value was due to the increase in the price of cost-pre-minute advertising rates that were used in the comparison. This increase off-set the decrease from 2011 in the overall number of brand exposures, the total on-screen duration time, the number of brands tracked, and audience viewership. Chevrolet had the highest monetary value of any sponsor in this evaluation. Sprint, title sponsor for the NASCAR racing series, had the second highest monetary value of any sponsor in this evaluation (Broughton, 2013). Sprint having a high monetary value is not a surprising result as Sprint has one of the largest investments with NASCAR through its title sponsorship of the racing series.

Beyond an estimated dollar amount for brand exposure, obvious legitimate questions can still be raised in relation to these examples, such as did the readers notice the Nike logo or the viewers of the NASCAR races notice any of those brands? Were the readers able to associate Nike with the proper university or the viewers of NASCAR able to associate brands with the proper drivers? Were the readers influenced to think positively about Nike or the viewers of NASCAR influenced to think positively about the brands that they witnessed? Were the readers more inclined to purchase Nike products or the viewers of NASCAR more inclined to purchase any of the brands that they witnessed? Did the readers actually purchase a Nike-branded product or did the viewers of NASCAR actually purchase any of the brands that they witnessed?

The problem with using media impressions as an evaluative measure is that while they can be used to illustrate exposure and penetration of a particular message, these impression figures only report the size of the audience and do not measure impact (Cornwell, 2008; Speed & Thompson, 2000). Speed and Thompson (2000) point out that media exposure can provide an evaluative measure in terms of comparing the cost of media exposure through the sponsorship to traditional spot advertising buys in that location, but it will not provide direct evidence of the sponsorship's effect on a targeted audience's level of brand awareness or image. Cornwell (2008) adds the exposure measurement in relation to a media-buy price does offer sponsors some comfort in providing a value on the sponsorship investment, but the exposure does not equate to the quality of the message being delivered. Thjomoe et al. (2002) contend that while the measurement of brand exposure "might be an appropriate method for measurement of such sponsorship goals as building brand awareness, it is clearly not appropriate for more advanced goals such as changing brand image or enhanced relationships with stakeholders/customers" (p. 13).

Traditional media metrics of CPM (cost per thousand), CPP (cost per person), CPI (cost per insertion), GRP (gross ratings points), or CTR (click-through rates) can thus no longer be the only evaluative measures for promotional communication (Burns, 2011; Nelson & Katz, 2011; Russell, 2011). Crompton (2004) believes that one of the obstacles to effective sponsorship measurement is that often only traditional advertising evaluations are being used. Dan Donnelly, executive vice president and managing director with Starcom MediaVest, describes quantitative exposure measurements such as television rating points as "a given" and that larger questions need to be addressed: "Are people talking about your brand? And, are they talking about it with the brand message behind it?" (personal communication, December 19, 2011).

Evaluation: Digital Technologies

Evaluation along quantitative methods of brand exposure might be stressed because of the simplicity; however, any information ascertained about impact on consumers is more meaningful, especially for the companies with promotional communication goals other than mere exposure. Russell (2011) makes a distinction between "assumed engagement, in which the audience metrics count the number of people who could potentially pay attention to a message, and earned engagement, in which the audience engages with the message in a real or imagined way because the message is perceived to merit interaction" (pp. 125–126).

One area where some of these engagement evaluations can be conducted is through digital media. The emergence of digital technologies has led to greater opportunities for more precise measurement and evaluation. Researchers contend that digital media offer the capability to automatically collect information about audience exposure, gather invaluable personal information directly from customers, and quickly adapt communication campaigns (Bianco, 2004; Russell, 2011).

Nelson and Katz (2011) provide a summary listing of Internet measures that do include brand exposure, but also feature more progressive consumer behaviors. The evaluations are impressions, time spent viewing, retention rate of viewers revisiting a site, registration rates of people who sign up at a Web site, and conversion rates that result in a sale. They classify the two main Internet measures as click-through rates, "obtained by dividing the number of users who clicked on an ad on a web page by the number of times the ad was delivered (impressions)," and conversion rates, "the percentage of search-generated visitors who make a purchase or answer a call to action" (p. 317).

Researchers contend that companies need to be using social media and online vehicles to also measure brand recommendation and advocacy (Pope, 2010; Russell, 2011; Steyn, 2009). The word-of-mouth communication that has always influenced consumers' brand preference has now been shifted to digital media. Pope (2010) states, "Satisfied consumers tell their friends, dissatisfied ones tell online communities" (p. 243). Steyn (2009) points out that now through online and social-media technology, consumer opinions are "digitally amplified" and that an online brand recommendation now has a global audience. He states, "Sponsors need an understanding of the consumer's online engagement with their brands and the extent to which consumers will promote, or demote, the sponsor brand through online channels" (p. 317).

Steyn (2009) found that sponsorship recall can have a positive impact on both brand image and brand recommendation. Evidence also exists that the intention to promote (or recommend) a brand is highly correlated with a company's growth and profitability (Keiningham, Cooil, Andreassen, & Aksoy, 2007; Reichheld, 2003; Steyn, 2009). Therefore, one communication objective of a sponsorship could be to facilitate ways to increase the likelihood that consumers will recommend their brand (Reichheld, 2003; Steyn, 2009; Yu & Hui, 2007).

Burns (2011) simply states, "marketers are seeking new and better ways to measure the effectiveness of their programs and justify their marketing spend" (p. 308). He comments that "new metrics that are precisely defined and are both valid and reliable, will be critical for the monetization of alternative media, as well as helping us understand the ways in which we relate to mediated content delivered in accordance with contemporary technology and life style" (p. 310). Russell (2011) adds, "With valid and actionable metrics, new media channels can be appropriately priced and advertisers will have a rational basis for recommending advertising strategies and media buys for their clients" (p. 126).

Return on Investment (ROI)

Beyond the evaluation method used, the standard for the success of the promotional communication is questioned. Sponsorship evaluations are conducted on economic outcomes compared to the cost of the entire sponsorship program, referred to simply as Return on Investment (ROI). Green (2008) contends that ROI "should be viewed as a precise financial accounting term, namely the incremental profit generated by a given level of marketing expenditure" (p. 358). Similarly, Maestas (2009) defines, "True ROI is determined by taking the bottom-line profit that can be attributed to a sponsorship and dividing it by the total sponsorship investment" (p. 99). He summarizes, ROI should be an "educated approximation of how much additional profit the company has earned based solely on the sponsorship" (p. 99). Crompton (2004), therefore, claims the ideal measurement to evaluate a sponsorship is indeed sales. He then recognizes important steps in the process toward sales with evaluating intent to purchase and brand awareness or recall studies as the next most effective measurements.

Another economic evaluation measure of sponsorship is the stock price of a corporation. Researchers have found that sports sponsorships can enhance the stock price of the sponsoring corporation (Clark, Cornwell, & Pruitt, 2002; Miyazaki & Morgan, 2001; Pruitt, Cornwell, & Clark, 2004). In studying sponsorship through stadium signage, Clark, Cornwell, and Pruitt (2002) found, "Many investors clearly believe that stadium sponsorship can indeed serve as an important element in a company's overall marketing strategy" (p. 30). Their results indicate that sponsorships can "significantly enhance the stock price of sponsoring companies" (p. 16). Clark et al. (2002) claim, "Sponsorships are able to add direct financial value to the firm and help differentiate the brand" (p. 30). Cornwell, Pruitt, and Van Ness (2001) found that there may be more of an effect for sponsors whose brands are functionally congruent with the event. The research results are, however, not unanimous. In studying Olympic sponsorship, Miyazaki and Morgan (2001) found evidence of an impact for some sponsors, but not a general effect. Kinney and Bell (2004) also found no significant stock price effects because of sponsorship.

There is evidence that individual endorsers being associated with positive events can have a positive influence on the stock price of a company as well (Agrawal & Kamakura, 1995; Mathur, Mathur, & Rangan, 1997; Russell et al., 2005). Mathur, Mathur, and Rangan (1997) indicated that on average the companies that were endorsed by Michael Jordan had their stock prices increase by 2 percent after his return to the NBA in 1995. Conversely, there is evidence that individual endorsers associated with negative events can have a negative influence on the stock price of a company (Louie & Obermiller, 2002; Russell et al., 2005). Louie and Obermiller (2002) reported that a company's financial performance increased when it released an endorser who was identified as highly blameworthy for a negative event.

Similar to product purchasing consumer behavior, there are many variables that influence the increase or decrease of a stock price, making a definite attribution to a sponsorship program problematic. If economic success is achieved, the measurement might be able to demonstrate that the promotional communication strategy should be credited with having played a role.

Return on Objectives (ROO)

Measuring the success of a promotional communication campaign along a singular ROI criterion is only one approach. In addition to evaluating a sponsorship on its ROI, some scholars emphasize evaluation on Return on Objectives (ROO) (Maestas, 2009; O'Reilly & Madill, 2009; Savary, 2008; Watt, 2010). Savary (2008) claims ROO "serves as an alternative to the traditional ROI metric, which tries to attribute a set number of units sold to a given marketing program. Instead of forcing marketers to focus on immediate sales as a measure of success, ROO allows marketers to count customers at each step of the purchase process" (pp. 218–219). Savary (2008) explains that this approach, measuring ROO, evaluates consumers' movement from brand familiarity, to usage of the brand, to becoming a brand advocate. She claims that measuring the consumers' movement helps evaluate the success of the entire campaign. She indicates that comparative measurements need to be conducted with both pre- and post-exposure to the campaign and adds that it is helpful to have a group that has not been exposed to the campaign. Savary (2008) summarizes, "Ultimately, marketing success occurs when a change in beliefs, knowledge, affinity or advocacy can be directly correlated with exposure to a specific campaign" (p. 220).

Similarly, Maestas (2009) identifies the elements of ROO that are often measured are the level of brand awareness, customer satisfaction, and customer intent. He too argues that companies should ideally perform research before the sponsorship begins to establish an initial baseline measurement so that comparisons can be made throughout the sponsorship and the changes identified after exposure to the promotional communication campaign to decipher a more accurate measurement of the sponsorship's impact. Nielsen (2011) emphasizes the immediacy of evaluation, claiming that "companies wait months into a new mega-sponsorship before deciding to get serious about measurement, missing the opportunity to establish key baselines from the get-go" (p. 22).

It is important to note that measurement of ROI and measurement of ROO are not mutually exclusive. It is up to the sponsor to evaluate all of the measurement data collected and determine which are the most important. Maestas (2009), however, contends that all ROO measurements are merely a step to the needed ROI outcome. He explains that ROO measurements "are only valuable if one understands how these changes affect the bottom line" (p. 99). Nielsen (2011) adds, "A return is a monetary term, meaning you put in dollars and get a certain amount of more dollars in return" (p. 22).

Evaluation and Planning

In an ROO-based marketing process Savary (2008) explains that once an objective is determined, communication strategies to achieve that objective and the metrics to evaluate their effectiveness need to be developed. There are difficulties in both planning and evaluating sponsorship in that through one promotional communication campaign each customer that is reached has a different relationship with the brand. Russell (2011) adds that "for campaigns with more complex objectives such as loyalty or brand building, evidence of success requires several metrics that each address an aspect of the customers, their contexts, the media used, and the scope of changes sought. The more complex the objectives of the campaign, the more complex are the metrics needed to assess interim results and overall success" (p. 129).

Mike Singer, consulting director for the Marketing Arm, stresses the coordination of the brand's goals, selecting the property, creating the activation programs, and determining the evaluative methods in the initial negotiation of the sponsorship agreement. Singer notes that all sponsorships cannot be measured along the same criteria because each might have a very different goal. He contends that an evaluation model must be developed that is unique to each client and that clearly reflects the company's goals for the promotional campaign. For example, a company needing brand exposure would value stadium signage differently than a company that has significant brand awareness. Singer too believes in the importance of conducting the evaluation prior to and after the program's implementation with benchmarks placed on what the sponsorship overall, or any of its activation programs specifically, is expected to achieve.

Some examples can illustrate how the brand's goals, the activation programs developed, and the evaluation measures used are all in alignment. John Knebel, vice president and managing director of corporate partnerships and business development for the Washington Nationals, details the process. For example, if a car company has a business goal of having its local dealerships acquire customer leads, an activation program could be set up at the ballpark where a fan can get a co-branded giveaway item, such as a T-shirt, by simply providing his or her information. The car company with that customer information now has a potential lead. The program could then include that if that fan visits the local dealership and test drives a car within the next 30 days, he or she would get two free tickets to a game. To incorporate the goal of sales, the program could include that the fan gets two premium tickets to a game if he or she actually buys a car. In this example, the number of leads, the number of cars test driven, and the number of sales are all based on the sponsor's goals, they are all measurable, and they can be compared to the cost of the program (personal communication, February 14, 2012).

Through its sponsorship of the United States Olympic Committee BMW provides a practical example. In activating around the London Olympics in 2012 BMW created "Drive for Team USA" events at more than 300 dealerships across the United States. BMW sent fliers to perspective buyers where if they test-drove a BMW at one of these events they would receive $1,000 toward the purchase of a new car while BMW would make a $10 donation to the USOC for every test drive taken. A member of Team USA was present at every "Drive for Team USA" event. The result was more than 26,535 people test drove BMW cars with approximately twenty-five percent becoming buyers, giving the program an estimated more than $150 million in sales. Trudy Hardy, manager of marketing communications and consumer events for BMW North America, commented, "as a car company, we always do a summer sales event, but this was a great way to tie in with the Olympic movement. It generated such a spirit and energy. It really gave us a great message and allowed all of our dealers to operate under a giant umbrella" (Mickle, 2012d, p. 38).

In another example, John Knebel points out that teams use ticket stubs as a measurable incentive program in response to a brand goal of retail purchases or restaurant visits. The Papa John's Miami Heat home game deal mentioned in Chapter Six that includes a coupon for a pizza at a Papa John's restaurant can easily be tracked. Some teams even tie the team's performance, such as points or runs scored, to the retail or restaurant promotion. For these retail or restaurant promotions, just getting the customers to visit their locations is the key, as the customers will often spend more than the discount provided in the program. In some instances, the measurement could reveal that the sponsorship paid for itself.

Tony Ponturo, former head of media and sports marketing for Anheuser-Busch, indicates that as a beer company one evaluative measure it would examine is where point-of-sale displays were being used. If these retail displays were only being used in certain states, some conclusions could be drawn that the particular geographic area might not have as much interest in that property.

The extensive evaluation helps put a value on the many aspects of a sponsorship. This information is essential in both the initial negotiation and the renewal process. By having an accurate value placed on a sponsorship program, with larger companies negotiating many sponsorship agreements for multi-millions of dollars, the ability to accurately determine the value for a sponsorship or one of its activation elements could result in millions of dollars of savings for the company.

To illustrate this point of proper evaluation and interpretation of the measured results serving as the basis for future sponsorship decision making, UPS provides an example. For the 2012 NASCAR season UPS decided to shift from being the primary sponsor of a car, signified by the car having the UPS paint design, for 36 races to only being the primary sponsor for driver Carl Edwards' number 99 Ford car for one race at Kentucky Speedway. UPS was an associate sponsor for Edwards for the entire season. Ron Rogowski, UPS vice president of sponsorship and events for UPS, commented, "The shift in our program was a strategic business decision that allows us to focus on the elements that drive the best return on our investment. We are always evaluating ways to refine and enhance all of our sponsorship programs to ensure they are aligned with our business strategy and objectives" (UPS press release, October 27, 2011).

Who Should Measure?

Because of the complexity and importance of evaluation Pearsall (2010) contends that measurement needs to occur by both the sponsor and the property. Maestas (2009) explains, "As a property, there is no better validation than to show a client how a partnership benefits their business, especially in challenging economic times" (p. 101). In the annual IEG and Performance Research survey in 2013, however, only 40 percent of respondents reported that they thought it was valuable if the property assisted in measuring ROI and ROO (IEG Sponsorship Report, April 22, 2013).

In addition to the simple question of who is going to conduct the evaluation, there is the issue of interpreting the data. With so much money at stake, when these two entities renegotiate a contract they will each try to obtain the best deal possible. Evaluating the sponsorship in a way that might benefit a particular position certainly would impact that negotiation. If the property is measuring the sponsorship effectiveness it might interpret the data in a way that is beneficial to itself so as to be more attractive and more expensive for the sponsor to renew (Seiferheld, 2010). If the property conducted an evaluation that showed the sponsorship was not effective, it might not want to share that information. Conversely, if a sponsor was receiving tremendous, measurable results through its sponsorship of a property, it might want to downplay that fact a little bit so that the property does not ask for a steep increase in the price of that sponsorship. The sponsor would not want to cede all of its negotiation leverage.

Perhaps gathering data is largely for the company's own use in effectively negotiating the deal rather than developing data that will be shared, although the use of objective measurements can help alleviate this concern. It is in the evaluation process where the concepts of relationship building and trust between the property and the sponsor might be the most important. In the end, the sponsorship industry is only as good as the people working in it. The evaluation process is one area where the need for professionalism is paramount.

Ultimately, to not conduct extensive evaluation is a missed opportunity. Still, resources need to be committed to evaluation. Burton, Quester, and Farrelly (1998) identify the dual problem for sponsorships not being successful, claiming that many corporations are naïve about purchasing sponsorship packages and many are not sufficiently evaluating their sponsorship investments. Green (2008) argues that if "R" for return is important in the Return on Investment evaluation, the "I" indicating the level of investment, including an investment in measurement, is equally vital and must be considered in realistically evaluating the returns. The examples provided here that demonstrate the value of investing in measurement can influence more sponsors and properties to commit the necessary resources. As these examples indicate, these investments in evaluation can impact future planning and more efficient sponsorships can be the result.

Conclusion

In documenting the principles and practices of the sponsorship industry there are some conclusions that can be drawn with a high degree of certainty. The first is that sponsorship will continue to be a viable promotional communication strategy and an instrumental part of any integrated communication campaign. Properties will continue to need revenue, and sponsors in an ever changing media-use environment will continue to need these properties as a vehicle to reach their desired target audience. Companies will always need brand exposure, brand recall, desire a brand association, creative ways to communicate brand themes, and consumer behavior; in many instances sponsorship answers those needs. Sports properties will remain a viable destination for sponsors because of the demographic variables of the audience, the fact that sports is one of the few DVR-proof television genres, and the sports fans' emotional characteristics of loyalty and passion dictate their behavior.

The sponsorship characteristic of negotiation making anything possible offers unlimited opportunities for sponsors. The sponsorship negotiation process must be driven by the achievement of specific brand goals. As brand goals are established the two primary decisions for sponsors are the selection of the property and developing an activation program. Sponsorship selection of the property is conducted along the criteria of the target audience and brand association, with cost obviously being a factor. In the negotiation process, the advantageous characteristic of product category exclusivity with the property or event location is obtained. Through an exclusive sponsorship an association between the sponsor and the property, and thus the audience that the property attracts, is formed. A brand association can be communicated through sponsors putting the league or team logo on their product packaging. The hope for the sponsor is that fans will transfer their passion and loyalty from their favorite teams to supporting its brands.

To assist with the brand transfer, property selection will occur on dimensions of brand fit or congruence. In a functional congruence there is the opportunity for customers to witness the brand being used in support of or during the event. Functional congruence is not possible for all companies; thus many sponsors' selection of properties is based on image congruence, when the sponsor and the property have similar brand images. Finally, some companies have the advantage of purchase congruence, where there is an opportunity for point-of-purchase sales. The soft drink industry is one where point-of-purchase sales at the stadium or arena are possible.

Beyond the investment to acquire the rights to a property, the sponsor needs to spend money to activate the sponsorship. An activation program should be developed based on the sponsor's goals. The sponsorship activation must be a flexible and customized program that is unique to the sponsor. There are activation strategies for each brand goal. If, for example, exposure to increase brand awareness is the goal, stadium signage or naming rights would be effective. If product trial is the goal, a contest could be developed where to enter, the person did have to first try the product. Overall, the sponsors have the ability to provide fans or other constituency groups with experiences that would have not otherwise been possible. The negotiation of the activation program is where the concept of anything being possible and sponsorship truly being an "ideas business" is realized.

Finally, in the negotiation process evaluation methods should be set up to measure the sponsorship's effectiveness in achieving the brand's goals. There should be coordination between the brand's goals, the activation programs developed, and the evaluation methods used. Ideally, there will be an acceptable return on investment for the sponsor, with perhaps in some instances evidence that the sponsorship paid for itself.

Theories of persuasion and promotional communication lend themselves to a better understanding of the sponsorship industry. The Elaboration Likelihood Model attributed to Cacioppo and Petty (1979, 1981, 1984) can be applied. The main premise of the Elaboration Likelihood Model is that individual involvement with a product category will determine the extent of evaluating the arguments presented in the promotional communication message. As high-involvement individuals will focus on the quality of the message and the brand features, low-involvement individuals will focus on heuristic cues, such as attractiveness or source credibility or a brand association. Sponsorship is an ideal promotional communication strategy because of its unlimited possibilities that allow for creative activation programs that appeal to both the high-involvement and low-involvement individual.

For example, the low-involvement individual might be persuaded simply through the association that was created between the sponsor and the property. The low-involvement individual in that product category could be swayed because he or she is a fan of a team, and that sponsor now supports that team as well. If the product category is one of low involvement, the brand association between a sponsor and a property could serve as that company's unique selling proposition.

Through the possibilities of sponsorship activation, a brand theme that appeals to high-involvement individuals can also be conveyed. The examples in this book showed brand themes being demonstrated in opportunities of functional congruence, such as technology equipment providers assisting in the production of the Olympics or athletes using Nike products or drinking Gatorade during competition. Other brand themes have to be more creatively communicated to the audience. In some of these examples, the brand theme was effectively communicated through a corporate social responsibility initiative, such as the MasterCard Stand Up to Cancer Program that reflected the brand theme of moments that are priceless.

In applying the Elaboration Likelihood Model to the practice of sponsorship, it has to be noted that individual involvement is not a static condition with people moving along the spectrum of interest in a product category. Also, when one message is being sent, the sender cannot definitively know how much of the audience is of a high-involvement or low-involvement characterization. Therefore, the use of quality argument activations that stress brand features and themes should be used in conjunction with ideas that stress the association between the sponsor and the property. Ideas to reach all potential customers become the cornerstone of the sponsorship industry.

What a sponsorship entails is only limited by the ideas that the representatives of the sponsor and the property agree to implement. In this light, sponsorship is a relationship business built on trust with constant dialogue serving as the foundation of a more effective sponsorship. Practitioners from the sponsor perspective are constantly thinking about the next innovative activation program that addresses and satisfies the brand's goals. Practitioners from the property perspective are constantly thinking about how they can apply the property's assets in a way that will help the sponsors achieve their brand goals, while at the same time increasing revenue for the property.

Practitioners from both the property side and the sponsor side will continue to be creative in developing the next effective sponsorship idea. All of the different ideas put forth in this book were thought of by some industry professional. Someone thought of Deloitte using Olympic athletes in a university tour to talk about its brand and meet potential employees. Someone thought of Qualcomm using its Snapdragon brand as the name of the stadium in San Diego for the two weeks that included three football games on prime-time television. Someone thought of the Doritos "Crash the Super Bowl" campaign.

Finally, the audience reaction to sponsorship plays a factor in the industry. At first, there might be an adverse reaction to the notion that certain events or locations have a sponsor's name attached. For example, it was probably awkward to hear a bowl game or a stadium have a sponsor's name; now it is customary. When the next major sports league sells a uniform sponsorship, there will be some degree of criticism, but soon after it will be accepted as a function of the business.

Sponsorship is a promotional communication strategy; when executed properly, both the sponsor and the property should accrue major benefits. For all of the possibilities and complexities of the sponsorship industry and the fact that it will continue to change as new technologies and ideas emerge, Tony Ponturo, former head of media and sports marketing for Anheuser-Busch, stresses that the fundamental principles of sponsorship have not changed. It is still about "knowing who is the customer, finding the property to reach that customer base, knowing the value of the property, and taking that asset and exciting consumers about it" (personal communication, February 21, 2012).

The challenge for current and future sponsorship practitioners is simply to continue to understand the opportunities that are presented in a complex industry. This book intended to provide a clear way to properly approach and implement a sponsorship. It was designed to detail the possibilities and the potential impediments to a successful sponsorship. It tried to point out some of the missed opportunities if not included in the sponsorship process, such as not activating the sponsorship to achieve brand goals, not having a corporate social responsibility activation component, or not investing in evaluation. With the money as substantial as it is to acquire rights and execute a sponsorship, the industry will continue to have a demand for people who have a passion and desire to maintain their knowledge of what brands are thinking, an awareness of the latest trends in the field, and a talent for developing creative ideas and solutions to business problems. Hopefully, this book has encouraged and helped the readers begin to answer that demand.

References

Aaker, D. A. (1991). *Managing Brand Equity*. New York: The Free Press.

_____. (1996). *Building Strong Brands: Capitalizing on the Value of Brand Name*. New York: The Free Press.

_____, and E. Joachimsthaler. (2000). *Brand Leadership*. New York: The Free Press.

Aaker, J. L. (1997). Dimensions of brand personality. *Journal of Marketing Research, 34*(3), 347–356.

Agrawal, J., and W. A. Kamakura. (1995). The economic worth of celebrity endorsers: An event study analysis. *Journal of Marketing, 59*(3), 56–62.

Ahluwalia, R. (2000). Examination of psychological processes underlying resistance to change. *Journal of Consumer Research, 27*(2), 217–232.

Amato, C. H., C. L. O. Peters, and A. T. Shao. (2005). An exploratory investigation into NASCAR fan culture. *Sport Marketing Quarterly, 14*(2), 71–83.

Amis, J. (2003). "Good things come to those who wait": The strategic management of image and reputation at Guinness. *European Sport Management Quarterly, 3*(3), 189–214.

_____, T. Slack, and T. Berrett. (1999). Sport sponsorship as distinctive competence. *European Journal of Marketing, 33*(3/4), 250–272.

Ang, S. H., and S. Y. M. Low. (2000). Exploring the dimensions of ad creativity. *Journal of Marketing Research, 33*(2), 835–854.

Ansons, T. L., F. Wan, and J. P. Leboe. (2011). The influence of immersion on product placement effectiveness: A synthesis and review of product placement in traditional and digital media. In M. S. Eastin, T. Daugherty, and N. M. Burns (eds.). *Handbook of Research on Digital Media and Advertising: User Generated Content Consumption* (pp. 109–124). Hershey, PA: Information Science Reference.

Armstrong, M. (2010, June 8). A new source for NFL team credit cards. *Philadelphia Inquirer*, C1.

Arnett, D. B., and D. A. Laverie. (2000). Fan characteristics and sporting event attendance: Examining variance in attendance. *International Journal of Sports Marketing & Sponsorship, 2*(3), 219–238.

Arnold, K. A., and C. Bianchi. (2001). Relationship marketing, gender, and culture: Implications for consumer behavior. *Advances in Consumer Research, 28*(1), 100–105.

Arthur, D., D. Scott, T. Woods, and R. Booker. (1998). Sport sponsorship should ... A process model for the effective implementation and management of sport sponsorship programs. *Sport Marketing Quarterly, 7*(4), 49–60.

Artsitas, G. (2010, June 21). Nike steals Adidas' World Cup thunder. *USA Today*, 3C.

Atkin, C., and M. Block. (1983). Effectiveness of celebrity endorsers. *Journal of Advertising Research, 23*(1), 57–61.

Atkin, D. (2004). *The Culting of Brands When Customers Become True Believers*. New York: Penguin Group.

Atkin, D. J., and L. W. Jeffres. (1998). Understanding Internet adoption as telecommunications behavior. *Journal of Broadcasting & Electronic Media, 42*(4), 475–490.

Auty, S., and Lewis, C. (2004). Exploring children's choice: The remainder effect of product placement. *Psychology & Marketing, 21*(9), 697–713.

Bae, J., and G. T. Cameron. (2006). Conditioning effect of prior reputation on perception of corporate giving. *Public Relations Review, 32*(2), 144–150.

Baker, W. E. (1999). When can affective conditioning and mere exposure directly influence brand choice? *Journal of Advertising Research, 28*(4), 31–46.

Bal, C., and S. Boucher. (2011). Venue sponsorship and customer journey: A case study of the O_2. *Journal of Sponsorship, 4*(3), 236–244.

Balasubramanian, S., J. A. Karrh, and H. Patwardhan. (2006). Audience response to product placements: An integrative framework and future research agenda. *Journal of Advertising, 35*(3), 115–141.

Barboza, D. (1995, August 7). Dallas Cowboys' stadium ousts Coke, despite NFL deal, and gives Pepsi "pouring rights." *New York Times*, D8.

Barry, T. (2002). In defense of the hierarchy of effects: a rejoinder to Weilbacher. *Journal of Advertising Research, 42*(3), 44–47.

_____, and D. Howard. (1990). A review and critique of the hierarchy of effects in advertising. *International Journal of Advertising, 9*(2), 121–135.

Basil, D. Z., and J. Erlandson. (2008). Corporate social responsibility website representations: A longitudinal study of internal and external self-presentations. *Journal of Marketing Communications, 14*(2), 125–137.

Basinger, J. (2004). How one president fielded a football crisis. *Chronicle of Higher Education, 50*(29), A1–A4.

Becker-Olsen, K. L. (2003). And now a word from our sponsor. *Journal of Advertising, 32*(2), 17–32.

Bee, C. C., and L. R. Kahle. (2006). Relationship marketing in sports: A functional approach. *Sport Marketing Quarterly, 15*(2), 102–110.

Bell, J. (1995, August 15). Cola wars bubbling: Cowboys' Jones shakes things up with separate deal. *USA Today*, 12C.

Bellamy, R. V., Jr. (1998). The evolving television sports marketplace. In L. A. Wenner (ed.), *Mediasport* (pp. 73–87). London: Routledge.

_____, and P. J. Traudt. (2000). Television branding as promotion. In S. T. Eastman (ed.), *Research in Media Promotion* (pp. 127–159). Mahwah, NJ: Lawrence Erlbaum Publishing.

Belson, K. (2010a, October 13). Nike will dress the NFL. *New York Times*, B14.

_____. (2010b, October 26). Knicks add tequila to roster of sponsors. *New York Times*, B16.

_____. (2010c, December 20). American Express ends five-year absence as NBA's official charge card. *New York Times*, D5.

_____. (2011, November 25). Hints of a comeback as Woods secures deals. *New York Times*, B9.

_____. (2012, April 11). Judge orders Reebok to recall Tebow jerseys. *New York Times*, B18.

Benoit, W. L. (1995). *Accounts, Excuses, and Apologies: A Theory of Image Restoration Strategies*. Albany, NY: State University of New York Press.

_____. (2000). Another visit to the theory of image restoration strategies. *Communication Quarterly 48*(1): 40–44.

Benson, J. A. (1988). Crisis revisited: An analysis of the strategies used by Tylenol in the second tampering episode. *Central States Speech Journal 39*: 49–66.

Berger, B. K, and D. J. Park. (2003). Public rela-

tion(ship)s or private controls? Practitioner perspectives on the uses and benefits of new technologies. *New Jersey Journal of Communication, 11*(1), 76–99.

Bianco, A. (2004, July 12). The vanishing mass market: New technology. Product proliferation. Fragmented media. Get ready: It's a whole new world. *Business Week*, 61–68.

Biswas, D., A. Biswas, and N. Das. (2006). The differential effects of celebrity and expert endorsements on consumer risk perceptions: The role of consumer knowledge, perceived congruency, and product technology orientation. *Journal of Advertising, 35*(2), 17–31.

Blackston, M. (2000). Observations: Building brand equity by managing the brand's relationships. *Journal of Advertising Research, 40*(6), 101–105.

Botta, C. (2012, June 4–10). Kings' run good for business, even in Canada. *Street & Smith's Sports Business Journal, 15*(8), 6.

_____. (2012, June 18–24). Sponsors get piece of MLS rivalry. *Street & Smith's Sports Business Journal, 15*(10), 4.

Boyd, T. C., and T. C. Krehbiel. (2003). Promotion timing in Major League Baseball and the stacking effects of factors that increase game attractiveness. *Sport Marketing Quarterly, 12*(3), 173–183.

_____, and M. D. Shank. (2004). Athletes as product endorsers: The effect of gender and product relatedness. *Sport Marketing Quarterly, 13*(2), 82–93.

Bradish, C., and J. J. Cronin. (2009). Corporate social responsibility in sport. *Journal of Sport Management, 23*(6), 691–697.

Bradshaw, T., and V. Kortekaas. (2011, September 3). Olympic sponsors seek podium for brands. *Financial Times*, 12.

Brennan, C. (1995, September 20). Jones states his case at owners meeting: Peers skeptical of deals by Cowboys' boss. *Washington Post*, D1.

Bressoud, E., J. M. Lehu, and C. A. Russell. (2010). The product well placed: The relative impact of placement and audience characteristics on placement recall. *Journal of Advertising Research, 50*(4), 374–385.

Bright, L. F. (2011). Media evolution and the advent of Web 2.0. In M. S. Eastin, T. Daugherty, and N. M. Burns (eds.). *Handbook of Research on Digital Media and Advertising: User Generated Content Consumption* (pp. 32–51). Hershey, PA: Information Science Reference.

Brinson, S., and W. L. Benoit. (1999). The tarnished star: Restoring Texaco's damaged public image. *Management Communication Quarterly 12*, 483–509.

Broughton, D. (2010, December 20–26). Lower

ad rates drive down exposure value. *Street & Smith's Sports Business Journal, 13*(34), 13–15.

_____. (2011, May 2–8). Sports ad spending roars back: AT&T Mobility ousts A-B from top spot. *Street & Smith's Sports Business Journal, 14*(3), 1,26–27.

_____. (2012a, May 2–8). Verizon tops among ad spenders. *Street & Smith's Sports Business Journal, 15*(8), 1,26–27.

_____. (2012b, November 12–18). Everybody loves bobbleheads: Popular giveaway climbs past t-shirts, headwear to top spot on promotions list. *Street & Smith's Sports Business Journal, 15*(30), 9.

_____. (2012c, November 19–25). In a first for survey, MLB completes the sweep. *Street & Smith's Sports Business Journal, 15*(31), 16–17.

_____. (2013, January 7–13). Higher ad rates lift NASCAR exposure value. *Street & Smith's Sports Business Journal, 15*(36), 9.

Brown, P. (2011, July 25–31). Effective, creative activation gives naming rights more impact. *Street & Smith's Sports Business Journal, 14*(14), 32.

Brown, S. P., and D. M. Stayman. (1992). Antecedents and consequences of attitude toward the ad: A meta-analysis. *Journal of Consumer Research, 19*(1), 34–51.

Brown, T. J., and P. A. Dacin. (1997). The company and the product: Corporate associations and consumer product responses. *Journal of Marketing, 61*(1), 68–84.

_____, and M. L. Rothschild. (1993). Reassessing the impact of television advertising clutter. *Journal of Consumer Research, 20*(2), 138–146.

Bruell, A. (2011, January 14). Integrated effort puts Head & Shoulders above the rest. *PR Week*, 15.

Buffalo News (2011, January 22). Budweiser still sole beer advertiser for Super Bowl, C6.

Burns, N. (2011). Point of involvement, purchase and consumption: The delivery of audience engagement. In M. S. Eastin, T. Daugherty, and N. M. Burns (eds.). *Handbook of Research on Digital Media and Advertising: User Generated Content Consumption* (pp. 300–313). Hershey, PA: Information Science Reference.

Burton, N., and S. Chadwick. (2009). Ambush marketing in sport: An analysis of sponsorship protection means counter-ambush measures. *Journal of Sponsorship, 2*(4), 303–315.

Burton, R., P. G. Quester, and F. J. Farrelly. (1998). Organizational power games. *Marketing Management, 7*(1), 27–36.

Bush, A. J., C. A. Martin, and V. D. Bush. (2004). Sports celebrity influence on the behavioral intentions of generation Y. *Journal of Advertising Research, 44*(1), 108–118.

Cacioppo, J. T., and R. E. Petty. (1979). Effects of message repetition and position on cognitive responses, recall, and persuasion. *Journal of Personality and Social Psychology, 37*(1), 97–109.

Cameron, G. T., L. Sallot, and P. A. Curtin. (1997). Public relations and the production of news: A critical review and a theoretical framework. In B. Burleson (ed.). *Communication Yearbook 20* (pp. 111–115). Thousand Oaks, CA: Sage.

Cameron, N. (2009). Understanding sponsorship and its measurement implications. *Journal of Sponsorship, 2*(2), 131–139.

Campbell, M. C., and K. L. Keller. (2003). Brand familiarity and advertising repetition effects. *Journal of Consumer Research, 30*(2), 292–304.

Cancel, A. E., G. T. Cameron, L. M. Sallot, and M. A. Mitrook. (1997). It depends: A contingency theory of accommodation in public relations. *Journal of Public Relations Research, 9*, 31–63.

Carey, J., and M. Elton. (2010). *When Media Are New: Understanding the Dynamics of New Media Adoption and Use*. Ann Arbor: University of Michigan Press.

Carison, B. D., and D. T. Donavan. (2008). Concerning the effect of athlete endorsements on brand and team-related intentions. *Sport Marketing Quarterly, 17*(3), 154–162.

Caroom, E. (2011, August 24). MetLife Stadium shows economic optimism. *Newark Star-Ledger*, 26, 28.

_____. (2012, January 25). Even with Super Bowl in store, some jerseys won't be. *Newark Star-Ledger*, 1, 10.

Carp, S. (2011, October 6). Race driver, rapper form unique partnership. *Las Vegas Review-Journal*, 2C.

Carrillat, F. A., E. G. Harris, and B. A. Lafferty. (2010). Fortuitous brand image transfer: Investigating the side effect of concurrent sponsorships. *Journal of Advertising, 39*(2), 109–123.

_____, B. A. Lafferty, and E. G. Harris. (2005). Investigating sponsorship effectiveness: Do less familiar brands have an advantage over more familiar brands in single and multiple sponsorship arrangements. *Brand Management, 13*(1), 50–64.

Casey, N. (2007, July 20). Nike delays Vick's shoe after NFL star is indicted. *Wall Street Journal*, B3.

Cauberghe, V., and P. De Pelsmacker. (2010). Advergames: The impact of brand prominence and game repetition on brand responses. *Journal of Advertising, 39*(1), 5–18.

_____. (2011). Adoption intentions toward interactive digital television among advertising professionals. *Journal of Interactive Advertising, 11*(2), www.jiad.org.

Chadwick, S., and D. Thwaites. (2005). Managing

sport sponsorship programs: Lessons from a critical assessment of English soccer. *Journal of Advertising Research, 45*(3), 328–338.

Chaiken, S. L., A. Liberman, and A. H. Eagly. (1989). Heuristic and systemic processing within and beyond the persuasion context. In J. S. Uleman and J. A. Bargh (eds.). *Unintended Thought* (pp. 212–252). New York: Guilford Press.

Chandy, R., G. J. Tellis, D. MacInnis, and P. Thaivanich. (2001). What to say when: Advertising appeals in evolving markets. *Journal of Marketing Research, 38*(4), 399–414.

Chevrolet (2011, November 28–December 4). Special advertising section. *Street & Smith's Sports Business Journal, 14*(31), 39–46.

Chiesa, A. (2007, October 24). Nike buys UK football kit giant Umbro in GBP285m deal. *The Herald* (Glasgow), 11.

Cho, S., and W. L. Benoit. (2005). 2004 primary presidential election campaign messages: A functional analysis of candidates' news releases. *Public Relations Review, 31*(2), 175–183.

_____. (2006). 2004 Presidential campaign messages: A functional analysis of press releases from President Bush and Senator Kerry. *Public Relations Review, 32*(1), 47–52.

Choi, J., and S. Park. (2011). Influence of advertising on acceptance of press releases. *Public Relations Review, 37*, 106–108.

Cialdini, R.B., R. J. Borden, A. Thorne, M. R. Walker, S. Freeman, and L. R. Sloan. (1976). Basking in reflected glory: Three (football) field studies. *Journal of Personality and Social Psychology, 34*, 366–375.

Clark, J. M., T. B. Cornwell, and S. W. Pruitt. (2002). Corporate stadium sponsorships, signaling theory, agency conflicts, and shareholder wealth. *Journal of Advertising Research, 42*(6), 16–33.

Clow, K. E., and D. Baack. (2012). *Integrated Advertising, Promotion, and Marketing Communications,* 5th ed. Boston: Prentice Hall.

Collett, P. (2008). Sponsorship-related hospitality: Planning for measurable success. *Journal of Sponsorship, 1*(3), 286–296.

Coombs, W. T. (2006). Crisis management: A communicative approach. In C. H. Botan and V. Hazleton (eds.). *Public Relations Theory II* (pp. 171–197). Mahwah, NJ: Lawrence Erlbaum Associates.

_____, and S. J. Holladay. (2010). *PR Strategy and Application.* Malden, MA: Wiley-Blackwell.

Cornwell, T. B. (1995). Sponsorship-linked marketing development. *Sport Marketing Quarterly, 12*(4), 13–24.

_____. (2008). State of the art and science in sponsorship-linked marketing. *Journal of Advertising, 37*(3), 41–55.

_____, and L. V. Coote. (2005). Corporate sponsorship of a cause: The role of identification in purchase intent. *Journal of Business Research, 58*(3), 268–276.

_____, M. S. Humphreys, A. M. Maguire, C. S. Weeks, and C. L. Tellegen. (2006). Sponsorship-linked marketing: The role of articulation in memory. *Journal of Consumer Research, 33*(3), 312–321.

_____, and I. Maignan. (1998). An international review of sponsorship research. *Journal of Advertising, 27*(1), 1–21.

_____, S. W. Pruitt, and R. Van Ness. (2001). The value of winning in motorsports: Sponsorship-linked marketing. *Journal of Advertising Research, 41*(1), 17–31.

_____, G. E. Relyea, R. L. Irwin, and I. Maignan. (2000). Understanding long-term effects of sports sponsorships: Role of experience, involvement, enthusiasm, and clutter. *International Journal of Sports Marketing and Sponsorship, 2*(2), 127–143.

_____, D. P. Roy, and E. A. Steinard. (2001). Exploring manager's perceptions of the impact of sponsorship on brand equity. *Journal of Advertising, 30*(2), 41–51.

_____, C. S. Weeks, and D. P. Roy. (2005). Sponsorship-linked marketing: Opening the black box. *Journal of Advertising, 34*(2), 21–42.

Cowley, E., and C. Barron. (2008). When product placement goes wrong: The effects of program liking and placement prominence. *Journal of Advertising, 37*(1), 89–98.

Crimmins, J., and M. Horn. (1996). Sponsorship: From management ego trip to marketing success. *Journal of Advertising Research, 36*(4), 11–20.

Crompton, J. (1996). The potential contributions of sports sponsorship in impacting the product adoption process. *Managing Leisure, 1*(4), 199–212.

_____. (2004). Conceptualization and alternate operationalizations of the measurement of sponsorship effectiveness in sport. *Leisure Studies, 23*(3), 267–281.

Cropp, F., and J. D. Pincus. (2001). The mystery of public relations: Unraveling its past, unmasking its future. In R. L. Heath (ed.). *Handbook of Public Relations* (pp. 189–203). Thousand Oaks, CA: Sage.

Cunningham, S., T. B. Cornwell, and L. V. Coote. (2009). Expressing identity and shaping image: The relationship between corporate mission and corporate sponsorship. *Journal of Sport Management, 23*(1), 65–86.

Cutlip, S. M., A. H. Center, and G. M. Broom. (2006). *Effective Public Relations,* 9th ed. Upper Saddle River, NJ: Pearson Prentice Hall.

Dalakas, V., R. Madrigal, and K. L. Anderson. (2004). "We are number one!" The phenomenon of basking-in-reflected-glory and its implications for sports marketing. In L. R. Kahle and C. Riley (eds.). *Sports Marketing and the Psychology of Marketing Communication.* Mahwah, NJ: Lawrence Erlbaum Associates.

Dater, A. (2000, January 20). Cola giants put feud on ice for one big day. *Denver Post,* D10.

Daugherty, E. L. (2001). Public relations and social responsibility. In R. L. Heath (ed.). *Handbook of Public Relations.* Thousand Oaks, CA: Sage.

Daugherty, T., M. Eastin, and L. F. Bright. (2008). Exploring consumer motivations for creating user-generated content. *Journal of Interactive Advertising, 8*(2), 1–24.

David, P., S. Kline, and Y. Dai. (2005). Corporate social responsibility practices, corporate identity, and purchase intention: A dual process model. *Journal of Public Relations Research, 17*(3), 291–313.

Davies, G., R. Chun, R. V. da Silva, and S. Roper. (2003). *Corporate Reputation and Competitiveness,* New York: Routledge.

Davis, S. M. (2002). *Brand Asset Management: Driving Profitable Growth through Your Brands.* San Francisco: Jossey-Bass.

Dawkins, J. (2004). Corporate responsibility: The communication challenge. *Journal of Communication Management, 9*(2), 108–119.

Dean, D. H. (2002). Associating the corporation with a charitable event through sponsorship: Measuring the effects on corporate community relations. *Journal of Advertising, 31*(4), 77–88.

DeFleur, M., and E. E. Dennis. (2002). *Understanding Mass Communication,* 7th ed. Boston: Houghton Mifflin.

Degaris, L., C. West, and M. Dodds. (2009). Leveraging and activating NASCAR sponsorships with NASCAR-linked sales promotions. *Journal of Sponsorship, 3*(1), 88–97.

Deitsch, R. (2013, March 18). A shot at the champ: Fox promises to come out swinging with a new 24/7 channel, but can FS1 really challenge ESPN? *Sports Illustrated, 118*(12), 16.

Demetriou, M., I. Papasolomou, and D. Vrontis. (2010). Cause-related marketing: Building the corporate image while supporting worthwhile causes. *Brand Management, 17*(4), 266–278.

Diaz, J. (2010, October 13). Nike bests Reebok: Apparel maker loses NFL deal worth millions. *Boston Globe,* B7.

Donegan, L. (2011, October 6). Woods looks back in the game. *The Irish Times,* p. 28.

Dorman, L. (2010, July 1). This year at AT&T National, Woods has a different role. *New York Times,* B14.

Drane, D., D. Phillips, A. Williams, and B. Crow.

(2005). Sports celebrities as endorsers: An analysis of Tiger Woods. In B. G. Pitts (ed.). *Where Sport Marketing Theory Meets Practice* (pp. 179–187). Morgantown, WV: Fitness Information Technology, Inc.

Dreier, F. (2010, November 22–28). P&G puts spotlight on Olympic moms. *Street & Smith's Sports Business Journal, 13*(30), 20.

_____. (2011a, March 14–20). In K.C., naming right mix with doing right. *Street & Smith's Sports Business Journal, 13*(45), 3.

_____. (2011b, March 21–27). A-B stays in soccer with MLS renewal. *Street & Smith's Sports Business Journal, 13*(46), 4.

_____. (2011c, April 18–24). Sponsorship drives NHL to $2.9B in revenue. *Street & Smith's Sports Business Journal, 14*(1), 4.

Drumwright, M. (1994). Socially responsible organizational buying: Environmental buying as a noneconomic buying criterion. *Journal of Marketing, 53*(3), 1–19.

Duke, T. (2001, March). Playing to win. *Ad Age Global, 1*(7), 43–45.

Eagly, A. H., and S. Chaiken. (1993). *The Psychology of Attitudes.* Fort Worth, TX: Harcourt, Brace, Jovanovich.

_____. (1998). Attitude structure and function. In D. T. Gilbert, S. T. Fiske, and G. Lindzey (eds.). *Handbook of Social Psychology,* (4th ed., Vol. 1), pp. 269–322. Boston: McGraw-Hill.

Eastin, M. S., T. Daugherty, and N. M. Burns. (2011). *Handbook of Research on Digital Media and Advertising: User Generated Content Consumption.* Hershey, PA: Information Science Reference.

Edelman, D. C. (2007). From the periphery the core: As online strategy becomes overall strategy, marketing organizations and agencies will never be the same. *Journal of Advertising Research, 47*(2), 130–134.

Ehrenberg, A., N. Barnard, R. Kennedy, and H. Bloom. (2002). Brand advertising as creative publicity. *Journal of Advertising Research, 42*(4), 7–18.

Elkington, J. (1994). Towards the sustainable corporation: Win-win-win business strategies for sustainable development. *California Management Review, 36*(2), 90–100.

Elliot, M., and P. Speck. (1998). Consumer perceptions of advertising clutter and its impact across various media. *Journal of Advertising Research, 38*(1), 29–41.

Elliot, P. (2002). The loveable rogues who devalue sporting events: Brands that do not want to fork out on expensive sports sponsorship often turn to ambush marketing. *Marketing Week, 25*(26), 14.

Ellis, D., M. Gauthier, and B. Seguin. (2011). Ambush marketing, the Olympic and Paralympic

Marks Act and Canadian national sports organizations: Awareness, perceptions, and impacts. *Journal of Sponsorship, 4*(3), 253–271.

Entman, R. (1993). Framing: Toward clarification of a fractured paradigm. *Journal of Communication, 43*(4), 51–58.

Erdogan, B. Z. (1999). Celebrity endorsement: A literature review. *Journal of Marketing Management, 15*(4), 291–314.

_____, M. J. Baker, and S. Tagg. (2001). Selecting celebrity endorsers: The practitioner's perspective. *Journal of Advertising Research, 41*(3), 39–48.

Fahy, J., F. Farrelly, and P. Quester. (2004). Competitive advantage through sponsorship: A conceptual model and research propositions. *European Journal of Marketing, 38*(8), 1,013–1,030.

Farhi, P. (1988, December 31). Big business creating bowls full of money: Sponsors pouring dollars into college football finals, other events. *Washington Post*, A1.

Farrelly, F. J., and S. A. Greyser. (2007). Sports sponsorship to rally the home team. *Harvard Business Review, 85*(9), 22–24.

_____, P. G. Quester, and R. Burton. (1997). Integrating sports sponsorship into the corporate marketing function: An international comparative study. *International Marketing Review, 14*(3), 170–182.

_____, P. G. Quester, and S. A. Greyser. (2005). Defending the co-branding benefits of sponsorship B2B partnerships: The case of ambush marketing. *Journal of Advertising Research, 45*(3), 339–348.

Fearn-Banks, K. (2001). Crisis communication: A review of some best practices. In R. L. Heath (ed.). *Handbook of Public Relations* (pp. 479–485). Thousand Oaks, CA: Sage.

Ferguson, D. A., and E. M. Perse. (2004). Audience satisfaction among TiVo and replay TV users. *Journal of Interactive Advertising, 4*(2), http:www.jiad.org/vol4/no2/ferguson.

Finch, D., N. O'Reilly, P. Varella, and D. Wolf. (2009). Return on trust: An empirical study of the role of sponsorship in stimulating consumer trust and loyalty. *Journal of Sponsorship, 3*(1), 61–72.

Fink, J. S., G. B. Cunningham, and L. J. Kensicki. (2004). Using athletes as endorsers to sell women's sport: Attractiveness vs. expertise. *Journal of Sport Management, 18*(4), 350–367.

Fishbein, M., and I. Ajzen. (1975). *Belief, Attitude, Intention and Behavior: An Introduction to Theory and Research*. Reading, MA: Addison-Wesley.

_____. (1981). Acceptance, yielding, and impact: Cognitive processes in persuasion. In R. E. Petty, T. Ostrom, and T. C. Brock (eds.). *Cognitive Responses in Persuasion* (pp. 339–359). Hillsdale, NJ: Lawrence Erlbaum Associates.

Fisher, E. (2012, February 13–19). Live NBC games part of Verizon-NHL renewal. *Street & Smith's Sports Business Journal, 14*(41), 4.

_____, and T. Lefton. (2012, July 16–22). K.C. delivers for league, fans, sponsors. *Street & Smith's Sports Business Journal, 15*(13), 3, 39.

_____, and _____. (2013, January 14–20). Persistence pays off as MLB and T-Mobile overcome complexities of partnership. *Street & Smith's Sports Business Journal, 15*(37), 4.

_____, _____, and D. Kaplan. (2013, May 27-June2). Microsoft-NFL relationship "will evolve over time." *Street & Smith's Sports Business Journal, 17*(7), 4.

Foltz, K. (1991, March 20). Does Bo, hurt, know as much? *The New York Times*, D1.

Fortunato, J. A. (2001). *The Ultimate Assist: The Relationship and Broadcast Strategies of the NBA and Television Networks*. Cresskill, NJ: Hampton Press.

_____. (2004). The rival concept: An analysis of the 2002 Monday Night Football Season. *Journal of Sport Management (special issue on sports media), 18*(4), 383–397.

_____. (2006). Scheduling promotional events in Major League Baseball: Examining team and sponsor desires. *International Journal of Sports Marketing & Sponsorship, 7(2)*, 104–114.

_____. (2008). Using message content to communicate a brand association: Olympic television advertising. *Journal of Sponsorship, 1*(3), 248–257.

_____. (2009). Using sponsorship as a form of public relations: A case study of Chevrolet and Major League Baseball. *Journal of Sponsorship, 4*(2), 330–339.

_____. (2011). Digital media and sports advertising. In M. S. Eastin, T. Daugherty, and N. M. Burns (eds.). *Handbook of Research on Digital Media and Advertising: User generated Content Consumption* (pp. 491–506). Hershey, PA: Information Science Reference.

_____, and A. E. Dunnam. (2004). The negotiation philosophy for corporate sponsorship of sports properties. In B. G. Pitts (ed.). *Sharing Best Practices in Sports Marketing* (pp. 99–111). Morgantown, WV: Fitness Information Technology, Inc.

_____, and S. E. Martin. (2010). American Needle v. NFL: Legal and sponsorship implications. *University of Denver Sports and Entertainment Law Journal, 9*, 73–82.

_____, and J. Melzer. (2008). The conflict of selling multiple sponsorships: The NFL beer market. *Journal of Sponsorship, 2*(1), 49–56.

_____, and J. Richards. (2007). Reconciling sports sponsorship exclusivity with antitrust law. *Texas Review of Entertainment & Sports Law, 8*(1), 33–48.

_____, and D. M. Windels. (2005). Adoption of digital video recorders and advertising: Threats or opportunities. *Journal of Interactive Advertising* (www.jiad.org), *6*(1), 137–148.

_____, and M. A. Yost. (2006). Evaluating sports sponsorships through media impressions: Nike exposure in Sports Illustrated's college football coverage. In B. G. Pitts (ed.). *Sport Marketing in the New Millennium* (pp. 105–114). Morgantown, WV: Fitness Information Technology, Inc.

Friedman, H. H., and L. Friedman. (1979). Endorser effectiveness by product type. *Journal of Advertising Research, 19*(5), 63–71.

Funk, D., and J. James. (2001). The psychological continuum model: A conceptual framework for understanding an individual's psychological connection to sport. *Sport Management Review, 4*(2), 119–150.

Futterman, M., & S. Ante. (2013, June 5). Verizon pads NFL deal. *Wall Street Journal*, p. 1.

Gardner, M. P. (1985). Does attitude toward the ad affect brand attitude under a brand evaluation set? *Journal of Marketing Research, 22*(2), 192–198.

Gearty, R. (2012, March 29). Hands off Tebow! Nike suing Reebok over jersey sales. *New York Daily News*, 18.

Gerrard, B., M. M. Parent, and T. Slack. (2007). What drives the value of stadium naming rights? A hedonic-pricing approach to the valuation of sporting intangible assets. *International Journal of Sport Finance, 2*(1), 10–24.

Geue, M., and C. Plewa. (2010). Cause sponsorship: A study of congruence, attribution and corporate social responsibility. *Journal of Sponsorship, 3*(3), 228–241.

Glenn, B. (2011, May 30–June 5). How to validate jersey sponsorship value. *Street & Smith's Sports Business Journal, 14*(7), 22.

Godfrey, P. C. (2009). Corporate social responsibility in sport: An overview and key issues. *Journal of Sport Management, 23*(6), 698–716.

Golding, B. (2012, March 29). Nike sacks Reebok in Tebow $$ tussle. *New York Post*, 32.

Golob, U., and J. L. Bartlett. (2007). Communicating about corporate social responsibility: A comparative study of CSR reporting in Australia and Slovenia. *Public Relations Review, 33*, 1–9.

Grady, J., and S. McKelvey. (2012, October 22–28). Ambush marketing lessons from the London Olympic games. *Street & Smith's Sports Business Journal, 15*(27), 25.

_____, _____, and M. J. Bernthal. (2010). From Beijing 2008 to London 2012: Examining event-specific Olympic legislation vis-à-vis the rights and interests of stakeholders. *Journal of Sponsorship, 3*(2), 144–156.

Graham, J. P. (1997). Ambush marketing. *Sport Marketing Quarterly, 6*(1), 10–13.

Green, A. (2008). Planning for effective evaluation: Are marketers really doing it? *Journal of Sponsorship, 1*(4), 357–363.

Greenwald, A. G., and C. Leavitt. (1984). Audience involvement in advertising: Four levels. *Journal of Consumer Research, 11*(1), 581–592.

Grimm, M. (1991, March 25). Pitchman Bo Jackson sits on the sidelines. *Adweek*, p. 5.

Grohs, R., and H. Reisinger. (2005). Image transfer in sports sponsorships: An assessment of moderating effects. *International Journal of Sports Marketing & Sponsorship, 7*(1), 42–48.

Gruen, T. W. (2000). Membership customers and relationship marketing. In J. N. Sheth and A. Parvatiyar (eds.). *Handbook of Relationship Marketing* (pp. 355–380). Thousand Oaks, CA: Sage.

Grunig, J. E., and L. A. Grunig. (1992). Models of public relations and communication. In J. E. Grunig, D. M. Dozier, W. P. Ehling, L. A. Grunig, F. C. Repper, and J. White (eds.). *Excellence in Public Relations and Communication Management* (pp. 285–326). Hillsdale, NJ: Lawrence Erlbaum Associates.

Gupta, P. B., and K. R. Lord. (1998). Product placement in movies: The effect of prominence and mode on audience recall. *Journal of Current Issues and Research in Advertising, 20*(1), 47–59.

Gwinner, K. P. (1997). A model of image creation and image transfer in event sponsorship. *International Marketing Review, 14*(3), 145–158.

_____, and J. Eaton. (1999). Building brand image through event sponsorship: The role of image transfer. *Journal of Advertising, 28*(4), 47–58.

_____, and S. R. Swanson. (2003). A model of fan identification: Antecedents and sponsorship outcomes. *Journal of Services Marketing, 17*(3), 275–294.

Haney, D. (2013, March 25–31). How college brands can lose their way amid March Madness. *Street & Smith's Sports Business Journal, 15*(47), 23.

Harris, R. (2005). When giving means taking: Public relations, sponsorship, and morally marginal donors. *Public Relations Review, 31*(4), 486–491.

Harris, T. L. (1998). *Value-Added Public Relations: The Secret Weapon of Integrated Marketing.* Chicago: NTC Business Books.

Harvey, B. (2001). Measuring the effects of sponsorship. *Journal of Advertising Research, 41*(1), 59–65.

Heath, T. (1996, December 14). NFL, Cowboys settle suits. *Washington Post*, F3.

Hickman, T. M., and K. E. Lawrence. (2010). The

halo effect of goodwill sponsorship versus the pitchfork effect of supporting the enemy. *Journal of Sponsorship*, *3*(3), 265–276.

Hiestand, M. (1996, June 6). Atlanta officials hope shame threat ends ambush ads. *USA Today*, p. 11C.

_____. (2011, January 12). Under Armour scores big with Auburn's BCS title. *USA Today*, C3.

Ho, P. (2011). Making your Chinese sponsorship strategy work. *Journal of Sponsorship*, *4*(3), 214–219.

Hoeffler, S., and K. L. Keller. (2003). The marketing advantages of strong brands. *Journal of Brand Management*, *10*(6), 421–445.

Hoek, J., and P. Gendall. (2002). Ambush marketing: More than just a commercial irritant? *Entertainment Law*, *1*(2), 72–91.

Hogan, N. (2011, October 3). New Orleans Saints sell Superdome naming rights to Mercedes-Benz. www.nola.com.

Hollis, S. (2008). Stadium naming rights — A guided tour. *Journal of Sponsorship*, *1*(4), 388–394.

Homer, P. M. (2009). Product placements: The impact of placement type and repetition on attitude. *Journal of Advertising*, *38*(3), 21–31.

Hopwood, M. (2007). Sports public relations. In S. Chadwick and J. Beech (Eds.), *Marketing of Sport* (pp. 292–317). Upper Saddle River, NJ: Prentice Hall

Horovitz, B. (2011, September 21). "X Factor" revives the cola wars; it gets Pepsi, Coke sticks with "Idol." *USA Today*, 3B.

Howard, D. J. (1997). Familiar phrases as peripheral persuasion cues. *Journal of Experimental Social Psychology*, *33*(3), 231–243.

Husted, B. W., and J. D. J. Salazar. (2006). Taking Friedman seriously: Maximizing profits and social performance. *Journal of Management Studies*, *43*(1), 75–91.

Imbriano, L. and E. King. (2011). *Winning the Customer: Turn Customers into Fans and Get Them to Spend More.* New York: McGraw-Hill.

Irwin, R. L., T. Lachowetz, T. B. Cornwell, and J. S. Clark. (2003). Cause-related sport sponsorship: An assessment of spectator beliefs, attitudes, and behavioral intentions. *Sport Marketing Quarterly*, *12*(3), 131–139.

_____, W. A. Sutton, and L. M. McCarthy. (2002). *Sport Promotion and Sales Management.* Champaign, IL: Human Kinetics.

Ito, T. A., J. T. Larsen, N. K. Smith, and J. T. Cacioppo. (1998). Negative information weighs more heavily on the brain: The negativity bias in evaluative categorizations. *Journal of Personality and Social Psychology*, *75*(4), 887–900.

Jackson, K. (2010). Achieving value from sponsorship in a new world order. *Journal of Sponsorship*, *3*(3), 215–219.

Jain, S., and D. Maheswaran. (2000). Motivated reasoning: A depth-of-processing perspective. *Journal of Consumer Research*, *26*(4), 358–371.

James, J. D., R. H. Kolbe, and G. T. Trail. (2002). Psychological connection to a new sport team: Building or maintaining the consumer base? *Sport Marketing Quarterly*, *11*(4), 215–225.

Jensen, M. (2003, September 16). After three seasons, WUSA goes under. *Philadelphia Inquirer*, E1.

Jensen, R. (2007). Public relations lessons from how the Houston Astros got "Enron-ed." *Journal of Sports Media*, *2*(1), 103–108.

Jewler, A. J., and B. L. Drewniany. (2001). *Creative strategy in advertising,* 7th ed. Belmont, CA: Wadsworth.

Joachimsthaler, E., and D. A. Aaker. (1997). Building brands without mass media. *Harvard Business Review*, *75*(1), 39–50.

Johar, G. V., and M. T. Pham. (1999). Relatedness, prominence, and constructive sponsor identification. *Journal of Marketing Research*, *36*(3), 299–312.

_____, _____, and K. L. Wakefield. (2006). How event sponsors are really identified: A (baseball) field analysis. *Journal of Advertising Research*, *46*(2), 183–198.

Johnson, G. (2006, September 18). When logos are a no-go: Athletes' endorsement deals conflict with sponsorships of leagues, teams and venues, leading to tension, fines and mixed messages. *Los Angeles Times*, D1.

Johnson, R. L., and C. J. Cobb-Walgren. (1994). Aging and the problem of television clutter. *Journal of Advertising Research*, *34*(3), 54–62.

Jones, M., and D. W. Schumann. (2004). The strategic use of celebrity athlete endorsers in print media: A historical perspective. In L. R. Kahle and C. Riley (eds.). *Sport Marketing and the Psychology of Marketing Communication* (pp. 107–131). Mahwah, NJ: Lawrence Erlbaum Associates.

Jones, S. (2011, June 22). Making a play at Rutgers: High Point Solutions will up its exposure with its name on football stadium. *Newark Star-Ledger*, 32,30.

Jones, S. A., T. A. Suter, and E. Koch. (2006). Affinity credit cards as relationship marketing tools: A conjoint analytic exploration of combined product attributes. *Sport Marketing Quarterly*, *15*(3), 138–146.

Jowdy, E., and M. McDonald. (2002). The FUTURES Golf Tour case study: Sponsorship sales and eduselling. *Sport Marketing Quarterly*, *11*(4), 248–250.

Kahle, L. R. (1996). Social values and consumer behavior: Research from a list of values. In C. Seligman, J. M. Olson, and M. P. Zanna (eds.). *The Psychology of Values: The Ontario Symposium*

(Vol. 8, pp. 135–151). Mahwah, NJ: Lawrence Erlbaum Associates.

_____, and P. M. Homer. (1985). Physical attractiveness of the celebrity endorser: A social adaptation perspective. *Journal of Consumer Research, 11*(4), 954–961.

Kamins, M. A. (1990). An investigation into the "match-up" hypothesis in celebrity advertising: When beauty may be only skin deep. *Journal of Advertising, 19*(1), 4–13.

_____, M. J. Brand, S. A. Hoeke, and J. C. Moe. (1989). Two-sided versus one-sided celebrity endorsements: The impact on advertising effectiveness and credibility. *Journal of Advertising, 18*(2), 4–10.

_____, and K. Gupta. (1994). Spokesperson and product type: A matchup hypothesis perspective. *Psychology and Marketing, 11*(6), 569–586.

Kapferer, J. N. (2001). Is there really no hope for local brands. *Brand Management, 9*(3), 163–170.

Kaplan, D. (2011a, January 17–23). Nike report hints at big NFL check. *Street & Smith's Sports Business Journal, 13*(37), 7.

_____. (2011b, June 20–26). Mercedes endorsement won't be the last for Li; "We could do 25 deals," agent says. *Street & Smith's Sports Business Journal, 14*(10), 3.

_____. (2011c, September 5–11). U.S. Open mad as ale over ads. *Street & Smith's Sports Business Journal, 14*(19), 8.

_____. (2012, April 16–22). NFL gives OK for teams to accept casino advertising. *Street & Smith's Sports Business Journal, 11*(1), 3.

_____. (2013, January 7–13). ATP allows for more, bigger logos on apparel. *Street & Smith's Sports Business Journal, 15*(36), 1, 27.

_____, and T. Lefton. (2005, September 5–11). Molson Coors renewing with NFL. *Street & Smith's Sports Business Journal, 8*(18), 1, 59.

Karla, A., and D. Soberman. (2010). The forgotten side of marketing. *Brand Management, 17*(4), 301–314.

Karrh, J. A. (1998). Brand placement: A review. *Journal of Current Issues and Research in Advertising, 20*(1), 31–49.

Katz, D. (1993, August 16). Triumph of the swoosh. *Sports Illustrated*, pp. 54–73.

Kaynak, E., G. G. Salman, and E. Tatoglu. (2008). An integrative framework linking brand associations and brand loyalty in professional sports. *Journal of Brand Management, 15*(5), 336–356.

Keiningham, T. L., B. Cooil, T. W. Andreassen, and L. Aksoy. (2007). A longitudinal examination of net promoter and firm revenue growth. *Journal of Marketing, 71*(3), 39–51.

Keller, K. L. (1993). Conceptualizing, Measuring, and Managing Customer-Based Brand Equity. *Journal of Marketing, 57*(1), 1–22.

_____. (1998). *Strategic Brand Management: Building, Measuring, and Managing Brand Equity.* Upper Saddle River, NJ: Prentice Hall.

_____. (2001). Mastering the marketing communications mix: Micro and macro perspectives on integrated marketing communication programs. *Journal of Marketing Management, 17*(7–8), 819–847.

_____. (2003). Brand synthesis: The multidimensionality of brand knowledge. *Journal of Consumer Research, 29*(4), 595–600.

_____, and D. A. Aaker. (1992). The effects of sequential introduction of brand extensions. *Journal of Marketing, 29*(1), 35–50.

Kelley, S. W., and L. W. Turley. (2004). The effect of content on perceived affect of Super Bowl commercials. *Journal of Sport Management, 18*(4), 398–420.

Kent, R. J., and C. T. Allen. (1994). Competitive interference effects on consumer memory for advertising: The role of brand familiarity. *Journal of Marketing, 58*(3), 97–105.

Kerr, K. (2012, December 31). Oh, what a year. *Sports Illustrated, 117*(26), 12–13.

King, B. (2011, August 1–7). Tecate goes big on boxing promo. *Street & Smith's Sports Business Journal, 14*(15), 4.

Kinney, L. (2006). Sports sponsorship. In A. A. Raney and J. Bryant (eds.). *Handbook of Sport and Media* (pp. 295–310). Mahwah, NJ: Lawrence Erlbaum Associates.

_____, and G. Bell. (2004). Do sport sponsorship announcements influence firm stock prices? In L. R. Kahle and C. Riley (eds.). *Sports Marketing and the Psychology of Marketing Communication* (pp. 223–239). Mahwah, NJ: Lawrence Erlbaum Associates.

_____, and S. R. McDaniel. (1996). Strategic implications of attitude-toward-the-ad in leveraging event sponsorships. *Journal of Sport Management, 10*(3), 250–261.

_____, and _____. (2004). American consumer attitudes toward corporate sponsorship of sporting events. In L. R. Kahle and C. Riley (eds.). *Sports Marketing and the Psychology of Marketing Communication* (pp. 211–222). Mahwah, NJ: Lawrence Erlbaum Associates.

_____, _____, and L. DeGaris. (2008). Demographic and psychographic variables predicting NASCAR sponsor brand recall. *International Journal of Sports Marketing & Sponsorship, 9*(3), 169–179.

Kintner, E. W. (1973). *An Antitrust Primer: A Guide to Antitrust and Trade Regulation Laws for Businessmen,* 2d ed. New York: MacMillan Company.

Kiousis, S., M. Mitrook, X. Wu, and T. Seltzer. (2006). First- and second-level agenda-building and agenda-setting effects: Exploring the linkages among candidate news releases, media coverage, and public opinion during the 2002 Florida Gubernatorial Election. *Journal of Public Relations Research, 18*(3), 265–285.

Kiszla, M. (2001, February 3). Cola wars: Coca-Cola, official sponsor of the NHL, invades enemy territory for all-star weekend, forcing Pepsi to retreat. *Denver Post,* D1.

Kitchen, P. J., I. Kim, and D. E. Schultz. (2008). Integrated marketing communications: Practice leads theory. *Journal of Advertising Research, 48*(4), 531–546.

Koernig, S. K., and T. C. Boyd. (2009). To catch a Tiger or let him go: The match-up effect and athlete endorsers for sport and non-sport brands. *Sport Marketing Quarterly, 18*(1), 25–37.

LaBletta, N. (2001). If *per se* is dying, why not in TV tying? A case for adopting the rule of reason standard in television block-booking arrangements. *Fordham Intellectual Property, Media & Entertainment Law Journal, 12*(1), 195–234.

Lachowetz, T. M., T. McDonald, W. A. Sutton, and D. G. Hedrick. (2003). Corporate sales activities and the retention of sponsors in the National Basketball Association (NBA). *Sport Marketing Quarterly, 12*(1), 18–26.

Ladousse, C. (2009). How Lenovo deploys powerful creative sponsorship activation techniques for a global brand. *Journal of Sponsorship, 2*(3), 199–205.

Lapio, R. L,. Jr., and K. M. Speter. (2000). NASCAR: A lesson in integrated relationship marketing. *Sport Marketing Quarterly, 9*(2), 85–95.

Lardinois, T., and P. Quester. (2001). Attitudinal effects of sponsorship on television audiences and the influence of sponsors' prominence interaction and main effects of two types of sponsorship. *Journal of Advertising Research, 41*(1), 48–58.

Larson, B. V., K. E. Flaherty, A. R. Zablah, T. J. Brown, and J. L. Wiener. (2008). Linking cause-related marketing to sales force responses and performance in a direct selling context. *Journal of the Academy of Marketing Science, 36*(2), 271–277.

Lavidge, R. L., and G. A. Steiner. (1961). A model for predictive measurements of advertising effectiveness. *Journal of Marketing, 25*(6), 59–62.

Law, S., and K. A. Braun. (2000). I'll have what she's having: Gauging the impact of product placement on viewers. *Psychology & Marketing, 17*(12), 1059–1075.

LeBlanc, M. S. (2010). American Needle Inc., v. NFL: Professional sports leagues and "single-entity" antitrust exemption. *Duke Journal of Constitutional Law and Public Policy Sidebar, 5*, 148–160.

Leckenby, J. D., and P. Stout. (1985). Conceptual and methodological issues in persuasion management. In M. J. Houston and R. J. Lutz (eds.). *Marketing Communication—Theory and Research* (pp. 7–12). Chicago: American Marketing Association.

Ledingham, J. A. (2006). Relationship management: A general public relations theory. In C. H. Botan and V. Hazleton (eds.). *Public Relations Theory II* (pp. 465–483). Mahwah, NJ: Lawrence Erlbaum Associates.

_____, and S. D. Bruning. (2000). *Public Relations as Relationship Management: A Relational Approach to the Study and Practice of Public Relations.* Mahwah, NJ: Lawrence Erlbaum Associates.

Lee, C. W., and K. D. Aiken. (2010). Changing brand associations in Taiwan: Nike's sponsorship of high-school basketball. *Journal of Sponsorship, 3*(3), 249–259.

Lee, M., and R. J. Faber. (2007). Effects of product placement in on-line games on brand memory: A perspective of the limited-capacity model of attention. *Journal of Advertising, 36*(4), 75–90.

_____, D. Shani., and D. Sandler. (1997). Attitudinal constructs towards sponsorship. *International Marketing Review, 14*(2/3), 159–169.

Lefton, T. (2006, March 20–26). Anheuser-Busch takes big role in Cardinals' new football stadium. *Street & Smith's Sports Business Journal, 8*(45), 9.

_____. (2010a, May 10–16). Strong Brew: A-B flexes its muscles with "big bet" on NFL. *Street & Smith's Sports Business Journal, 13*(4), 1,32.

_____. (2010b, October 25–31). Addition of banking partner part of NBA offseason highlight reel. *Street & Smith's Sports Business Journal, 13*(26), 11.

_____. (2011a, May 30–June 5). Sponsorship: The gatekeepers: Jackie Woodward. *Street & Smith's Sports Business Journal, 14*(7), 19.

_____. (2011b, May 30–June 5). Sponsorship: The gatekeepers: John Price. *Street & Smith's Sports Business Journal, 14*(7), 19.

_____. (2011c, June 17–July 3). Chevrolet renews MLB deal; other sponsors step up. *Street & Smith's Sports Business Journal, 14*(11), 4.

_____. (2011d, August 29–September 4). NFL is USAA's big play. *Street & Smith's Sports Business Journal, 14*(18), 1, 27.

_____. (2011e, October 31–November 6). Title helps UConn boost sponsorship revenue by 20 percent. *Street & Smith's Sports Business Journal, 14*(27), 12.

_____. (2012, August 27–September 2). NFL shifts Super Bowl merchandise game plan. *Street & Smith's Sports Business Journal, 15*(19), 10.

_____. (2013a, April 1–7). MLB sponsors step to plate for new season. *Street & Smith's Sports Business Journal, 15*(48), 4.

_____. (2013b, April 1–7). Pepsi adds players to

NFL marketing roster. *Street & Smith's Sports Business Journal, 16*(9), 12.

_____. (2013c, June 17–23). Marketers hail 'sense' of USAA deal with Griffin. *Street & Smith's Sports Business Journal, 16*(10), 3.

L'Etang, J. (2006). Public relations and sport in promotional culture. *Public Relations Review, 32*(4), 386–394.

Li, H., and J. D. Leckenby. (2007). Examining the effectiveness of Internet advertising formats. In D.W. Schumann and E. Thorson (Eds.). *Internet Advertising, Theory and Research* (pp. 203–224). Mahwah, NJ: Lawrence Erlbaum Associates.

Lombardo, J. (2006, April 17–23). Plan for global stores part of Adidas' NBA plans. *Street & Smith's Sports Business Journal, 9*(49), 8.

_____. (2009, September 7–13). PNY, Nets do first NBA practice jersey deal. *Street & Smith's Sports Business Journal, 12*(19), 3.

_____. (2010, May 24–30). After two years, NBA China on steady course. *Street & Smith's Sports Business Journal, 13*(6), 1, 24–25.

_____. (2011a, June 27–July3). Hugo Boss likes the look. *Street & Smith's Sports Business Journal, 14*(1), 17.

_____. (2011b, August 22–28). WNBA lands Boost Mobile as top sponsor. *Street & Smith's Sports Business Journal, 14*(17), 1, 33.

_____. (2013, June 10–16). NBA clubs to sell ads high, low. *Street & Smith's Sports Business Journal, 16*(9), 1, 47.

Louie, T. A., and C. Obermiller. (2002). Consumer response to a firm's endorser (dis) association decisions. *Journal of Advertising, 31*(4), 41–52.

Luicci, T. (2011, June 22). What's in a name? Big bucks. *Newark Star-Ledger, 41,* 47.

Lundy, L. K. (2006). Effect of framing on cognitive processing in public relations. *Public Relations Review, 32*(3), 295–301.

Lutz, R. J. (1985). Affective and cognitive antecedents of attitude toward the ad: A conceptual framework. In L. F. Alwitt and A. A. Mitchell (eds.). *Psychological Processes and Advertising Effects: Theory, Research, and Application* (pp. 45–63). Hillsdale, NJ: Lawrence Erlbaum Associates.

Lyberger, M. R., and L. McCarthy. (2001). An assessment of consumer knowledge of, interest in, and perceptions of ambush marketing strategies. *Sport Marketing Quarterly, 10*(3), 130–137.

Macchiette, B., and A. Roy. (1992). Affinity marketing: What is it and how does it work? *Journal of Services Marketing, 6*(3), 47–57.

MacKenzie, S. B., R. J. Lutz., and G. E. Belch. (1986). The role of attitude toward the ad as a mediator of advertising effectiveness: A test of competing explanations. *Journal of Marketing Research, 23*(2), 130–143.

Madrigal, R. (2000). The influence of social al-

liances with sports teams on intentions to purchase corporate sponsors' products. *Journal of Advertising, 29*(4), 13–24.

Mael, F. A., and B. E. Ashforth. (2001). Identification in work, war, sports, and religion: Contrasting the benefits and risks. *Journal for the Theory of Social Behavior, 31*(2), 197–222.

Maestas, A. J. (2009). Guide to sponsorship return on investment. *Journal of Sponsorship, 3*(1), 98–102.

Maignan, I., and D. A. Ralston. (2002). Corporate social responsibility in Europe and the US: Insights from business' self-presentations. *Journal of International Business Studies, 33*(3), 497–514.

Marketing Weekly News (2012, January 7). Qualcomm incorporated unveils temporary renaming of Qualcomm Stadium to promote Snapdragon processors, 185.

Mathur, L. K., I. Mathur, and N. Rangan. (1997). The wealth effects associated with a celebrity endorser: The Michael Jordan phenomenon. *Journal of Advertising Research, 37*(3), 67–73.

Matuszewski, E. (2002, January 4). Even traditional Rose needs corporate help. *Houston Chronicle,* 1.

Maxwell, H., and N. Lough. (2009). Signage vs. no signage: An analysis of sponsorship recognition in women's college basketball. *Sport Marketing Quarterly, 18*(4), 188–198.

McAllister, M. P. (1996). *The Commercialization of American Culture.* Thousand Oaks, CA: Sage.

_____. (1998). College bowl sponsorship and the increased commercialization of amateur sports. *Critical Studies in Mass Communication, 15*(4), 357–381.

_____. (2010). Hypercommercialism, televisuality, and the changing nature of college sports sponsorship. *American Behavioral Scientist, 53*(10), 1,476–1,491.

McCarthy, M. (2003, July 10). Nike laces up Converse deal. *USA Today,* 1B.

_____. (2005, August 22). Beer sponsorship worth big bucks to NFL. *USA Today,* 1.

McClellan, S. (2010, October 20). Vizio scores Rose Bowl sponsorship deal. *Brandweek.com.*

McCracken, G. (1989). Who is the celebrity endorser? Cultural foundations of the endorsement process. *Journal of Consumer Research, 16*(3), 310–321.

McDaniel, S. R., and L. Kinney. (1998). The implications of recency and gender effects in consumer response to ambush marketing. *Psychology & Marketing, 15*(4), 385–403.

_____, and _____. (1999). Audience characteristics and event sponsorship response: The potential influence of demographics, personal interests and values on brand awareness and brand image. *International Journal of Sports Marketing & Sponsorship, 1*(2), 125–146.

McKelvey, S. (2003). More tales of body art and "branding." *Brandweek, 44*(3), 23.

McMurphy, B. (2006, December 22). What's in a name? Lots of exposure for sponsors. *Tampa Tribune*, 1.

McShane, L. (2010, February 27). Gatorade powers off Tiger: Sports drink giant breaks off reported $100M deal. *New York Daily News*, 16.

McWilliams, A., D. S. Siegel, and P. M. Wright. (2006). Corporate social responsibility: Strategic implications. *Journal of Management Studies, 43*(1), 1–18.

Meenaghan, T. (1991). The role of sponsorship in the marketing communications mix. *International Journal of Advertising, 10*(1), 35–47.

_____. (1994). Point of view: Ambush marketing: Immoral or imaginative practice? *Journal of Advertising Research, 34*(5), 77–88.

_____. (1996). Ambush marketing: A threat to corporate sponsorship. *Sloan Management Review, 38*(1), 103–114.

_____. (2001). Understanding sponsorship effects. *Psychology & Marketing, 18*(2), 95–122.

_____, and D. Shipley. (1999). Media effect in commercial sponsorship. *European Journal of Marketing, 33*(3/4), 328–347.

Mickle, T. (2010, February 1–7). Revival of Olympic ambush marketing shows power of Games. *Street & Smith's Sports Business Journal, 12*(39), 4.

_____. (2011a, July 25–31). Tiffany to sponsor USSA's Gold Pass ski resort program. *Street & Smith's Sports Business Journal, 14*(14), 6.

_____. (2011b, September 12–18). Decade-long deals pay off for Lowe's, Reebok: Winning partnership with Johnson roll on. *Street & Smith's Sports Business Journal, 14*(20), 1, 26–27.

_____. (2011c, October 3–9). Goodyear keeps its NASCAR deal rolling. *Street & Smith's Sports Business Journal, 14*(23), 3.

_____. (2011d, October 17–23). McD's close to TOP extension. *Street & Smith's Sports Business Journal, 14*(25), 1,8.

_____. (2012a, February 13–19). NBC Olympics ad sales blow past Beijing. *Street & Smith's Sports Business Journal, 14*(41), 1,10.

_____. (2012b, August 6–12). McDonald's get kids in the Games. *Street & Smith's Sports Business Journal, 15*(16), 1,33.

_____. (2012c, September 24–30). Gatorade to extend deal with ISC, maintain victory lane sponsorship at 12 NASCAR tracks. *Street & Smith's Sports Business Journal, 15*(23), 7.

_____. (2012d, November 19–25). BMW: USOC deal drives strong sales. *Street & Smith's Sports Business Journal, 15*(31), 1, 38.

_____. (2013a, April 1–7). Visa extending World Cup for eight years. *Street & Smith's Sports Business Journal, 15*(48), 1,38.

_____. (2013b, May 13–19). Sherwin-Williams signs NASCAR deal. *Street & Smith's Sports Business Journal, 16*(5), 3.

_____, and J. Ourand. (2012, April 30–May 6). NBC's digital rivals line up with their own London 2012 sites. *Street & Smith's Sports Business Journal, 15*(3), 4.

Miller, F. M., and G. R. Laczniak. (2011). The ethics of celebrity—athlete endorsement: What happens when a star steps out of bounds? *Journal of Advertising Research, 51*(3), 499–510.

Mills, J. (2011). Performance-enhancing media: Virtual advertising in sports. In M. S. Eastin, T. Daugherty, and N. M. Burns (eds.). *Handbook of research on digital media and advertising: User generated content consumption* (pp. 507–520). Hershey, PA: Information Science Reference.

Miloch, K. S., and K. W. Lambrecht. (2006). Consumer awareness of sponsorship at grassroots sports events. *Sport Marketing Quarterly, 15*(3), 147–154.

Mitchell, C. (2002). Selling the brand inside. *Harvard Business Review, 80*(1), 5–11.

Miyazaki, A. D., and A. G. Morgan. (2001). Assessing market value of event sponsoring: Corporate Olympic sponsorship. *Journal of Advertising Research, 41*(1), 9–15.

Money, R. B., T. A. Shimp, and T. Sakano. (2006). Celebrity endorsements in Japan and the United States: Is negative information all that harmful. *Journal of Advertising Research, 46*(1), 113–123.

Morgan, R. M., and S. D. Hunt. (1994). The commitment-trust theory of relationship marketing. *Journal of Marketing, 58*(3), 20–38.

Mullen, L. (2011a, January 10–16). Delta Air Lines signs multiyear deal with Lakers. *Street & Smith's Sports Business Journal, 13*(36), 5.

_____. (2011b, December 5–11). Crosby back on ice and breaking new ads. *Street & Smith's Sports Business Journal, 14*(32), 12.

_____. (2012a, March 5–11). Stella's off to the races with new Churchill-Derby deal. *Street & Smith's Sports Business Journal, 14*(44), 3.

_____. (2012b, August 13–19). Teams try to link sponsors, athletes. *Street & Smith's Sports Business Journal, 15*(17), 8.

Mullin, B. J., S. Hardy, and W. A. Sutton. (2007). *Sport marketing*, 3rd ed. Champaign, IL: Human Kinetics.

Muret, D. (2010a, October 18–24). Penguin palace: Pittsburgh brings high-tech to new home. *Street & Smith's Sports Business Journal, 13*(25), 1, 34–35.

_____. (2010b, November 8–14). Magic's kingdom: At Orlando's Amway Center premium is for everyone. *Street & Smith's Sports Business Journal, 13*(28), 1, 34–35.

_____. (2011, April 4–10). Lexus buys naming rights

to Panthers' rink. *Street & Smith's Sports Business Journal, 13*(48), 4.

_____. (2013, May 13–19). Gold and blue: Dinner meeting started Levi's, 49ers on the road to stadium naming deal. *Street & Smith's Sports Business Journal, 16*(5), 1, 33.

Murphy, J. H., I. C. M. Cunningham, and L. Stavchansky de Lewis. (2011). *Integrated Brand Promotion Management: Text, Cases, and Exercises.* Dubuque, IA: Kendall Hunt Publishing.

Murray, K. B., and C. M. Vogel. (1997). Using a hierarchy of effects approach to gauge the effectiveness of CSR to generate goodwill towards the firm: Financial versus nonfinancial impacts. *Journal of Business Research, 38*(2), 141–159.

Myers, G. (1995, September 19). Jones dealin' forces NFL to just sue it. *New York Daily News*, 48.

Myerson, A. R. (1996, May 31). Olympic sponsors battling to defend turf. *New York Times*, D1.

Nelson, M. R. (2002). Recall of brand placements in computer/video games. *Journal of Advertising Research, 42*(2), 80–92.

_____, and H. Katz. (2011). Digital metrics: Getting to the other 50 percent. In M. S. Eastin, T. Daugherty, and N. M. Burns (eds.). *Handbook of Research on Digital Media and Advertising: User Generated Content Consumption* (pp. 314–334). Hershey, PA: Information Science Reference.

_____, R. A. Yaros, and H. Keum. (2006). Examining the influence of telepresence on spectator and player processing of real and fictitious brands in a computer game. *Journal of Advertising, 35*(4), 87–99.

Nelson, T. E., R. A. Clawson, and Z. M. Oxley. (1997). Media framing of a civil liberties conflict and its effect on tolerance. *American Political Science Review, 91*, 567–583.

Neumeister, L. (2012, April 5). Tebow Reebok jerseys still banned. *Newark Star-Ledger*, 40.

Newark Star-Ledger (2011, August 19). Coca-Cola announces major investing in China. *Newark Star-Ledger*, 23.

Newell, S. J., and K. V. Henderson. (1998). Super Bowl advertising: Field testing the importance of advertising frequency, length, and placement on recall. *Journal of Marketing Communication, 4*(4), 237–248.

_____, _____, and B. T. Wu. (2001). The effects of pleasure and arousal on recall of advertisements during the Super Bowl. *Psychology and Marketing, 18*(11), 1,135–1,153.

Newman, A. A. (2009, June 18). NASCAR sponsors find customers in other sponsors. *The New York Times*, p. B4.

Nielsen, G. (2011). Companies find there's no substitute for real ROI measurement. *Street & Smith's Sports Business Journal, 13*(37), 22.

Norcross, L. (2011). Best defense against ambush marketing is a good offense. *Street & Smith's Sports Business Journal, 13*(43), 15.

O'Guinn, T. O., C. T. Allen, and R. J. Semenik. (2006). *Advertising & integrated brand promotion,* 4th ed. Mason, OH: Thomson.

Ohanian, R. (1990). Construction and validation of a scale to measure celebrity endorsers' perceived expertise, trustworthiness, and attractiveness. *Journal of Advertising, 19*(3), 39–52.

_____. (1991). The impact of celebrity spokespersons' perceived image on consumers' intention to purchase. *Journal of Advertising Research, 31*(1), 46–54.

Ohl, C. M., J. D. Pincus, T. Rimmer, and D. Harrison. (1995). Agenda-building role of news releases in corporate takeovers. *Public Relations Review, 21*(2), 89–101.

O'Keefe, M., and J. Zawadzka. (2011). Does passion for a team translate into sales for a sponsor? The Irish case. *Journal of Sponsorship, 4*(2), 190–196.

O'Keefe, R., P. Titlebaum, and C. Hill. (2009). Sponsorship activation: Turning money spent into money earned. *Journal of Sponsorship, 3*(1), 43–53.

Olson, E. L. (2010). Does sponsorship work in the same way in different sponsorship contexts? *European Journal of Marketing, 44*(1/2), 180–199.

_____, and H. M. Thjomoe. (2003). The effects of peripheral exposure to information on brand performance. *European Journal of Marketing, 37*(1/2), 243–255.

_____. (2011). Explaining and articulating the fit construct in sponsorship. *Journal of Advertising, 40*(1), 57–70.

O'Reilly, G. (2010, July 30). Warning for Olympic brands. *PR Week*, 3.

O'Reilly, N., and J. Madill. (2009). Methods and metrics in sponsorship evaluation. *Journal of Sponsorship, 2*(3), 215–230.

Ourand, J. (2010, December 20–26). GE partnership caps productive year for PGA Tour. *Street & Smith's Sports Business Journal, 13*(34), 1, 43.

_____. (2012, June 25–July 1). CBS: Game already 80% sold. *Street & Smith's Sports Business Journal, 15*(11), 1, 52.

_____, and T. Lefton. (2010, March 15–21). Verizon-NFL deal: Convergence is here. *Street & Smith's Sports Business Journal, 12*(45), 1, 42.

Palomba, M. (2011). Ambush marketing and the Olympics 2012. *Journal of Sponsorship, 4*(3), 245–252.

Pankratz, H. (2011, September 9). Sports Authority name officially unveiled at Mile High stadium. www.denverpost.com.

Papadimitriou, D., and A. Apostolopoulou. (2009). Olympic sponsorship activation and the creation of competitive advantage. *Journal of Promotion Management, 15*(1/2), 90–117.

Pava, M. L., and J. Krausz. (1996). *Corporate Social Responsibility and Financial Performance: The Paradox of Social Cost.* Westport, CT: Quorum Books.

Pearsall, J. (2009). Tightening our belts: What research tells us about corporate sponsorship in the current economic crisis. *Journal of Sponsorship, 3*(1), 23–34.

_____. (2010). Sponsorship performance: What is the role of sponsorship metrics in proactively managing the sponsor-property relationship. *Journal of Sponsorship, 3*(2), 115–123.

Pedersen, P. M., K. S. Miloch, and P. C. Laucella. (2007). *Strategic Sports Communication.* Champaign, IL: Human Kinetics.

Perloff, R. M. (2008). *The Dynamics of Persuasion: Communication and Attitudes in the 21st Century.* New York: Lawrence Erlbaum Associates.

Perone, T. (2007, July 28). Endorse biz giving Vick the boot. *New York Post*, 8.

Peterson, R. A. (1995). Relationship marketing and the consumer. *Journal of the Academy of Marketing Science, 23*(4), 278–281.

Petty, R. D. (1992). *The Impact of Advertising Law on Business and Public Policy.* Westport, CT: Quorum Books.

Petty, R. E., and J. T. Cacioppo. (1979). Issue involvement can increase or decrease persuasion by enhancing message-relevant cognitive responses. *Journal of Personality and Social Psychology, 37*(10), 1,915–1,926.

_____. (1981). *Attitudes and Persuasion: Classic and Contemporary Approaches.* Dubuque, Iowa: W. C. Brown.

_____. (1984). The effects of involvement on responses to argument quantity and quality. *Journal of Personality and Social Psychology, 46*(1), 69–81.

_____, J. T. Cacioppo, and K. J. Morris. (1983). Effects of need for cognition on message evaluation, recall, and persuasion. *Journal of Personality and Social Psychology, 45*(4), 805–818.

_____, _____, and D. Schumann. (1983). Central and peripheral routes to advertising effectiveness: The moderating role of involvement. *Journal of Consumer Research, 10*(2), 135–146.

_____, and D. T. Wegener. (1999). The Elaboration Likelihood Model: Current status and controversies. In S. Chaiken and Y. Trope (Eds.). *Dual Process Theories in Social Psychology* (pp. 41–72). New York: Guilford Press.

Pham, M. T., and G. V. Johar. (2001). Market prominence biases in sponsor identification: Processes and consequentiality. *Psychology & Marketing, 18*(2), 123–143.

Phau, M., and H. H. Wan. (2006). Persuasion: An intrinsic function of public relations. In C. H. Botan and V. Hazleton (eds.). *Public Relations Theory II* (pp. 101–136). Mahwah, NJ: Lawrence Erlbaum Associates.

Phillips, P. A., and L. Moutinho. (1998). The marketing planning index: A tool for measuring strategic marketing effectiveness. *Journal of Travel and Tourism Marketing, 7*(3), 41–57.

Polonsky, M. J., and R. Speed. (2001). Linking sponsorship and cause-related marketing: Complementarities and conflicts. *European Journal of Marketing, 35*(11/12), 1,361–1,385.

_____, and G. Wood. (2001). Can the overcommercialization of cause-related marketing harm society? *Journal of Macromarketing, 21*(1), 8–22.

Pope, N. K., and K. E. Voges. (2000). The impact of sports sponsorship activities, corporate image, and prior use on consumer purchase intention. *Sport Marketing Quarterly, 9*(2), 96–101.

_____, _____, and M. Brown. (2009). Winning ways: Immediate and long-term effects of sponsorship on perceptions of brand quality and corporate image. *Journal of Advertising, 38*(2), 5–20.

Pope, R. (2010). The making of social sponsorship. *Journal of Sponsorship, 3*(3), 242–248.

Pornpitakpan, C. (2003). Validation of the celebrity endorsers' credibility scale: Evidence from Asians. *Journal of Marketing Management, 19*(1/2), 179–195.

Prendergast, G. P., D. Poon., and D. C. West. (2010). Match game: Linking sponsorship congruence with communication outcomes. *Journal of Advertising Research, 50*(2), 214–226.

Pruitt, S. W., T. B. Cornwell, and J. M. Clark. (2004). The NASCAR phenomenon: Auto racing sponsorships and shareholder wealth. *Journal of Advertising Research, 44*(3), 281–296.

Prunty, B. (2011, August 22). Top-flight golfers get the free ride: More than 150 BMW's shipped in for week. *Newark Star-Ledger*, 27, 35.

Pyle, G. (2010, October 13). New Era part of major deal with NFL: Among vendors that would share a total of $1 billion. *Buffalo News*, B8.

Quester, P. (1997). Awareness as a measure of sponsorship effectiveness: The Adelaide Formula One Grand Prix and evidence of incidental ambush effects. *Journal of Marketing Communications, 3*(1), 1–20.

Quester, P. G., and B. Thompson. (2001). Advertising and promotion leverage on arts sponsorship effectiveness. *Journal of Advertising Research, 41*(1), 33–47.

Raju, S., H. R. Unnava., and N. V. Montgomery. (2009). The moderating effect of brand commitment on the evaluation of competitive brands. *Journal of Advertising, 38*(2), 21–35.

Raney, A. A. (2006). Why we watch and enjoy mediated sports. In A. A. Raney and J. Bryant (eds.). *Handbook of Sport and Media* (pp. 313–329). Mahwah, NJ: Lawrence Erlbaum Associates.

Raynaud, J., and G. Bolos. (2008). Sport at the heart of marketing: The integration debate. *Journal of Sponsorship*, 2(1), 31–35.

Real, M. R. (1996). Is television corrupting the Olympics? *Television Quarterly*, 28(2), 2–12.

Reese, J. T., and M. S. Nagel. (2001). The relationship between revenues and winning in the National Football League. *International Journal of Sport Management*, 2, 125-

Reeves, R. (1961). *The Reality in Advertising*. NY: Knopf.

Reichheld, F. F. (2003). The one number you need to grow. *Harvard Business Review*, 81(12), 46–54.

Rhoden, W. (1995, September 6). Cowboys' owner takes a stand against the NFL welfare state. *New York Times*, B15.

_____. (2009, May 22). Humane society sees Vice as an ally, not a pariah. *New York Times*, B11.

Rifon, N., S. M. Choi, C. Trimble, and H. Li. (2004). Congruence effects in sponsorship: The mediating role of sponsor credibility and consumer attributions of sponsor motive. *Journal of Advertising*, 33(1), 29–43.

Ritchie, C. (2011). Technology enabled sponsorship strategies. *Journal of Sponsorship*, 4(2), 105–115.

Robinson, T., and L. Bauman. (2008). Winning the Olympic marketing game: Recall of logos on clothing, equipment and venues at the 2006 Winter Olympics. *International Journal of Sports Marketing and Sponsorship*, 9(4), 290–305.

Roehm, M. L., H. A. J. Roehm, and D. S. Boone. (2004). Plugs versus placements: A comparison of alternatives for within-program brand exposure. *Psychology & Marketing*, 21(1), 17–28.

Rogan, M. (2008). Building the business case for internal sponsorship activation. *Journal of Sponsorship*, 1(3), 267–273.

Rogers, P. (1998, June 26). Rose Bowl gives in, finally goes corporate. *Atlanta Journal and Constitution*, 7E.

Rosner, S. (2013, March 18–24). NRA sponsorship a mistake for NASCAR. *Street & Smith's Sports Business Journal*, 15(46), 10.

Roush, C. (1995, August 4). Pepsi deal breaks Coca-Cola's NFL monopoly. *Atlanta Journal and Constitution*, 1G.

Rovell, D. (2004, February 23). NFL drinks up Gatorade money. www.espn.go.com.

_____. (2005, May 4). One moment worth $20 million a year. www.espn.go.com.

Roy, D. P., and T. B. Cornwell. (2004). The effects of consumer knowledge on responses to event sponsorships. *Psychology & Marketing*, 21(3), 185–207.

Rucci, A. J., S. P. Kirn, and R. T. Quinn. (1998). The employee-customer-profit chain at Sears. *Harvard Business Review*, 76(1), 82–97.

Russell, C. A. (2002). Investigating the effectiveness of product placements in television shows: The role of modality and plot connection congruence on brand memory and attitude. *Journal of Consumer Research*, 29(3), 306–318.

_____, and M. A. Belch. (2005). A managerial investigation into the product placement industry. *Journal of Advertising Research*, 45(1), 73–92.

Russell, M., J. Mahar, and B. Drewniak. (2005). Examination of stock market response to publicity surrounding athletic endorsers. *Marketing Management Journal*, 15(2), 67–79.

Russell, M. G. (2011). Evolving media metrics from assumed attention to earned engagement. In M. S. Eastin, T. Daugherty, and N. M. Burns (eds.). *Handbook of Research on Digital Media and Advertising: User Generated Content Consumption* (pp. 491–506). Hershey, PA: Information Science Reference.

Ruth, J. A., and B. L. Simonin. (2003). Brought to you by brand A and brand B: Investigating multiple sponsors' influence on consumers' attitudes toward sponsored events. *Journal of Advertising*, 32(3), 19–30.

_____. (2006). The power of numbers: Investing the impact of event roster size in consumer response to sponsorship. *Journal of Advertising*, 35(4), 7–20.

Ryan, N. (2011, October 20). Sponsorship prices plunge; Teams scramble as deals expire. *USA Today*, 9C.

St. Petersburg Times (2009, November 5). Son's Air Jordans lead Adidas to end UCF sponsorship. *St. Petersburg Times*, 1c.

Sandler, D. M., and D. Shani. (1989). Olympic sponsorship vs. "ambush" marketing: Who gets the gold? *Journal of Advertising Research*, 29(4), 9–14.

Sandomir, R. (1996, December 10). Jones-NFL lawsuits may end in a draw. *New York Times*, B17.

_____. (2007, August 1). In endorsements, no athlete is a sure thing. *New York Times*, D5.

_____. (2009, February 4). Congress zooms in on Mets' naming deal. *New York Times*, B12.

Savary, J. (2008). Advocacy marketing: Toyota's secrets for partnering with trendsetters to create passionate brand advocates. *Journal of Sponsorship*, 1(3), 211–224.

Schiller, H. I. (1989). *Culture, Inc: The Corporate Takeover of Public Expression*. New York: Oxford University Press.

Schneider, L. P., and T. B. Cornwell. (2005). Cashing in crashes via brand placement in computer games. *International Journal of Advertising, 24*(3), 321–343.

Schwaiger, M. (2004). Components and parameters of corporate reputation: An empirical study. *Schmalenbach Business Review, 56*(1), 46–71.

_____, M. Sarstedt, and C. R. Taylor. (2010). Art for the sake of the corporation: Audi, BMW group, DaimlerChrysler, Montblanc, Siemens, and Volkswagen help explore the effect of sponsorship on corporate reputation. *Journal of Advertising Research, 50*(1), 77–90.

Schwartz, D. A. (2011). Shutting the back door: Using American Needle to cure the problem of improper product definition. *Michigan Law Review, 110*, 295–317.

Sciullo, M. (2010, September 1). Eat your heart out, Samson: Troy's hair worth $1M. *Pittsburgh Post-Gazette*, A1.

Seguin, B., and N. O'Reilly. (2008). The Olympic brand, ambush marketing and clutter. *International Journal of Sport Management and Marketing, 4*(1), 62–84.

_____, K. Teed, and N. O'Reilly. (2005). National sport organizations and sponsorship: An identification of best practices. *International Journal of Sport Management and Marketing, 1*(1/2), 69–83.

Seiferheld, S. (2010, July 26–August 1). Is measurement up to sponsors or properties? Answer: Yes. *Street & Smith's Sports Business Journal, 13*(14), 20.

_____. (2013, April 22–28). Total recall: Which on-site factors make fans remember brands?. *Street & Smith's Sports Business Journal, 16*(2), 15.

Seitel, F. P. (2004). *The Practice of Public Relations,* 9th ed. Upper Saddle River, NJ: Pearson Prentice Hall.

Sen, S., and C. B. Bhattacharya. (2001). Does doing good always lead to doing better? Consumer reactions to corporate social responsibility. *Journal of Marketing Research, 38*(2), 225–243.

Shani, D., and D. M. Sandler. (1998). Ambush marketing: Is confusion to blame for the flickering of the flame. *Psychology & Marketing, 15*(4), 367–383.

Shank, M. (2008). *Sports Marketing: A Strategic Perspective.* 4th ed. Upper Saddle River, NJ: Pearson Prentice Hall.

Shaw, S., and J. Amis. (2001). Image and investment: Sponsorship and women's sport. *Journal of Sport Management, 15*(3), 219–246.

Sheehan, B., and A. Young. (2011). Convergence, contradiction, and collaboration: Case studies on developing creative strategies for digital components of integrated campaigns. In M. S. Eastin, T. Daugherty, and N. M. Burns (eds.). *Handbook of Research on Digital Media and Advertising: User Generated Content Consumption*

(pp. 275–298). Hershey, PA: Information Science Reference.

Sherif, M. (2001). Superordinate goals in the reduction on intergroup conflict. In M. A. Hogg and D. Abrams (eds.). *Intergroup Relations: Essential Readings. Key Readings in Social Psychology.* New York: Psychology Press.

Sherman, A. (2010, August 25). Tiger's losing streak is wearing on his Nike apparel line. *Newark Star-Ledger*, 32.

Sherry, J. G. (1998). The key to maximizing your sports sponsorship. *Public Relations Quarterly, 43*(1), 24–26.

Sheth, H., and K. M. Babiak. (2010). Beyond the game: Perceptions and practices of corporate social responsibility in the professional sport industry. *Journal of Business Ethics, 91*(3), 433–450.

Sheth, J. N., and A. Parvatiyar. (2000). *Handbook of Relationship Marketing.* Thousand Oaks, CA: Sage.

Shimp, T. A. (2003). *Advertising, Promotion. Integrated Marketing Communications.* Mason, OH: Thompson South-Western.

Shipley, A. (2010, January 28). USOC sees fool's gold in some advertising: Committee upset by commercials suggesting sponsorship of Games. *Washington Post*, D8.

Simmons, C. J., and K. L. Becker-Olson. (2006). Achieving marketing objectives through social sponsorships. *Journal of Marketing, 70*(4), 154–169.

Singh, M. A., S. K. Balasubramanian, and G. Chakraborty. (2000). A comparative analysis of three communication formats: Advertising, infomercial, and direct experience. *Journal of Advertising, 24*(4), 59–75.

Sirgy, M. J., D. Lee, J. S. Johar, and J. Tidwell. (2008). The effect of self-congruity with sponsorship on brand loyalty. *Journal of Business Research, 61*(10), 1,091–1,097.

Sisario, B. (2011, August 5). Pepsi takes active role in 'X Factor.' *New York Times*, p. B2.

Skalski, P., C. Campanella-Bracken, and M. Buncher. (2011). Advertising: It's in the game. In M. S. Eastin, T. Daugherty, and N. M. Burns (eds.). *Handbook of Research on Digital Media and Advertising: User Generated Content Consumption* (pp. 437–455). Hershey, PA: Information Science Reference.

Slater, J., and C. Lloyd. (2004). It's gotta be the shoes: Exploring the effects of relationships of Nike and Reebok sponsorship on two college athletic programs. In L. R. Kahle and C. Riley (eds.). *Sport Marketing and the Psychology of Marketing Communication* (pp. 191–210). Mahwah, NJ: Lawrence Erlbaum Associates.

Sloan, L. R. (1989). The motives of sports fans. In J. H. Goldstein (ed.). *Sports, Games, and Play:*

Social and Psychological Viewpoints (pp. 175–240). Hillsdale, NJ: Lawrence Erlbaum.

Smith, A. C. T., and H. M. Westerbeek. (2007). Sport as a vehicle for deploying social responsibility. *Journal of Corporate Citizenship, 25*, 43–54.

Smith, M. (2011a, August 1–7). Sprint to sponsor Notre Dame football game. *Street & Smith's Sports Business Journal, 14*(15), 4.

_____. (2011b, August 22–28). In a tough spot, PGA Tour nails title sponsor challenges. *Street & Smith's Sports Business Journal, 14*(17), 1, 33.

_____. (2011c, October 3–9). FedEx Cup up-and-down on TV despite finish. *Street & Smith's Sports Business Journal, 14*(23), 41.

_____. (2011d, November 21–27). Penn State crisis pushes business into background. *Street & Smith's Sports Business Journal, 14*(30), 1, 47.

_____. (2012a, February 27–March 4). Learfield, IMG in the race for Illinois' rights. *Street & Smith's Sports Business Journal, 14*(43), 31.

_____. (2012b, March 12–18). Coke boosts NCAA digital, social media efforts. *Street & Smith's Sports Business Journal, 14*(45), 4.

Smolianov, P., and D. Shilbury. (2005). Examining integrated advertising and sponsorship in corporate marketing through televised sport. *Sport Marketing Quarterly, 14*(4), 239–250.

Solomon, A. (2011, October 10–16). Why athletes aren't always best choice. *Street & Smith's Sports Business Journal, 14*(24), 11.

Spanberg, E. (2012a, March 5–11). Teams toast the benefits of beer category. *Street & Smith's Sports Business Journal, 14*(44), 17.

_____. (2012b, March 26–April 1). Employee benefits: Companies use sports sponsorships to motivate employees and recognize their accomplishments. *Street & Smith's Sports Business Journal, 14*(47), 13–14.

Speed, R., and P. Thompson. (2000). Determinants of sport sponsorship response. *Journal of the Academy of Marketing Science, 28*(2), 226–238.

Stanwick, P. A., and S. D. Stanwick. (1998). The relationship between corporate social performance and organizational size, financial performance, and environmental performance: An empirical examination. *Journal of Business Ethics, 17*(2), 195–204.

Steinberg, B. (2011, August 8). Fox-NBC: Program rivals but promo partners thanks to NFL, PepsiCo: An unusual deal between "X Factor," Super Bowl and the beverage giant is creating strange bedfellows. *Advertising Age*, 2.

Stevens, P. (2008, September 3). Maryland is going all Under Armour. *Washington Times*, C8.

Steyn, P. G. (2009). Online recommendation as the ultimate yardstick to measure sponsorship effectiveness. *Journal of Sponsorship, 2*(4), 316–329.

Stipp, H. (1998). The impact of Olympic sponsorship on corporate image. *International Journal of Advertising, 17*(1), 75–87.

_____, and N. P. Schiavone. (1996). Modeling the impact of Olympic sponsorship on corporate image. *Journal of Advertising Research 36*(4), 22–28.

Stone, G., M. Joseph, and M. Jones. (2003). An exploratory study on the use of sports celebrities in advertising: A content analysis. *Sport Marketing Quarterly, 12*(2), 94–102.

Stotlar, D.K. (1993). Sponsorship and the Olympic Winter Games. *Sport Marketing Quarterly, 2*(1), 35–43.

_____. (2001). *Developing Successful Sport Sponsorship Plans*. Morgantown, WV: Fitness Information Technology.

Stryker, S. (1980). *Symbolic Interactionism: A Social Structural Version*. Menlo Park, CA: Benjamin/Cummings.

Sutherland, M., and J. Galloway. (1981). Role of advertising: Persuasion or agenda-setting? *Journal of Advertising Research, 21*(5), 25–29.

Sutton, W. A., T. Lachowetz, and J. Clark. (2000). Eduselling: The role of customer education in selling to corporate clients in the sport industry. *International Journal of Sports Marketing and Sponsorship, 2*(2), 145–158.

Swaminathan, V., and S. K. Reddy. (2000). Affinity partnering: Conceptualization and issues. In J. N. Sheth and A. Parvatiyar (eds.). *Handbook of Relationship Marketing* (pp. 381–405). Thousand Oaks, CA: Sage.

Szykman, L. R., P. N. Bloom, and J. Blazing. (2004). Does corporate sponsorship of a socially-oriented message make a difference? An investigation of the effects of sponsorship identity on responses to an anti-drinking and driving message. *Journal of Consumer Psychology, 14*(1/2), 3–20.

Tajfel, H. (1982). *Social Identity and Intergroup Relations*. Cambridge: Cambridge University Press.

Tanier, M. (2011, September 14). There's an exciting clash on the field. Oh, that's the uniform. *New York Times*, 1.

Tauder, A. R. (2006). Getting ready for the next generation of marketing communications. *Journal of Advertising Research, 45*(1), 5–8.

Tellis, G. J. (2004). *Effective Advertising: Understanding When, How, and Why Advertising Works*. Thousand Oaks, CA: Sage Publications.

Tharp, P. (2010, June 19). Tiger's $30m tail — Golfer's agent, IMG, also take$ hit in scandal. *New York Post*, 23.

Tharpe, J. (2010, January 3). Can Tour de Georgia bike race be saved? Organizers cancel meet, pin hopes on 2011 — if a sponsor can be found. *Atlanta Journal-Constitution*, 1B.

Thjomoe, H. M., E. L. Olson, and P. S. Brom.

(2002). Decision-making processes surrounding sponsorship activities. *Journal of Advertising Research 42*(6), 6–16.

Thomas, K. (2009, September 1). U.S. team seals a deal with Procter & Gamble. *New York Times*, B16.

Thomaselli, R. (2011, September 5). IMG offers national marketers regional access to NCAA sports: UPS, Old Navy ink deals that will allow them to tap potential of rabid fan bases of 68 schools. *Advertising Age*, 2.

Till, B. D. (2001). Managing athlete endorser image: The effect of endorsement product. *Sport Marketing Quarterly, 10*(1), 35–42.

_____, and D. W. Baack. (2005). Recall and persuasion: Does creative advertising matter? *Journal of Advertising, 34*(3), 47–57.

_____, and M. Busler. (2000). The match-up hypothesis: Physical attractiveness, expertise, and the role of fit on brand attitude, purchase intent, and brand beliefs. *Journal of Advertising, 29*(3), 1–14.

_____, and T. A. Shimp. (1998). Endorsers in advertising: The case of negative celebrity information. *Journal of Advertising, 27*(1), 67–82.

_____, S. M. Stanley, and R. Priluck. (2008). Classical conditioning and celebrity endorsers: An examination of belongingness and resistance to extinction. *Psychology and Marketing, 25*(2), 179–196.

Torre, P. S. (2012, August 6). Cost of doing nothing: The financial ramifications of Penn State's failure to take action in the Sandusky scandal could haunt the school for years. *Sports Illustrated*, 33.

Turley, L. W., and S. W. Kelley. (1997). A comparison of advertising content: Business to business versus consumer services. *Journal of Advertising, 26*(4), 39–48.

Tutko, T. A. (1989). Personality change in the American sport scene. In J. H. Goldstein (ed.). *Sports, Games, and Play: Social and Psychological Viewpoints* (pp. 111–127). Hillsdale, NJ: Erlbaum.

Underwood, R., E. Bond, and R. Baer. (2001). Building service brands via social identity: Lessons from the sports marketplace. *Journal of Marketing Theory & Practice, 9*(1), 1–13.

Van Reijmersdal, E., P. Neijens, and E. G. Smit. (2009). A new branch of advertising: Reviewing factors that influence reactions to product placement. *Journal of Advertising Research, 49*(4), 429–449.

Varadarajan, P. R., and A. Menon. (1988). Cause-related marketing: A coalignment of marketing strategy and corporate philanthropy. *Journal of Marketing, 52*(3), 58–74.

Vega, T. (2011, June 2). Nike tries to enter the niche sports it has missed. *The New York Times*, B3.

Vorkunov, M., and T. Luicci. (2011, June 21). NJ tech company to pay $6.5 million for naming rights to Rutgers Stadium. *Newark Star-Ledger*, 1, 5.

Waddock, S. A., and S. M. Graves. (1997). The corporate social performance-financial performance link. *Strategic Management Journal, 18*(4), 303–319.

Wakefield, K. L., K. Becker-Olsen, and T. B. Cornwell. (2007). I spy a sponsor: The effects of sponsorship level, prominence, relatedness, and cueing on recall accuracy. *Journal of Advertising, 36*(4), 61–74.

Walker, A. K. (2008, July 25). Under Armour in public eye. *Baltimore Sun*, D1.

_____. (2011, July 26). Up and comers: Sports apparel company Under Armour goes with a rookie strategy in the vital endorsement game. *Baltimore Sun*, C1.

Walker, M., and A. Kent. (2009). Do fans care? Assessing the influence of corporate social responsibility on consumer attitudes in the sports industry. *Journal of Sport Management, 23*(6), 743–769.

Walliser, B. (2003). An international review of sponsorship research: Extension and update. *International Journal of Advertising, 22*(1), 5–40.

Walters, L. M., and T. N. Walters. (1992). Environment of confidence: Daily newspaper use of press releases. *Public Relations Review, 8*(1), 31–46.

Wang, A. (2007). Priming, framing, and position on corporate social responsibility. *Journal of Public Relations Research, 19*(2), 123–145.

Wann, D. L., J. Royalty, and A. Roberts. (2000). The self-presentation of sports fans: Investigating the importance of team identification and self-esteem. *Journal of Sport Behavior, 23*(2), 198–206.

Washington Post (2002, August 29). Lack of funding does in Blue-Gray, D2.

Watt, K. (2010). The future of sponsorship integrated with CSR/CSI strategy. *Journal of Sponsorship, 3*(3), 220–227.

Weaver, M. (2009, December 15). Nike stands by Woods as other sponsors distance themselves from troubled golfer. *The Guardian, London*, 19.

Webb, P. H., and M. L. Ray. (1979). Effects of TV clutter. *Journal of Advertising Research, 19*(3), 7–12.

Weigley, S. (2011, July 1). Nike and NFL's Vick team up. *Wall Street Journal Online*.

Weisman, L. (1995, September 20). Interpreting why Jones did what he did. *USA Today*, 3C.

Wenner, L. A. (1989). Media, sports, and society: The research agenda. In L. A. Wenner (ed.). *Media, Sports, and Society* (pp. 13–48). Newbury Park: Sage.

_____, and W. Gantz. (1998). Watching sports on television: Audience experience, gender, fanship, and marriage. In L. A. Wenner (ed.). *Mediasport* (pp. 233–251). London: Routledge.

Werther, W. B., Jr., and D. Chandler. (2006). *Strategic Corporate Social Responsibility: Stakeholders in a Global Environment.* Thousand Oaks, CA: Sage.

Wharton, D. (2010, June 22). Rose Bowl loses sponsor. *Los Angeles Times*, C6.

Whitehouse, L. (2006). Corporate social responsibility: Views from the frontline. *Journal of Business Ethics*, 63(3), 279–296.

Wilson, B., C. Stavros, and K. Westberg. (2008). Player transgressions and the management of the sport sponsor relationship. *Public Relations Review*, 34(2), 99–107.

Winkler, T., and K. Buckner. (2006). Receptiveness of gamers to embedded brand messages in advergames: Attitudes toward product placement. *Journal of Interactive Advertising*, 7(1), 37–46.

Winters, P. (1995, August 15). Pepsi invading Coke turf: Foxboro second stadium to switch colas. *New York Daily News*, 23.

Woisetschlager, D. M., A. Eiting, V. J. Haselhoff, and M. Michaelis. (2010). Determinants and consequences of sponsorship fit: A study of fan perceptions. *Journal of Sponsorship*, 3(2), 169–180.

_____, and V. J. Haselhoff. (2009). The name remains the same for fans — Why fans oppose naming right sponsorships. *Advances in Consumer Research*, 36, 575–576.

Wong, T. (2009, August 14). Tennis events vie for dollars. *The Toronto Star*, B1.

Woo, K., H. K. Y. Fock, and M. K. M. Hui. (2006). An analysis of endorsement effects in affinity marketing: The case for affinity credit cards. *Journal of Advertising*, 35(3), 103–113.

Wood, W. (2000). Attitude change: Persuasion and social influence. *Annual Review of Psychology*, 51(1), 539–570.

Wright, J. B. (1999). The Supreme Court of the United States and First Amendment protection of advertising. In J. H. Jones (ed.). *The advertising business.* Thousand Oaks, CA: Sage.

Yang, M., and D. R. Roskos-Ewoldsen. (2007). The effectiveness of brand placements in the movies: Levels of placements, explicit and implicit memory, and brand choice behavior. *Journal of Communication*, 57(3), 469–489.

Yerak, B. (1999, December 30). Virtual TV ads to appear during Rose Bowl: Company to insert trademarks, logos of five sponsors. *Detroit News*, B1.

Yoon, S., and Y. Choi. (2005). Determinants of successful sports advertisements: The effects of advertisement type, product type and sports model. *Journal of Brand Management*, 12(3), 191–205.

Yoon, Y., Z. Gurhan-Canli, and N. Schwarz. (2006). The effect of corporate social responsibility activities on companies with bad reputations. *Journal of Consumer Psychology*, 16(4), 377–390.

Yu, C., and D. Hui. (2007). Welcome to the world of Web 2.0. *CPA Journal*, 77(5), 6–10.

Ziehm, L. (2003, September 16). No fund league: WUSA folds. *Chicago Sun-Times*, 105.

Zillmann, D., J. Bryant, and B. S. Sapolsky. (1989). Enjoyment from sports spectatorship. In J. H. Goldstein (ed.). *Sports, Games, and Play: Social and Psychological Viewpoints* (pp. 241–278). Hillsdale, NJ: Lawrence Erlbaum.

Index

Index